/2012

To my friend Lereen
with best wishes,

Anna

Isabel: The Secret Diary of a Discreet Secretary

Isabel Szlavik

iUniverse, Inc.
New York   Bloomington

Isabel: The Secret Diary of a Discreet Secretary

The views expressed in this work are solely those of the author and do not necessarily reflect the views of the publisher, and the publisher hereby disclaims any responsibility for them.

iUniverse books may be ordered through booksellers or by contacting:

iUniverse
1663 Liberty Drive
Bloomington, IN 47403
www.iuniverse.com
1-800-Authors (1-800-288-4677)

Because of the dynamic nature of the Internet, any Web addresses or links contained in this book may have changed since publication and may no longer be valid.

ISBN: 978-1-4502-0151-3 (sc)
ISBN: 978-1-4502-0152-0 (dj)
ISBN: 978-1-4502-0153-7 (ebk)

Printed in the United States of America

iUniverse rev. date: 1/11/2010

Contents

ACKNOWLEDGEMENT

I thank my family for their support during the laborious, creative process of this book, and their ongoing incentive to bring it to completion.

I also wish to thank my editor and friend, Sharon Crawford, for her invaluable guidance and professionalism in the editing of this first—and hopefully, not last—book of mine.

INTRODUCTION

En route to secretarial stardom, I sailed through different work experiences which took me to three continents: South America, Europe and North America.

In 1957, I was but a sixteen-year-old humble Jill-of-all-trades, learning about the multi-faceted manufacturing aspects of a small fashion company in Petrópolis, Brazil. It led me into the world of fashion modelling, and for a short period of time, the entertainment world as a lady crooner for a local jazz band.

A couple of years later my family moved to Niterói, a beach resort across from fascinating Rio de Janeiro, where I soon found employment, once again, as a fashion model. Fame and fortune, however, were not written in the stars for me. Perhaps because I was not willing to pay the less-than-glamorous price because I refused to accept the notion I was nothing more than a pretty dumb blond.

I decided to try out the world of a secretary, which had always been the largest job category for women anywhere in the world. It was considered a prestigious and elegant profession, which has since been tarnished, thanks to a few Hollywood flicks portraying secretaries as dumb blonds with nothing better to do than apply nail polish between calls and hop into bed with the boss.

In the early '60s in Rio, all that was required from an average secretary was a typing speed of at least forty-five to fifty words per minute along with some stenography—better known as shorthand. Regrettably, my first job interview turned out to be a total disaster as I had absolutely no training in any of the necessary secretarial skills. Luckily, however, I was given a second chance. Thanks to my boss's patient coaching and my eagerness to succeed, I was on the way to a new working universe.

I learned to use an IBM Selectric typewriter; to handle the messy and unforgiving mistakes with carbon papers and to properly use the mimeograph machine. I also had fun tackling the Pitman's shorthand course and later some

Speedwriting as this art form was still very much in demand at the time. Later on I was introduced to computers: big noisy boxes using large magnetic disks. Sometimes entire office floors housed the giant machines, which only skilled programmers and trained technicians knew how to use. Key punch operators were in charge to put in data into a machine-usable format.

The situation was similar in Milano, Italy. By the late 1960s and early 1970s, everybody had electric Olivetti typewriters. Some offices also had telex machines and Xerox copiers, which slowly replaced the old mimeograph equipment. Computers began to shrink in size but were affordable only to businesses. Dictaphones were popular among those who disliked the shorthand dictation method.

From the time I arrived in Canada in the early 1980s, the office world had undergone significant changes. At a rapid succession, many products and equipment became obsolete and were replaced with better, faster and more efficient ones. Electric typewriters turned into electronic typewriters with word processing capabilities. Telex machines became fax machines and copiers. In most cases carbon paper was replaced by carbonless, multi-paged writing forms and pads. Rotary phones became touch-tone phones, available in a choice of colors other than the depressing, standard black. Computers shrank even more and became affordable to the public as PCs—Personal Computers. Laptops followed and then came cell phones and Blackberries with camera, TV and Internet capabilities. Printers and photocopiers produced color copies and you could even process your high quality matte or glossy photographs. The buzz words were then and will remain: *Total Automation.*

Some of the other important aspects of my secretarial ride included the humorous side of the secretary-boss relationship as well as the customs and idiosyncrasies of the various company CEOs and co-workers. It was a colorful palette of American, Brazilian, German, Italian, Hungarian, Chinese, French and Canadian nationals; each with his or her particular cultural background and mindset.

Among the various challenges encountered on a daily basis between work and family —problems familiar to most working moms—there was also my handicapped mother with special needs, which were in constant disagreement with the medical establishment. It was always very difficult to remain focused on a particular issue or task when other pressing problems seemed to intrude in an otherwise well-organized schedule. A new word for an old, well-known concept by most working mothers was multi-tasking, which simply translates into doing many things at the same time, and doing them fast and well.

Another challenge I had to deal with was the emotional and psychological adjustment needed each time I started new employment. Next there was the necessary relocation of geographical areas within the same country or abroad.

And to spice up these challenges even more was the work-related stress itself, including office politics, gossip, envy and rivalry.

In retrospect, however, it has been a fascinating and educational roller coaster of experiences, which have enriched me professionally and as an individual, and for which I will always be very grateful to each of my former bosses, co-workers and people I had the privilege to meet along the way—even those with extreme idiosyncrasies!

As expected from a discreet secretary, I have changed most names in my story to respect individual privacy. Unfortunately, most former employers have closed their business or have passed away. There are only a few, in their late 80s and 90s, with whom I still communicate on a regular basis via phone or by mail. And they are always so happy and grateful that I did not forget them. I am grateful, too, for the many good memories.

1

LILLI FASHIONS – 1957 – Petrópolis

WWII had ended. Europe was nothing but rubble and even if there was the promise of reconstruction and a bright future for all, my parents decided to leave behind the horrendous memories of war by immigrating to Brazil. They settled in a beautiful mountain city named Petrópolis. For about three months, my brother and I visited a private school to learn some Portuguese before entering regular public school. We already spoke Hungarian and German and unlike my parents, we picked up the Portuguese language quickly and moved along in our schooling.

Higher education, however, was not an option, at least not for me, because of my family's financial difficulties. Besides, the mentality at the time was that a girl would marry eventually, and would not require a university degree to cook, clean, wash dishes, and bear children. Therefore, I decided to look for a job. I wanted to have those niceties my friends and other girls had such as fashionable clothes, shoes and cosmetics. But who would be willing to hire a person without skills or experience? I was sixteen at the time, believed I could do almost anything and had no limit in enthusiasm.

It just happened that my grandmother was selling hand-printed skirts for a small local fashion manufacturer. Some of those were rejects with minor imperfections, to be sold at low prices on a door-to-door basis. After grandmother promised to give me a small commission on every skirt sold, I decided to try out the sales world.

One early morning I left home with a small suitcase filled with skirts. I knocked on every door along my way, with the endless hope to sell all the skirts I had on consignment. I was lucky that first day, again the day after and even the week after that, returning home with an empty suitcase every time and a pocketful of money. I could finally afford to buy some of the long dreamed-of things such as a lipstick, a pale pink one, almost unnoticeable to my father's strict eye; my first bra with pink lace, a bottle of "Alfazema" cologne (lavender scent), and some candy for my family.

The results were stimulating and I felt overwhelmed with joy and goals that were even more ambitious. Soon, however, the beginner's luck turned into an almost daily defeat. Many doors slammed in my face while some others did not bother to open at all. I tried many other areas of the village; walking for miles in the continuous hope that perhaps, the next door would open and bring me luck.

Before knocking on the doors, I would study a new approach; select the proper words and even facial expressions. Instinctively I knew that I had to apply a different technique for different people. Luck, however, was not always on my side and often, I would return home tired and frustrated. The suitcase, light as a nutshell at the start, was becoming heavier, as if it were filled with lead. My feet, agile and restless at first, were also growing heavier and heavier. I felt as if the entire world had collapsed over me and I was merely at the beginning of it all.

One day, I decided to accompany my grandmother to the manufacturing plant and get to know Lilli, the owner. Tall, in her mid-30s, she was an attractive, vibrant human being. She had curly, copper red hair, high cheekbones, a slightly aquiline nose and fleshy lips. Her dark brown eyes had a charming twinkle and the gift of speaking on their own. Every gesture, every word was followed by a smile.

After Lilli had finished talking to grandmother, she turned in my direction and started a lively conversation. Although I was the timid type, I soon felt at ease and was offered a job of factotum by the time we were ready to leave. Without hesitation and without even knowing what I was getting myself into, I accepted Lilli's offer. Like magic, the entire world that had threatened to crumble over me vanished. New hopes and dreams appeared on the horizon.

Once back home, it took the combined efforts of my mother, grandmother and myself to convince father to allow me to take the job. In his opinion, and many others in those days, it was the responsibility of the man to provide for the financial needs of the family; however, in light of our difficult economic situation, it would have been plain stupid to refuse the opportunity of another, even though minimum, salary. My childhood dream of becoming a doctor would also just continue to be nothing more than a dream. My immediate priority was to start making money.

Monday morning, dressed in my best Sunday outfit, I showed up punctually at the office, followed by Lilli a few minutes later. With a bright, happy smile, Lilli unlocked the door and showed me into the little Spanish-style bungalow, which served as office and warehouse for their activity. The first room, originally a living room, was set up as an office. It contained a large desk, two chairs, and a small desk with an Olivetti typewriter, a couple of dark grey filing cabinets and a large shelf packed with folders, binders, books and stacks of photographs. A young, handsome blue-eyed blond German named Arnold was the bookkeeper.

The second room, a former bedroom, was set up as stock room. Three of the four walls had wooden shelves mounted to them, which were packed with neatly folded skirts divided by pattern and sizes. Under the small window, there was a long, narrow table, lined with brown packing paper. It was crammed with order forms, scissors, pens, pencils, ashtrays, fabric samples, sketches and piles of fashion magazines and more photographs. Two old chairs completed the furnishing. At the far end of the narrow corridor, there was a small kitchen used as a packaging area and storage room for different rolls of fabric samples. On the left side, a small door opened into a yet smaller washroom.

We then returned to the stockroom and took a seat. Lilli lit a cigarette—the world was not smoke free in 1957—and offered me one also. To my own surprise, I accepted with nonchalance. Hiding behind the house, away from our father's eyes, I had experimented, along with my brother, to puff on a cigarette or two but had never seriously considered taking up smoking. In that particular instance, however, I felt it was necessary to add a more sophisticated touch and self-confidence to my image, characteristics I knew I lacked at times. My brief, suffocating cough must have betrayed me as Lilli glanced in my direction with a smile, discreetly ignoring my inexperience. It must have been clear to her that I wanted to appear older than I really was.

Lilli placed an armful of skirts on top of the table and began telling me about the work I was to do. Starting out as a Jill-of all-trades, I would slowly learn everything I had to master about the business. Lilli also explained that, because the factory was still at its beginning, they were unable to offer great wages. I hoped to get at least 200-300 cruzeiros per month and my mind raced through all the possible goodies I would be able to afford with that amount—which in reality was not much at all—when the sound of a voice announced 3,000 cruzeiros (approx. US$ 40 in 1957) per month. For an instant, I stood still, breathless. Then forgetting the role of sophisticated adult with a cigarette between my fingers, I began hopping, laughing and clapping my hands as a child in front of an unexpected new toy. Surprised at first with my enthusiastic reaction, Lilly soon joined in my happiness by giving me a big hug.

Later that evening at the dinner table, my family also cheered my success. My mother said I had always been a smart kid, with a built-in talent for many skills and always eager to learn and experience new challenges. I was indeed a fast learner, had a good memory and a special knack for detail. I often noticed the most insignificant things as, for example, the worn- out shoe soles of a customer's left shoe, and so forth. Lilli thought it was funny.

I enjoyed every moment of my daily activities and could not be more grateful to Lilli for having given me the chance to learn and work in such a friendly atmosphere. I also enjoyed visiting the plant, a few blocks away from the office, where all the fabric dying, washing and printing took place. Lilli's brother-in-law, Jorge, was in charge of the entire operation. Jorge was a tall, skinny, ever smiling blue-eyed blond man in his forties and a real workaholic. On weekends, however, his attention focused mainly on fishing, real fish, as well as those of the human female gender. He considered himself a God-given gift to the ladies and was openly proud of his *Casanova* exploits.

A small corner of the plant was reserved for Lilli's husband, Lucas. There he would nurse his beloved fleet of Citroen cars. He loved to dismantle and re-assemble the parts to bring the cars to a unique spotless shine and efficiency. He was a private person, in his late forties, medium height, with balding grey hair, a beer belly and dreamy blue eyes. His apparent absent-minded gaze was nothing but concentration. He always seemed to be absorbed in thought. A restless character, he would never sit anywhere for more than a minute or two. He disliked arguments and simply left the scene when the situation threatened to develop into a polemic.

Everyone around me seemed to be so pleasant; especially Lilli who, lacking a daughter of her own—she had two sons—treated me as her own child. She taught me to dress with elegance, to apply proper make-up and eye shadow, how to relate to customers and many other useful tips that would come in handy in the following years. My admiration and affection for her grew as time went on. During hot summer days, she would send me to the corner store to pick up cigarettes, candy and cold beer, which we would share as two good friends of the same age and the same social status. On weekends, Lilli would squeeze some extra money into my hand for a movie, a new lipstick, mascara or some yummy chocolate. On occasion, she would take me to the hairdresser and even pay for my hair styling. It was always a treat to be invited for dinner at Lilli's place. The food was mostly simple but tasty. My favorite was fresh crusty bread, sardines, cheese and cold beer. After dinner, we often played a few hands of Canasta and about 9 p.m., Lucas always drove me back home—an approximate twenty-five minute car ride.

At that point I had almost become a family member and had even taken part in business trips. My first six-hour long trip with Lilli, her husband and Jorge, took us as far as São Paulo. I had been there before spending school holidays, along with my brother, at our uncle's place. Unlike my previous trips in a bus crowded with strangers, I was proud and happy to sit with Lilli in the back seat of Jorge's pea-green Pontiac. The men exchanged the driving task while Lilli and I played trivia games.

Upon our arrival in São Paulo, they checked into a hotel downtown and I hoped to be able to stay with them. I had never before been inside a luxury hotel and I would have loved to spend, even if only one night, among a bunch of elegant, well-to-do people. I could not keep my eyes off the glamorous surroundings, the crystal chandeliers that glittered as giant diamonds, oriental carpeting, heavy crimson damask drapes and the comfortable sofas and armchairs upholstered in heavy crimson velvet. I enjoyed watching the many well-dressed people walking in and out of the hotel. Elegant bejeweled ladies with fancy hairdos, walked by with a stately posture, while others sat gracefully with their legs crossed wearing expensive high heels and blowing blue smoke in the air. I wished to become an elegant lady too, some day. Soon, however, I had to snap out of the daydreaming and return to reality. I had promised to call my uncle as soon as we arrived in town because I was to spend the night at his place.

After Lilli and the men refreshed themselves from the long trip, they drove me over to Uncle's. As usual, they were extremely happy to see me and welcomed me with the usual hugs and kisses. With pride, I introduced them to my bosses. They talked about their activities and business in general while I wondered why the guests were sitting in the entrance hall instead of the more comfortable living room downstairs and perhaps offered a drink or a coffee. Most probably my relatives were not too keen to make new friends and tried to cut the encounter short. I was sad when Lilli left, even though I knew it was a matter of only two nights.

At the dinner table later that evening, I told Uncle and Auntie about the family and all that was new at home. I could not conceal my enthusiasm when telling them about my job at Lilli's but as usual, Uncle and Auntie only saw what was not right in their eyes.

"What's with all that make-up on your face? You don't really need to put on all that stuff," Uncle said.

To avoid arguments, I decided not to reply, and kept any thoughts to myself. With the exception of some carefully applied mascara, some powder on my nose and cheeks, and a light lipstick, in my view, there was no excess make-up on my face.

"And remember what I told you about wearing a bra," Aunt Mary said. "It will only contribute to the loss of elasticity of the breasts."

Again, I did not argue. Perhaps Aunt Mary was right, but she kept forgetting that my breasts were twice the size of hers and that I wore the bra for support mainly. Or was there another reason for their disapproval? Maybe with a bra it was more difficult for Uncle to fondle me when he and Auntie had a few too many shots of Chivas Regal.

I spent the whole next day with Lilli. After visiting several customers during the morning, she decided it was time to have some lunch. She had chosen an elegant restaurant in the downtown core of São Paulo. Thanks to my mother's disciplinary rules, in addition to the more fussy ones at Uncle's place, I was at ease with the good table manners. Yet there was always room for improvement.

"Look here, Isabel. This is how you do it." Lilli whispered across the table with a smile, showing me how to just dab the sides of my mouth with the candid linen napkin without smearing lipstick all over it. "Maybe you should just break the bun in small pieces like this." Lilli showed me while buttering a small piece and gently bringing it to her mouth, chewing almost imperceptibly. Another lesson was how to sip a glass of wine instead of swallowing it in great thirsty gulps.

Even though I had always been an incorrigible rebel, never really accepting rules—which I considered useless means to complicate one's life—I accepted Lilli's instructions with docility and gratefulness. Lilli did not impose, she simply suggested, gently. There was still so much to learn and Lilli was willing to teach me. The business meetings finally ended and we returned to Petrópolis.

There were days when nothing much was happening at work; business was slow and Lilli would run errands while I reshuffled skirts on the shelves or chatted with Arnold. He would often let me use the old Olivetti typewriter to copy, with two fingers, letter texts for exercise or teach me to prepare invoices and to file documents. Arnold was not always busy either nor had he work for me to do, so I would sit in the stock room and doodle skirt patterns. Soon Lilli realized that, even though lacking the basics, I had a natural gift for drawing and decided to send me to a silk-screening shop in the downtown area. The shop, which also did their artwork and screens, was a good place to learn new skills. I didn't like to be away from Lilli's protective wings, but because it was, apparently, just a temporary arrangement, I agreed. Slowly, I advanced through the different stages of the silk-screening process. It was new. It was fun.

I learned how to trace the original pattern onto celluloid sheets and then fill each color with a dark brown ink — for each color a separate sheet. Those were transferred photographically onto coated screens stretched onto heavy metal frames. Back at the plant, the framed screens were hooked onto rails installed on both sides of long, narrow tables, where the fabric to receive the prints was already stretched into place. The printing process required two laborers, one on each side of the table. They would pour the lighter colors first and by means of a large squeegee, push the ink back and forth inside the screen. After two to three swipes they would lift the screen and place it into the next section and so forth, until the entire length of approximately thirty feet (or 12 meters) was completed. Usually by the time they were finished with the last section, the ink at the beginning of the table was dry and allowed the second color to be applied and so forth, until completion of all colors. Once they all were properly dried, the fabric was boiled, set to dry and finally, rolled up and taken to the seamstresses in charge of cutting and sewing the skirts to the sizes required by the different orders.

At the studio I was fascinated by the many talented artists that worked all around me. I was particularly impressed by an older Japanese artist. He hardly ever opened his mouth and smiled even less. He worked tirelessly from early morning until late in the afternoon, at times forgetting his lunch break, creating new, intricate, colorful masterpieces. His hand was steady, every line a precision stroke. Aware of my interest, he would occasionally glance at me and with a motion of his head invite me to approach his bench to watch more closely. It was during one of those sessions that he taught me how to draw straight lines without the aid of a ruler. "You must hold in breath and then quickly draw line." He demonstrated the action with a large gesture of his hand. He invited me to try on a separate piece of paper. I tried several times. Mr. Hakimoto was not very tolerant of mistakes and watched impatiently. I then tried harder and once I succeeded in drawing a straight line, Mr. Hakimoto expressed his satisfaction with a smile that almost stretched from ear to ear.

Three months later, as business picked up, I was recalled to the office. Lilli's sister-in-law, Dolly, the genius behind all the creative design, had developed a new set of patterns for the summer collection. Lilli had great plans in mind to improve the promotion of their products. A photo catalog with fabric samples attached to the price list page was the main idea and I was chosen to act as the fashion model in the pictures. I was thrilled, to say the least. Like most teenagers in those days, I often flirted with the idea of becoming a famous singer or movie star and to become a fashion model was close enough to the idea of stardom.

I enjoyed posing in the many beautiful skirts and dresses. Each time it was a different pose and a different background: seated on a late model motorcycle, the hood of a brand new white Cadillac or stepping into a motor boat, aboard a luxury yacht and even traveling to different towns with breathtaking sceneries. Initially, the pictures were all in black and white and did no justice to the beautiful colors of the different patterns but color pictures in the 1950s were extremely expensive and Lilli had to respect the available budget. The photographer hired for the job was an elderly gentleman with the classic old-fashioned ideas about modeling. Mr. Toth preferred the statue-like stiff, inexpressive poses whereas I pushed towards using the more professional poses I had seen in fashion magazines. Luckily, Lilli shared my preferences and the end-result was quite attractive. I was extremely proud to see myself depicted and circulating—even if only in pictures—throughout the entire country. Soon these new experiences would drastically interfere with my otherwise steady and peaceful daily existence.

One lazy summer afternoon, Lilli's older son, Stan—a tall, skinny, blue-eyed blond young man—dropped in for a brief visit to his mother. Aside from the height, he took after his father. He was extremely nervous and a little short-sighted. A university student, he was involved in countless social activities as well as in smart business transactions to pay for his own studies. After a little chitchat with Lilli and Arnold, he briefly leafed through the photo catalog of the new garment collection. While turning the pages, he quickly glanced in my direction, as if making sure I was the same person portrayed on those pictures.

"How would you feel like to participate in a beauty contest for charitable purposes?" he said. "You would run for the title of 'Glamour Girl' along with twenty-five other contestants. The income from the sale of the tickets is going to be donated to a local charity."

I listened attentively, but had no idea what a beauty contest was all about and simply shrugged with a timid smile. Stan then asked me to walk down the corridor, and back. With critical eyes he screened my every move and then with his usual dry humor remarked:

"Almost as graceful as a baby elephant," he chuckled. "But not bad. Not bad at all."

I remember blushing and wished the earth would swallow me that very instant. With Lilli's encouragement, however, they all agreed that I should go for it and a few days later, Stan introduced me to the various sponsors among which was, Annie Braga, the wife of the city's mayor.

Annie was a beautiful, intelligent and refined lady. She totally lacked the arrogance and snobbish behavior so typical among the females of similar rank and position. She was generous, patient and compassionate. Her short, curly white hair, with a slight tinge of blue, framed a perfect face with two limpid blue eyes. There must have been an immediate good vibration between the two of us as she did not hesitate to offer to sponsor and help me with the show. During the following weeks, I met Annie at her home, where she taught me proper posture by putting a couple of heavy books on my head and then had me walking up and down the corridor and the staircase. A big problem, however, threatened to kill a newly born dream. The participants were to provide their own evening gowns. My salary was far from enough to buy a suitable dress; the family's finances had also not improved yet, and an evening gown was definitely a non-essential item on our list of priorities. My mother, however, thirty-seven years of age at the time and tempered by a string of tragic events, was not easily put off by difficult situations. With confidence, she declared, "Just as I managed to sew your first communion dress from an old piece of parachute silk, so I will figure out a way to make you an evening gown."

Mother's assurances, however, were not enough and many sleepless nights were to follow due to the uncertainty of my dream and because time was drawing short. There were no more silk pieces or any other fabric for that matter left anywhere in the house that could have been used for an evening gown. How could I possibly tell Annie and Lilli about my big problem? How could all those people grasp, even slightly, what it meant to be less fortunate? How could they understand the type of problems my family and I were facing? I tried very hard to hide my anguish from the two women but somehow, Lilli—an extremely perceptive person—sensed that something was wrong with me. Gently and tactfully, she succeeded in convincing me to reveal my great torment.

"You little dummy," Lilli said, while giving me a big hug. "What made you think that I wouldn't understand your problem?"

At that point I could no longer hold back my tears and broke into a bitter sob.

"Don't you worry little girl. I'll see what I can do for you," Lilli said, while ruffling up my hair and handing me a handkerchief.

I blew my nose, took a deep breath and then rewarded Lilli with a wide, bright smile.

The next day after work, I went over to Lilli's house. From an old box, she pulled out a beautiful, emerald green chiffon dress that I immediately tried on. It was a perfect fit except for the hem, which due to storage time had become uneven and needed some touch-up. It also needed a petticoat to enhance the richness of the skirt. It was a full-length halter gown with a deep V-cut opening in front with the back bare to the waist. Lilli pulled up my long, blond hair and pinned it on top of my head. The effect was sexy and glamorous.

"You'll have to find a good seamstress to fix a little here and there," Lilli said, pleased with what she saw.

"I'm sure my sewing teacher will be able to help me with the hem," I told her, happily. I was taking sewing lessons twice a week in the evenings.

Two days before the event, I rushed over to the school to pick up the dress. I tried it on as soon as I got home. What a bitter disappointment that was. The hem hadn't been touched and the petticoat was so stiff that I could hardly move. It was too late to bring the dress to another seamstress and I was tired, frustrated and struggling with the stream of tears flooding my pillow.

The day of the big event had finally arrived. Stan picked me up along with my parents and drove us to the club site, already lit up and crowded with elegant people and prominent personalities of the local high society. I showed my parents to their table and then rushed to the dressing room. Gorgeous-looking groups of young ladies were getting busy with their outfits. Some were already dressed and looked like queens. Others were getting the last touches from a Max Factor make-up artist. A few had trouble with a zipper, or were looking for a lost shoe amidst the chaos of beauty cases, flowers and people. The entire atmosphere was dense with tension and excitement. Each girl hoped to become the one and only "Glamour Girl" of the night. Only a few were true professionals, while the rest, like myself, were about to experience the apparent sweet taste of celebrity for the very first time.

Soon, a voice from the stage began calling the contestants one by one. For the first appearance, I wore a turquoise shantung tailleur, donated to the event by a boutique in the city. White high heeled pumps, three-quarter long white gloves and a tiny flower corsage of baby breath on the left lapel completed the outfit. My hair was set into a very elegant chignon by Lilli's own hairdresser. The applause I received during the first run repaid the anguish I endured in those last weeks. The second and last appearance took place with the evening gown. I climbed the few steps onto the stage and almost tripped because of the rigid petticoat. My heart pounded wildly and I felt my face burning from embarrassment. Never before did I have to concentrate so hard in order to give my walk a free and natural appearance. Along the runway the crowd cheered with enthusiasm. Flashlights were popping everywhere I turned, and despite my dreams of fame and glory, I suddenly felt embarrassed and somewhat uncomfortable up there, with hundreds of eyes screening my every movement. Annie had instructed me to smile, smile always. People cannot fight or resist a smile, but I felt my jaws getting weaker, contracting into what soon could become a grimace. My steps, firm at the beginning, felt like faltering, and my knees threatened to fail me at any moment. My eyes spotted mother's glowing face and the dissimulated pride in father's expression. Then there was Lilli, applauding frantically while Annie winked an eye in my direction from the jury seat. Those were my real friends and true fans, and their enthusiasm gave me enough strength to finish the runway with all the grace and dignity

I could master. It had been a breathtaking experience. Technicalities such as the dress's hem and my being a foreigner hindered my winning the title, but I was happy with the second place.

After the participants had received their prizes and posed for photographs, we each joined our families and friends.

"In my book, you are the true winner," said Annie Braga while giving me a big hug.

Lilli hugged and kissed me and showered me with compliments. At last, my parents, who beamed with pride, congratulated me on this wonderful event, as did many other people, known and unknown, shaking hands and tapping my shoulders. More flashlights, flowers, music, dance and champagne followed. I was in seventh heaven and enjoyed every instant of my momentous popularity.

All good things, however, end too soon. I returned to the normal daily routine, occasionally dreaming about my personal success. I began receiving invitations for more fashion shows, cocktail parties and other social events, which I always accepted enthusiastically. It was during one of those events that Stan introduced me to Koruba, a middle-aged well-known musician and leader of a local jazz band. I told him about my passion for singing and so he invited me for an audition at the studios of the local broadcasting station.

Koruba and I arranged to meet on a Saturday afternoon at the studio. After a brief chat about my preferences, Koruba began playing *The Autumn Leaves*. He re-played the song a few times until I got into the right rhythm. The more I repeated the song, the stronger my voice became. I learned quickly and soon Koruba was able to play freely without confusing or deflecting my attention from the main theme. After an hour of rehearsing, Koruba was satisfied and engaged me for his weekly evening show, *Cocktails at Ten*. It was not a real job and therefore no money was involved. Somehow, the monetary aspect, even though useful and welcome most of the time, never seemed to matter much to me, as long as I was happy with the activity. I confess I never knew how to market my talents. In this case, I was simply overjoyed with the perspective of singing on radio.

The smile on my face soon faded into a grimace as I suddenly remembered that there would be an obstacle waiting at home. My father would certainly object to my new plan, as he always did in the past. So my answer to Koruba at that point was a hopeful "maybe." Wisely, I shared the news with my mother and grandmother first. I could always count on their support for whatever new and interesting enterprises I undertook, whereas my father—perhaps because more experienced in the ways of the big, ugly world—would immediately point out all the dangers and negative aspects of a deal. Invariably, he foresaw catastrophe and failure.

"You just don't worry my child," grandmother said with firm determination. "You will tell your father that we are going to the movies and that's it."

The solution was apparently very simple and grandmother was so persuasive and secure that I did not hesitate to follow her suggestion. Being in a particularly good mood that evening, father also approved, and let me go. I agreed with mother that she would stay home, listen to the radio and call father from the workshop when it was time to listen to my singing.

While climbing the stairs to the auditorium, my heartbeat accelerated. I was facing a completely new situation. For a brief moment I thought I would not be able to go through with it and contemplated a fast retreat but Koruba's reassuring, smiling face, overpowered my cowardly feelings. He immediately introduced me to Roberto at the contrabass, Carlos at the drums, Giorgio with the sax, Luiz at the vibraphone, Pedro with the maracas and Antonio who played the bongos. Except for Koruba, the boys were all very young, between eighteen and twenty-eight years of age. They were all very friendly and pleased with Koruba's idea of a female addition to their group. I therefore rehearsed with the orchestra and they all agreed that I could become an asset to the band and increase their ratings.

Moments later, Freddie the announcer joined us, and Koruba introduced me to him. Freddie then asked how the group was to be introduced to the public that evening and what my art name was to be. They had forgotten about that detail. Everybody suggested a different name and I was beginning to worry. People were already taking their places in the auditorium and the boys were still trying to find the perfect name for me. In those days artists always had different names from their real ones and I couldn't stop wondering why they had to complicate their lives with such silly details. Finally, Koruba came up with the name Peggy Doll. He explained that Peggy came from Peggy Lee, his favorite singer, and doll because he thought I was as cute as a doll.

In the meantime, the auditorium had completely filled with people and I was now very nervous. I could feel it in my bladder. It was a live program without margin for error. Freddie noticed my discomfort and as we still had fifteen minutes before the start, he suggested that I get a quick drink at the studio's bar. We ran downstairs and Freddie, knowing Zeca the bartender, instructed him to serve me a shot of *Leite de Onça* (Wild Cat Milk). It was nothing more than some Pernod mixed with water. The mixture turned the liqueur into a white substance; extremely effective in calming my shaking body. Five minutes later, we were back on stage. Standing next to the piano, glancing at the hundreds of anxious faces, I experienced, if just for a brief moment, the cold feet syndrome once again. At that point, however, it was too late to chicken out. The red pilot light came on; the lights were dimmed, and Freddie announced the program, listing the names of the various sponsors and then introducing the group and Peggy Doll. The crowd responded with a generous applause as I stepped forward, slightly bowed my head, and then moved back to my spot near the piano.

"Don't worry sweetheart; you'll be all right. Just wait for my signals," Koruba whispered reassuringly and then moved his attention back to the keyboard.

I never tired watching him play and envied his dexterity, the ease with which his fingers caressed the black and white keys of the piano. I hoped to one day master the keyboard as he did. Two more arrangements were played and then it was my turn. Koruba's hand signal and reassuring smile was all I needed. Initially, the staring eyes of the audience disturbed my concentration and I chose to sing with my eyes slightly closed or turned towards the ceiling. Soon, however, I got carried away by the rhythm of the music and the Wild Cat drink I had before, did also kick in, contributing with additional encouragement. My voice acquired more power, more confidence. I even grabbed the microphone and slowly walked across the stage, just like the real singers, and not even when the boys introduced variations into the theme did I lose a beat. Interestingly enough, not even my bladder disturbed me anymore. After a short intermission, it was my turn again and I sang *Night and Day*. I was even more confident at that point and the enthusiastic applause from the spectators confirmed the successful performance.

At the end of the program, after the red pilot light went off and the audience had left the auditorium, Koruba and the boys gathered around me and congratulated me for work well done. They then had the recording played back and I could hardly believe that what I was hearing was actually my very own voice. I would have loved to accept the band's invitation to join them for a drink to celebrate the occasion but it was late and I had to go home. Grandmother, who had been following the entire performance with great admiration and enthusiasm, telling everyone around her that she was related to "the artist," was also signalling that it was time to take off. Before leaving, Koruba reminded me about the next rehearsal. I was to become their official mascot. On my way out along the corridors and stairs of the building, several people who had been in the audience, stopped me to express their appreciation. I was not only flattered but also very, very happy.

Along the way home, grandmother couldn't stop praising my exhibition and my talent, while my mind was taken over by apprehension about my father's reaction once we arrived home. Would he be happy? Would he be proud? I hoped that he would, this one time, understand his relentless enterprising daughter and greet me with words of praise and encouragement.

Once at home, I was warmly received by mother who exhorted me to go see father. With my heart pounding, I walked over to the workshop. There was my old man, with the face covered in sweat, bent over heavy wooden planks, working away long hours every day to make ends meet for the entire family. I felt so much compassion that it almost spoiled my happiness. Finally, father noticed my presence.

"Well, what is it?" he asked, pretending indifference.

"Oh, nothing," I replied in a tone that betrayed both nervousness and eagerness to learn about his reaction. "Did you listen to the radio?" I dared asking.

"Yes, indeed. Your mother called me saying you were singing, but all I heard was a record with this person named Peggy something," he said without lifting his eyes from work.

"Well, believe it or not, that was me singing there," I said, extremely excited. "It was a real band playing and Peggy Doll is now my art name. They chose it for me."

"And if that is true, who gave you permission to get into such an arrangement? He said giving me an icy glance. "I was made to believe that you went to the movies with grandmother. You know very well how much I hate lies."

"Well, would you have let me go if I had told you the truth?" I asked defiantly.

"Who knows? You'll never know unless you ask. Maybe yes, maybe no," he replied after a long thoughtful pause.

"The fact that I did not ask is because you always say *No* to everything," I said frustrated.

"All right, all right, let's just drop the argument. Go to bed now. We'll talk it over tomorrow." He turned his attention back to his work.

I was disappointed with another cold shoulder. It was so darn difficult to please father, no matter how hard I tried. Only one good thing resulted from our short squabble, and it was that no matter how angry he might have been with my sneaky way of carrying out the plan, he thought that Peggy Doll had a good voice. After all, he thought he was listening to a record. With that in mind, I walked back to my room and went to sleep.

The next day we were fairly busy at work but I could not conceal my enthusiasm for too long and told Lilli about my new adventure. Lilli was enthused with the good news and showed interest in my future plans. Somehow, Lilli felt that sooner than later, I would part to follow my own destiny.

"You're still so young," she used to say with a shade of sadness. "You've got the right to live your own life now."

One Saturday afternoon, I decided to pay a short visit to the studio where Freddie worked as an announcer. He was sitting in his small cubicle advertising products and sponsors for the birthday program. He seemed pleased to see me and signaled for me to wait. As soon as the red pilot light went off, he opened the door and let me in, offering the stool next to him. We chatted away between announcements and I asked him if I could try to make one announcement. Freddie didn't think it was such a good idea, as he had never heard me doing it before and he could get into trouble for it.

"First you need some training, sweetheart. If you want, I am willing to teach you," he said with a cheerful smile.

I was so enthused with the idea that I immediately agreed. My first and subsequent lessons took place at Freddie's deluxe bachelor apartment. At each session, I learned new tricks and soon my pronunciation became crisp and clear. During one of my last lessons, after having read countless newspaper lines and decidedly showing exhaustion, Freddie offered me a cocktail and since it was already late in the evening, he ordered a pizza. I enjoyed the cocktail and the pleasant background music for the relaxing feeling it was giving me, and naturally, the pizza, because I was hungry. I was also sensitive to Freddie's flatteries but felt apprehensive when he took a step longer than his leg by stealing a kiss. It caused me to immediately retreat into my shell of defensiveness.

Freddie was a good-looking man in his late twenties with brown eyes and brown hair; he wore double-heeled shoes to disguise his height. He confirmed his Italian background through the choice of fine tailored Italian-styled suits. However, he was engaged to a girl named Laura. The whole town knew about it and so did I, and it would not be me to come between the two lovers.

"I am not going to eat you, you know?" he said. "It's just a friendship kiss."

"I know you won't eat me, but I prefer that you don't kiss me," I said.

"Why?" he asked. "Am I so repulsive?"

"No, not at all, I find you very handsome but you are also very engaged and I do not snatch other people's boyfriends, you know?"

"Oh, you wouldn't snatch me away with just a little kiss."

"Well, that's usually how trouble begins, my teacher used to say."

"Yeah, especially when a pretty and sexy young lady accepts to visit a young man in his bachelor apartment, did she mention that, too?"

"I don't see anything wrong with it. After all, we are working, aren't we?"

"If that is how you call it..." Freddie ruffled my hair and then gave me a quick peck on the cheek. He then walked over to the bar and poured himself another drink. Returning to my side, he grabbed my face into his hands and looked into my eyes for a moment and smiled. "You know what? Better listen to this old man here. In the future, don't accept invitations from anyone, not even from me, to go to their place, unless you want to get hurt."

"I guess this means you will not help me anymore, right?" I said with a tone of resignation.

"Well, let's just put it this way," he smiled widely. "It's not really up to me but to the station's director. If he approves, you can do anything you want. I will say a good word on your behalf, but from there on, it's between you and the boss."

Damn it, I thought to myself. There always had to be a price for everything in life. But I was not going to give up easily. Aside from my strict upbringing, which did not include familiarity with malice, I also inherited stubbornness, which would not allow me to play around unclean business.

Two weeks later, Freddie introduced me to his boss, Mr. Cordeiro. In his late forties, he was of medium height, black hair, balding at the front crown, black beady eyes, bushy moustache, fleshy lips and a double chin. His overall appearance was that of a debonair type. Impressed with my eagerness and enthusiasm, he agreed with Freddie in giving me a chance. It was to be a training period for which, however, I would not get paid.

In time, I proved to be talented and successful and Freddie, very graciously, took all the merit upon himself. Mr. Cordeiro was especially pleased with me as more and more clients requested that I be the announcer of their products. Again, I was not aware of the profitable side of my performance and never even dreamed of touching the financial aspects of the business. Mr. Cordeiro showered me with little gifts instead, gifts such as cosmetics, American lipsticks, French perfumes and so forth. I was only too proud of the fact that I worked for the station and one evening was even invited by the boss himself to go up to his flat for a drink and to get better acquainted. I took the invitation as a great honor. After all, he was an authority figure and a very important personality in town.

We chatted about various subjects, mainly about my dreams and aspirations. Throughout our conversation, my attention wandered around the surroundings. Definitely in contrast with his financial means, the place was in shambles. The doors to the various rooms were left open. I noticed his bedroom was furnished with a large king-sized bed and the sheets and blankets were thrown everywhere. There was a wardrobe and two run-down armchairs piled up with old magazines, newspapers and dirty socks. In one corner, there were suitcases and shoeboxes. The living room had a sofa covered with a dusty grayish-green plaid, a round table crowded with dirty ashtrays, glasses and documents of all kinds. Four chairs, packed with more magazines, a tray on wheels packed with wine bottles and dirty glasses, and a glass shelf crammed with all sorts of liquor bottles and souvenirs. The kitchen looked more like a battlefield. Dirty pots, pans, dishes and dozens of glasses still with the imprint of red lipstick marks, cluttered the countertop, sink and the kitchen table. It was a real wonder that amidst that mess he could produce two clean glasses and prepare his favorite concoction, a Manhattan.

I did not care much about the liquor but I certainly enjoyed the cherries, which I had not tasted since my family and I had left the old country many years ago and were too expensive for our family budget. I pointed that out to Mr. Cordeiro who immediately filled up a little bowl and offered it to me. I was extremely happy and proud to be in the company of the big boss until he began with the "to know you better" ritual. His puffy, nervous, hairy hands began squeezing my knees, sliding down the curves of my legs. Next, he placed an arm around my shoulders, pulling me towards him. He kissed my temple while forcing my face in his direction in the attempt to kiss me on the lips. I quickly turned my face to avoid the contact. I had a real hard time to fend off the man's kisses and at the same time keep my skirt from being pulled up. My heart began to race and to pound stronger.

"Why are you so malicious, my child?" he suddenly asked, panting excitedly.

"I just don't like you to touch me this way or kiss me," I replied, still trying to fend off his advances.

"Oh, c'mon now, what is a little kiss after all? I'm not going to eat you."

I remembered Freddie using the same line and wondered if all males would use that refrain in their approach to me.

"Listen, Mr. Cordeiro, you are a very nice man and I thank you for the chance you have given me to work at the station but I still don't like to be touched or kissed like you are doing."

"Oh you silly girl. Why did you accept my invitation then?"

"I thought you had invited me for a drink and a chat," I said softly. Then suddenly I snapped. "I really can't understand why you guys must always see only the lower half of a female person. Why can't you simply talk, conduct a normal conversation, exchange ideas, instead of only thinking of sex all the time. I find it very annoying and so primitive. And to top it all off, you accuse *me* of being malicious. Aren't there any other values you appreciate in a girl besides what she covers up with her panties?"

"Of course there are, but they all boil down to the same thing. I am a man who appreciates beauty and I find you beautiful and extremely sexy. Besides, as I said earlier, you should not have come up here in the first place."

Damn, damn, damn. I mentally reproached myself. Once more, I was the one to be blamed. Who else? Why did I have to be so foolish, trusting and naive? My father had been right all along. It just wasn't safe out there and yes, it was extremely difficult to find a male friend to just share feelings and thoughts without falling into unpleasant, ambiguous situations.

"Well, I guess I am leaving now," I said jumping to my feet and heading towards the door. Before opening it, I turned towards Mr. Cordeiro: "I imagine this is the end of my career as announcer, right?"

For a moment, Mr. Cordeiro left me in limbo. "What do you think I should do?" he asked.

"I don't know," I replied with a sigh of resignation. "You are the boss. It is your decision."

"Oh c'mon Isabel, I'm not as evil as you think," he said. "You may continue working as announcer. You are doing a good job. Too bad I still can't put you on the payroll, at least not for the time being." He joined me at the door and ran his hand along my bare arm.

I thanked him and left the apartment hurriedly. During the following weeks, I worked at the station in the late afternoon shift, right after leaving work. My performance had been so good, that in appreciation, Mr. Cordeiro allowed me to use a small publicity spot for my father's carpentry. I considered that a fair trade for my work. Only then, did father give me the official consent to continue with my broadcasting activities. Had he known about the unsafe encounters with Freddie and Mr. Cordeiro, he would certainly have had reservations about it.

During the time I worked for the station, I met many people including professional fashion models. One of them, a pretty brunette named Alice, asked me if I felt like taking over the in-house modeling position at Gentile's, the largest fashion manufacturer in town. The salary would have been 12,000 cruzeiros, more than double of what I was earning at Lilli's place. For me it represented both a small fortune and a great dilemma. How could I possibly abandon my friend Lilli, after all she had done for me? On one hand there was a new challenge and a better financial retribution, on the other, the guilt feeling.

For many days I lived my torment and ardently wished to be swallowed by the earth rather than having to confront Lilli and confess that I was leaving. I was facing my very first major decision. Time was running out because the management at Gentile's needed their replacement as soon as possible. Somehow, I finally found the lacking courage and told Lilli about my new project. Both, Lilli and I sat in front of each other with watery eyes, reminiscing about the beautiful days we had spent together. It was Lilli who first snapped out of the depression with a bright, encouraging smile.

"You must go, you dummy. There is a lot of world out there to see, new things to experience and to learn every day. I honestly can't afford to pay you more and neither can I promise a raise in the near future. Therefore, you must accept the offer." She wiped her eyes and then blew her nose. "You know, I am very sorry to lose you, but somehow, I knew it would happen sooner or later. Anyhow, be very careful anywhere you go and keep me posted, always. After all, we are still friends, aren't we?" She smiled warmly.

"We sure are," I replied with a great sense of relief while giving Lilli a big hug.

"Oh, there is only one more thing I'd like to ask you. Keep the child within you and that shiny personality of yours, always alive."

For several days, Lilli's words kept echoing in my head and somehow, I wished that none of that had happened. It was mother to give me the final push that would help me decide and finally accept the new job offer. Soon, however, I would find that the world was not all populated by Lillis and would many times regret my decision.

2

GENTILE FASHIONS

I had mixed feelings as I walked up the long driveway leading to the three-storey building occupied by Gentile Fashions. There was a small retail outlet attached to the main entrance. I was about to introduce myself to the sales lady when Alice spotted me and came running to get me and introduce me to a tall, well-built woman in her late forties, whom everybody called Madame. She was the owner and in charge of the creation of new fashion lines; she was also proud of the success the company achieved nationwide, year after year. I was then introduced to her husband, Mr. Starnowsky, a 5'3" tall man with a face furrowed by countless wrinkles. His temples were slightly grizzled and his inquisitive brown eyes peeked from over his brown rimmed eyeglasses. He stretched out his right hand and gave me a robust handshake.

"I understand you will be working for us now," he said with a quiet smile. "So, welcome to Gentile's. I hope you will like it here."

"Let me show you around," said Madame, leading the way.

We moved from the ground floor, where the administrative offices and the retail showroom were located, up to the first floor.

"Up here we have the cutting section," Madame said while pointing to a large table with patterns placed over layers of fabric. "Over there is the sewing section." She followed her words with an ample gesture of one hand.

There were about one hundred employees immersed in their sewing task. They glanced up briefly to check out the newcomer.

Madame then led the way up another flight of stairs.

"Up here we have the ironing and packaging department. And these are our most hardworking little helpers." She pointed to Nilza and Tata.

The two girls smiled timidly and continued folding a pile of blouses. We then moved up one last flight of stairs, to the stockroom, which housed hundreds of different fabric rolls, accessories, threads, buttons and so forth. Madame noticed that my attention was captured by a 12 x 12 foot locked enclosure, holding several hundred paper patterns.

"Oh, yes," she said. "Here we keep all the paper patterns of every piece we ever created. Aside from me and Emma, no one else is allowed in here."

We then returned to the office where I was told about my duties. The most important feature for them was that I was pretty, had a good body with the required measurements and would keep it that way for as long as I worked for them. One of my main tasks was to gracefully wear and show the various creations to the buyers and reps who would occasionally visit the showroom. The rest of the time, I was to care for the showroom's appearance. I had to keep all the sample pieces clean and nicely lined up, with name and price tags attached for easy identification. Once this task was completed and not much was happening in the little retail outlet attached to the reception area, I was sent up to the first floor to help write labels, fold garments and neatly tuck them into transparent plastic sleeves or stand boring hours for Emma, the Junoesque German stylist.

Emma appeared to be a strong, resolute, self-sufficient woman. Deep inside, however, she was a sensitive, suffering human being who would often sink into bouts of depression. Having become a widow recently, she had to fend for her own survival and that of her teenage son, Kurt. Such depression would then worsen with the frequent outbursts of malcontent from Madame, and naturally, reflect on everyone else around her. Whenever I sensed tension in the air, I would run up to the packaging department and join Tata and Nilza with the folding of garments. To put some spice into such tedious work, I introduced the speed-packing game. Whoever folded the most garments within a given time, would be declared folding champion of the day. Throughout the competition, we would tell each other a joke or two, especially Nilza. Tata was the more serious type, seventeen years old, very hard working. Yet she said that she loved my bubbly disposition because it turned work into a more pleasant task. Nilza was a petite, eighteen-year-old black girl who loved to clown around just like me. Her expressive little face and her inner beauty sparkled through her small, lively eyes and through her contagious open character. Her specialty was telling ghost stories. She knew many and knew how to tell them to raise one's hair in the back of the neck.

I was always very busy during the sampling season, shuttling between ground floor and first floor. Every half hour or so, I had to run to the dressing room to try on a dress once for Madame, then for Emma. Madame was a perfectionist, extremely fussy at times and not very concerned about feelings. Whenever dissatisfied with the way a dress looked on me, she would throw it back at Emma.

"You better check these sleeves, Emma," she said. "The girl cannot even lift her arms properly without pulling up the entire dress. This is absolutely not acceptable."

In tears, Emma would march back to her cutting table to fix the problem or start all over again. She would repeatedly call me for yet another fitting to check on the corrected piece. During those occasions, she would suddenly discover a multitude of defects in my body.

"It looks like your left shoulder is hanging lower than your right shoulder," she once said. "I also noticed that your hips are a little uneven and what about this fatty pad around your waist?"

Emma's unjustified remarks clearly irritated me because interestingly enough, the dresses I was given to try on the very first day, still fitted as a glove months later. To vent my frustration, I would seek refuge on the first floor with Tata and Nilza.

"Oh, c'mon buddy, there's nothing wrong with you. It's all in Emma's head. It's all envy. She's just envious...and old." Nilza whispered the last word.

The girls ended up laughing and I soon forgot the whole incident. Amazingly, the garments did not fit me only when Emma was in a bad mood.

The production increased considerably in the following months, but instead of hiring extra labor, the management decided to have the existing workforce do overtime in exchange for small incentives. The machines rattled away for endless hours, filling the air with their monotonous, deafening sound. The workers, mainly females of all age groups, did not dare lift their heads from their work field. There was no time to waste. One sole female supervisor was in charge of the entire crew.

I was kept busy all day long and by the end of the day, I felt tired and hardly in the mood to run over to the station to take care of my other commitments. It was not easy to hold a full-time job and at the same time juggle other activities. Unfortunately, I had to give up my short-lived fame of lady crooner and announcer. Unlike Lilli, my new bosses had an entirely different view of my "other" activities and aspirations and did not appreciate or encourage me towards other directions other than what concerned the interests of their own company. There were days when I would have gladly traded a year or two of my life for an extra hour of sleep in the morning but a commitment was a commitment and my parents, especially my father, would see to it that I respected it to the fullest. Flu, sore throat, tummy ache or a slight fever were never considered good enough reasons to skip school or work. Since I was a little girl, I was taught and trained to react with energy to any form of weakness. Mr. Starnowsky often needed me to do some overtime, helping with the last-minute labeling, yet my willingness in doing so seemed to be taken for granted most of the time. I was not even paid, let alone did I receive a ride home when late at night. It happened several times that my father would call the office to find out if I had left already. Only then would the boss realize how late it was and excuse himself.

"She will be leaving real soon," was his quick answer.

I could not call home because we did not have a telephone at home. My father would run down the hill to a neighbor's house and call from there. In the 1950s, there was still a fifteen-year-long wait in Brazil to have an ugly, black rotary telephone installed in a private residence. Only the wealthier homes in the area had one. They obviously had what was necessary to speed up the bureaucratic process. The same applied to transportation. Not many families could afford an automobile; the majority of the population traveled by bus. I was one of the many. Late at night, however, buses would not run frequently, if at all, especially not in the outskirts of town where I lived: Quarteirão Brasileiro. Streetlights along dirt roads cutting through parts of jungle were also scarce, and to walk alone as a young girl was frightening and dangerous. The boss could obviously not be bothered with such details.

"Never mind, hard work is good for you. Small trees grow more vigorously when straightened out from the beginning," was my boss's favorite motto, whether it applied or not to a particular situation.

One day, Madame was in one of her chatty moods and asked me if I liked dogs. Of course I did. We already had a couple of German shepherds and a dachshund. Madame seemed extremely pleased and asked if I would like to buy a newborn Boxer puppy with Pedigree. All for a measly one month's salary. It would certainly make my mother very happy, and perhaps, help me win over more of Madame's esteem as well. When I finally agreed to purchase the dog, I saw a happy smile appear on Madame's face for the very first time. My grandmother always said that people who loved animals were generally warm-hearted, understanding good people, and if that was true, then Madame must certainly be a good lady, I thought to myself.

A few days after our conversation, Madame drove me over to her house, showed me the way to the kennel where she picked up a wonderful, sleepy puppy. She wrapped it in a little blanket and very gently handed it over to me.

"There you go," she said with tears running down her cheeks. "This is our little Tatiana. Take good care of my baby." She also handed me the official Kennel Club papers.

I wondered about Madame's little tragedy as I could see several dogs in her kennel. I tried to place myself in Madame's shoes. With so many pets, it was still very hard to give up even just one. I definitely knew the feeling as I grew up on a mini farm where even chickens, ducks and pigs had a pet name. I handed Madame the agreed amount, thanked her, and then hurried away holding on tightly to my puppy. Luckily, a cab had just pulled up from around the corner. Once at home, everybody welcomed Tatiana, whose name shortly after was changed to Gigi, after the motion picture with Leslie Caron and Maurice Chevalier. Even the other four-legged family members came closer to sniff and scrutinize the new arrival. That night, Gigi shared the bed with me. Thanks to Tatiana, aka Gigi, Madame would spend a full ten minutes chatting with me every morning. Once the subject ran out of news, the smile would again desert her lips, replaced by worry and stress and it was business as usual.

One late afternoon, Madame asked me if I could spend a few hours on Saturday to help her reorganize the stockroom. It meant missing a terrific cocktail party I had been invited to. Madame's eyes were almost begging and even though I knew that my efforts would most likely not be acknowledged, I did not know how to refuse. That Saturday afternoon passed rapidly as Madame and I worked silently alongside each other. We finished a lot sooner than planned and Madame was immensely pleased and grateful. As we walked through the large, silent sewing room and before reaching the stairs, Madame turned around and with an ample gesture pointed towards the hundred, silent, perfectly aligned sewing machines.

"There, you see? This is my life," she said. "We came here from Poland shortly before the war exploded in Europe. Whatever we had we sold and invested in the purchase of an old Singer sewing machine, then another and another, one machine at a time; sacrifices, sleepless nights." Her gaze caressingly swept over the various departments. Tears were about to flood her eyes when she moved on to the ground level and remarked with a gloomy voice, "Yes, life is very hard, most of the time."

She thanked me by shaking my hand and then walked away to join her husband in the office. I left the building still impressed with Madame's momentary emotional weakness.

It was not too late to join my friends at the cocktail party but I really did not feel like rushing home, changing and then dashing back into town. Besides, I was tired. That evening, my father was particularly tense. For some time, business hadn't been as good as expected. Clients would fail to pay, and among them a couple of large accounts went under and dragged along my father in the process. He sold what he could to pay the taxman, the bank and some suppliers. We then all decided that it was better to start a new life elsewhere and so we moved close to Rio de Janeiro, to a city named Niterói right across the Guanabara Bay.

Although I looked forward to something new and perhaps even exciting, I was sad to leave behind a nice chunk of my heart. Friends I loved, experiences that had enriched my life and a marvellous city dipped in a giant garden of sky-blue Hydrangeas. Heartbroken, I jumped onto the mover's truck along with Gigi. For a while my eyes caressed the majestic mountains surrounding the valley and the old house that had promised us a happier and more peaceful life. Left behind were the garden, the workshop, the painful hardworking long hours, the sweat, the tears and fears. It was all over now. I held on to Gigi and let my tears flow freely. No one could see me huddled between pillows and furniture. The noise of the truck engine was so loud that I did not have to refrain from sobbing aloud. Smart and sensitive, Gigi tried eagerly to cheer me up by licking off the tears from my face.

A couple of hours later, the truck stopped at a four-storey apartment building located two blocks away from the São Francisco Beach in Niterói. It was a two-bedroom, living room, bath and kitchen apartment, small but cozy and within the family's new budget. Maybe now mother would stop complaining about the vast areas to be kept clean.

From the São Francisco beach, looking across the Guanabara Bay was Rio de Janeiro, the city of a million lights, charms and hopes. To cross to the other side there were motorboats. The older ones, some locals called *Barcaças*, resembled the old Mississippi paddleboats. The average travelling time was twenty to thirty minutes, depending on tides and weather conditions. Up until then, I had known Rio only by fame, through postcards or pictures in magazines. The initial fear of the big city was soon replaced by wonder and love. I quickly adapted to the ferment of its streets and stores, the grandeur of its skyscrapers, monuments and variegated luxurious gardens. The splendid stretches of white, sandy beaches of Copacabana, Ipanema, Botafogo, Flamengo, Leblon and Barra da Tijuca, dotted with thousands of colorful umbrellas and perfectly suntanned bodies. The *Pão de Açucar* (Sugar Loaf) Mountain is the most famous landmark of Guanabara Bay, a solid granite prominence that rises at its entrance. I soon fell in love with the *cariocas*, so endowed by human warmth and genuine extrovert gaiety. Their every gesture turned into music, each set of words into a poem. At times, the entire city seemed to move at the unmistakable rhythm of Samba. Rich and poor, white and black, pretty and less pretty, all under the same blue sky, the same magnificent flag protected and blessed by the towering Cristo Redentor statue on top of the Corcovado Mountain.

The enthusiasm of the family was as great as the hope, which had spurred us to a new beginning. The job market, however, was not very promising for my father who, at the time was recuperating from a deep depression caused by the recent bankruptcy episode. Money, as usual, was short, yet life had to go on, the rent had to be paid and food had to be purchased. A brand new chapter was to begin in our lives and, once more, we had to resort to our inner strength and faith in God.

3

Prince of Whales Fashion House –
Rio de Janeiro

Luckily, it took me only two weeks to land a job interview at the Prince of Whales Fashion house and Boutique located in Rio's downtown core.

Sitting behind a desk cluttered with papers, pencils, fabric samples, catalogs, an unfinished sandwich, half a glass of water and piles upon piles of fashion magazines, was Mr. Aaron Rosenbaum. To me he appeared as a good-natured older gentleman. He had a large, bald spot on the crown of his head, a prominent nose and thin lips. The chin was almost inexistent whereas his big belly did compensate for the lack of other anatomical forms. His speech was confusing, like a constant mumble, difficult to understand at times. The suffocating February heat caused him to perspire abundantly. Pearls of sweat dripped down his big nose, which he wiped with a huge dirty, white handkerchief.

Between constant telephone interruptions, he would ask me a number of questions about my origins, experiences and references. I was slowly losing hope of getting the job when Roberto Guy, a former sales rep for Gentile Fashions walked into the premises and immediately recognized me.

"Well hello, sweetheart," he exclaimed, surprised. "What are you doing here?"

"Oh my, Roberto, do you know her?" Mr. Rosenbaum asked, wide-eyed.

"Do I know her? Of course I know her," Roberto replied with his powerful baritone voice. "She was one of the best models Gentile Fashions ever had."

Mr. Rosenbaum smiled sheepishly. Roberto Guy was a small man with grayish hair, bushy dark eyebrows and piercing green eyes. He always dressed elegantly and smelled good. Such attributes added to his convincing sales pitch turning him into a much searched-after sales person. He immediately asked Mr. Rosenbaum if he could occasionally borrow me for the Catalina swimwear exhibit.

"I don't think it is much to ask in exchange of having found you this jewel of a girl, right?" Roberto said.

Mr. Rosenbaum had obviously already forgotten that I had applied for the job based on his own ad and believed in Roberto's quick talk and agreed to the good deal. He was now eager to see me in their dresses and called in his assistant, Ruth, to help me with it. The collection was beautiful and each dress fit me as a glove. He also liked the way I walked back and forth and swirled around his desk, making him turn around in his swivel chair.

When I finished the presentation, Mr. Rosenbaum asked me to follow him. Without even telling me first, he simply introduced me to the different departments as their new official model. He then took me over to their luxury boutique, about half a block away from the atelier, where mainly the wealthier people could afford to buy. All I could do was admire the magnificent outfits on display in the shop window while mentally calculating the number of pay checks it would take me to purchase one of the items. *Maybe one day*, I teased myself. Mr. Rosenbaum introduced me to the various sales ladies who would occasionally need my services to model outfits for selected clients. The most important part of that day was that I got the job, thanks to Roberto, with a slightly higher salary than that at Gentile Fashions.

My job unfolded a little all over the place, but mainly in the tailor shop where I posed for two stylists. One was a slim, black beauty and the other, a stubby, middle-aged white woman. There was constant bickering between the two and I could clearly sense the tension and a certain rivalry between them, tinted with a fair amount of racism. The black female was proud to have succeeded in crossing the threshold of the slums and managed to enter the glamorous world of high fashion for people with means and to be paid generously for her performance. She was fast and very knowledgeable in her field. I admired and respected her for her talent and character. The white female was much older and less aggressive and her ambitions were apparently limited to the strictly necessary. However, the uninhibited efficiency and the growing professional achievements of her colored counterpart seemed to annoy her. Consequently, envy and frustration interfered with her performance.

Both girls competed for my cooperation and complicity and would do anything to gain my support during their often petty disputes. My impartiality, however, would leave them disappointed and at times even very angry. Out of spite, they would have me pose for endless hours in woollen outfits while the thermometer indicated a 38°C – 40°C in the shade and not even apologize for pinches or the sting of needles, wilful or not. I simply hated both girls in those occasions. But my lucky star never failed to help. Usually it was the handsome tailor Alberto Santos who came to my rescue, even though that meant more posing and sweating. I often tried to seek Mr. Rosenbaum's company and follow him in his visits to the various showrooms, which was not always a good idea though. I would often get stuck having to show off an evening gown, a fur coat or a tailleur to a snobbish, fussy *Madame* of the local high society. In spite of the many air conditioners and fans available in the various departments, the heat was still unbearable. I would have hardly applied a layer of make-up and already the perspiration would erase it all.

Occasionally, I was asked to run over to Roberto's office to show off some swimwear to a new buyer. There I was allowed to refresh myself by taking a quick shower in Roberto's deluxe bathroom and was able to redo my make-up before slipping into the latest swimsuit models. For my modeling job, Roberto would always squeeze a generous amount of money into my hand or give me a new bikini or, when extremely busy with his client, just press a quick peck on my cheek.

As I progressed in my job, I was also invited to participate in several fashion shows at the prestigious Copacabana Palace Hotel, situated along the Avenida Atlantica and right in front of the Copacabana beach. Upon request by Mr. Rosenbaum, I also appeared in various national fashion magazines. I was very pleased with my new success story but unlike the other professionals, my extra hour's services were not paid separately as they were "included" in the overall salary. So was transportation, cabs or buses. I felt bitter about it but did not argue.

"It's built in, in their race," my mother explained. "That's why they are mostly rich. They do not spend money foolishly and they know the art of bargaining." In time, I found out that mother was right.

Mr. Rosenbaum would often go up to the atelier to check on the new creations and patiently wait until I slipped into the various outfits and pirouetted around him. His satisfaction seemed to touch the sky whenever he brought along a friend or a special customer. His eyes would sparkle and a true smile would emerge from his lips, while he would point out each creation like had he done it himself. Before leaving, he would always tap me on a shoulder and mumble a "Good girl. Good girl." Whenever he visited the atelier alone, he would choose a corner or lean against one of the cutting tables and observe the activities in silence. His mind must have been wandering, pondering on something as he would suddenly jump out of his trance, pound his fist on the table and swear in Yiddish. His face would turn red and his eyes bulge out of their sockets while rivulets of sweat would run down his forehead.

I often wondered about the many strange thoughts criss-crossing his mind in those moments, responsible for triggering those sudden reactions of bad temper. As everyone in the room was deeply absorbed in their work, his explosions of anger must have been caused by other sources and directed to those same sources. Overall, he was not a bad man, simply a commander who not always knew how to command. The real commanders were his sisters-in-law, in charge of the boutique and the sales in general. Esther and Miriam were both very talented businesswomen, capable of persuading a client to buy an item normally considered an aesthetic monstrosity. I envied their creativity and often tried getting closer to them, to gain their trust and friendship, but the ladies were always too busy with business. Once again, I missed Lilli.

For a while, I did some freelance work for other companies and photographers. The extra income was good but not as good as some of my colleagues were making. I was not meant to climb the steps of stardom because I was not willing to pay the steep price required to reach the top. My strict upbringing did not include hopping into bed with an individual in exchange for favors. Show business, the fashion world and most of the entertainment industry were based on sexual favors. Apparently, my desire to succeed was not strong enough, and so, tired of the glamorous world of fashion, to be driven from pillar to post, considered nothing but a beautiful head without brains, I felt it was time to move on in a different direction.

One evening, while crossing the Guanabara Bay, enjoying the spectacular view of a purple-red sky and the million twinkling lights of the great city, I was approached by Mario, a neighbor who travelled the same route as I did. While chatting away, I touched the subject of changing my job to something less demanding and a little better paid.

"Well, that can be arranged," Mario said with a big smile. "My company could use a good secretary and the fact that you are familiar with the fashion industry is even better."

"Hey, I might just give it a try," I said with a hearty chuckle. "When do I start?"

"Tomorrow, if you wish," Mario replied.

"That's great. But I must give at least a week's notice to the boss."

According to Mario, there was not only the possibility to earn a lot more money, but also room for advancement. I would soon find out what Mario's Modas Brasileiras had in store for me.

Mr. Rosenbaum was very upset when I submitted my resignation; not as much for my leaving as for having to spend more money for a new ad to find a replacement. Between remarks, Mr. Rosenbaum kept pounding his desk while swearing in Yiddish. His favorite expression sounded like "May the lightings strike you." I tried to explain to him the better offer I had received, but he simply ignored my reasons. He told me about his hardships instead; on how broke he had been and still was. He did indeed always look very poor in his appearance. More than that, he looked sloppy. On my last day, Mr. Rosenbaum assured me of his support.

"Should you ever regret having left us, come back," he said with a big grin on his face. "I'll re-hire you and even give you back your old salary."

I thought he was just joking and laughed heartily about his offer, whereas Mr. Rosenbaum was dead serious about his proposition.

4

Mario Modas Brasileiras

Along with his younger brother and a retired acquaintance, Mario owned a small sales office in downtown Rio. They represented several fashion manufacturers. Mario reiterated the need for a good secretary who could keep their records organized, samples updated and orderly, and occasionally, accompany him on short business trips.

My initial enthusiasm dropped considerably when my eyes met the chaotic surroundings in which I was supposed to work, but I soon overlooked the mess and got down to business. For an entire week I filed letters, invoices, bills, catalogs and address cards. I cleaned up the showroom, placing all outfits on proper hangers or racks, just as I did at Gentile's. I dumped old empty boxes and beer and other liqueur bottles. Mario was impressed and visibly pleased after he returned from a one-week business trip. Used to disorder, it took him a while to adapt to the new environment and he relied heavily on my assistance to hand him the necessary documents.

Once the office was up and running properly, Mario decided to take me along on some of his local field trips. We travelled mostly by cab or bus. The fact that Mario, as a sales person, covering a rather large territory, did not own a vehicle surprised and disturbed me initially, and triggered my suspicion about his ability to even pay me a salary. Maybe I was just imagining things and quickly brushed aside any negative thoughts and scenarios.

I very much enjoyed watching Mario's sales pitch and tried learning from him. He would generally start with a resolute handshake, followed by a friendly embrace and loud greetings. For starters, he would ask about the client's family, then came weather, a pocketful of jokes, which he would tell with such ability, to cause incessant laughter by anyone present, followed by sports—Soccer, of course—and a *cafézinho*, similar to an Italian espresso, from the bar at the corner. While sipping on the coffee or a drink, Mario would pull out his purchase order booklet and easily fill a page or two with orders, applying overwhelming discounts, which would give the client the impression of having closed the deal of the century. He rarely walked out of a sales meeting without a substantial order in his hands. My contribution was helping him remember appointments and occasionally showcase a new piece of garment. Mario was grateful and showered me with gifts such as chocolate boxes, a dress or two from the collection sample set, shoes and matching purses. Each time, I refused and each time Mario said, "Never mind, you deserve it. I want you to have it."

Even though I liked the idea of getting free merchandise, especially pretty outfits, I felt awkward in accepting them because Mario was not a rich man after all. Even the books in the office revealed a precarious financial situation. It was only after Mario started sending me long-stemmed red roses that I began to worry. He was a married man, had a child and was not even my ideal for a boyfriend. Gently, but firmly, I explained to him that I had no intention of deviating from our professional relationship. Mario, however, was not willing to accept rejection.

"All I ask you is to give it a chance," he said. "In time, you'll learn to love me."

"And what if I don't, then what?"

"You will, I just know it."

I began to feel uncomfortable and decided to avoid his company as much as possible, pretending to be busy with paperwork or after work, making up a date to avoid traveling with him back home. With more time spent in the office, I noticed Mario's brother withdrawing money from the petty cash box, often without leaving a voucher or a simple note. The older partner instead wasted time in slumbering behind his desk or getting drunk at the corner store bar. Even I, who at the time was still inexperienced in business matters, recognized the fact that the company could not survive like that in the long run. Actually, it was a rather short run. My pay check always came late and once did not arrive at all. I realized that I was sailing on a sinking ship and confronted Mario about all that I had observed. I also stressed the fact that I could not continue working for him if the company was unable to pay me. I had a family to help, which needed food and rent money. Under pressure, Mario fell apart and began to sob.

"I'd rather have my family starving than you and your folks," he said.

"Oh, come on. Don't exaggerate now. That is a very stupid thing to say."

"You just can't do this to me. You can't just simply leave me. If you just knew how much I love you. My every thought revolves around you." His eyes flooded by tears.

His emotional outburst left me extremely uncomfortable. I was not used to seeing adult males crying and did not know how to react to that scene. A long silence followed.

"Your feelings are very flattering, but as I already told you before, you are just a good friend to me, a neighbor and a boss," I said with mixed feelings of revulsion and compassion.

"You are being selfish and cruel. After all I've done for you."

"Oh, for heaven's sakes Mario, stop that nonsense. You should rather concentrate on your business and your family."

"Oh, give me a break with this family thing, always the family. You have become part of my family, too." He hit the desk with his fist. "I simply don't know what I would do without you."

"You would do just fine, like you always have, even before knowing me."

"But it wouldn't be the same, don't you understand?"

"No. I don't understand. I came to work for you because you had promised me the possibility of pursuing a career in the sales field and a better salary. The better salary lasted only two months." I could barely control my temper.

"But I've been working so hard, can't you see?"

"I sure can, but that does not solve my problem. Besides, I feel extremely uneasy with you breathing down my neck at all times. You've become possessive, jealous and we don't even have a romantic relationship. If you don't stop this behavior, I will definitely leave." I was still holding back the anger that was building up.

"But I love you very dearly."

"You should reserve that love for your wife and your child."

Mario then promised to refrain from his amorous advances and again begged me to be patient and remain a little longer. I decided to give him one last chance. However, in the following weeks the situation precipitated with a serious government crisis and a general decline in the business world. Nobody was buying or investing. To complicate things even more, Mario's brother disappeared with all the company's cash while the older partner spent his days in a blissful stupor, littering the office with empty bottles of *cachaça* (Brazilian sugar cane brandy).

It became obvious that the company was close to bankruptcy, so I started searching for another job. When Mario found out, he tried desperately to stop me and even threatened to commit suicide and it was then that I rebelled against his oppressive nature and called it a definite quits. Once again, I had learned new lessons and promised myself to be less credulous, less trusting, taking more control over my emotions, refrain enthusiasm for a particular task, gift or invitation and never to talk about my innermost feelings or mix idealism and poetry with business.

After two long weeks of inactivity, filled with more anguish than moments of rest, I realized that it was time to pick up the broken pieces and start all over again. While leaving the Sunday service at the local São Francisco parish one evening, my mother stopped to chat with Father Joseph, who had become a good friend of the family. During their conversation, my mother brought up the subject of my job hunting. After pondering for a moment, the priest remembered that an American welfare organization was looking for a capable, bi-lingual secretary with good typing skills. For a moment, a cold chill traveled down my back. I had never worked as a real secretary before; my typing skills were practically non-existent and my knowledge of the English language wasn't much better. No large company would hire such a dumbbell, I figured. I was about to reject the possibility when my father's favorite saying came into my mind.

"Trust yourself. Our lucky star has never let us down."

The thought of our precarious financial situation, along with mother's reassuring blue eyes, gave me the necessary incentive to give it a chance and try.

5

C R S – Father Anthony

I went to the appointment arranged for me by Father Joseph with the mind in turmoil and the heart pounding wildly in my chest. I possessed no office skills or certificates and was doubtful if goodwill and enthusiasm alone would qualify me for the position. The elevator stopped at the seventh floor. I rang the bell at Suite 701 and a beautifully tanned young man opened the door.

"May I help you, Miss...?" he said with a bright smile, revealing impeccable white teeth.

I barely introduced myself and already a tall, handsome Stewart Granger look-alike priest in a long black cassock came along and welcomed me in.

"Hello, there," he said with a hint of a smile on his face. "You must be the girl Father Joseph sent over, right?"

"Yes Sir," I whispered.

Somehow, I was intimidated by his towering height, the authority in his voice, and his social position. Father Anthony had brown hair with some grey speckles on the temples. His vivacious hazel-brown eyes screened me from head to toe. Between questions, he took quick drags on his pipe, which surprised me, as I had never seen a priest smoking before. Having attended a nun's institute, I grew up with the notion that a priest was a representative of God on earth and therefore almost a perfect being, not in need of the common earthly pleasures as were smoking, drinking or overeating. In my eyes they were some sort of holy men or close to it anyway.

Father Anthony was a missionary who had devoted his life to the cause of the needy all over the world. His background was German, and therefore, he spoke that language, even if with a heavy American accent. From South America he picked up some Spanish and Portuguese. At times he would just mix all these languages in the hope of making himself better understood without realizing, that it just confused the recipient even more. With great interest, he listened as I told him, in my very scholastic English, about myself and my previous work experiences. He then handed me a sheet of paper and invited me to read the text aloud. Taking it as a diction test, I read it with the American accent I had acquired by watching Hollywood movies, hoping to impress Father Anthony. As soon as I finished, he removed the paper from my hands.

"Good," he said. "Now tell me, what was it you just read there?"

My first reaction was that of panic. A sudden memory blank prevented me from recalling any of the contents of the text. I blushed, felt my ears burning and wished to be swallowed by mother earth that very instant. Father Anthony concealed his disappointment and invited me to copy a letter on the typewriter. I could sense his eyes pointed towards my back and felt almost as paralyzed. To top it all off, the typewriter was an IBM Selectric I had never touched before. My eyes ran over the entire machine surface trying desperately to figure out a way to turn it on. Again, Father Anthony was disappointed but merciful and showed me how to "turn the darn machine on."

With some hesitation, I handed over my "work of art" to Father Anthony who gazed over the piece of paper, shaking his head in slow motion. The typing errors suddenly appeared even worse as he went on underlining them with a big red pencil. Again, I felt my face burning and was convinced of having lost my chance. Father Anthony thanked me for coming and promised to let me know soon about his decision. Never before had my return home been so long and painful. I blamed myself for my stupidity and inability but rejected the idea of being just a pretty, empty-headed blond. I would work on it and be somebody someday, I told myself, while crossing the Guanabara Bay and staring over the glittery surface of its waters.

At home, my father and mother tried to minimize my disappointment. Somehow, they refused to believe that I wasn't capable of handling that job or any other job for that matter. They suggested that I contact Father Joseph and honestly tell him what happened. After some hesitation, I decided to do just that. In the meantime, I also borrowed an old Underwood typewriter and practiced for hours every day. If I was to be given a second chance, I had better be well-prepared this time. My tenacity and the ambition to advance in life would be rewarded a few weeks later with a second interview.

Father Anthony welcomed me with a generous smile.

"I hope you are less nervous this time," he said, and gave me a text to copy. "Now, try to take it easy and relax." Then he walked away.

At least this time I knew how to switch the darn machine on. I took a deep breath and devoted all my concentration to the test. I definitely wasn't a fast typist but I finished with very few errors. Father Anthony seemed satisfied and invited me to start working the following Monday. Working hours were 9 a.m. to 5:30 p.m., with an hour for lunch. The salary was considerably higher than what Mario had last paid me.

Overjoyed with the outcome of this second meeting, I could hardly wait to get home to tell my folks the good news. While waiting for the boat to arrive, I stopped at the nearby bar, ordered a big glass of beer and drank it in a few quick gulps. I had felt the urge to celebrate and the way home was long. Once aboard the boat, I chose a seat near a window to let the sea breeze and the sunshine caress my face. Between the beer and the new job, I was overcome by a sense of euphoria and well-being and even the people and the world around me seemed prettier and less threatening.

Close to home, I saw mother and father looking out the window. They both displayed a large, happy smile as I gave them a thumb up signal, meaning the interview went well. That weekend we all celebrated. Even my brother, Frank, whose only love and interest centered on math and infinitesimal equations, made an exception and accompanied me to collect oysters from the nearby beach cliffs.

On Monday morning, I showed up at the office at 9 o'clock sharp. A while later, the lady I was to replace, arrived and began teaching me all the things I should know and do. Her instructions went straight through my ear tunnel—in one end, and out the other side. The lady spoke too fast and garbled most of her instructions. A good source of information instead was Paulo, the beautifully tanned office boy. He was my same age, twenty. Medium height, slim, shiny black hair and eyes, a boxer nose and fleshy lips, he was familiar with office routines, with Father Anthony's habits, desires and, most importantly, his undecipherable handwriting.

Initially, my task consisted in translating Father Anthony's sermons from English into Portuguese. The chapel where he would celebrate daily Mass was mainly attended by Portuguese-speaking worshippers. The text had to be typed in double space and capital letters for easy reading. For the translations, I had to make constant use of a dictionary, which helped me to develop and enrich my English vocabulary.

A few weeks later, I started to take dictation but as I had no formal shorthand skills, Father Anthony would dictate slowly and patiently to allow me time to write down each word and sometimes, even correcting my spelling. My greatest torment was to speak English on the telephone. I feared not understanding or being understood, and the more I worried about it, the worse it became. I would avoid long conversations or messages, passing on the call to Father Anthony almost immediately or, in his absence, telling the caller that the boss wasn't in and then hurriedly hanging up.

One day, Father Anthony was truly upset with me. Had I not only omitted the reason of a certain call, but I also failed to ask for the caller's name.

"Why the heck don't you make an effort to speak English, damn...." he said slapping his lips like reprimanding himself for the cursing. "Are you or aren't you my secretary?"

"I was afraid I wouldn't understand," I muttered, shaking from head to toe.

"And you never will if you keep doing things your way. You must insist, and if you did not understand something the first time, well, you ask the caller to repeat it again, till you get everything clear, understand?"

I acknowledged with a nod.

Father Anthony's outbursts were similar to those of my father, who was his same age, 49. They would both punch the table with their fist to come across to the listener. I hated their expressions of anger or ironic remarks, which easily threw me into deep depressive moods. As with all good-natured people, however, Father Anthony would never sulk for too long. After a while, he would walk over to my desk and humbly apologize.

"You know, I was a little nervous," Father Anthony said.

I was always ready to forgive, firstly because I knew he was right and I was wrong, and secondly, because I was eager in keeping up a harmonious relationship with the boss. When there was peace and quiet, my work produced better results.

One small problem, however, would remain unchanged for another while and that was the boss's handwriting. Father Anthony would often write drafts of letters and reports and then have me type another draft. In Paulo's absence, I had to bother Father Anthony about a scribble. Most of the time he did not mind the interruptions, but there were moments when he would enact impatience and angrily re-write the word in a corner of the good copy. I had to re-type the whole letter or report, instead of just correcting the one word I could not decipher. It was more time and paper waste but certainly a good exercise for me.

Like every beginning, it was not easy, especially in a field I knew so little about. I would often get angry at myself for not being a fast enough learner and consequently fell into deep bouts of depression, which pushed me close to suicidal thoughts. While looking to the street down below from the seventh floor window, I once wondered how it would feel like jumping. My nerves had become fragile and I would feel hurt even with the slightest criticism. I was convinced that only death could release me, and everyone else for that matter, from all the unpleasant earthly sufferings. Luckily deep down, Father Anthony was also a sensitive person who recognized a tormented soul. With a friendly pat on my shoulders, he would find a way to cheer me up.

"Take it easy kiddo. Don't take things so hard. You're still so very young. You'll learn in time. You'll learn."

It was indeed so. Slowly, but steadily, I climbed the ladder of knowledge and experience, thanks also to Father Anthony's generous patience and guidance. After a full year with the organization, I had become sufficiently fluent in English and was capable of taking care of the office without Father Anthony's constant supervision. I was no longer afraid to write letters or to entertain English-speaking guests over the phone or in person.

Life, however, could not always run smoothly. Occasional problems and mishaps would still occur due mainly to my naivety. While Father Anthony was away one day, in a meeting at the American Embassy, I received a phone call from a certain Mario Machado who would only leave his phone number without any particular message. I relayed the call as soon as Father Anthony returned to the office.

"Who is this Mario Machado?" he asked.

"I don't know. He refused to leave a message. He just wants you to call him back," I replied.

"Well, is he a priest?" Father Anthony asked.

"Oh, no, he is just a man."

"What the heck are you saying there?" Father Anthony said, slightly annoyed. "Do you mean to say that a priest is not a man?"

For a moment we stood silently, staring at each other. Then realizing the humorous overtone of the incident, we both cracked up laughing.

As time went on, working for Father Anthony became more pleasant. He would entrust me with new responsibilities such as the bookkeeping part of the office. Morton Page, working out of the sixth floor office and in charge of the import of surplus goods for the needy, was the man who would patiently teach me the basics of bookkeeping. Morton was a very friendly man in his mid-thirties, extremely dedicated and hard-working. He was also a very good teacher as I quickly picked up his instructions, even though anything related to figures had never been one of my favorite subject matters. Preferences, however, change with age and I learned to like my task so much, that I never minded working overtime or even taking work home when there were minor discrepancies to be cleared. What pride and joy filled my ego, whenever I would trace a given error without Morton's assistance.

Through the assiduous reading of memos and reports received from the New York headquarters, I became more and more familiar with the very nature and structure of the welfare agency. This also reinforced the professional bond between Father Anthony and me. With my parent's consent, I would invite him for lunch or dinner. The very first Sunday that he came for lunch, he appeared at the door with a large carton filled with all sorts of canned food, cookies and bottles of beer. He enjoyed every bit of the Hungarian *paprikás* my mother had prepared and did not hesitate to go for seconds. He returned many more Sundays after that one. He spent the afternoon telling about his experiences as chaplain in the United States Air force during WWII and about his ordeal in Korea. Having traveled extensively around the globe, he had collected countless memories of good and bad events, which he generously shared with whomever was willing to listen. I was one of his fascinated listeners and often wished he was a little younger and not a priest.

In addition to my admiration for Father Anthony, I was also extremely grateful to him for the chance he had given me within the organization, for the patience with which he taught me all I knew about office work at that point, as well as for his constant interest in my professional development. In my opinion, a simple "Thank You" was not enough. He deserved something special as a token of my gratitude, something like an oil-painted portrait. I was cleaning up a section in his office shelves when a shoebox filled with hundreds of pictures came tumbling down. Father Anthony helped to collect them and put them back in the box. He would show the odd picture of himself explaining where it had been taken. I really liked one of the pictures where he displayed a happy smile and must have been a lot younger. I asked if I could keep the picture. Father Anthony gave it to me but asked me to be discreet with it. I could now continue with my sketching and the painting. When the canvas was finally dry, I wrapped it in gift paper and gave it to him.

"A little gift for you in appreciation for all you've done for me," I said blushing while watching excitedly as he opened the package.

Father Anthony was definitely surprised. He leaned back in his swivel chair and stuck the pipe in his mouth while holding up the picture with both hands.

"Very nice Isabel, very nice indeed," he said while standing up to shake my hand. "Thank you so very much."

A few weeks later, however, he brought the picture back to the office. He chose a moment alone with me.

"Would it be possible for you to touch up my cheeks a little?" he whispered. "See, I have the impression that the way you painted them makes them seem a lot chubbier than what they really are. Don't you agree?"

Somewhat surprised with his request, I agreed to fix the cheeks even though I could not see much difference between the painting and the model.

Weeks later he was invited to participate in a local TV show to promote the organization's welfare campaign in order to raise more public funds for the needy. He seemed very nervous that morning, pacing up and down in the office and occasionally retiring into the washroom from where he would walk out shortly after with his hair brushed to a perfect shine. The fact that he would ask Paulo's opinion about his appearance only confirmed that image was an important issue as well. The show turned out to be quite successful and by the time he returned to the office later that afternoon, he displayed a smile of great satisfaction.

Like most Americans, Father Anthony loved sports and in particular baseball. In vain he would try to explain the technicalities of a curve ball to either Paulo or myself because neither was familiar with the baseball game. He did, however, come to appreciate soccer as well, Brazil's national sport and number one favorite along with carnival and samba. When in 1962 Brazil won the championship 3-1 against Czechoslovakia, Father Anthony had a fun time watching the crowd parade on the city streets, celebrating in style with confetti, drumbeats, whistles, samba and *caipirinhas* (sugar, lime and cachaça). That day, he even allowed Paulo to bring his small portable transistor radio to the office so he could follow the game. After each goal, Paulo would jump from his chair, run over to the boss and yell "Goal, Father, big goal of Brazil." Father Anthony would smile happily while dragging on his pipe. When later Brazil was declared champion, Paulo's screams joined that of the jubilant crowds on the streets. It was like one giant thunderous roar. People were delirious with joy, dancing, singing and drinking. Many hugged, kissed or cried due to the emotion. From skyscraper windows, more people would drop confetti, shredded paper or even toilette paper rolls. Carried away by the rapture of the moment, Father Anthony picked up his waste paper basket and emptied its contents through the window, laughing away like a mischievous kid who had just committed a prank.

In time, Father Anthony had become more than just a boss to Paulo and me. He had become our best friend and we both would do just about anything to keep the man happy. Small attentions such as a fresh coffee in the morning prepared by Paulo or a particularly tidy desktop done by me were always very much appreciated. It then would take Father Anthony a whole five minutes to turn tidiness into chaos again. Papers spread all over the desk's surface, pens and pencils disappearing under piles of documents, coffee spills, ashes blown over paperwork and so forth. Noticing my disappointment one day, he tried to come up with the best explanation he had.

"Not that I do not appreciate an orderly desk top, but most people would be inclined to think that you haven't got enough work to do," he said with a mischievous smile. He took a deep drag from his pipe and glanced at me sideways. "If I'd see your desk too tidy, I would think that you haven't got enough work to do and would obviously feel tempted to find you some additional tasks to keep you busy with. Remember that for the future." He winked an eye. I would forever treasure his observation.

There was a period of restlessness as Father Anthony learned about his mother's illness and decided to spend some time in the United States with her. The few weeks without his presence seemed endless and I often prayed for his mother's recovery just so he would return and everything would get back to normal again, without the constant intrusions of Morton who in the meantime had taken it upon himself to look after Father Anthony's business. I was relieved when the boss finally returned, even though he was a different man. His face was pale and emaciated and his usual bright smile was replaced by only a faint outline of a smile. His apathy, however, vanished as per magic when a few weeks later he was promoted and appointed General Director for all South American branches of the organization. Such appointment involved extensive traveling and although I was proud and happy for him, I was at the same time sad with the perspective of seeing a lot less of him.

Father Anthony's hectic schedule slackened only with the arrival of one particular hot summer. He would often feel very uncomfortable in his long, black cassock so he switched into the more practical clergyman suit. He looked a lot less clumsy and could easily stretch his long legs on top of his desk.

Considering the religious environment and my own upbringing, I respectfully dressed in very conservative long sleeved, ankle length dresses, but summer was an entirely different story. There was no air-conditioning in the office and the couple of small fans would just stir up the warm air even more. The clothing sticking to one's body parts was extremely uncomfortable. Despite a great deal of initial hesitation and apprehension, I showed up one day in a light, sleeveless colorful summer dress. Father Anthony screened me briefly, smiled and then nodded in approval. I was relieved. While working with Father Anthony, I noticed that the American clergy in general, was far more tolerant, open-minded and flexible towards human needs than their Latin American counterparts.

Towards the middle of May, Father Anthony was overjoyed in learning that he was to be assigned the title of Monsignor by His Holiness, the Pope. In June he flew back to the United States for the investiture ceremony. When he returned to Rio, he gave me a picture of him dressed in his new purple Monsignor robes.

"I imagine I will have to call you Monsignor from now on," I said.

"Well, so it should be, but I can make an exception for you. Just call me Father, as usual. In a way, I feel a little like a father to you anyway." He laughed and gave me a big hug.

In the meantime, he kept wearing his black or white cassock or the clergyman, leaving the purple outfit for special occasions.

During the entire months of July and August, Father Anthony kept busy with reports and new projects. Consequently, my workload also increased. I was happy with my career choice and also with the self-esteem I managed to build up thanks to the appreciation I received not only from third parties but especially from Father Anthony, who at times bragged to his visitors about having the most loyal and efficient secretary. My skills had improved to the point that Father Anthony would approve most of my initiatives. Unlike the earlier outbursts, when finding an occasional typo, he would call me aside and gently point to the mistake with a winking eye. Most of the time, however, I was able to catch my own mistakes and correct them before submitting my work to the boss. Both Paulo and I would work in such harmony that a glance was sufficient for us to capture Father Anthony's minimum desires.

As it often happens in life, good things always end too soon and so the feelings of bliss and happiness vanished as Father Anthony was requested to move to new headquarters in Lima, Peru. I felt as if the ground had been removed from under my feet. I was angry with my boss's superiors. Initially, not even Father Anthony was too thrilled with yet another transfer and had mixed feelings about it. He would certainly miss the daily routine and the familiar surroundings, yet on the other hand, he was excited to meet with new challenges in a different country. Despite all efforts, I was unable to conceal my disappointment and dismay as the departure date arrived, too soon.

"Well, this is it, I guess," Father Anthony said with a sigh of resignation. "My mission here is completed. It is now up to you people to carry on and continue the good work."

It was an emotional moment for everyone. Father Anthony hugged and bid farewell to a teary-eyed Paulo, shook hands with Morton and all the others including Bill, Father Anthony's replacement who later became known as the "Gentle Giant" because of his height and peaceful, gentle manners. At last, he hugged me.

"Take care of yourself kiddo and don't work too hard," he said, while giving me a peck on the forehead.

We then escorted him to the Galeão International Airport and remained until the PanAm plane disappeared behind angry gray clouds.

6

CRS - Bill, the Gentle Giant

A Canadian layman, Bill was a 6'3" tall man with reddish-brown hair and blue eyes like peaceful northern lakes. A devout Catholic, he was married to a Canadian lady who had already given him six children. Professionally, Bill was an architect, but his wealthy background allowed him to be compassionate and to donate some time to the cause of the less fortunate. He was a very soft spoken, relaxed man in his mid-forties, who disliked being bothered with silly things. Just as he would never bother anyone as long as the work was carried out properly and on time. The only changes Bill introduced were transferring the offices. Along with Morton, they would move up to the seventh floor. Paulo would stay with them. I joined Marianne instead, the senior secretary on the sixth floor.

Marianne was a tall, middle-aged lady of German background whose motto was precision and efficiency. Aside from my usual bookkeeping tasks, I was to become her assistant. I was to help her with typing and filing. Even though it was not easy to please Marianne, I knew that I could learn a fair bit from the lady. My ambitions and desire to succeed were strong and helped me to accept Marianne's demanding and perfectionist nature. She would have me retype any letter or report in case of the slightest error or cancellation marks. Everything had to be impeccable.

Despite her fluency in three languages, German, English and Portuguese, Marianne would still make use of the various dictionaries, exhorting me to do the same in order to improve and enrich my vocabulary. Thanks to Marianne, I learned numerous, valuable tricks pertaining to the secretarial field such as the proper use of an electric typewriter, obtaining perfect margin distances, erasing mistakes without leaving a trace at a time when liquid paper was not yet invented, to use several layers of carbon paper without getting the ink all over one's hands and documents. She taught me about the different letter and memo styles. Contrary to one's belief, there was no standard format for the entire world. The Americans had one style, the Brazilians, the Germans, the Italians had yet another, and so forth. Marianne taught me to write more impressive reports, which would definitely impress the reader, and a sophisticated filing and follow-up system.

"Don't ever rely on your memory alone," she would tell me. "No matter how young you are or how smart you think you are, always write things down. You might come across a situation when a note may become extremely handy, even save you from trouble." Marianne had an excellent memory herself, yet would make notes all the time, even for the most irrelevant things.

One day, during a coffee break, talking about weather and work, Marianne gently suggested, "You know Isabel, you really should take a shorthand course. For a professional secretary, it is an indispensable skill."

I was somewhat surprised with her suggestion as not too long ago she had mentioned that if she had to keep on using her shorthand skills, at the rate Bill was dictating, she would end up forgetting the skill altogether. Bill was very slow dictating. Marianne could have easily written down everything in long hand, instead, she would often just doze off while waiting for the next sentence. I decided to accept Marianne's advice, nonetheless, and enrolled in the Pitman's shorthand course. I thought it would be fun to learn some modern hieroglyphics that the public in general would not be able to understand.

Initially, my interaction with Bill was very sporadic. It was mainly Marianne's job to bring him the mail and other documentation to view and sign. I would see him only once or twice a month to submit the balance sheets or to ask his opinion about the proper allocation of a given expense. The preparation of the monthly financial statement would take me only a few hours. Once finished my own tasks, I would help Marianne. I enjoyed typing the endless, long reports. Not only would I have to proofread them twice, but also Marianne would read them over one more time before submitting them for Bill's approval and signature. The original was then mailed to the headquarters in New York; one copy was filed in the project's file, another in the master file in chronological order, and the fourth and last copy in the follow-up file.

Marianne's files resembled an army of soldiers perfectly aligned, neat and clean. No scribbles or coffee spills were allowed on documents, or more than one staple. Excessive staples would not only increase the volume of a folder on the upper left corner, but could hurt one's hand while manipulating the document. It could also end up tangled up with other pages or documents unrelated to that particular file. There was no waste of time in searching for a particular letter or document because everything was meticulously numbered and recorded. A project could be identified and located in chronological order by date, title or category. Only in exceptionally rare cases would Marianne allow anybody to access the master file, and if a document had to leave the office, even if for only half hour, Marianne would record date, time, reference and the name of the person who took the document. The same procedure was followed upon return of the document. After a few months, I had mastered Marianne's job to the point where I felt quite comfortable in replacing her during the holidays or whenever she couldn't make it in to work.

Not always, however, would the working environment be a relaxed one. Marianne could at times be just as nasty and irritating as she was sweet and understanding, showering me with little gifts to gain even more of my support and cooperation. At times her possessive character was overpowering and oppressive. She often tried to force her lifestyle upon me and not always did I know how to handle the situation. She truly believed that her type of balanced diet was essential to the upkeep of a balanced physical and mental elasticity. True to my own age, however, I preferred what was to become known as junk food in later years such as hamburgers, hotdogs, milkshakes and the like. Besides my preference for that type of food, it was also more compatible with my daily food allowance. Only every so often, to please Marianne, did I go with her to a local eatery to taste some of her balanced foods such as black beans, rice, fries, steak and salad. I liked the Brazilian staple food, but the portions served at that eatery, and easily devoured by Marianne, were enormous. Besides, I was not used to having such large quantities of food during lunchtime and especially not during the hot season. Even though I did not share most of Marianne's views on daily life and disliked her over-protectiveness, I did not have the heart to reject her concerns.

One of those concerns, true to Marianne's own concept of *mens sana in corpore sano*, was that I should practice more sports, do more exercise and stay in touch with nature. She suggested that I join her son and friends in their nature walks. To get Marianne off my back, I accepted one of their invitations and met with the boys one Sunday morning at the Red Beach, close to the Sugar Loaf. From there, we proceeded towards the planned nature's walk. After all, how bad could a nature walk be, I wondered. Walking in a tropical forest couldn't be but beautiful, observing all the lush vegetation, listening to the songs of the various birds and maybe even collect wild orchids to take home for my mother. What the boys had in mind, however, was entirely different. After a long walk through a dense patch of vegetation, we reached a small clearing where I was faced with a huge rock formation. Marianne's son, Karl, opened his rope bag and pulled out a harness fitted with carabiners and a long, strong rope.

"What are you going to do with that?" I asked.

"Watch me carefully," Karl replied and proceeded to fit himself with the equipment and to show off his climbing ability. His agility made the climb seem so easy, that when he asked me, "Do you think you can do this?" I did not hesitate to reply that I could. Karl came back down, helped me with the harness and showed me how to use the carabiner on the steel cable that ran along the entire mountain surface. He then exhorted me to try climbing the rock in front of me. I tried a couple of times and did not think of it as being a big deal. Being a fairly strong swimmer, I had developed healthy, strong muscles and could easily pull myself up. Karl was the first one to climb, followed by me and then Gilberto, who would act as safety net in case I would slip and fall.

After a half hour climbing, I began to wonder how much longer. I did not dare look around me, nor backwards or downwards and concentrated entirely on the rock surface ahead of me.

"Depending on how fast we move on, it should take us at least another hour from this point," said Karl.

"Is there a chance to rest a little?" I asked. "My hands are getting sore."

"There is a little nook further up. We'll rest there."

I did not want to let the boys think that I was a coward, afraid of climbing, and carried on, clenching my teeth and concealing the exhaustion that was taking over. At a certain point we had to climb over a bulge in the rock, which to me seemed an impossible feat. My arms were achy, my feet bruised because I had to remove the leather sandals to get a better grip on the stone. After all, I was dressed for a nature's walk, not for mountain climbing. My hands were bruised and bleeding from the friction on the steel cable. Twice I almost lost my grip on the cable and slid backwards, also scraping my knees. Karl prevented me from sliding further by holding on to the rope that connected the three of us. Then with a last super human effort and Karl's supportive coaching, I overcame the protruding bulge and finally landed on a ledge with access to a small recess in the rock, big enough for the three of us to sit and relax for a while. Only then, did the boys disclose to me that we were climbing the famous Sugar Loaf, a granite and quartz mountain rising 396 metres (1,299 feet) above sea level. The view from that point was breathtaking. The mountain below was surrounded by luxurious vegetation and the Atlantic Ocean ran into the bay with its shimmering deep blue waters. A cable car was on its way up to the top carrying a load of tourists. It was a warm, sunny day with a most beautiful, cloudless blue sky. While sitting inside the nook, I noticed a metal plaque bolted on the rock wall in front of me that had a date inscribed.

"What is that metal plate all about?" I asked.

"Oh, there is a telephone inside," Karl said, convincingly.

Setting aside my pride, I jumped at that revelation.

"Oh, good, so we can call in the rescue team because I am not moving from here," I said with determination.

There was a long moment of silence, followed by laughter from Karl and Gilberto.

"I was just kidding," said Karl. "There is no telephone in there. It's a plaque for some guy who fell from here and died. We will have to continue the climb. Another fifteen-twenty minutes and we should be on the top. This is actually the shortest stretch, right under the cable car line. So, hang in there."

Disappointed, angry, tired and sore, I had no other way out but to follow the boys to the very top. I was also very thirsty but Karl allowed me only a few sips saying, that if I drank too much, I would lose the necessary energy to complete the ascent. I began to feel a little better when the people from the cable cars, now much closer to us, waved and snapped pictures of the three of us climbers. At our arrival on the top, we were received like heroes, with much fanfare, applause and taps on our shoulders.

I ran to the washroom. My bladder needed urgent relief; my hair was a mess and the make-up had disappeared from the perspiration. I did not hesitate to splash water all over myself. I also cleaned up my bloodied hands, knees and feet. Since I had to climb barefooted, the friction on the sharp edges of the rock, as well as glass chips from broken bottles tossed down by negligent tourists, caused me several cuts. I then joined Karl and Gilberto at the terrace bar. Instead of water, I ordered and drank a whole 750 ml bottle of ice-cold Brahma Chopp beer. It had never tasted so good in all my life.

"So, which route should we take to climb down now?" Karl teased.

"Oh, you guys just go ahead without me," I said. "This was my very first and last nature walk of this kind. I'll be taking the cable car down, thank you very much."

We all took the cable car back down. Instead of waiting around for the bus, I took a cab to the ferry terminal. I chose a bench on the upper deck of the boat from where I had the best view of Rio's landscape. As the boat slowly passed by the Sugar Loaf, I could hardly believe that just a few hours ago I had been struggling to climb that remarkable monument of nature. I was filled with sudden pride and satisfaction. The next morning, my muscles were so sore and stiff that I needed mother's assistance to get dressed.

While Bill thought I was a funny sight, walking and moving like a robot, with hands and feet wrapped in gauze, Marianne was furious at the boys for having taken me on an outing that could have become a dangerous, if not fatal adventure. For me instead, it would remain a life-long memory and whenever I was faced with problems that seemed insurmountable at the time, I would whisper to myself: "if you were able to climb the Sugar Loaf in Rio, you can overcome this hurdle, too."

The relative peaceful harmony was broken one day by the unexpected visit of Paula, Morton's wife. Both Marianne and I were surprised with her visit, asking for her husband on the sixth floor. He had been working on the seventh floor for several months and must have certainly informed her accordingly. I invited her to have a seat while grabbing the phone and dialling Morton's extension. Not receiving an answer, we assumed that he was still out for lunch. Instead of heading to the seventh floor, however, Paula decided to wait at the sixth floor. Marianne and I returned to our work. Occasionally, I glanced over at Paula. She seemed nervous, constantly checking her watch. She did not remove her dark glasses, perhaps to better see without being seen. She was of medium height, brown hair and no remarkable traits or particulars aside from a severe case of rosacea around her nose and chin.

Marianne and I tried to establish a friendly conversation with her, but she would answer only in monosyllables. She was definitely not in the mood to socialize. To alleviate the tension, I tried Morton's extension again.

"Hey, Morton, your wife is here to see you. Are you coming down here or should I send her up there?" I had hardly hung up the phone, when suddenly all hell broke loose.

"How dare you call my husband by his first name?" Paula yelled from the top of her lungs while the red spots in her face became even more congested. "Has no one taught you good manners, Missy? You will call my husband Mr. Page, not Morton, understand?"

Both Marianne and I stood speechless, totally shocked by the uncalled for, dramatic performance.

"You secretaries are all the same—a bunch of no-good hookers," Paula said, obviously without using common sense and blinded by her anger.

Marianne seemed to have had enough of Paula's insults and motioned to take a stand, but she soon realized that even the best psychiatrist could not have stopped the hysterical outbursts and the sea of profanities leaving Paula's holier-than-thou mouth. Morton arrived shortly after wondering about all the commotion and the yelling. Paula simply ignored him and continued her tirade. Somehow, he succeeded in calming her down and with a protective arm around her shoulders escorted her out of the office. Visibly irritated, Marianne had, for a very first time, lost her temper and slammed the door shut after them. I was definitely shaken and after a while, I just couldn't hold back my tears any longer.

"What did I do wrong?" I asked. "It was Morton himself who told me to stop addressing him as Mister and just call him Morton from the first day I was introduced to him by Father Anthony."

"I know, I know," said Marianne patting me gently over the head. "Just don't take it so hard, my dear. Paula is just a very frustrated lady who is extremely jealous of her husband. See, she can't have kids and so she's afraid that Morton is going to find another woman. At this point, any female is her enemy."

"You may be right, but it still does not justify her vulgarity and rudeness."

"I know. She is envious and jealous. You, instead, are not only intelligent and sensitive, but also very pretty and you understood what I just told you. So now wipe your tears and let's get back to work. In time, you'll forget this unpleasant incident, you'll see."

Paula's behavior, like other acts of injustice, would haunt me for many years to come. *It was easier to forgive than forget*, I thought.

Morton showed up a while later to find out more about what really happened. Marianne took it upon herself to explain the incident in detail. Extremely mortified, he apologized for Paula's behavior and said that she frequently suffered bouts of mood swings and depression.

"See, my wife is essentially a good woman," Morton said. "She is obsessed by the fact of being unable to have children and thinks that she is a lesser person because of that."

He also told us about his wife's strict religious background. I wondered if Paula's Christian feelings and sensitivity included profanity and obscenity. Poor girl, if she had only given me a chance to speak I could have assured her that Morton was far from what I considered an ideal boyfriend. However, some women, when under emotional stress, tormented by insecurities, fanaticism or *furor Uterinus*, would never listen to whatever reason. Marianne blamed Hollywood instead and all those silly pictures where secretaries were always depicted as the super sexy blond, dumb temptress, stealing bosses from their wives and having steaming affairs with them. Paula's ghosts of unfaithfulness could easily thrive on such fertile grounds. Ironically, a few months later, she also joined the ranks of the no-good hooker secretaries.

"She would have never made it, had it not been for her husband's recommendation at the Caritas office," Marianne said with a touch of sarcasm.

There was not much affinity between Marianne and Morton and they did not bother to conceal their feelings either. Morton thought of her as a conceited, domineering, fussy old bitch, whereas Marianne looked down at him as a weak, slimy non-entity, whose disgusting bootlicking techniques erased any traits of good character and personality.

One day, Bill had sent Morton to pick up the correspondence to be signed but since Marianne was in the process of recording the letters, she refused to release the bundle until she was ready. For the sake of fun at first, Morton teased her by saying that there was so much waste of time with such elaborate procedures. He briefly leafed through the pile of letters and grabbed the one Bill was interested in. Marianne instantly jumped off her chair to snatch back the letter from Morton's hand, but he was a lot faster and succeeded in running away, up the stairs to the seventh floor. Marianne was livid but finished recording the rest of the letters before bringing them up to Bill. She then complained to Bill about Morton's behavior but with little success.

"That despicable, two-faced toad," she said upon returning to her desk, "with his cunning, hypocrite character. For years my system has proved to be efficient and now, all of a sudden, it has become a waste of time. Things aren't supposed to be done properly anymore," she screamed while throwing papers all over the place.

"Have you not told Bill about Morton's intrusion?" I asked.

"Sure did, and you know what his answer was? Morton, that.... that vermicular son-of-a-bitch convinced Bill that I was wasting my time with stupid, unnecessary things," Marianne pounded her fist on the desk.

"How ironic though. Wasn't it Bill who first praised your system, hailing it to be the most efficient he had ever seen?"

Marianne stared at the wall in front of her desk, biting her lower lip. She broke the silence.

"Do you know what those two, excuse the expression, sons of bitches dared tell me? Well, you know, Bill spoke for both of them. He said that a secretary was far from indispensable and could be replaced any time, whereas a key man, such as Morton, with all his political contacts and knowledge of the socio-economic status of the country, was one in a million. That's what he told me."

There was a rather long silence before Marianne continued talking and rambling about what had just happened.

"I always failed to understand why a secretary was frowned upon, like an inferior being, a replaceable object, even when smart, efficient and many times just as competent as her male counterpart. They simply don't get it that a female can do more than just wash dishes and underwear, clean house and dirty diapers, cook and bake and be dutifully ready when Mr. Dick feels like having a quickie."

I listened attentively without quite comprehending the enormity of Marianne's verbal outburst.

"On one hand they look down at you; on the other hand they love to brag about having a secretary and use every opportunity to show them off to friends and business partners by dictating heaven knows what, important two liners or reports that will find their way into a dead file anyway."

Later on that same day, I was summoned to Bill's office. He wanted to see the checks and petty cash records. It was an unusual request and for a moment, I worried, even though I always made sure to update and balance all my records. I only hoped that Bill would not find something to pick on. Sometimes, too much adrenaline can ignite or add to an already tense situation and the two men upstairs could have very well been fuelling each other's frustrations and needed an outlet to heal.

When I arrived upstairs, the two men stopped talking. Morton returned to his desk and busied himself with the pile of papers in front of him.

"So, let me see those books, Isabel," Bill said with a faint smile. "Do you know the balance in our cruzeiros fund?"

I announced the total without hesitation.

"What about the US dollar balance?" Bill asked.

I once again replied with the exact figure.

"Don't tell me you memorize the figures," Bill said in a more relaxed tone.

"Most of the time," I replied, less worried.

"That is good. That is really very good." Bill returned the books to me.

Morton glanced in my direction, grabbed a bunch of files and then smiling, left the room.

"Would there be anything else, Bill?" I asked eager to get back to my office.

"No, thank you, dear," Bill said, but as soon as I crossed the threshold, he called me back. I wondered why they always do that—call you back when you are walking out, or going halfway up or down the stairs.

"How is Marianne doing by the way?" he asked. "Has she calmed down yet?"

"Not really."

"Oh, I'm sure she will calm down, at least, so I hope."

"I don't no. She is mighty angry with Morton and for what was said to her earlier."

"Oh, is that right? So what do you think will happen?"

"Well, I feel that she will not rest until Morton stops interfering with her work. He seems to enjoy making her nervous by poking his nose in everything she does."

"You mean like recording every piece of paper that lands on her desk?" Bill chuckled.

"Well, I must say it is a laborious procedure, but once it is in place, it is quite easy to maintain and so far has proven to be an extremely efficient system. At any given moment you are able to find anything related to the organization complete with details from beginning to end. I do not understand why this bothers Morton so much. After all, the clerical aspects of the office are not of his competence. He has more important things to take care of I assume, right?"

"I understand, and I'm sure we will settle this little dispute sooner or later." Bill smiled and returned his attention to the papers in front of him.

I returned to my office. Marianne was so busy between phone calls and the typing of reports that it did not even occur to her to ask me about my visit to Bill's office. For some time after that incident, Morton kept away from the sixth floor and Marianne was definitely relieved and returned to be the efficient, self-sufficient top secretary as before.

Maybe it was too much to ask for a perennial peaceful atmosphere because a few weeks later all hell broke loose again when Morton walked in with his usual crooked smile, heading towards Marianne's desk. After a few seconds, he grabbed the pile of letters that had just arrived and were being recorded and pulled out the one he had apparently been expecting. As he was about to leave the office, Marianne jumped to her feet and ran after him, demanding that the letter be returned to her. If Bill needed it that badly, Marianne would take it to him immediately and personally. Still smiling, Morton invited Marianne to calm down.

"Save your breath and a trip up the stairs," he said, trying to be funny.

Marianne was livid and went after Morton who laughed, jumping back and forth, waving the letter above his head while Marianne desperately tried to snatch it from his hand. Marianne was a lot taller than Morton, at least by a foot, and could have easily taken the letter out of his hand but Morton was a lot faster on his feet and like a soccer player, dribbled quickly and easily. I was left speechless, following the scene without knowing whether to laugh or cry. There were two grown ups, behaving like two children, quarrelling and shouting over the same toy. While Morton was getting a kick out of the whole circus, Marianne was dead serious, offended in her dignity and authority over her own territory. She had enough. She turned around, walked over to her desk, quickly picked up her few belongings and without uttering another word, walked out, slamming the door behind her.

Morton returned a while later to pick up the rest of the correspondence. He did not even bother to ask about Marianne or her whereabouts and walked out with a victorious smile on his face. When Bill learned about the incident, he seemed somewhat displeased and annoyed but as in the past, also this time he would not interfere in personal disputes because he was after all, Mister Nice Guy.

The only one missing Marianne was me, swamped by additional work while Bill had no intention to hire a replacement. Despite the heavy workload, however, I loved everything I was expected to do. It was a challenge to my abilities. I worked hard and enthusiastically, sometimes as late as 11:00 p.m., without ever receiving a penny more. It was, after all, a charitable organization and my extra work could be considered as my personal time donation to the cause.

My contact with Bill became more frequent. His dictations were indeed so slow that I did not have any trouble in writing everything in long hand. My efforts in learning shorthand at that point in time did not seem worth my while and so I stopped going to night school. Unlike Marianne, I would not doze off during dictations, but occasionally let out a sigh or a yawn while sketching cartoon characters around the edges of my shorthand pad. It was indeed boring, just as when Bill insisted on teaching me the use of his fascinating slide ruler. Patiently he would go on forever illustrating the many advantages of the wooden precision device.

Everything in Bill translated serenity; his speech, his gestures, his actions. Whoever was not familiar with Bill's true nature would take him as an individual deprived of energy or afflicted by some sort of tropical disease. Even his complaints were carried out in the same, incredible slow motion. Gentle Giant remained the nickname Paulo and I had coined for him. A man of many talents, he personally prepared the Christmas cards he would send out to friends, relatives and business connections. He would draw them and have them printed by the hundreds. He showed me the collection he had from previous years, which were all very beautiful. He also loved to play guitar and once even took me with him to find a music store to buy chords for the instrument. He was a happy guy who also loved surprises.

One afternoon, he buzzed my intercom inviting me to join him on the seventh floor for a surprise party he organized for his own birthday.

"Come on in, Claudia," he said with a large happy smile as I entered the door.

"How come you're calling me Claudia?" I asked, puzzled.

"Because you look so much alike, you and Claudia Cardinale, the Italian movie star," he answered.

I had to laugh. It wasn't the first time that someone pointed out my likeness to that actress. Maybe it was the hairstyle. Since I was myself a fan of Claudia's, the comparison couldn't be but flattering.

The party consisted of only four people: Bill, Morton, Paulo and me. The surprise party was after all not a surprise, because Bill had prepared everything himself. He offered everyone a large glass of orange juice, keeping the milk for himself. Joined by me and Paulo, Morton began singing "Happy Birthday to you." We had some pastry while Bill performed as singer and guitar player. As expected from a tall, well-built man, his voice was a beautiful and powerful baritone. Soon also Paulo and I pitched in singing some of the popular samba and bossa nova tunes. Morton watched approvingly, but without participating. He didn't have a good voice he claimed, and preferred to stay in a corner, munching away on the pastry. It was a beautiful way to begin the weekend.

One day I heard knocking at the door and went to open it.

"Good Heavens, Marianne. Where have you been?" I said, inviting her in.

"Well, you know, I was in the area and I thought I'd pay you a visit."

"I'm glad to see you again."

"So am I," she said. "How is Bill? What is new? What is that slimy toad Morton doing?"

"Oh, they are both Ok," I replied.

"And how is your work coming along?"

"Oh, gee, I got plenty of work now. I'm doing your job as well as mine. Bill does not seem to want to hire extra help for the time being."

"Of course not, you dummy. They see you can handle everything and so they take advantage of you, the work of two for the salary of one. Don't you get it? The more you do the more they'll expect from you. The enthusiasm you put into whatever you consider, for one reason or another, as a challenge, is taken for granted after a while. Believe me. Listen to your old friend here. I went through all that crap before, not once or twice, several times. I should know."

"Are you going up to see Bill?" I asked.

"Oh, yes. I want to get all the monies they still owe me. I know I should have come before but I just didn't have time to do so."

Marianne then went into a frenzy, telling me about the terrific job she had found with an important insurance company as well as a new apartment she had rented close to her work.

"I was just thinking," Marianne said. "What if we shared the apartment? We could also share the homework. I would cook one day and the next you would do it. Same for the cleaning and the shopping and you'd be more free and independent."

The proposal caught me by surprise. I had never considered the possibility of leaving my parents to go live on my own let alone with a stranger. Even less attractive was the prospect of having to clean, shop and cook, all tasks my mother had been doing for me.

"I really don't think it would work, Marianne. The idea does not attract me. I am happy at home, even if sometimes we do not see eye to eye, I wouldn't feel comfortable anywhere else."

"I know," Marianne cut in, "but I still think that you should be able to make your own decisions. And look, I would really charge you very little for rent and food."

I just shook my head. Who needed double expenses, more work and more hassle?

"Oh, come on, Isabel. Talk to your parents. You'll see, they'll agree."

"I honestly don't feel like moving out of my parent's home," I said politely but firmly.

"Sooner or later you will leave them anyway," Marianne said, checking her wristwatch. "I guess I've wasted enough time already. I have to go see Bill now. In case you change your mind about my proposal, just give me a call." She handed me a piece of paper with a phone number scribbled on it.

Marianne was definitely not her usual self. She seemed deeply troubled and confused and I was definitely not eager in getting involved in her problems and soon forgot the incident; and so must have Marianne because she never showed up again.

One afternoon, Morton popped in and handed me the mail he had just picked up from the lobby.

"Got news for you," he said without a smile.

"Is that why you look like you've come from a funeral?"

"I just heard that Bill is being transferred elsewhere," Morton said. "Most likely he'll return to the States."

I was more upset than surprised. Another change, another face to please and heaven only knew whatever else there was in store for me and the others.

"Do you know who is going to replace Bill?" I asked.

"No. Not yet," Morton replied, scratching his head.

"Too bad, Now that everything was flowing so well, those New Yorkers are throwing the dice again."

"Yeah, tell me about it. That means having to start everything all over again. Anyway, have faith and courage. I'm telling this to myself." He walked out slowly, slamming the door behind him.

For the next couple of weeks I couldn't but speculate about the next boss. Would he be pleasant or rude; good-looking or ugly; young or old? What new changes or systems would be introduced? It was all interconnected. Questions and more questions formed in my mind without me receiving an answer, just yet.

Thinking back in time, I can still see Bill's gentle blue eyes and could only imagine his surprise had he known I would end up moving to Canada, his native land. I always think of him when I hear the tunes of the *Canadian Sunset*. Regrettably, Bill passed away a few years back. I never had a chance to say *hello* from Canada—may his soul rest in peace.

7

CRS - Father Nielsen, the Dynamo

One Friday morning I received a telegram announcing Father Anthony's visit. Thrilled with the good news, I could hardly wait until Monday to tell him about the various changes that had occurred during his absence, and the professional progress I had made during the same period. He would officially introduce Bill's replacement and new director for the Brazilian agency, an American priest from Buffalo named Father Nielsen.

I was the first to arrive in the office on Monday morning. On the way I also picked up some flowers to brighten my office. I quickly dusted the furniture, and for a third time re-arranged chairs and the objects on top of the desks. After almost two hours of impatient waiting, there finally was the expected knock on the door. I answered the door and there stood Father Anthony with his arms stretched out and a big bright smile on his face. Morton and Father Nielsen looked on with a grin on their faces as Father Anthony hugged me and swept me off my feet, making a half turn around.

"So, how is my favorite secretary doing? You're looking good, kiddo." He put me back on the ground.

"This is Isabel," he said, introducing me to Father Nielsen. "She has been my secretary for several years and I am sure you two will get along just fine. She knows everything about our work. Just ask her or Morton. They both are very good and efficient."

"I'm sure it will be as you say," said Father Nielsen, winking in my direction.

"Unfortunately, I do not have much time at my disposal," said Father Anthony. "I still have many things to discuss with Father Nielsen here. But I promise to see you for a brief chat before I leave." Father Anthony patted me on a shoulder.

The three men left for the seventh floor and I did not see them for the rest of the day.

The next morning, Father Anthony walked in with two cups of coffee, one for me and one for himself. He took a seat in front of my desk. He then asked about my family and work, and I gladly told him everything he wanted to know. He seemed very impressed with my progress and praised me for it.

"How do you like Father Nielsen?" he suddenly asked me. "What is your impression of him?"

I was surprised with the question. What kind of input or opinion could I possibly have on a person I had just met once and only for a few minutes? It was flattering nonetheless. Not too many people bothered to ask my opinion on anything.

"He looks like a very friendly person," I said. "He also looks like he is a very dynamic individual. I'm sure we will work well together."

Our conversation ended when interrupted by a phone call asking Father Anthony to attend a meeting on the seventh floor. He gulped down the remaining coffee and ran to the door. He stopped briefly and turned around.

"I'll be back later on or tomorrow morning," he said, winking an eye in his usual mischievous way and then ran up the stairs.

Time passed fast and the next morning, as promised, Father Anthony returned to chat with me. He had many questions about everybody and everything and again, he was impressed with the quantity and quality of information I was able to give him.

"See, I always knew that one day you'd be able to handle things on your own," he said. "You're still so young and have a whole life ahead of you. I'm really proud of you."

Suddenly, Father Anthony remembered that he had brought me a little gift. He frantically searched in the chaos of his suitcase when he finally found the little box and handed it to me. Eagerly, I opened the nicely wrapped box. It was a beautiful heart-shaped manicure set in red leather. As always, when given a gift, I was unable to hold back my joy and gratefulness and gave Father Anthony a big hug. He reciprocated with equal enthusiasm. On many occasions in the past, he gave me little gifts, mainly empty boxes of all sorts, because he thought they were pretty. A knock on the door interrupted the magic. It was Morton and Father Nielsen ready to escort Father Anthony to the airport.

"Oh, heavens, I wouldn't want to miss my plane," Father Anthony exclaimed, checking his wristwatch and zipping up his suitcase. "You are coming with us are you not, Isabel?"   "Sure, if I'm allowed," I replied glancing at one and then at the other priest for approval.

"Fine with me," said Father Nielsen, smiling.

"Ok then, lets get the show on the road," said Father Anthony while grabbing his suitcase and heading towards the elevator.

Paulo was allowed to join the party as well and so the offices remained closed for a couple of hours. There was not much waiting when we arrived at the airport. Passengers had already boarded the plane and as soon as Father Anthony checked his luggage, he proceeded to say his farewell speech. He hugged everybody, leaving me for last.

"And you, little girl, take care of yourself. Don't work too hard and keep me updated, ok?" He gave me a quick peck on one cheek.

"I'll do that," I whispered, fighting back the tears swelling up in my eyes.

Father Anthony waved often on his way to the plane and then once more from the top of the stairs before disappearing inside the aircraft.

"Would you like to stay 'til the plane takes off?" I heard Father Nielsen whispering into my ear.

"I'd love to, if you don't mind."

"No problem," said Father Nielsen winking an eye and tapping gently on my shoulder. We watched the plane take off and slowly disappear behind thick, fluffy clouds.

Back in the office, sitting at my desk, I stared gloomily at the flowers I had purchased for Father Anthony's visit. In a way, his brief visit had depressed me more than the news of his transfer. Everything happened so fast. There was silence all around me and I felt so terribly lonely. I knew, however, that he would return for his periodical inspection visits and that thought, re-tempered my spirit. I wondered why I was so eager to see him again. I realized that some of my reactions while in his presence revealed a little more than the sentiment of friendship. Could I be in love with him? How could that be possible? I was only twenty and Father Anthony was forty-nine at the time. I blushed while imagining how it would feel kissing him on the lips. I caressed the idea for a moment even though the thought alone was a forbidden dream. Priests were not supposed to be messed with, not the Catholic priests anyway. It was considered a sin. I had a hard time understanding the fuss. After all, did not Christ himself preach that one should love his or her neighbor as oneself? So what could be so wrong in loving Father Anthony after all? I didn't have to tell my feelings to anybody. I would keep it as my innermost very special secret. My daydreaming ended when Father Nielsen's voice came through the intercom asking me to come up to the seventh floor for a meeting.

Throughout the meeting, I found Father Nielsen to be an extremely dynamic person. He lived most of his life in Brazil. Two sky blue eyes peered from his youthful, ever-smiling face. Tall, slim and very athletic, he loved sports, especially tennis, swimming and horseback riding. He had been chosen by the organization for his vast knowledge of the country, the people and for his past successful and dynamic performance in similar operations.

He had great plans for the future of the organization and decided not to waste time with irrelevant details or financial obstacles. He showed a vast knowledge of the problems he had inherited by clearly exposing some of the alternatives and tracing the outline of new plans to be carried out within the next few months. To fight poverty was his main goal, and to become more efficient and faster, action had to be taken on a much larger scale than what his predecessors had been doing. An intense fundraising campaign was to be implemented immediately, not only throughout the eastern board of the United States but also and mainly in Brazil itself, where the wealthier class would be invited to help the needy in their own backyard.

Father Nielsen possessed not only charisma but also an extraordinary power of persuasion, easily obtaining the enthusiastic participation and approval of his co-workers. The goal of that meeting was precisely to obtain the staff's full support for the new plan. Numerous changes were introduced in the following weeks and months. The organization moved the offices to much larger premises in Botafogo. Through his various connections, Father Nielsen obtained donated office furniture and equipment. He also hired more personnel such as social workers, secretaries, typists, a receptionist, an engineer, an agronomist, a medical doctor and a nurse, an expert in cooperatives, and a lawyer.

Fund-raising campaigns were to take place in local parishes as well, and for the purpose, Father Nielsen hired two more priests: Fathers Francis and Manuel. Father Manuel was slim, with shiny black hair and sparkling black eyes. The deep dimples on his rosy cheeks enhanced even more the charm of his smile. Father Francis was a little older, perhaps in his mid-fifties. He was tall, with dark brown hair, grizzled at the temples and hazel brown eyes smiling from behind black-framed glasses. He appeared to be a very calm, understanding person. Each time Father Nielsen would hire a new employee, he would introduce me as: "my right hand and in charge of the accounting and personnel departments. She organizes and distributes the tasks to the various sections, checks all correspondence, statistics, some PR and most importantly," —he would add chuckling—"she is the one who will hand over your pay check."

Some time later, two British volunteers, Jean and Janet would join the organization as social assistants and so I transferred to them the project files with all the pertaining information. Despite my heavy workload, I felt betrayed whenever I had to hand over any of the tasks I had been responsible for, to another person. Yet, I had to agree with Father Nielsen that I could not manage the workload all by myself. His plans and ideas were not only imposing but also quantitatively too many. He insisted that I learn to delegate.

Father Nielsen not only possessed a volcanic mind in constant eruption, he was also a great speaker. He knew how to expose boring subjects in an interesting, captivating manner. He often called for meetings with the various departments and naturally, each time, I had to be present even though I was not always a willing participant. My desk drawers and desktop were still the target of overflowing paperwork, which did not seem likely to diminish, rather the opposite. At the rate the program was developing, work would only increase for all. When unable to sit in at the meetings, I would receive a typed report, "for your info only," on what was discussed during a given meeting.

The office was what is known as an open concept environment. As in a huge classroom, the desks were lined up in four rows, six desks in each row. Like teachers, Father Nielsen and I had our desks facing the other desks. I often felt awkward being stared at all day long, especially by some members of the opposite sex and was happy when Father Nielsen decided to place Father Francis' desk in front of mine.

Even though Father Nielsen persistently begged me to delegate more of my tasks to other employees, I would fall behind and often do overtime just to make sure that a particular task was done properly. I did not always have the patience to explain elementary details to beginners or wait for a letter to be re-typed for a third time because of improper grammar or punctuation and so I would just do it myself. I also hated being blamed for others' errors. But as more and more important work piled up on my desk, I had to overlook my own obsessions and let the other typists deal with the details.

Aside from the regular daily routine, there were occasional incidents disrupting my schedules such as the visit of a missionary from a poor village in the Acre territory, hoping to be included in the organization's donation program. Other times there was an employee facing a difficult moment in need of advice or some quick cash. Dealing with very poor individuals and being myself of a compassionate nature, I would often skip the bureaucratic aspect of my job and act on impulse by handing out a little cash here and there to a begging priest or a hungry shoeshine boy. The gratefulness I would read in their eyes would promptly erase my sense of guilt towards my petty cash.

One incident involved Lina, a young receptionist-typist. Her curvy, sensuous full figure, her red curly hair, fleshy lips and flirting big brown eyes exuded sexuality all over. I often listened patiently to the various problems she would share with me. Her father had died when she was fifteen years of age and her mother, not being able to provide for their upkeep, decided to re-marry. Her new husband was a black man who up to a couple of years before proved to be a good provider and a loving step-father. Something, however, triggered his behavior to degenerate into violence. He became addicted to drinking and to practicing of black magic. Lina was afraid of him and for several times, she had tried to run away from home but did not know where to go. She feared her stepfather's wrath and decided to hang in there until she'd found a nice guy to marry. She did try very hard indeed. She had a remarkable array of admirers.

One early morning, Lina walked into the office, pouting and clearly upset with something. There was hardly any make-up on her freckled face. She threw her purse in one drawer of her desk and then walked over, plopping herself in the chair next to my desk, expecting to be asked about what was wrong. And I did ask. As usual, Lina was depressed with her situation. Her eyes were flooded with tears and her speech was incoherent. She needed to borrow some money urgently; otherwise the next alternative would be suicide, Lina said. I first tried to calm her down and slowly talked her out of the crazy idea. I gave her the loan, which fortunately, wasn't a large amount. Lina phoned in sick the next morning and showed up for work only one week later. She then confessed that the money she had borrowed had been used to get an abortion. Her story was interlaced with sadness, relief, happiness and anger. Despite my disappointment, I did not feel easy to judge Lina's motivations but was adamant in having the money returned to my petty cash, which Lina did two days later. I tried to imagine Father Nielsen's reaction had he known about that incident. In the past, he had singled out Lina as an example of sheer gaiety and worry-free happiness and wished that I be more like her—relaxed, outspoken and sociable. I was essentially very shy and would loosen up only among people I had known for a while. I definitely did not aspire to become a second Lina.

I felt the need to erase that incident from my mind. Lina was not a bad kid but her behavior disturbed me. As on many other occasions, when stressed due to a particular situation, I would just tour the various departments for a quick chat with one or the other. I stopped to talk a little with Father Francis who loved to describe to me the many beautiful spots of Rio. He invited me, along with Jean and Janet, the two volunteers who happened to join our conversation, for a tour around Rio the next Sunday. The girls, who were new to Brazil, were thrilled with the opportunity. Jean was a very sweet, twenty-five-year-old Londoner, dedicated to Social Services. She did not need any make-up to beautify her smart little freckled face, the naturally red lips and expressive, luminous dark brown eyes, which had the power to dart straight into one's heart. She was very dedicated to the organization and worked very hard on her reports to New York, hoping to get the best possible donation for a particular worthy project. Jean and I would become good friends and stay friends, at least while we both lived in the same country. Janet was also a pretty girl with blue eyes, light brown hair and very fair skin. She thought that working as a social assistant in a third world country would contribute to her acting experience, because her ultimate goal was to become an actress.

I returned to my desk and shuffled through the paperwork. Shortly before quitting time, Lina came over to my desk.

"I really hope you are not too upset with me, Isabel."

"Just forget it. I don't want to talk about it anymore. I don't want to blame you or judge you. I'm just a little disappointed. Anyway, don't do it again. There are ways to prevent it. You should know better."

"I know. Perhaps I was too tipsy when it all happened."

"Why didn't you tell me about what the money was for?"

"I was afraid you wouldn't understand and perhaps convince me to keep the baby."

"How would you know that? How would you know what my reaction would have been? I don't think you know me that well."

"Oh, Isabel, I know you. I just know."

"How often have you done this before?"

Lina bowed her head and blushed but ignored the question.

"Don't you feel like having a beer this evening?" Lina asked with a sudden fresh smile on her face.

"No, thank you. I have other plans for tonight."

Lina seemed disappointed but did not insist. There was a long silence while I tidied up my desk and locked the safe.

"I feel I must tell you something," Lina said with a little hesitation.

"And what is that?" I asked while tucking away the keys in my purse.

"I think I'll be leaving the organization."

"And why is that? Have you found another job?"

"Well, actually, I have a few possibilities. Nothing definite, so I can't tell you anything just yet."

"Well, I guess you're entitled to choose whatever is best for you. Just let me know when exactly you are planning to leave." I gave no further thought to the matter.

Lina's expression revealed surprise and disappointment again. She probably expected me to give her the "I'm so sorry, don't leave us" speech, but it did not happen. I did not insist and at that point did not consider Lina to be an asset to the organization. Lina tried to keep up the chit-chat but pointing towards my wrist watch, I politely showed her off.

Happy and sad days frequently took turns. One afternoon, we received the visit of an extraordinary missionary stationed in the remote territory of Roraima in Northern Brazil. Months before, he had allegedly sent a detailed report describing the precarious situation of the people in his area and had never received a reply to his plea for help. I immediately asked Jean to check into the matter.

Father Marcos was an extremely outspoken individual. He was not tall but his presence was imposing nonetheless. His angular face showed a deep leathery tan. His hair was a glossy, unkempt black bushy mess and his eyes were of a magnetic pitch-black color. The initial impression he left with people was that of a rough, primitive nature that vanished, however, as soon as he opened his mouth to speak, revealing a generous human being capable of housing the entire humankind in his heart. When moments later Jean returned explaining that the report had been re-written into the form of a project, and forwarded to the headquarters, but that no reply had been received to date, Father Marco's face turned from hopeful into an irate grimace.

With quick movements he rolled up his sleeves, showing powerful biceps. "Here, look at these," he said. "Look at these arms." He pulled up his trouser legs, exposing a pair of tanned, well built strong legs. "And look at these legs. These, my friends, are not the result from simply reading the Breviary in the cool shadow of a chapel. These muscles are the result of my daily struggle, carrying rocks up to a hundred pounds to help build foundations and roofs over the heads of my poor flock. I'm not asking help to build a citadel. I only want to improve the living conditions of my village, but how would you people imagine, even remotely, the conditions in which some of our people live? You are so far from reality here in the big city." He shook his head from side to side.

I felt so much compassion for his cause but all I could do was listen and hope that his project would soon be approved. Father Marco adjusted his sleeves and pants and then grabbing his patched little suitcase, walked out with the same dignity he had on his way in.

Hundreds of reports and heart-breaking cases would flood the office on a weekly basis and each case was important and deserving prompt attention. But nothing could be done by anybody without following the proper procedures. Each report had to be evaluated and re-worked into a project and then sent to the headquarters for further evaluation and prioritized accordingly. Every penny, donated by the thousands of generous American citizens, was carefully applied towards food, clothing, education, health and housing for the least fortunate all across Brazil. The program was huge and the challenges even greater. The funds had their limitations and there were many who would cross the threshold with their hearts full of hope and had to depart empty-handed. I suffered along with each rejected case and many a times walked over to Father Nielsen's desk to seek advice for the emotional turmoil my job was creating in my mind and soul. Father Nielsen was of the opinion that compassion, when properly balanced, was a beautiful human property, but compassion without logic behind it, could only prove to be harmful and counter-productive.

"But isn't it useless to teach an individual to fish if, while he's learning, he's dying of hunger?" I argued.

"Hunger also urges men to find means to gather food for them," Father Nielsen replied with his usual calm smile.

I would never forget the gloomy look in the eyes of a local Florence Nightingale named Anesia, as she told about the atrocious sufferings she had witnessed during a particular trip to northern remote areas of the interior, where there was no medical assistance, clean water or electricity. Where little children's eyes were filled with tears instead of hope, their mouths echoing cries instead of laughter; their tummies bulging with disease instead of food; where hunger was a daily spectre and some even resorted to nibble on their own fingers. Scenes of crude reality, so different from those of the shores of Copacabana populated by throngs of beautiful, well nourished, spoiled brats.

I often found myself thinking about the extreme differences between the social classes surrounding me. There were the many unfortunate yet wise, the snob insensitive ignorant, the greedy self-centered smart ass and the hardworking, generous law-abiding specimen who make it all possible for the other categories. And then there were angels such as Anesia, a specimen as rare as honesty among corruption, who truly fought for the poorest and did not turn her eyes when a stretched hand begged for help, nor did she shiver in horror while reassuring a person affected by leprosy with a comforting, soothing touch of her hands.

As the months passed by, I developed a particular love-hate relationship with my job. I was tiring of the emotional stress involved. Instead of getting tougher after reading countless heart-breaking reports, I felt weaker and weaker. I began to hate all the bureaucracy involved, the statistics, the legal jargon and most importantly, the feeling of impotence as an individual. Attentive Father Francis noticed my depression and invited me over to his place for dinner along with Jean and Janet.

Father Francis lived in an apartment complex near the office with his twenty-two-year-old niece Marcia. She was extremely cute in her red and white polka dot dress. She had curly brown hair and sparkly brown eyes. Her pink cheeks were graced with deep dimples every time she smiled. Shy by nature and new to the big city, she did not venture out on the streets by herself. She was therefore thrilled to meet with us and finally make friends with girls of her own age group.

Except for Marcia, everybody smoked. Father Francis served cold beer as it was a hot, sticky evening. We chatted about numerous subjects before sitting at the table to enjoy the exquisite dinner Marcia had prepared for the occasion. After we had finished, Marcia proudly refused our help to clean up and exhorted us to join her uncle in the living room where after a piping hot *cafézinho*, we played a few hands of Canasta. We were interrupted a while later by the arrival of Father Manuel who happened to live in the same building, just one floor up. He invited everybody over to his place for a quick drink. He also introduced his sister, a fifty-five-year-old spinster whose face resembled that of a person who had just bitten into a lemon. With detached courtesy, she showed us into a very tidy living room. She reappeared after a while with a tray of goblets filled with Port wine. She placed the tray on the table and vanished into her bedroom, ignoring the guests for the rest of the evening. Father Manuel was visibly embarrassed with his sister's rude behavior, but all he could do was blush, smile and shrug his shoulders. Coming from a strict, religious background, his sister did not consider it appropriate for a priest to receive female friends in the house and she was there to prevent her brother from falling into temptation.

The group talked a little about each other's work and what was happening on the work scene before Father Francis brought up the excursion the following Sunday. Once again, Marcia's eyes sparkled and so did Jean's and Janet's. They could hardly wait to see some of the famous beauty spots of Rio de Janeiro. Even I was enthused with the idea of tagging along and being able to finally see the Christ the Redeemer statue atop the 710 meter (2340 ft.) high Corcovado mountain. The granite statue itself stands at 30 meters (100 ft.) high and can be seen from every corner of the city of Rio de Janeiro. The only party pooper was Father Manuel.

"How could I, for heaven's sake," he said. "She'd kill me." He referred to his sister.

"Oh, darn. You're well over eighteen," Father Francis said. "I guess you can decide for yourself what you want to do."

"Oh, I know, but she is so jealous and protective of me. What can I say, it's her upbringing. Maybe some other time," he replied with a sigh of resignation.

I quickly checked my watch and realized that it was getting late. Not having a phone at home, I could not notify my parents of last minute delays or programs. To avoid having them worried sick, I often decided to break up the entertainment and head home. The group parted happily, looking forward to the next weekend. There was something interesting to look forward to, finally.

I woke up early Sunday morning and prepared sandwiches to take along for my friends and me. Jean, Janet, Marcia and Father Francis were already waiting for me at the other end of the Guanabara Bay and without further delay we drove up to the Corcovado. A more unique than rare scenery spread before our eyes as we reached the very top of the mountain and the feet of the statue. The sky was an intense blue and the sun sprayed its golden rays over the shimmering surface of the deep blue ocean. Way below, streets were crowded with cars and the beaches populated by myriads of colorful living dots.

"Hey, we could also go swimming later," Jean suggested happily.

"Why not," agreed Father Francis while inviting the girls to pose for a picture. "I brought my swim trunks along anyway," he added, giggling.

Everybody had brought their swimwear because they all hoped for the same thing.

From the Corcovado we drove to a location named *Mesa do Imperador* (Emperor's Table). It was said that at the time of the Portuguese Empire in Brazil, Emperor Dom Pedro the Second, had chosen that very spot for the family picnics. The area was surrounded by thick, luxurious vegetation and the breathtaking landscape extended infinitely, touching the sky from our viewpoint. Another view, but from a different angle, could be seen from the location named *Vista Chinesa* (Chinese View), which took its name after the Chinese pagoda that had been erected there. We then drove through the enchanting Tijuca forest, a tropical reserve that includes 100 Km (60 miles) of narrow, two-lane dirt roads, winding through crisp, thick vegetation, occasionally broken by a sparkling waterfall or a tapestry of multi-colored impatiens, which grow freely in the shady Brazilian forests. I loved nature, the creatures of the forest and deeply enjoyed every instant of our outing. What better prayer to the Creator than admiring and loving the magnificence of His creation, I pondered.

The day was beautiful but very hot and humid and even worse inside the Jeep Father Francis had borrowed for the occasion. Unanimously, we decided to head towards Barra da Tijuca. Back in the 60s, it was simply a giant 11-mile stretch of white sandy beaches, kissed by the open, majestic Atlantic Ocean. With the exception of a couple of small kiosks at a few hundred feet apart from each other, there was nothing else in sight. No bars, restaurants, beach benches. One at a time, we changed inside the Jeep and soon we entered the jade-colored ocean waves where we jumped, splashed and laughed like happy, worry-free children.

Walking in the sand and swimming in that magnificent ocean was good but also tiring. Hunger did set in. While Father Francis walked over to the kiosk to pick up some cold beverage and beer, Jean, Marcia, Janet and I prepared the food spread. There were plenty of sandwiches, fried chicken, boiled eggs and fresh fruit for all. It didn't take long before we'd polished up the food and stretched out in the sand, lazily watching the seagulls floating effortlessly against a stupendous blue sky. A little while later, Janet picked up her guitar and soon we all pitched in singing the warm tunes of the bossa nova.

Not much was needed for happiness and serenity. Seen from that angle, the world was so simple, uncomplicated and beautiful. We remained to watch the unique spectacle of a typical Brazilian sunset, when the sky catches fire, mutating colors from gold to red and deep purple to the instant when the golden fireball slowly sinks into the deep, dark ocean. We were all very tired as we fared goodbye to each other, but also extremely peaceful and happy.

Life was back to normal on Monday morning. Father Nielsen gave me a few additional tasks, hoping I would do a good job as usual. As to the details on how, when and why, was entirely my problem. He was the mastermind, the others were his executioners. I did not mind and kept treading on, extracting renewed energy from the well of my enthusiasm.

Although Father Nielsen could be the nicest person on earth, there were occasions when I just couldn't get across to him. Personnel matters were mostly my responsibility as were the annual salary reviews which, after careful evaluation were submitted and ultimately approved by Father Nielsen. He generously rounded up certain amounts and certain others a little less or not at all. He had his reasons, I figured.

I never paid too much attention to the different pay structures to avoid feeling greedy in the first place. I didn't feel offended when a newcomer earned more than I did even if there was an overall difference of workload between the parties. There were times, however, when I wished I could bring home a little more money to help my father quit the second job he had taken on. The gap between my pay check and that of Jose, the engineer, was obvious. He was an engineer after all, whereas I was a self-made secretary-bookkeeper-Jill-of-all-trades employee. My total was never brought to a round figure.

"You see, Jose besides being an engineer is the head of a large family. And he has really done a terrific job this year," was Father Nielsen's explanation after noticing my disappointment. I just nodded and smiled. Who was in the mood of arguing or getting tangled up in lengthy polemics? Yet it bothered me and thought that Father Nielsen's merit rating stunk because I had worked just as hard that year and all the previous years, and as to family, well, I had a handicapped mother, a father working two jobs and a brother who was in college full-time and could not work because of that. Every penny had to be accounted for. Luckily, my mother had learned to sew during the war and cotton fabric was not expensive in Brazil, so I had a number of pretty dresses which made me feel good and supported my self-esteem. The family could certainly not make ends meet without my contribution.

I grabbed the papers and returned to my desk. I spent the rest of the morning and part of the afternoon writing up pay checks and then distributing them to smiling, happy employees. It was that particular day of the month I was loved the most and I felt good about it, too.

Later that afternoon, I snapped out of my gloomy state of mind as Father Thom made his usual noisy bi-monthly entrance, greeting everyone by name and heading straight to Father Nielsen's desk where he plopped himself into a chair.

"Howdy brother," he said. "I'm pleased to see you alive and well, as usual."

He then turned towards me with a wide grin and said, "I'll be seeing you a little later, dear."

I thought he was a funny man. Tall, slim, blue eyes, thin nose and narrow lips, his originally red hair had become grizzled from the first time I had met him some three years before. I loved his characteristic southern drawl and his walk, shaking his hips like a girl. He was outspoken, generous and adored by a large number of followers. He loved his job as missionary in the Amazon region but would also enjoy socializing with lay people in general. Every two months he would fly in from Manaus to personally follow up on his many projects. Father Thom was a human dynamo just like Father Nielsen, constantly on the go, with a thousand irons in the fire. He certainly left an indelible mark of his accomplishments in the Amazon jungle.

After a good hour talking with Father Nielsen, Father Thom took his little tour around the office. He chatted with almost everyone, especially with Jean, about his projects and their latest development. He spoke to Father Francis about the possibility of having one more Jeep donated to the parish that would increase the help to the needy in more remote areas. At last, exhausted, he plopped into a chair next to my desk.

"Have you mailed out the bucks yet, dear?" he asked with a big sigh.

"No, but I have everything ready for you to take along," I said, handing him over a large Kraft envelope.

"Good girl. Thank you." He smiled with relief and in turn presented me with a carton of Salem menthol cigarettes, which he picked up from a duty free store in Manaus. "You'll love these, but go easy with your smoking. It's not really good for you."

I thanked him and immediately lit one, offering one to him as well.

"What about having dinner with me this evening?" he asked.

"I'd love to but I'm afraid it won't be possible this evening. I have to let my folks know ahead of time."

"Well, give them a call."

"Can't. Remember the phone? We don't have one?"

"Ok. Well then, what about tomorrow?"

"Tomorrow evening will be fine," I happily agreed.

"All right then, it's a deal," he said while collecting his belongings. "Seven o'clock at the Red Beach Restaurant. And wait for me even if I may be a little late, eh?"

Then he left in the same happy, noisy manner as he arrived.

The Red Beach Restaurant was located at the base of the Sugar Loaf Mountain and was a favorite of many celebrities as well, because of its romantic and private location, the ambiance and the exquisite seafood cuisine.

The next morning I continued distributing the pay checks to all those who were absent the day before. Among these, Fathers Francis and Manuel who were obviously very happy in returning to the office after a weeklong travelling to the interior. Father Manuel was always in a good mood; always smiling and ready to tell a good joke or to innocently flirt with me by reciting the verse of a poem or singing a little song, which I liked so much. It said: "Teus olhos castanhos de encantos tamanhos são os pecados meus...." (Your chestnut brown eyes, so enchanting, are my sins). It sounded even more attractive with his authentic Portuguese accent.

After that short intermezzo, I returned to my desk and started on my books. I was still fascinated by the accounting aspect of my job and was able to concentrate so deeply that I would often neglect my biological needs or a cramp in the leg I was sitting on for almost an hour. I would hardly notice the people standing in front of my desk, waiting for me to lift my head from the paper work. Had it not been for Father Francis reminding me of the time, I would have forgotten my dinner date with Father Thom that evening. I quickly piled up my papers and books, locked the safe and the desk drawers and ran out in the street to catch a cab. A quick look in the purse mirror, a touch of lipstick, a dab of "Ma Griffe" behind the ear lobes and I was ready to go.

Father Thom was already sipping on his gin and tonic when I arrived at the restaurant. I apologized for the delay and ordered a gin and tonic too, with lots of ice. I didn't have to check on the gin because the barmen in Rio were usually very generous with the dosages. Father Thom seemed to be in an excellent mood. Relaxed and quite handsome in his bright, colorful cotton shirt, white linen pants and sandals. I often wondered why good-looking males such as my superiors ended up choosing the priesthood. It certainly wasn't for the lack of female admirers. The fact that the Catholic clergy was not allowed to marry was another mystery that puzzled me. Protestants, Evangelical, Methodists and others did marry, and yet their civil status did not interfere with following Christ's commandments and taking care of their flock. I also wondered at how a priest could express an opinion about a situation, such as a family crisis or a conjugal problem, when he himself has had no hands-on experience to support his preaching. Reality is as different of fiction as theory is different of practice. One day, I thought to myself, I would approach one of them and ask about all these issues.

Over dinner that evening, Father Thom told me about his family back in Nebraska and more about his work and projects in the jungle.

"I wonder if you could approach our friend Nielsen and somehow get him to accelerate some of my most urgent projects," he said.

For a moment, I was flattered, as he was giving me more importance and power than I had.

"What makes you think that I have any influence with Father Nielsen?" I asked, giggling.

"Who else if not you, he likes you. It is so obvious. The way he looks at you and talks to you...."

"Yeah...right. My seniority with the organization doesn't mean that I have influence and power. Too many people think that all they have to do is sweet-talk me so that in turn, I sweet-talk the boss and ...poof...magic... the project will be suddenly approved. I'm sorry, but I don't have a magic button." I laughed heartily.

I finished my gin and tonic and lit another cigarette. "Sometimes, the only thing I can do is to ask a typist to type up a given project before another one and mail it out faster, with Jean's complicity. However, that's about it, and at the end, we all feel guilty for doing so because all projects are worthy causes. As for approval of the project itself, well, you know that all depends on the Bishop's evaluation and decision at the New York headquarters."

After a brief silence, Father Thom explained his request.

"You see, I consider myself a great optimist. I love to joke and have fun, to live with and among people, listen to their problems and within my possibilities, meet their needs, but I can't do it all by myself. Personally, I do not own a stinking dime. That is the reason for my begging. I realize that Jean is doing her best, but I wish Father Nielsen would show more interest in all this, too. So I just thought that maybe you could have a word with him in my favor."

"What makes you think that he does not care, and why would he listen more to me than you?"

"Well, as I said earlier, he likes you and always speaks so highly about your abilities and dedication."

"And you truly believe all that, right?" I said, while the salary increase incident flashed through my mind.

"Oh, yes. And I share his opinion completely," said Father Thom with a wide, bright smile.

I shook my head from side to side while taking a drag from my cigarette and glancing over my plate filled with shrimp shells. Deep in my heart I knew that there were more urgent projects to take care of and it simply wouldn't feel right to override the sequence of urgencies. But that secret, I kept to myself.

Noticing my distress, Father Thom grabbed my hand and said, "Don't worry, Isabel. I have many friends and if Father Nielsen won't help, they will. I'm sure. So don't think about it anymore. Not this evening, anyway," he said.

We decided to forget about work and for the rest of the evening chose to talk about Rio, philosophy and religion. I could have spent the entire night listening to Father Thom's fascinating way of clearing foggy religious concepts, but it was getting late and I had to go home and rest because morning was always back too soon.

Weeks filed by fast; work increased, and employees came and went. Father Nielsen was constantly on the move, busy with meetings, interviews, parties and fund-raising campaigns or travelling. I could often sense his stress and always wondered when, if ever, he would blow his top. Father Nielsen would never shout or show his true state of mind. He would always cover up with his charming, disarming smile. I often wished to be able to penetrate the intricate meanders of his thoughts, to break into the inner sanctum of his heart and feelings, but that was obviously, forbidden territory. He so much reminded me of my mother, who would never reveal her innermost turmoil, pain or sadness. She would even fight sleep just so no one ever surprised her dozing off occasionally. In her view, only lazy people dared and had time to doze off during the day. To be ill and miss a day's work was shameful and was very unacceptable. Most probably, Father Nielsen was raised with the same principles. On the scale of values, first came his work, then his image as priest, then all the rest. I often envisioned him not as a priest, but as a talented, clever, business executive, maybe sitting in a nice red leather chair behind a large mahogany desk, spoiled by an efficient legion of assistants.

One day, to my surprise, he offered to drive me to the ferry terminal. Along the way, he told me about the various meetings he had that day as well as the outcome of each. As we approached the terminal, Father Nielsen entered the parking lot and while searching for a spot, he asked me, "Would you mind if we had a little chat?"

I thought his request to be very unusual, considering that he had had plenty of time while driving but my female curiosity was stronger and so I agreed. He parked the car in a corner of the lot and began to talk about my contribution to the organization, praising my loyalty, goodness, naivety and last but not least, my "charming beauty."

"How can I tell you this? You are this young, pretty thing and I noticed how the guys in the office just can't keep their eyes off you. Do you think you could do something about it, like maybe covering up a little more?" he said blushing and visibly embarrassed.

For a moment, I was left speechless.

"What do you mean by cover up a little more? Cover up what?"

"Well, you know," he mumbled and gesticulated around his chest. "Maybe a little less cleavage, you know, the breasts." He sounded extremely uneasy.

I peeked at myself but couldn't understand his complaint.

"You know, I really don't see anything wrong with my dress here," I said with a pinch of annoyance.

"Of course you don't, but when you bend over someone's desk...you know? Mind you, there is nothing wrong in having a good-looking body. It's just that some people react a little more than they should." He still sounded very uneasy.

I had never thought of it that way. Most of my dresses were sleeveless, round or square-cut necklines, so pretty and comfortable to wear in that hot Brazilian summer and no one, up until then had found fault in my dress code, not even Father Anthony.

"I just thought that you should be aware of what is going on. I don't want people to keep on gossiping."

"Gossiping? Who, on earth is gossiping?"

"Well, you hear comments here and there and I don't want anybody to hurt you and I truly hope that you are not angry with me for telling you this. I'm just saying these things for your own good."

At that point he tapped me on the shoulder as if comforting me and finished by giving me one of his charming smiles. I could detect a sense of relief on his side and wondered how difficult it must have been for him to approach me about it.

I was still furious, however, and felt my anger building up. I was eager to give free rein to my feelings, but I refrained because after all, Father Nielsen wasn't the one trying to look at my breasts, or was he? I thanked him for the ride, slammed the car door and walked towards the terminal without looking back once. I was very upset at that point and decided that an ice cold beer was the answer to that nuisance. I ordered a double *Chopp sem Colarinho* (a large beer without the foam), and let the nice, golden fluid cool down my anger.

Who the hell could have gossiped about my dress, I wondered. In comparison to what Lina used to wear, skin tight, generously low-necked dresses, mine were just common, prêt-a-porter outfits, a tight upper bodice and wide skirts enhanced by a petticoat and a beeline waist. I could simply not get over the incident. To gossip and make a big issue about a simple dress in a country where streets and beaches were populated by all kinds of sexy, gorgeous creatures in truly adamitic outfits; where public carnival scenes and magazine pictures were the clear expression of pure eroticism was real stupidity and hypocritical bigotry. Sin resides where sin is seen. Not all eyes were trained to, at all costs, uncover sin and insinuate malice where there was none. I was angry at all the religious nonsense, which turned some humans into dangerous fanatics, capable of destroying the true nature of God's earthly creations and promoting hatred, falsehood, mistrust and betrayal.

On the boat, I chose a window seat. The ocean breeze acted as a relaxing balm to my upset nerves. Soon, the usual noisy, happy crowd filled the seats and platforms. What were the various individuals up to, I wondered while studying the crowd. Were they all heading back home? Were they returning to a world of happiness or sadness? My attention was captured by a small group of black teenagers, dancing and singing while beating the rhythm on wooden matchboxes. Brazilians do not need fancy percussion instruments. Any object will do and if one listens carefully, one can even hear the musician's heart lead the main beat. One of the boys began singing a popular Carnival song, which so well described my mood that evening. The translation sounded like "Sadness has no end, happiness does. The happiness of the poor is like the great illusion of the Carnival. The people work the entire year for a moment of dream, to make the costume of a king or a gardener, and then all ends on Ash Wednesday."

That evening after dinner, I took a long walk with Gigi—my little four-legged boxer friend—along the seashore. The night was warm and the sky was studded with myriads of glittering stars. How extraordinarily wonderful and grand was the world around me, the universe and its mysteries, in comparison to the petty human problems. Gigi jumped happily in the sand, running back and forth, as if inviting me to run along with her. For a while, I obliged, but Gigi was so much faster and resilient. Sensing my inability to keep up with her, Gigi would stop, look back, wag the little stump of a tail and then run back towards me. She would bend down, her head touching her front paws, eyes rolled up in my direction, inviting me to catch her, but as soon as I would take a step towards her, she would sprint away again like a thunderbolt, raising big clouds of sand around her. She would race around a few more times and come to a halt again, with her tongue hanging out, panting wildly and with an authentic smile of happiness all over her face.

I crashed into the sand next to my grateful, drooling pooch. It had been a good race and I was tired. Intermittently, a light breeze would rustle the palm leaves bringing along the brinish scent of the ocean and the spectacular sound of waves breaking against the cliffs. After a while, I got to my feet, shaking off the sand from my clothes and started walking back home. I turned around a few times to take a last glimpse of the throbbing lights of Rio across the Guanabara Bay, a breathtaking scene that I would cherish forever.

The next morning, I showed up in the office with my usual poise and dress style. The only thing I would no longer do is to bend down while sorting documents or talking to anybody. Father Nielsen was already busy in a meeting with a group of early bird visitors and very briefly waved in my direction. Father Francis immediately asked me for some gasoline money and at the same time invited me for another card game the next Friday. He then handed me a paper bag saying, "Marcia made this for you and hopes you'll enjoy it." I immediately opened the bag and found a large piece of tempting Banana cake in it. I thanked him while handing him over the requested money.

"I'm not too sure about next Friday, but I'll let you know ahead of time," I said.

I had hardly settled down when Tia Marta, the black housekeeper whom everyone affectionately called Auntie, came to ask for money to purchase coffee and some cleaning material. After she had tucked away the money in her apron pocket, Marta gave me a folded piece of paper.

"I wrote this poem last night. Would you please read it and tell me what you think of it?" she said.

Marta was a tall, well-built woman in her late fifties. Even though lacking the privilege of schooling, she had made every effort to learn reading and writing, assisted by her former employer's children. Sensitivity and color were the main ingredients of the poems she wrote in her spare time, and the one she had handed over to me was just one more of her masterpieces. I wrote a small note of praise, clipped it to her poem, re-folded the paper and left it at a corner of my desk where Marta would pick it up later. Many times, I would invite her to sit for a while, to chat about her poems, her feelings and inspirations. There was so much love, understanding and wisdom in her philosophy of life, which was very simple. Love everybody, laugh off problems, sing, write poems and do not forget a daily prayer, of course.

Until about noon, I was very busy. I even stayed in for lunch because Dora's mother had sent me a special regional dish to taste. It had become almost a regular occurrence that some of the girls and sometimes the men, too, would spoil me with little gifts in sign of their appreciation. I must admit that I enjoyed the fuss and the attention and was flattered as long as that attention remained on neutral grounds and did not turn into possessive territorial disputes. Dora was at times a little too pushy. It came to a point where she would bring me lunch almost every day. Those were specialties ranging from the occasional titbit to a complete meal. Dora was becoming too possessive and I had the tendency of running from those characters. Besides, I liked to go out on my own sometimes and eat what I felt like eating, even junk food, without having to socialize with anyone.

One afternoon, while pausing from my paperwork, I gazed over the various workstations and remembered Father Nielsen's remarks and wondered who, among the co-workers, could be the famous gossiper. I scanned desk after desk, men and women. There was Maria, a middle aged, and still very good-looking lady, recently separated from her husband. She was very keen on her appearance. The quality of her outfits revealed that she had no particular financial worries. Despite her inner turmoil, caused by her husband's rejection—he had left her for a much younger female—she was still able to master a happy, youthful smile. Separations were becoming a common occurrence, especially in a country populated by sun-kissed gorgeous females, where faithfulness had become every male's challenge. For some reason, Maria had chosen me as her confidante and our entire relationship excluded petty morality. We shared our passion for Ian Fleming's James Bond books. It could definitely not have been Maria to spread gossip.

Then there was Antonio, the man with the "payday smile"—the only time, or almost, his face was graced by a smile. Skinny, medium height, black hair and eyes, he was renowned as a hard-working, good Catholic. An excellent family man, he had been married eight years and had seven children. He was of the opinion that a woman's ultimate and only goal in life was marriage and family. Once, during a conversation with a group of males he proudly stated that his wife was forbidden stupidities such as make-up, nail polish or fancy hairdos and he personally looked after her wardrobe. A married woman was not supposed to play the coquette and therefore did not need to be attractive. He also took care of all the shopping, so she did not have to show her face around. I thought that perhaps he should have just bought her a burka.

Anyway, I had very little contact with Antonio. I never really liked him because of his chauvinistic tendencies but I respected his serious work ethics nonetheless. Somehow, my suspicions landed on him because of his behavior and apparent prudishness. From that day onwards, I decided to leave his pay check, and whatever other documents he was to receive, on his desk early morning, before his arrival. The least contact I had with the man, the better.

Days kept flashing by and I was always busier, with more work and more friends. Invitations had to be programmed and I just didn't seem to be able to please everyone. Surprisingly, Father Nielsen also thought it was time to pay a visit to my parents.

"So why don't you come over for lunch next Sunday?" I said.

"I might just take you up on that," Father Nielsen replied, happily.

"No preaching, no sermons though, Ok?" I said, jokingly.

"No, no sermons," he agreed with a chuckle.

By eleven o'clock the following Sunday, Father Nielsen arrived with his executive briefcase. I hoped he would not talk about business. He seemed to be in an exceptional good mood. After a moment of hesitation, he accepted a dry martini, stirred, not shaken. He spent almost an hour chatting with my father who felt very honored by the visit. With enthusiasm, Father Nielsen explained to him the nature of the organization's work and the great projects that were being carried out. Finally, lunch was ready. Father Nielsen said a short prayer and blessed the food before we all started to dig in. He enjoyed every bit of the chicken paprikás and even went for seconds. We chatted some more 'til my parents left to attend the afternoon mass.

"Why don't we go to the beach for a swim?" Father Nielsen suggested.

"Sure, why not? Did you bring your swimwear?" I was surprised with my own stupidity. After all, he wouldn't have suggested it had he not come prepared. He used the bathroom to change while I used my parents' room.

"Do you know a nice little spot we can go to?" Father Nielsen asked, slightly embarrassed. "You know, discreet…"

"Oh, yes. There is a gorgeous little harbor further up, towards Samamguaiá. It is a very private enclosure and you still have the magnificent view of Rio across the Bay."

It was indeed a lovely corner, deserted at the time with the exception of a few couples too busy to care about the new arrivals. He must have been concerned about his priestly image but I was quite certain that nobody in that area would know or recognize him. Besides, what could be so terribly wrong about a priest going swimming with a girl, I pondered. Father Francis had never once expressed any concern about it. I pointed out my thoughts to Father Nielsen.

"Oh… Isabel, Isabel. It is not the swimming in itself, but the fact that I am accompanied by a pretty thing as you. The typical mentality will never understand or accept the fact that we are only good friends, working partners. Malice generates gossip, and there is much of that around. You do understand my position, right?"

"Gosh, why must life be so complicated," I said with a bored sigh.

Yet, I had to recognize that he was right. Mostly the bigots, wrapped tightly in religious rules and prejudices, had the uncanny ability to seeing sin where there was no sin, pointing out evil where there was no evil.

"Anyway, these people here don't know you. So relax. I'm going for a swim. Are you coming?" I jumped up and headed into the water.

Father Nielsen followed me shortly after. He was a very good swimmer and I had a hard time keeping up with his powerful strokes. We then swam back, closer to the beach, jumping, diving and splashing water at one another.

For a short while, instead of the Reverend Father, I saw a very happy, relaxed young boy, enjoying every bit of his short freedom.

The sun was nice and warm as we lay in the sand, side-by-side, drying up our swimsuits. He did not seem at all disturbed by the vision of my bikini clad body and even if he had been, he would not have shown it.

"Have you already been to mass today?" Father Nielsen asked, breaking the silence.

"Nope," I replied, with my eyes still closed.

"How come?"

"I'll be going later this evening," I lied, to avoid unnecessary possible polemics.

"I'm glad to hear that," he said, tapping slightly on my hand.

A while later, Father Nielsen consulted his watch and realized it was time for him to return home.

"Too bad it's time to go, Isabel," he said while pulling up his top shorts and putting on the shirt. "It was so good here. I really enjoyed every minute of it but I'm expected back in Rio this evening."

"Yes, it was very nice indeed. Too bad good things always end too soon." I said, while following Father Nielsen to the car. Fifteen minutes later we were back at home. I turned on the TV while Father Nielsen went to take a shower and change. When he was finished, he joined me for a beer in the living room while watching a Woody Woodpecker cartoon on TV. Half hour later Father Nielsen took off. I waved from the window until he disappeared around the corner. I then picked up another Brahma Chopp beer from the fridge and fell back onto the couch to watch some more cartoons. The heat, the swimming and naturally the beer, had drained my energy.

The following Monday morning, I crossed the bay with Luisa. We often travelled together on the same boat.

"Guess whom I saw last night?" Luisa said with a tone of suspense in her voice.

"No idea. Anyone I should know?"

"Yes. Someone you worked with some time ago."

"No idea. I've worked with so many people. How could I possibly remember everyone? Is it a girl or a guy?"

"It's a girl," Luisa teased.

"Oh, come on. Tell me already. Don't keep me guessing."

"Well, last night, my boyfriend and I went to this night club on Avenida Presidente Vargas and believe it or not, there was Lina, working as *entreneuse.*"

"You must be kidding. How do you know that she was working as an escort?"

"She told me so and she also asked me to say hello to you and tell you that now she is working in a more profitable environment." Luisa giggled.

"Yeah, right, a lady of the night."

"Oh, what do you care anyway?" Luisa said.

"Well, we used to be very good friends way back. But then several unpleasant incidents took place, of which I don't feel like talking."

"Like when she flirted with your boyfriend right in front of you?"

"Well, that was one of the things that pissed me off. It was my fault, too. I had one too many and didn't care much about what was happening around me. Only later, when the booze started to wear off did I realize how stupid I had been to allow it to happen."

"But your boyfriend was a jerk, too. He could have rejected her advances in respect of you."

"He could have, but you see, Lina oozed sex from every pore and I guess the guys had a hard time in keeping their cool, especially the hot blooded Brazilians. He was a little drunk that night also and Lina was horny, as usual. It was the perfect combination for the two of them."

"At least you got rid of her. Actually, now that I think of it, she was quite flirtatious with my boyfriend, too. Just that Valdir ignored her and pushed her away."

We kept silent for the rest of the trip, perhaps mentally rehashing all that we should or could have done better. I was still thinking of Lina as I walked into the office. Maybe intrigued by my gloomy looks, Father Nielsen called me over to his desk to find out more. I took a seat on the chair beside his desk and shared the news about Lina wondering how he would take it since he had always pointed her out to me as an example of bubbly, outgoing personality. She was bubbly all right, too outgoing and too bubbly for her own good.

"Well, it is a pity indeed," Father Nielsen said with a deep sigh while running his fingers through his hair. "All we can do is pray for her and hope for the best."

Later that afternoon, a social worker named Joaquim, returning from an extensive trip to the far north, shook up the place with his explosive personality. Despite his apparent physical fragility, Joaquim possessed a strong character and feared no one. His eyes had the ability to reach deep into the listener's heart. He smiled tenderly, emitted deadly sparks or fiercely underlined a statement. He even had some heated squabble with Father Nielsen. The problems were usually the same. The funds released were being delayed and diluted more and more.

"If you don't fork out the cash, I stop travelling. How do you think I can look in them people's faces? They wait, and wait and hope. And I promise and promise and nothing comes from the bag." Joaquim nervously paced back and forth in front of Father Nielsen's desk.

"Well, don't keep promising so much," Father Nielsen said.

"If I can't at least promise and therefore leave them a spark of hope, then what the hell am I doing, poking my nose in troubles we can't solve? Might as well stay home and chase some good looking chick instead." Joaquim was half-serious and half joking.

"In a way you are right, but you have to understand our situation also, and be a little more patient," said Father Nielsen with the hint of a smile on his face.

"Oh, I do understand all right; it is the patience part that doesn't understand me," Joaquim said, his two big brown eyes translating his emotional turmoil.

Joaquim's problems were not easily solved and were not the only ones. The files were overflowing with projects and each one seemed more important and urgent than the previous or the next one. The organization could no longer rely on the New York headquarters alone, which supported, thanks to the generous contribution of the American people, hundreds of thousands of humanitarian projects from all over the world. It was time for the locals to do something for themselves. It was in this line of thought that Father Nielsen launched a national campaign aiming to raise funds within the country itself. The entire staff applauded the initiative. There were plenty of wealthy people and organizations in Brazil who had the means to contribute handsomely to the less fortunate of their own country.

I often felt helpless and frustrated by the thousands of typed pages of letters, memos and reports as well as photographs illustrating the tragic conditions in which countless human beings were living. I would often share my feelings with Father Francis.

"Why do you think the almighty God allows so much misery and suffering, if he is the most powerful and compassionate God we are taught to believe in?"

"What can I say? It must be God's will," Father Francis replied a little uneasy. "This is one of the reasons why we pray and invite everybody else to join us."

He knew that I needed a much better explanation.

"Well, don't you think that it is cruel to let people die of hunger, especially the little ones? It is a form of killing isn't it, and if God is truly magnanimous and merciful, then how could he possibly be so insensitive?"

"See, God does not send hunger; neither did he create hunger. Hunger is a man-made condition. God did set man free to do as he sees fit and

God will not take that freedom away; otherwise everything would become a compulsory act."

Maybe Father Francis was right, but I still could not understand the logic behind his viewpoint. The problem was apparently a hard one, even for a priest to tackle and so I just kept the rest of my thoughts and feelings to myself. I walked back to my desk and tried in vain to concentrate on my work. The divine injustice kept creeping back into my mind. If God gave man freedom, why was it compulsory then to go to Mass, take communion and go to confession every Sunday? Why is an individual considered a lousy Christian and a lesser child of God, if he or she does not comply with such ritual? Why was it compulsory to have a newborn baby christened while the baby was still unable to chose and discern good from evil and vice-versa, justice from injustice, poor from rich, freedom from slavery — let alone decide in the case of religious matters? Why is a particular individual considered a good Christian just because he donates handsomely to the Church, while behind the bushes he screws around with other people's wives, husbands or business partners? Questions and more questions flashed through my mind. Yet I didn't feel like sharing these thoughts and feelings with any of the priests I had contact with, because I was convinced that neither would come up with a satisfying answer and would end up sending me to pray in some overcrowded chapel to overcome the sinful feeling of doubt.

Personally, I developed and preferred my own prayers, made up in my very own words and feelings. My church was all the space around me: the beach, a clearing in the forest, the waves in the ocean, a park and even my very own room. I also preferred to think of my God, Creator of all things, as a merciful, compassionate, understanding and forgiving higher power who would be pleased with my love and admiration for all the things He created and which surrounded me at any given time and anywhere. I believed that God resided in the green grass of the meadows, in the rocks of the mountains, in the deep blue oceans, in a fish, a flower, a pebble. I believed that whenever I stopped to admire even the infinitesimal objects of His creations, I would be admiring God himself and since God was everywhere at anytime, why did I need a particular chapel or church and on a particular day and time and have to listen to the same boring biblical passages over and over again. Despite the years of traditional religious teachings received at the college run by nuns, I often surprised myself with my lines of thought; yet was convinced I was following in the right track.

There was a time when I came to the realization that if I wanted to free myself from anguish and oppressive guilt feelings, I would have to free myself from the environment I lived in. The optimism and the load of enthusiasm were slowly fading and I no longer felt able to deal with the psychological and emotional stress the work encompassed. It was time to move on.

Through an acquaintance, I came to know about an opening for a bi-lingual secretary within a multi-national computer company. One day during lunchtime, I ran over to their personnel department to check out the possibility of being hired. The young man in charge for the interviews and selection of candidates was very pleasant and explained that the new secretary was expected to start in March. That would give me three months to find a replacement, train and leave all work properly updated.

After listening to the description of my activity, Roberto asked, "How come you are leaving this organization after so many years?"

"I must keep up with the cost of living, Sir. The organization I presently work for is mainly a charitable organization and cannot afford to pay more." I skipped the second reason that would have been my emotional upheaval—a problem Roberto did not have to know about.

Roberto seemed satisfied with my explanation and invited me for a series of aptitude tests as well as physical check-ups, all scheduled well ahead of time. Finally, he told me that the initial salary would be 450,000 cruzeiros. While I fought to keep my face perfectly composed, concealing my joy, my heart was doing somersaults for happiness. I was so confident in getting the job that I didn't give a second thought to all the tests I was expected to undergo.

For two weeks I struggled with the problem of how to tell Father Nielsen about my intention to leave the organization. I hoped that he would not try to persuade me to stay or for that matter, ask too many questions. The answer to my problem came through the annual salary review. While checking the names one-by-one on the review list and making notes about changes in the amounts, Father Nielsen's pen stopped at my name.

"So, let's see what we are going to do for this young lady here," he said, smiling mischievously into my direction. "You are now earning 195,000 cruzeiros. What if we round it up to 200,000?" he asked, probably feeling generous.

It was now or never, I thought, before his charming smile could have the chance to disarm my courage and will.

"You know, I really don't know how to tell you this, but I received an offer from another company and I did accept it," I said in one breath.

Father Nielsen was visibly surprised. He dropped his pen, removed his glasses and stared me straight into my eyes. There was an endless pause before he came to words again and wanted to know more about it. I only mentioned the name of the company to which he smiled, apparently very pleased.

"Jeez, you are very lucky to get in there," he said. "Congratulations. By the way, did you know that Anesia also got an offer for the position of head nurse at the General Hospital? That is why I am giving her a rather generous increase." He giggled. "And now let's see what about you? With how much are you going to blackmail me?" he chuckled.

"Four hundred and fifty thousand," I replied, proudly.

For a brief moment, Father Nielsen's smile froze on his face. He knew that the organization's budget could not afford to match that amount.

"Well, Isabel, I am truly very sorry in losing you. You know how much we all love you and appreciate your cooperation but I'd be a fool if I tried to dissuade you from such an improvement in your career. Besides, you know about our financial resources. We couldn't possibly afford this kind of salary for a secretarial position." He smiled faintly.

"I know, and I'm not asking for it either."

"My God, look at you, leaving us after all these years." He sighed. "I only hope you will not forget us."

"How could I?" I replied. How could I indeed, forget the several significant years that I had spent with the organization?

"And when do you intend to leave us?" he asked.

"Well, I am supposed to start by the first of March. So we still have plenty of time to search for a replacement and I was counting on at least two weeks off to recharge my own batteries."

"Naturally. At any rate, the intended raise stands. At least, I tried, right?"

Jean's arrival interrupted our conversation. She had to review an urgent project with Father Nielsen and so I returned to my desk. I felt a great sense of relief, as had I been freed from an incredible crushing weight, and pleased with myself for having dared to take an initiative without the interference of third parties. The news about my leaving the organization naturally leaked out, partially through Father Nielsen, then Father Francis and ultimately, me. An endless period of "why" and "how" followed, but I had an answer ready for everyone. "It was time to move on," I would simply say.

One of my extra tasks was the organizing of the annual Christmas party, to which I took much pride. Aside from the office personnel and their relatives, there were many other guests invited, as were donors, friends of the organization, and directors of other agencies as well as a few friends from the American Embassy. The party usually started right after work at about 6 p.m. I would put on the Christmas records on an old 33-rpm record player. Father Nielsen would remove his glasses, push aside any paperwork and then tour the various departments inviting some late bloomers or workaholics to drop whatever they were doing to join the celebration. Meanwhile, Alina, Jean, Janet, Dora, Tia Marta and I would provide the last touches to the beautiful buffet to which each participant had been asked to contribute. There were salads, tarts, cold cuts, fried chicken, regional specialties, cookies, cakes, fruit and a selection of beverages, beer and liquor. The tree, the decorations and the candles were recycled from year to year. Whoever wished to make a gift to a colleague or friend would place the gift under the tree. Towards 6:30 p.m., the relatives would slowly show up and shortly thereafter everyone else. Once the crowd was gathered together, Father Nielsen would initiate the festivities with his ritual Christmas speech and blessings. That particular Christmas, he ended his speech by officially announcing my resignation.

"Unfortunately, a less pleasant event this day is that our friend Isabel here will soon leave us to join a large company and I would like to take this opportunity to thank her, in my name and in the name of the entire organization for all the wonderful work she has done throughout these years. I would also like to assure Isabel, that despite her desertion..." Father Nielsen chuckled briefly, "we do love her and will always include her in our prayers. We also wish her all the best and so much success and happiness for the future."

Applause followed his speech. Father Neilson then approached me and gave me a big hug. He was followed by all the others, one at a time, offering their best wishes. Maria, Anesia, Janet, Jean and Tia Marta hugged me with watery eyes while Father Francis chose a corner to wipe his tears.

Although I was aware of being well-liked by most of the people I encountered and worked with, I could not have anticipated the commotion my departure would cause among my colleagues. It was all very flattering and at the same time sad, but that evening, I did not wish to be saddened and exhorted everyone to enjoy themselves. Jean began to play the guitar and Raimundo, the office boy, played the accordion while a bunch of us pitched in with our voices. As the atmosphere warmed up, records of samba and bossa nova, a rhythm that was irresistible even for those lacking dancing skills, replaced the voices. Joaquim instead was a real master and very few ladies were capable of keeping up with his intricate variations and twists. I loved to watch his exhibition. Soon everyone joined into dancing. In the meantime, Father Nielsen was busy entertaining the Embassy delegates, while sipping a gin and tonic. On and off, a small crowd would form around Joaquim who would perform his one-man show by telling jokes on a non-stop basis. No one seemed to be able to resist his terrific sense of humor. Father Manuel guffawed away with his face turning red as a ripe tomato. Even Antonio, the gloomiest of the gloomy, decided to set aside his zealot outfit to join the happy crowd. The only person decidedly out of place seemed to be Morton's wife, Paula, who had also been invited for the special occasion, even though Morton had been transferred to another branch of the organization years before. The unpleasant jealousy scene of a few years back was still vividly present in my mind, yet I tried to overcome any hard feelings by offering her a second chance. I approached her with the intention of starting a friendly conversation but time hadn't changed the woman. Her monosyllabic answers were proof that she preferred not to be bothered and preferred to be left alone in her own little misery. I did not insist and returned my attention to my friends.

At a certain point, Maria announced that I would sing a song. I fought the invitation as it had been a long time since I last sang in public, but my audience refused to accept the excuses and insisted by clapping their hands rhythmically. Even Father Nielsen, attracted by the noise, joined in clapping his hands exhorting me to sing. Suddenly, there was dead silence as I began to sing my favorite tune: "Sunny Side of the Street." For an instant, my voice threatened to falter since it was not easy to sing without accompaniment, but soon everybody around me pitched in with the rhythmic clapping of hands while Joaquim produced a percussion sound with a wooden matchbox. The crooner in me was finally back and I sang my heart out.

"Do you want all this talent going to waste in this office?" Maria said, elbowing Father Nielsen beside her. "She'll go a long way, you'll see."

Joaquim led the group to ask for an encore when everybody's attention was suddenly captured by a sobbing Paula standing near a window. She probably wanted to show everyone that she was just as modern and outgoing as all the other gals, and ended up having one too many shots of scotch. I ran to the kitchen to pick up a cup of coffee and offered it to her but the woman just simply turned away, ignoring the friendly gesture. Placing an arm around her shoulders, Morton led her away to the washroom. Her stomach was probably eager to get rid of some of the liquor she had ingested. I did not make an effort to understand Paula's behavior and rejoined the others until 10 p.m., when the festivity ended. Everybody who was not too tipsy pitched in with the clean-up, and everybody left happily looking forward to a full week off for Christmas.

My last month with the organization was chaotic. To find a replacement proved to be a little difficult. Not only was the older gentleman Father Nielsen had appointed for a trial period unable to find his way through the accounting system, but he also lacked the experience in the use of a typewriter. Another young lady thought the workload was excessive, and so forth. Father Nielsen therefore decided to hire a professional accountant for the accounting department alone and distributed all other tasks among several departments. On my last day, I dedicated the entire time to my co-workers.

Father Nielsen presented me with a generous bonus check and when I finally shook his hand and hugged him for the last time, all I was able to say was: "Goodbye and thank you." I felt that we would meet again some day and we made it a point to keep in touch, no matter how far we'd be from each other. And we did, to this day.

8

Big Blue

I was early for my appointment and the first battery of tests. Eagerly, I followed Roberto to a small room set up for the purpose. I had to translate various texts to and from English to Portuguese. Later, I had to compose commercial letters in both English and Portuguese. Based on Roberto's grin, I must have done well that day.

In the following weeks I had to undergo a few more tests including typing speed and accuracy. Not only did I enjoy the various fancy IQ and ability tests, measured according to scientific parameters, but rejoiced each time I completed a test before the timing clock rang. I was told that most large corporations used those methods to evaluate the abilities, speed and integrity of an applicant. Aware of being time measured, many applicants would lose their concentration and succumb to their nervousness. That was the case of Eliza, the only other candidate left at the end. I beat her on the typing test by 85 against 70 wpm.

"There is only one last thing before you can come aboard our company," Roberto said with a large grin.

"And what would that be?" I asked, confident that whatever it was, I would be able to handle.

"You have to go for a physical. It is one of the requirements." Roberto handed me an appointment slip.

The physical was carried out by a physician appointed by the company. Dr. Braga found that overall, I was in very good health and I would have passed with flying colors had it not been for a mild case of tonsillitis.

"How often do you suffer with tonsillitis?"

"Very rarely," I said, "only when I drink ice cold liquids."

Dr. Braga suggested the removal of my tonsils and management followed suit to his recommendations.

Aside from an appendectomy at age ten and painful visits to the dentists, I never had to see a doctor. The occasional flu or bellyache was taken care of by over-the-counter medicine prescribed by the pharmacist. Most pharmacists were considered as good as doctors for minor ailments and also because specialists in Brazil, at least in 1965, were for us common mortals, financially prohibitive. And we did not have a health insurance plan either.

To go under the knife, aside from the fear, meant to kiss my long-awaited vacation goodbye. In vain were my protests, pleas and assurances that I would never, ever miss a day of work due to tonsillitis. It was a sine qua non in order to get that position and the management's decision was final.

Their argument was that they could not afford to hire personnel prone to recurrent illnesses, with consequent time and financial loss. I had no alternative but to accept their conditions if I wanted the job. One week later, scared out of my wits, I was lying on a white stretcher in a private clinic, waiting for the anaesthesiologist. For a full week after surgery, I was miserable, in pain, couldn't swallow and had a front tooth chipped in the process. Luckily, the dentist fixed the problem with a crown, and two weeks after that I was ready to face a brand new lifestyle.

Born in Brazil, my new boss, Aldo Machado, was 5'8" tall with brown wavy hair and brown eyes. He had a master's degree in electronic engineering and was in charge of the distribution of software programs on large magnetic tapes or punched cards to their vast South American clientele.

"Your tasks will cover all the correspondence, both in English and Portuguese," he said. In a slow, calm manner he continued. "You will take care of the filing and the maintenance of the software library. I am not a demanding person, but I insist on punctuality and neatness." He smiled.

All in all, it promised to be a pleasant, relaxed environment, I thought.

Even though paperweights with the word "Think" were sitting on most desks, it wasn't really very necessary to use one's brain as there was an answer to most anything in a heavy, frequently updated Manual of Operations. Even if at times a certain situation or thing seemed illogical, the "Bible," as many referred to the Manual, would have the proper instructions on how to deal with the illogical situation or thing.

As with all large corporations, bureaucracy reigned sovereign. For example, a requisition for writing pads and pencils was typed in multiple copies to be distributed to the various departments, sections and divisions concerned. At times I felt as if my main occupation was filling in forms. I, who rarely needed to be told what to do, and had grown up to become a person with self-initiative, felt frustrated when unable to exercise that talent; everything had been predetermined, set up, programmed and the individual initiative seemed to be of lesser importance, at least on the clerical level.

I observed the other secretaries. None seemed overburdened with work or worried about having to use their mental resources. They all worked at a gentle, slow pace. They were mostly young, pretty girls, dressed in elegant, fashionable outfits. I compared my own homemade "Dior" ensemble, sewn by my mother with a fabric she had purchased on a liquidation sale at the street market, with those expensive dresses. I wondered if those girls could notice the difference. I hoped they didn't. After all, we were all there to work, not for a fashion show, which seemed to be the case almost every day.

At the beginning, I did not have much to do and wondered why Aldo needed a secretary in the first place. The few reports he would dictate on a weekly basis could have been easily typed by him, but heaven forbid, a director typing! That was a secretary's job. Anyone in a managerial position had to have a secretary. It was also a matter of status and prestige.

"Senhorita Isabel, would you come in for dictation?"

I would naturally drop whatever I was doing and go into his office, located right behind my desk. The room was surrounded by large framed glass panels. He could keep tabs on me and vice-versa. I would then sit in the chair across his desk. He would tilt his head forward so I could see his eyes peeking from above his tinted lenses.

"Are you ready?" he would ask and then start to dictate. The "dear so and so", with instructions as to the address and number of copies was always given in a big rush. The content of the letter instead was dictated slowly, every word carefully researched. Towards the end, his dictation gained momentum and I had to scramble to get it all down on my steno pad.

"Are we doing okay there?" he would ask, getting up from his chair, which meant we were finished, you can go now.

Most of my time, however, was still spent reading the company's "Bible," tidying the filing cabinets or begging the boss for more work to do. He must have been so annoyed with my pestering him for work, that one morning he threw an armful of folders on top of my desk and said, "There you go. Leaf through this material and type me a report on it, possibly in a chronological order."

"When do you need this for?" I asked. It was my standard question whenever a task was given to me just so I could program my activities and deadlines accordingly.

"For yesterday," Aldo said.

"Whew. Yesterday is gone."

"I know. I was just kidding, Miss. Take your time." He gave me a rare smile and then disappeared into his tiny office.

I was happy. There was finally something different and interesting to do. I read the content of all the folders in a couple of days. At the second reading, I started to make notes of all the points I considered important for the report. Then I classified the different subjects and operations carried out by our department. Aldo did not mask his surprise seeing me so enthused and enthralled with that little task. He probably did not expect me to take it so seriously and even felt embarrassed disturbing me with dictations or even just asking for a file from the filing cabinet. Executives such as Aldo were not supposed to help themselves to such simple tasks. That is why he had a secretary after all, and as I was always ready and willing to satisfy the master, Aldo slowly pushed aside the courteous "could you please" with a simpler "get me this, or that, will you?"

After a few days, I was ready and handed over my report to Aldo. Twenty neatly typed pages, which he read with great interest. He seemed satisfied because he read the report for a second time. It prompted him to think, jotting down notes, crossing out sentences and adding others here and there. He then returned everything to me for retyping, which I did for at least another three times before Aldo was completely satisfied. It was like one idea feeding the next and the next. What he initially had considered a little something, perhaps to keep me busy and off his back, had become a serious project, which he submitted to the attention of his superior who in turn was impressed and very pleased with the idea. Soon, also other departments were encouraged to submit similar reports, contributing to a better understanding of each other's purposes and operations within the company.

Some time later, Dr. Arpad, general manager of our division, selected me to temporarily replace his own secretary who was on an extended sick leave. For approximately two weeks, I had to divide my attention between Aldo and the sumptuous office of Dr. Arpad, who was also an electronic engineer. It was normal in South America, that whoever had a university degree was automatically recognized and revered as a doctor, and Arpad liked to be addressed as such.

I met him for the very first time when he came over to our office to attend a meeting with Aldo. He walked in with a sunny smile on his face.

"You must be Isabel; pleased to meet you," he said with a vigorous handshake and looking straight into my eyes as if he was reading something in them.

Dr. Arpad was about 5'6" tall, had blond hair and sparkling sky blue eyes. He was born in Hungary but there was no trace of the famous Hungarian accent, recognizable among millions, because he completed all his studies in Brazil. His parents had immigrated to Brazil shortly after the end of WWII.

I was early the first day I went over to his office and was told to just have a seat and wait for his arrival. There were two armchairs, a small desk with company pamphlets and a green desk lamp that gave the surroundings a cozy feeling.

"Hello, Isabel. How are you this morning? Come on in, please." He rushed into his office and dropped an armload of files and schematics on a small table next to his desk.

"Have a seat please," he said, pointing to the armchair across from his desk.

He was about to tell me something when he answered a phone call. His office was decorated in a very elegant, modern style. Soft, thick, dark green carpeting covered the floors. A lighter shade of green was used for the curtains covering panoramic windows. Magnificent tropical plants decorated almost every corner of his office. Shaded desk lamps gave the room a homely, cozy feeling. Documents, books, catalogs and folders covered the surface of his large black desk; yet everything was very neat and orderly.

"So this is what I need from you," he said after hanging up the phone. "I will give you letters and memos to type mainly in the morning. You will do some filing, take messages and keep an eye on my office until my return sometime in the afternoon. As you see, nothing major or complicated." He smiled.

"I sure can handle that," I said.

"So let's start with a couple of memos. You will find all the necessary tools in that desk over there." He pointed to a desk in the corner opposite to his and near a large window from where I had a panoramic view of part of the downtown core.

Dr. Arpad dictated at a steady pace, with occasional brief intervals. He had his elbows placed on the arms of his chair and both hands joined at his finger tips. His blue eyes fixed the wall across the room while his mind searched for the needed sentence or words. Once he was finished, he simply thanked me, made a few more phone calls and then disappeared till late afternoon.

Most offices in the main building had air conditioning and a device that would, at given intervals, release a pleasant fragrance in the air. Dr. Arpad had such a device. On the left hand side of his desk he had a panel with numerous colored buttons by which he could reach any other department or division at any given time. Opposite his desk, in a corner, there were two comfortable black leather armchairs, a small brass coffee table with a heavy bevelled glass top and a mini bar. Soft background music enhanced the environment and turned everything into a pleasant task. Labor relations authorities claimed that most people worked and concentrated better in a relaxed atmosphere, enveloped in a soft, caressing background tune.

At times, I felt like I worked for a movie set. Most girls in the main building looked like so many Miss Universe candidates, with perfect make-up and hairdos, wearing the latest fashions and rarely repeating an outfit. Even the guys were handsome, sexy movie star types with impeccable manners and dress codes. I often wondered why Dr. Arpad had chosen me for the replacement job. Any of those dolls could have done the job, as none seemed busy doing anything. I rarely typed more than five letters or memos per day and because I was fast, I often finished everything in a couple of hours. I was told to read "stuff" for the rest of the day and so I read the company's newsletters or boring technical magazines.

Dr. Arpad was a busy man, always on the go and spent only an hour, if that, each morning, dictating his letters, memos or reports. He was not at all a big talker. He kept his meetings and other business encounters short and to the point. Unlike Aldo, however, he was never too busy to remember the two magic words: "Please" and "Thank You." The fact that I was not always busy did not seem to bother him, as long as whatever I had to do was done properly and on time. I was, however, less satisfied with my rather monotonous activity. After the initial enthusiasm, due mainly to the elegant and sophisticated surroundings, I became bored, for which I was the only one to blame. Not being under any sort of pressure, there was definitely no need to rush and constantly show excessive efficiency. Like my colleagues, I could have spread my tasks throughout the day, chitchatting between one thing and another, but that was not my style. I was paid to work and anything else but work would not conform to my business ethics. Chitchatting and faking being busy was like stealing from the employer and I couldn't bring myself to do so.

One afternoon, Aldo told me that Dr. Arpad was extremely pleased with my work because unlike previous assistants, I was fast, precise and most importantly, silent. Even though the compliment caressed my ego, I was relieved when two weeks later Dr. Arpad's secretary returned and I was finally able to go back to my small, unsophisticated, uncarpeted office with a more active daily routine. Dr. Arpad thanked me for the great help I had been and said that he would call me again in the future for when an important event required specialized help. I confess I was proud of myself.

Aldo was happy to have me back, even though he hardly had work for me to do. I therefore fussed around the filing cabinets, my pride and joy and Aldo's obsession. In many ways, he was a perfectionist and craved aesthetic beauty. Everything had to be always in perfect order, placed or filed in a logical manner to impress anyone walking into his premises. I bet Marianne would have been proud of me, too.

I enjoyed most everything I did, especially organizing new filing systems for the hard copies of the many technical magazines and schematics for fast, easy retrieval. I was then always proud when Aldo would show off "his" creations to colleagues and other visitors, cleverly concealing his satisfaction from my view. He was an extremely meticulous person. His suits were mostly custom tailored, Italian style. His immaculate white shirts were perfectly pressed and starched. His hand-stitched loafers were always clean and shiny. His handwriting was precise and clear. His pencils had to be perfectly sharpened at any time of the day and punctuality was a must, regardless who the person was. Some of his idiosyncrasies could easily drive anyone nuts and I was no exception. One day, Aldo and I spent time arguing about a comma that had become a full point. Back then, people had to resort to erasers and did the best they could. Some executives were tolerant to minor typos; Aldo was not. After erasing the tiny tail of a comma, I typed over a full stop. Only trained or extremely fussy eyes would notice the correction.

"And what is this?" Aldo asked after reading the entire page and returning to the fatal comma-turned-dot. He removed his glasses, brought the paper closer to his eyes, and then pointed to the spot in question.

"Looks like a full stop to me," I said.

"Looks like or is?" Aldo asked.

"It is," I replied.

"You know what? I see the shadow of a comma instead." Very short-sighted, Aldo once more brought the paper even closer to his eyes, almost touching the tip of his nose.

"Ok. I accidentally typed a comma, erased it and typed over a full stop," I said to end the charade.

"Ahaaa!" Aldo said. "So it was a comma after all and not a real full stop."

"Exactly, and if you hadn't looked so hard, you wouldn't have noticed it either. I obviously didn't do a good enough job for you, right?"

"Right and I would appreciate it very much if you retyped the letter."

Aldo was so happy in catching my mistake, that if satisfaction could cause someone to levitate, he would have hit the ceiling.

Unlike Dr. Arpad, Aldo wasn't as fluent in writing or speaking English. He would handwrite his drafts and then ask me to correct his errors. I was always very cautious with my corrections, mainly because Aldo was extremely sensitive to criticism, which included possible corrections of his English texts. At times, I preferred to ignore some of his least noticeable mistakes, but Aldo was unpredictable and one afternoon, he called me into his office.

"How come you didn't notice such an elementary mistake?" he said sternly, pointing to the word in question.

Words such as whether and weather, wear, were, and where, which and witch, been and bean and so forth, were some examples that did at times create lively polemics.

"Well, I didn't dare correct too much," I once said, embarrassed.

"Do you mean to say that I would be capable of doing such a ridiculous mistake?" he replied visibly annoyed—as if the text had been written by another person.

He would then remind me that he went to the Berlitz School of Languages, where he was taught all the grammatical intricacies of the English language. I wondered why he would always ask me to check his letters and memos if that was the case. I simply smiled and retyped the document. Aldo loved to argue and I figured that somehow, he had to release his tension, his frustrations and underlying complexes. I frequently managed to forgive his tantrums because I knew that he had that desperate need of re-affirming his superiority and authority. It was probably included in my salary.

There was a time when Aldo was absent most of the time because of a series of meetings at an international level, held at the prestigious Copacabana Palace Hotel. For three days, I also had to show up at the hotel where I had a suite equipped with a typewriter, stationery and other materials necessary for the occasion. Aldo, however, did not seem to have much to say at those meetings, since I never had to type anything for him and spent most of my time indulging in the magnificent ocean view from the suite's terrace.

Aldo finally realized that my presence was unjustified and sent me back to the office. For several days, he would return to the office after hours and leave notes and memos with instructions on my desk. One morning, however, he was waiting for me with a great big smile and in an apparent good mood. He asked me to type a long report for the next day and gave me the necessary instructions on how he wanted it written and typed. I started on it as soon as Aldo left the office. I had all day, without having anyone watching over my shoulders. About three hours later, I had finished typing the eleven pages. I checked each page thoroughly watching for misspellings and typing errors. There were no mistakes and I proudly admired my impeccable work of art. I placed the report, with the ten carbon copies on Aldo's desk and returned to do some filing.

The next day in the morning, I arrived early, eagerly waiting for Aldo's word of approval. I did not have to wait too long. He arrived once again with a big smile on his face. He carefully examined the report and proceeded to sign each copy while complimenting me for a job well done. I could hardly believe that for a change, he was very satisfied with my work. I returned to my desk and was about to distribute the copies when Aldo called me back.

"Before you start sending out those copies, could I just have one last quick look?"

He grabbed the original and brought it to about three inches from his nose. Then he held it up straight ahead of him. He closed one eye first, then the other. At last, he took a ruler and started measuring. I began to feel extremely uneasy.

"Am I imagining things or do we have a slight discrepancy in the margins here?" he finally said.

I looked on, incredulous, yet there was a 1mm difference between the upper and the lower left-hand margin. The paper was not crooked and I always made sure to check that the upper and lower paper ends aligned after inserting the paper in the typewriter. I had never before encountered such a problem. I tried to explain it to Aldo, who was overtaken by a sudden bout of moodiness.

"You don't seem to be very familiar with this typewriter model, isn't it?" he said with badly concealed sarcasm.

For a brief moment, I was speechless. "Yet I've been using this same model the last two years but I never encountered this type of problem. It could be that after the alignment, while releasing the tension lever, the page slipped by 1mm."

"So how are we going to fix this problem?" Aldo asked.

"I don't know. Could be that the roller needs adjustment or something. After all, it is hardly noticeable."

"Well, I would suggest you send in a requisition and have a technician look after the machine immediately or replace it altogether. In the meantime, however, I want you to retype the report with exact margin measurements."

A brand new typewriter was delivered that same afternoon. That was the end of the matter. I was upset with myself for always lacking proper reaction time. Only hours later the "I should have said this or that," would pop into my mind. By then it was always too late and I would end up swallowing the bitter lesson and battle to forget the unjustified reproach. Aldo's emotional instability and often-sarcastic remarks slowly took the toll on my patience, goodwill and enthusiasm, and once I began losing interest in my work, no matter how important the company or how generous the pay, there was nothing that could hold me back.

To add to my emotional distress, my boyfriend had decided to leave me. We had met some eight months before in the same building where I had worked for CRS. Initially, I did not think much of the guy who kept staring at me with his brown beady eyes every time I passed by him. I found his glances to be almost intrusive and annoying, until one day, we were officially introduced to each other by a common friend. As they say, appearances can be deceptive. Mefisto, a nickname I had given him because of his love for the opera, revealed to be a very interesting, and at times quite fascinating character. He had many stories to tell and knew how to tell them in a most intriguing and captivating manner. We became good friends at first and ended up falling for each other, head over heels. He wanted to live with me and get married later, a condition that was completely unacceptable to my parents and frowned upon by the rest of society in those days. I found myself in an awkward position as I did not want to hurt either side, not my parents by eloping and not doing the right and proper thing, or Mefisto. In the meantime, I increased my intake of dry martinis, gin and tonics or scotch and sodas, hoping to erase all the problems from my mind and soul. The drinks acted as a temporary anaesthetic but certainly did not solve my problems, which would still be there the day after in addition to a painful headache caused by yet another hangover.

Tired of my endless wavering, Mefisto returned to his native Italy, leaving me with nothing more than a long, bitter goodbye letter, which a common friend of ours was to deliver to me after Mefisto's plane had taken off. In that letter, he pointed out that in his opinion, I had not yet done anything significant in my life and that efficiency alone was not enough to reach the apex of success. I definitely did not lack in initiatives, but was unable to let my character, abilities and personal rights prevail upon others. I was too attached to my family and my entire life had been organized in conformity to their personal needs and requirements. Even though I had completed 25 years of age, I had never dared to break the strong family ties that had kept me chained to a monotonous home-work-home existence, lacking, according to Mefisto, of deeper and more varied personal interests.

To a certain extent I could no longer pretend that my life was a paradise without problems. I had to decide fast and without the artificial support of a martini, to follow Mefisto to his native Italy. An action that meant breaking loose from all family ties. It meant leaving behind not only parents, but also grandparents, brother, friends and relatives as well as all those things that had surrounded me during my 25 years of life. I always wondered if Mefisto had ever realized the enormity of my action and decision in giving up everything to follow him. The rivers of tears and heartache it caused not to one, but to so many people. The challenge however, was on. To leave or not to leave, was my form of Hamlet's choice. How much did I love him? Enough to buy the airline ticket Rio to Rome via Aerolineas Argentinas.

Comforted by the idea that nobody on earth is entirely indispensable, I told my parents and grandparents about my decision to follow Mefisto to Italy. The news was initially received with outrage as they were convinced that Mefisto was nothing but a manipulative liar, stealing away a beloved daughter, sister and granddaughter. They would not let me go that easily and through their friends, Otto and Joseph had done a background check on the man to convince me of their suspicions. Not only justice is blind, love is too, and I proved it by following my impulsive heart. I submitted my resignation to a very perplexed Aldo whose main concern was how to explain to the main office about his inability to hang on to a secretary for more than a few months at a time. Dr. Arpad was very displeased.

"Are you not happy with us?" he asked. "Do you wish to work with someone else? Do you need a wage increase? Why throw away such a promising career?"

I was flattered by his concern but my decision was final. My destiny was in the making.

9

CIAO, Italia

It was June 1966 when I joined Mefisto in Milano where he had rented a small one-bedroom apartment at the end of Corso Lodi. All we had to start our new life together was a sofa bed, a small coffee table and two chairs. A big nail behind the door held our coats and sweaters.

Mefisto proudly showed me around Milano and I was touched in seeing places and monuments I had only seen in the movies and postcards: Duomo di Milano—the magnificent Cathedral with its spires and the golden Madonnina (little Madonna) statue towering in all majesty over the entire city. With reverence, I touched the walls of the Scala di Milano opera house. For a moment, I felt like hearing the voices of Maria Callas, Del Monaco, Tebaldi, Tagliavini and Di Stefano, echoing through the centuries' old stones as well as the powerful sounds of incomparable works by Verdi, Rossini, Puccini and so many other favorites. My brother and I always loved opera. For a short while we even took singing lessons from Lydia Nesterenko in Niterói. She thought that if I applied myself I could become a talented soprano. My favorite arias were Rigoletto's *Tutte le feste al tempio* and Verdi's *Libiamo ne' lieti calici* from La Traviata. My brother enjoyed singing Boito's *Mephistopheles* because he had a beautiful and powerful bass voice. Due to various reasons, including financial, we had to regretfully give up the lessons, and that was the end of our brief operatic careers.

Another time Mefisto and I strolled alongside the Naviglio, visited the Galleria, the Sforza Castle and the Brera Art Gallery. Each nook and cranny had a story to tell and I felt privileged in setting foot on the soil of such beautiful land.

For several months I tried to adapt to my new surroundings and lifestyle. Aside from the cultural aspect, I found Milano to be cold and impersonal.

Unlike in Rio, people on the streets hardly ever smiled. Everybody seemed to be rushing to an important destination. I put in all my effort to learn the language, not only to be able to communicate with the doorkeeper, the cashiers at the various shops, but also and mainly, to be able to apply for employment as a second salary would have been more than welcome at that point. A couple of months after my arrival in Milano, I had applied to IBM because I was already familiar with the organization. I thought that would help me to secure a position within the company, but my application was turned down because despite my fluency in Portuguese, German, some Hungarian and Spanish, I lacked the most important in this case, Italian.

I read anything I could lay my hands on, from the easier comic books to newspapers and even tried to initiate a conversation with anyone willing to help me. Some people were only too happy to teach me, trying to explain things with colorful sign language. The fact that I knew the Portuguese language helped quite a bit in picking up the Italian, even though there were differences. One such funny incident happened as we went shopping one Saturday and stopped at the dairy stand to pick up some cheese. I simply could not stop the need to laugh at the man serving us because he wore a white apron with the word "Burro" printed on it in bold red letters. While in Italian burro stands for butter, in Portuguese it means donkey.

Through Mefisto's business connections, I got a job interview at a pillow manufacturing company situated in the outskirts of Milano. On the day of my appointment, Mefisto and the couple that had recommended me also accompanied me to meet with Signor Marchetti. He showed us into a very elegant living room located on the upper level of the factory. Signor Marchetti had dark brown hair and hazel brown eyes. He was about 5'8" tall and rather robust. He was impeccably dressed in a tailored blue suit and black Gucci loafers. He invited us to take a seat and offered everyone a Cynar, which is a non-alcoholic herbal beverage. He then began describing the nature of his business and the work he hoped I would be able to perform.

"Practically, Signora, you would have to act as my *alter ego,* especially while I'm away from the office. You would have to take care of all my foreign correspondence and maintain regular contact with those clients. You would also make sure that business in the office runs smoothly, without any waste of time." Signor Marchetti spoke slowly, making sure that I understood everything he was telling me in Italian.

I understood his requirements but was apprehensive as to my ability in taking over such responsibilities, especially because of my still limited knowledge of the Italian language. While our acquaintances, Pupa and Carlo, distracted Signor Marchetti with a different topic, I took the opportunity to talk to Mefisto.

"How on earth could I demand or delegate to anyone without the fluency in their language?" I said, in a whisper. It didn't take a genius to realize that I was terrified and about to decline the job offer.

"I wouldn't pass the opportunity if I were you. Besides, you are more than capable of doing all that the man is asking you to do. Think positive, and consider also our need for money." Mefisto talked in English.

For whatever reasons, Mefisto always thought highly of my abilities and simply dismissed the possibility of me being overcome by fear and even terror whenever faced with a new situation, unfamiliar to me.

As Signor Marchetti did not seem to have a problem with my lack of Italian, I decided to fight my cowardice and even if with a certain reluctance, I accepted his renewed offer.

10

Pillows International

I began working for Pillows International in November 1966, but more than working, I mostly listened to what Signor Marchetti had to tell the other employees and read some of the foreign correspondence that the boss would occasionally show me. I shared a small office with two other people, Mirella the secretary, and Luigi Tozzi, the controller. Mirella was in her mid thirties, single, medium height and rather chubby. She had brown, watery eyes, copper red dyed short hair and was an extremely nervous chain smoker. Luigi Tozzi was in his late thirties, medium height and very thin. The paleness of his skin contrasted sharply with the absolute black of his hair and eyes. Even though perfectly shaved, his face always showed the grayish shadow of beard stubs. His eyebrows were thick and almost joined at the bridge of his nose. He hardly ever spoke and smiled even less. He also appeared to be a very nervous person.

The daily routine consisted of an early morning briefing between the two assistants and Signor Marchetti. For some unknown reason his "alter ego," that is me, had not been invited. I would have loved to find out a little more about all the commotion and yelling taking place in the boss' office. At one point, annoyed with the lack of real work, I decided to study the contents of the filing cabinets. It was, in my opinion, the best way to find out about the business, the filing methods, typing styles, etc. I was intent reading through one file when Mirella came storming through the door.

"No, no, no. You cannot touch the files. Signor Marchetti gets very upset, very angry. You understand?" She slammed the drawer shut, locked it and placed the key in her desk drawer. I was flabbergasted and wondered if they were ever told about my position within the company. Being an extremely busy person, Signor Marchetti must have forgotten to tell them. Perhaps I should clear the matter with him before things got worse, I thought, but whenever I knocked on the boss' door, he seemed either very busy or extremely annoyed with my intromission.

"What do you want? Anything you're looking for?" were his quick questions.

"I need to talk to you," I said one day.

"Is it very urgent?" he asked.

"It is, in a way, for me," I replied.

"Ok. Tell you what. Come back later, I'm quite busy now." He brushed me off with a phantom smile.

I returned to my desk, discouraged and frustrated. For awhile, I doodled on my writing pad, then I decided to write down a list of questions I intended to submit to Signor Marchetti's attention and to which I expected to receive precise answers. I wondered if acting as "alter ego" meant sitting behind a desk, blowing more hot air into a room. If that was the case, than it wasn't the right job for me. Besides, at that rate I would never learn anything. Maybe Signor Marchetti did not mind paying me a salary for doing nothing all day, but it made me feel uneasy and guilty. I also noticed that it would take considerable time and effort to win my co-worker's trust and cooperation. They often seemed to analyze me from head to toe as if I were an alien from outer space. Their behavior at times clearly revealed distrust and even hostility.

While Signor Marchetti kept on being very busy all the time, I decided to visit some of the other departments. There were people who smiled at me, while others didn't bother to acknowledge my presence. One day I peeked into the office of Giorgio Tognazzi. He was a handsome, tall man in his mid-forties, with blond hair and inquisitive brown eyes. He waved me in and introduced himself as Dr. Tognazzi, the engineer in charge of the plant's machinery. Also in Italy, having a title made a great deal of difference. Four of the most important titles were Dottore, (Doctor) Ingegnere, (Engineer) Ragioniere (Accountant) and Commendatore (a title of the Italian Republic).

I was invited to take a seat and tell him a little about myself, which I did, even if in a broken Italian. With the exception of Mirella, nobody really spoke fluent English. Only some of them spoke broken English just as I spoke broken Italian. I was surprised that Giorgio had not been informed about me joining the company. I told him about my frustration in not being able to be more useful to the company.

"I think I can help you with the work part. As a matter of fact, I need some translations from English into Italian. Do you think you can handle it?" He gave me a charming smile.

"I will try my best," I replied.

Giorgio then gave me the books where he had ear-marked the pages and underlined the passages he needed translated along with a huge English-Italian dictionary. I thanked him and returned happily to my desk. On my way back to the office, I noticed that Signor Marchetti's main office door was equipped with a device similar to a traffic light. Red light meant "do not disturb." Yellow meant "it better be good," and green was okay to knock and enter. I couldn't hold back a chuckle. Each individual was entitled to his or her own idiosyncrasies. Back at my desk, I started with the translations but soon realized that, due to their purely technical nature, they were not easy at all. Nevertheless, I enjoyed doing them, learning hundreds of new words in the process.

One early morning, I noticed that the traffic light on the boss' door was green and Signor Marchetti was alone. I took the opportunity to have a heart-to-heart talk with him, explaining my situation and the fact that I took over translation work from Giorgio. Signor Marchetti did not seem to have a problem with it. He told me to be patient, that in time I would learn to become his "alter ego." I also told him that I would like to know more about the company and its activities. How the many pillows were manufactured for example. I also asked permission to study the files and again, Signor Marchetti did not seem to have a problem with it. He actually thought that as I showed so much interest in the company, I should participate in the daily early morning office meetings. Our conversation was interrupted by the arrival of a supplier.

When Mirella and Luigi joined other employees in the boss' office for the ritual morning meeting, I pushed aside the translation work and joined them. Signor Marchetti sat like a king in his high-backed leather chair behind a very large mahogany desk crowded with four telephones, a color-coded button panel, books, magazines, documents and piles of folders. There was no boardroom as such or a table and chairs prepared for the meeting. The employees aligned neatly in front of the mahogany desk. There was total silence. The mail had just arrived, in time for the meeting and it was Signor Marchetti's pleasure and privilege to open the envelopes, one at a time, and to decide about the recipient of each document. Invoices and payments were handed over to Luigi with appropriate comments and instructions. Letters requiring answers in Italian were handed over to Mirella with the appropriate instructions, and so forth. I found it all to be very interesting but felt quite uneasy when some of the employees were publicly reprimanded and yelled at, as was the case of the production manager, the shipper or the purchaser. I hoped that Signor Marchetti's system did not reflect the entire Italian business community. Even though paradoxical, the scene bordered on the hilarious and I had to put in an extra effort to curb my urge to laugh.

Whenever Signor Marchetti was interrupted by a phone call, the entire group seemed to emit a breath of temporary relief. Except for me, everybody else had received something to look after. But then again, I already had enough work to do: translate and play "alter-ego." From that day onwards, I would regularly attend the daily meetings but instead of gathering a better understanding of the company's *modus operandi*, everything seemed to become more confusing and Mirella would still oppose my interest in the contents of "her" filing cabinets.

"The boss has not given me instructions in this regard," she would say very matter-of- factly.

"Well, then you better confirm with him, the sooner the better, because he did tell me that he had nothing against me learning more on what's going on here," I said, annoyed.

There were days when I felt like an intruder in the office, which could at times be compared to a real cuckoo's nest. No matter what they did, both the accountant and Mirella accompanied every gesture and every thought by endless sighs and moans. Luigi would often run back and forth, with the same piece of paper in his hand, like a hurried messenger about to deliver the most important document of his life. Sometimes he would simply roll the paper into a ball and with the typical moves of a professional soccer player, kick the ball into the wastebasket. Meanwhile, Signor Marchetti's yelling echoed through corridors and walls and became more frequent. Instead of getting used to it, like most of Signor Marchetti's employees, I still jumped up in my chair each time he yelled. Fortunately, he had no reason to yell at me but he did not hesitate to storm into the office to yell at Luigi or Mirella, who would then break out in tears and act miserable all day. Sometimes, while doing so, Signor Marchetti would stop for an instant, turn in my direction with a smile and quickly say: "How are you, Signora?" and then go back yelling at the other two. More often however, he had no time for niceties and did not refrain from slamming the door with such violence, that even the windows would rattle in the frames.

Signor Marchetti's friendly face did definitely not match his irrational temper tantrums. In private, he was an extremely courteous and refined individual. The many errors he blamed his employees for, were certainly caused by the ambiance of constant tension and fear in which they had to work. He reminded me of some barking political figures, such as dictators like the Führer and Mussolini. Those people loved to yell and scream, too, terrorizing the masses with their powerful vocal chords.

As Signor Marchetti's place of work was also his deluxe living quarters, he meant to treat his employees as his guests and likewise, demanded to be treated accordingly—greeted upon arrival in the morning and departure in the evening. Only if the traffic light on his door was red, and the employee could no longer wait, could she or he leave without expecting reprimands the day after. At least that is what I was told by Luigi and Mirella.

One evening, Signor Marchetti's late afternoon meeting did not seem to end and I started to worry as the minutes ticked away. Transportation was not frequent in that part of the outskirts. The bus serving the area would pass by only every forty minutes. To miss the 6:40 one at the corner bus stop upset my entire evening schedule. Mefisto being a sales agent, was mostly on the road and out of town and therefore unable to bail me out from this type of unpleasant situation. It had also been snowing all day, which disrupted all traffic even more. I hoped that nothing awful would happen to the boss overnight, so that we could still greet each other the next morning. Followed by numerous surprised glances, I finally left and arrived at the bus stop just in time to catch the bus.

The next morning, Signor Marchetti approached me.

"What happened yesterday evening?" he said. "You didn't come to greet me."

I almost took it as a compliment. I was noticed after all. I explained to him about the transportation problem to which he did not reply. He simply smiled, faintly, and without saying anything further, walked away.

"Mamma Mia, some courage you had there, girl," Mirella commented in a whisper.

I was surprised to hear her say that and broke out in a hearty giggle. Mirella tried to hush me up by bringing her forefinger to the lips. I wondered how that girl could live in an environment of constant fear and for her sake I limited my outburst of laughter and went back to the translations.

During the next few days, many more employees imitated my apparent violation of the greeting rule. Signor Marchetti considered such flagrant insubordination intolerable and almost flew through the roof during one of the morning ritual meetings.

"I must tell you this, by the way. I cannot tolerate anymore of this lack of respect towards my person. Remember, this is my house and you people here are my guests and as such are expected to behave accordingly by greeting me whenever you arrive in the morning and when you leave in the evening, no matter what excuses you have." He screamed and smashed the top of his desk with a powerful blow of his right fist.

It was obvious that he also referred to me who, once again, had to refrain from giggling. At times I wasn't quite sure if Signor Marchetti was for real or just a figment of my imagination. The poor guy must have had some serious psychological problems, maybe induced by an unhappy childhood or the bitter reminiscences of WWII events. I could easily picture him as being an actor. He was handsome enough to be one. He could very well play the role of a dictator in his own right, megalomaniac, in desperate need of spectators and downtrodden slaves. I wiped the thought from my mind and gave up, not only in trying to excuse his behavior, but also to understand him at all, period.

After his initial reprimand, he started the opening of the mail. The staff was already tense, hoping that no bad news would land on his desk and aggravate his particularly excitable disposition. He was so enraged that he did not even notice that he yelled throughout the mail distribution process and even while answering the phones, without giving it a thought that maybe it was an important customer on the other end. I noticed how badly Mirella's hands were shaking and felt sorry for her. One couldn't help wondering why, a man so self-sufficient, active and aware of his authority and power, needed an "alter-ego," and to make things even worse, by choosing a female, in a typically male-dominated society. Perhaps he was not entirely aware of the true meaning of the word *alter ego*.

A few weeks later Signor Marchetti took off on a business trip. I had learned about the news through the receptionist. Once again, I had to laugh. How ironic that Signor Marchetti's supposed *alter ego* had not been notified about his departure directly. For a moment, I fantasized playing the part of Signor Marchetti, sitting in his big leather chair, ripping open envelopes and sadistically yelling at the handful of pale, scared faces, shaking in front of me as willow trees on a windy day. Nay, I thought. That was not me. It was hard enough to be oneself, never mind slip in some other person's mindset.

For an entire week, the atmosphere at work seemed to be more relaxed, more cordial. People dared to smile even. Yet the relaxation was an artificial one and so were all other niceties. Signor Marchetti's spirit was ever present, like George Orwell's "1984 Big Brother," watching over everything and everybody. The brief interlude of serenity ended when Signor Marchetti returned in all his noisy glory and everything hurled back into the sad, scary daily reality.

Christmas had arrived and I hoped that Signor Marchetti would behave normally, at least during the holiday season. Snow had fallen, covering everything in sight. Signor Marchetti's kids had built a handsome snowman on the front lawn beside the large pine tree, decorated with colorful flashing lights. The day before Christmas Eve there was a huge line- up outside the boss' office. One by one the office employees and the plant laborers filed into his office to reappear soon after with a bright smile on their faces and a box of Panettone (Italian Christmas cake) in one hand.

"How nice of Signor Marchetti to remember everyone at Christmas time," I commented to Mirella.

"Yeah, once a year he feels the need to publicize his generosity," she said with slight sarcasm.

"Oh, shut up. It's better than nothing," remarked Luigi, rubbing his hands in contentment. "A Panettone always comes in handy," he added with genuine satisfaction. I agreed with Luigi. After all, there was no written law saying the company had to give anything to anybody at Christmas. It depended entirely on the company's generosity and ability to do so. In some cases, it was also a matter of prestige or show off and not so much for the pleasure of giving.

Holidays were always the fastest days of the year and soon, it was time to return to work. Once again, I decided to clear the situation with Signor Marchetti and as numerous times before, he was extremely busy and a few days later, he took off with the entire family for two weeks skiing in the mountains in the Aosta region. At that point I was truly fed up with all the puppet show at work. Everybody just hinted at their knowledgeable background, their courage and their titles but none was brave enough to stand up and say something. Their fatalistic and opportunistic submission was disgusting and Signor Marchetti's superficiality in relation to my desire of becoming truly useful to the company severed the last few strings of interest I had in the company. "Signor Marchetti is made like that. What can you do?" were invariably their words.

A few weeks later, Signor Marchetti called in Mirella and Luigi for an important meeting. All his meetings were very important all the time. Some thirty minutes later, they returned to their desk. Luigi's face was red, perspiring and he kept mumbling to himself. Mirella's face was pale and her eyes were watery. For a moment, I felt sorry for them as co-workers, but I did not show any particular interest in their situation and did not bother to ask questions. If they felt like it, they would tell me what was going on. I had just finished the thought when Mirella approached me.

"You know, I've got the impression that Signor Marchetti wants to fire me," she said, whispering while fumbling in the pocket of her jacket to retrieve a handkerchief and wipe the tears rolling down her cheeks. "I thought that maybe you could have a word with him and maybe suggest to him that in case of a choice, you wouldn't mind to leave instead of me." I was totally speechless while Mirella continued. "I have to take care of my old parents and if I lose this job, we will all go hungry." She now was sobbing heavily. "See, you are young, pretty and intelligent. It will be a lot easier for you to find another job and possibly even better than this one." She studied my reaction. "I would be eternally grateful to you." Her eyes drooped.

I was overcome by a certain degree of disgust and nausea. I could hardly believe my own ears. The girl who had so much power over the filing cabinets was now in tears, begging the alien to help keep her key role.

"I will think about it," I said sternly and turned my attention to the translations.

Occasionally, I gazed through the window in front of my desk while my mind kept recalling Mirella's words.

For a moment I allowed imagination to play with my thoughts. What if I approached Signor Marchetti and asked him about Mirella's employment. I could offer to replace Mirella and become his assistant, get used to his character and accept his idiosyncrasies, ignore all the sentimental crap, co-worker's opinions, and dedicate every effort to a new career. The language barrier could quickly be overcome. I had a knack for languages and before long I would be speaking Italian fluently. Then reality took over the imagination and brought me back to an even earlier unanswered question: what were the reasons that kept me going at this company? Aside from a small salary, there was nothing important to cling to or, at that point, to trigger my interest and enthusiasm.

It just happened that I fell ill and had to undergo surgery due to a fallopian tube pregnancy, which kept me away from work for at least three weeks, long enough to analyze my situation and decide whether to stay or resign. It was clear that Signor Marchetti did not need an "alter ego" and that my presence was superfluous and a definite waste of time for both parties.

To Mirella's immense joy and gratefulness, I submitted my resignation. I did not have to give two weeks notice either because there was no need for a replacement. I then thanked Signor Marchetti for the opportunity he had given me to learn about the varied aspects of his company, for improving my vocabulary and for one last time, bid him goodbye on the way out. The traffic control device on his door was still on Red when I left his office.

11

TeenStyle Fashions - Milano

Realizing that my knowledge of the Italian language was not sufficient to claim fluency and prevented me from aiming for better positions, I decided to search for a lesser assignment, a job where I did not have to be at the forefront. One ad called for a good-looking female with experience in modeling and a little knowledge of office work. Even though the modeling part did no longer trigger my interest, the idea of slowly slipping into an office environment wasn't such a bad idea after all. I mailed in the requested résumé and attached a small photo of myself.

A few days later I received a brief letter inviting me for an interview. I dressed carefully and spent time on my hairdo and make-up. I was raised with the notion that the first impression was the main impression. The first five minutes of one's talk, walk, handshake and eye contact, were supposed to reveal one's character and personality. I complied even if not entirely convinced of the truth hidden behind such rules. I knew of people who, even though well dressed, were not at all intelligent, truthful or compassionate, just as words and handshakes at times proved to be quite deceitful. Anyway, I needed a job and only hoped that not all Italian enterprises were like the previous unique, Duce-type company.

When I arrived at the given address, I found myself in front of an old but very well kept building, dating back to the 1800s. A massive wooden door opened towards a neatly kept courtyard, which had a small water fountain right in the middle and four small islands of flowerbeds. The entire courtyard was paved in cobblestones. The white marble stairs leading to the second floor were consumed at parts by time and use. I knocked on the Teenstyle Fashions door and a very elegant lady just happened to open it. She was carrying a purse and I thought she was on her way out and stepped aside, but the lady, after having asked the reason for my visit, invited me in.

"Oh, you are the Hungarian girl. Come in dear, come in," she said and showed me into her tiny, crowded office. The usual questioning followed about who I was, where I came from and what working experiences I had—even though all that information was listed in the résumé I had already sent in.

The lady's name was Myra. She was tall, well built, had black curly hair with a few gray strands and beautiful, magnetic green eyes. She smiled constantly and her voice was calm and warm. She told me that she had lived in Budapest for a while and that is why she spoke Hungarian. By birth, she was a Romanian Jew who was lucky enough to escape the persecution. After having separated from her perennially unfaithful husband, she established herself in Italy where she had been living for the last twenty years, and along with another woman, opened a successful small fashion atelier. After showing me the different sections in the large apartment and introducing me to the different people working for her, Myra took me back to the office to explain what was expected from me.

I was to act as a fashion model, pose for the various seamstresses and as there would not be enough modeling to fill my entire day, I was expected to help in the office and the showroom. My monthly salary was established at 120,000 Italian Lire with a possible increase after three to four months. Working hours were nine to six with one hour for lunch, five days a week. I was happy that I did not have to work on Saturdays, which I normally reserved for the house chores and the weekly shopping. Unlike in Brazil, most stores in Milano those days would close during lunch hours, which did not allow working people to catch up with the shopping list or other necessary errands. Everything had to be planned around Saturday or crammed into the few after-work hours, when the stores were mostly crowded with incredible line-ups, and to get onto a streetcar with a number of shopping bags was almost impossible. Moreover, the crowd did not believe in boarding the streetcars in orderly fashion but found enjoyment in elbowing their way into them. The force of the public was so powerful at times that my feet barely touched the ground as I was lifted up in a huge, big human squeeze. I often wondered what made those people turn into a desperate herd of Buffalos. Was it a natural instinct of running from the enemy? Was it to get a seat, perhaps? Was it to get home first or a desperate need to pee?

Myra asked me to try on a few of their outfits and smiled happily at what she saw.

"They look like they had been custom-made for her, isn't it?" she asked Linda, one of the stylists who had just stepped into the showroom and looked at the newcomer with a hint of mistrust. She stepped closer to me and with a professional touch adjusted the neckline and the sleeves of the dress. She then took a few steps back, twisting her head from side to side and declared that the fit was perfect. She pulled away the fitting room curtain and called the rest of her helpers who all seemed to agree with Linda and Myra's approval. I then changed back into my own clothes and followed Myra to the office where she introduced me to Giulia, the company's bookkeeper. She was a middle-aged lady with beautiful blue eyes and a timid smile. She was deaf and had speech impairment and despite wearing a hearing aid, Giulia still had trouble in hearing properly and understanding. Myra had great respect for her because she had been a very dedicated, hard working, individual since the inception of the company.

"A little handicap is not enough reason to kill a person emotionally and psychologically," Myra commented later.

Finally, I was shown to the room where I would have a desk, a chair and a small shelve beside my desk. There was a large wooden table packed with piles of fashion magazines, fabric rolls, button samples, sketching pads, pencils and a bright yellow telephone. In one corner, there was a large photocopier and next to it, a series of shelves packed with hundreds of different rolls of fabric. Once again, I would have to take a step back in my secretarial career. I could, however, not expect any better for the moment, but instead would take advantage of the situation and improve my spoken and written Italian. The fact that everybody spoke only Italian around me would help me to achieve that goal. My salary was going to be slightly higher than the previous one at Marchetti's and included a comprehensive health care coverage. In addition to all that, I liked Myra.

Two days later, I was at work leafing through some fashion magazines when around 10 o'clock, a sexy blond burst into the office. She seemed surprised in seeing me and there was a clear hesitation in her greeting. She sized me from head to toe and then pointed to the rubber boots behind the door.

"Who put those boots there?"

"They are mine," I said. "It was slushy out there this morning."

"Well, take them to the bathroom," the blond, named Sarah, snapped rather rudely. "This is no place to store dirty boots."

"If you'd be so kind to show me where in the bathroom you want me to store them," I replied, calmly.

Sarah rolled her large, protruding brown eyes and with a gesture of annoyance, simply pointed in the bathroom's direction.

Sarah, who I found out later happened to be Myra's partner, had a bony, elongated face with high cheekbones, a long, narrow nose, thin lips and a sharp, pointed chin. In her mid-thirties, Sarah had a good modeling body—

greatly due to her Spartan diet—and beautiful, strong cascading blond hair. Aside from arranging working capital for the company, she was supposed to sketch new outfits, which she normally copied from fashion magazines and then added a few changes here and there. She also travelled to Paris very often, to view the latest fashion shows and to gather inspiration from the display windows of Montmartre.

I realized that I was heading into yet another difficult beginning. To win over the trust and the friendship of the people I was to live with for a full eight hours per day, was definitely no small enterprise. Aside from organizing the catalogs and sketches, I had to pose for Linda because Sarah, even though pretending to be the company's top model, scorned the boring task of standing still for hours on end for the various stylists. She preferred the photo sessions and the runways but as soon as a client of a certain importance showed up at the showroom, she would immediately find something for me to do just so she could take over the modeling part herself. It was obvious that Sarah was terribly jealous and to avoid any possible frictions with her, I took it upon myself to just quickly disappear when customers showed up and let Sarah splash in the limelight entirely on her own. I could care less at that point, whether I was modeling or helping Giulia with some office work, whereas Sarah was obsessed with her modeling position, to the point of convincing Linda to produce all showroom pieces to her size just so I, who had slightly more generous curves, would not be able to wear them. It was definitely not in my plan to become flat as a board like Sarah and the various other cadaverous-looking modern fashion icons. While in town, Sarah rarely allowed me to access the showroom while entertaining a client, except when she needed help to get dressed, close buttons, pull zippers, pick up the dresses thrown on the floor and so forth.

The atelier was always very calm when Sarah was not present and I could peacefully work on my own little projects. In time, I organized a filing system with cards that allowed a proper inventory control of all the available fabric on the premises. I kept records of prices, customer orders and preferences, as well as notes on each showroom sample collection. I also kept a special file on sketches produced by Margit — a friend of Myra's who would come to Milano from Paris, to prepare the sketches for the various collections. There was evidently a strong rivalry between Sarah and Margit. Sarah was the fiercest and the most conceited one, constantly imposing upon Myra and Linda to have her own sketches produced before all the others.

As time progressed, I earned the trust and friendship of my co-workers and especially that of Myra who invited me often for an espresso at the corner bar and confided in me the various problems she had with the company as well as some of her very own, intimate personal struggles. It was during one of those coffee sessions that I learned about one secret. Sarah had an affair with Myra's former husband. While on the surface Myra did not show her resentment, I could tell that deep inside she was hurt. On the other hand, thanks to this strange liaison, Sarah was able to obtain financial help from Myra's ex-husband, a help that was sorely needed by the company in order to keep "the boat afloat." It was clear that the company was threading rough waters.

There were times when Myra seemed very confused in her reasoning. While on one hand she recognized the effectiveness of Sarah's contribution to the survival of the company, on the other hand she wanted to get rid of her.

"Why do you think she wants Linda to make all dresses in her size?" Myra asked. "Just so she can wear them and then charge the bill to a fictitious account, which she would never pay. Besides, she loves to spend money in extremely expensive fabrics which end up in stock, unsold, because very few people can afford to buy them."

Myra had apparently pointed out these dangerous spending habits to Sarah who, surprisingly, would always agree, but only for a day or two. Then she would fall back into the old trend. She considered herself a designer, an artist to whom anything is possible and conceded. Besides, she held the winning card in her hand, the money.

Sarah was overcome by jealousy as she noticed the friendship that had developed between Myra and me and decided to win over my favors by becoming extremely friendly, generous and chummy. Confidentially, she told me about some of Myra's very personal and intimate secrets hoping to weaken or even destroy some of the respect I had for Myra, but I was certainly no dummy and sensed Sarah's machinations. I was definitely not going to get involved in a web of jealousy and intrigue. To serve two bosses was not only arduous, but could also become dangerous.

One morning, Myra told me about her intention in hiring a business consultant to clean up the administrative mess that had been created throughout the years. It would be the only male in a company run entirely by females. I welcomed the idea. Maybe it was just what the company and Myra needed. A few days later therefore, David the new consultant joined the company. He was a tall, very handsome middle-aged gentleman of Romanian descent, just like Myra, who instantly attracted the interest of some of the girls in the atelier. He did not waste any time and immediately held several meetings with Myra and the bookkeeper. He also spent time chatting with the rest of the personnel, gathering every possible detail on how the company operated to aid him in the preparation of a cost analysis and then plan their finances accordingly. Considerable time was also spent in meetings behind closed doors. No one ever knew what those meetings were about or were leading to. I noticed that Myra, each time, reappeared distressed and only regained a smile on her face, when I went to offer her and David a cup of hot coffee.

A few weeks later, Myra invited me to accompany her on a business trip to Rome where she would meet with an important American buyer from New York. Myra was not fluent in English and thought that it would help in having someone along who could speak the language well. The idea of seeing Rome, the city of Caesars, just overjoyed me and I accepted the invitation without hesitation. Sarah had also been invited but she initially refused on the pretext that she had other more important things to do in Milano. Yet on the morning of the departure, she managed to materialize on time—maybe for the very first instance in her life, because punctuality was not exactly her cup of tea.

"I thought I'd come along for the ride," she said with an innocent smile. "I was actually invited by a friend to spend a couple of days in Rome."

Myra was an excellent driver and entertainer. She had many stories and jokes to tell and stopped only at an Auto grill along the Autostrada del Sole for a quick bite to eat. With the excuse of having to watch her waistline, Sarah refused everything.

"My diet includes only yoghurts, salads, tea and unsalted crackers," she said.

No one knew how much of all that was true. At last, she decided to have a couple of slices of veal with potatoes and vegetables and devoured everything with uncanny ferocity. Luckily for the restaurant, she left behind the plate and the utensils.

Arriving in Rome, we went directly to the hotel where Myra had booked a room with two single beds. While unpacking the luggage and hanging up the outfits, I heard Sarah trying to get hold of the alleged friend. She then asked Myra permission to take a shower. Myra looked at me and rolled her eyes towards the ceiling. I mastered a faint smile and continued to fix the rack with the outfits. When Sarah finished with her beautification procedure, she tried to contact her mystery friend again. She was lucky the second time around, but from the tone of the conversation it did not sound like she had been invited by him. She got him to invite her nonetheless, at least for overnight.

When Sarah finally left, Myra took a deep breath, shook her head from side to side and went to take a shower as well. At last, I also got to shower and dress up for the rest of the day.

"Have you ever been in Rome before?" Myra asked.

"No, I haven't," I replied.

"Well, then, I will show you Rome," Myra said with a bright, happy smile.

Because there was not enough time to see all that Rome had to offer, Myra decided to leave the task to a more experienced Roman taxi driver, familiar with sightseeing tourists and, therefore, with the main points of interests and short cuts.

I was deeply touched at the sight of the Colosseum. My mind instantly filled with images of the people and personalities who had lived among the centuries old walls: the emperors, the gladiators, the human and animal carnage, which took place on a soil drenched in blood. I imagined the glory and the decadence of the great Roman Empire. It had been the largest empire in the world and of all times and an empire that left behind a vast cultural imprint in history as well as a shameful barbaric past of excesses.

The cab zigzagged through heavy traffic and small, narrow cobblestoned streets with admirable dexterity. As they said over there, it takes a Roman to drive in Rome. I marveled at the grandeur of Saint Peter's, the architecture of the Campidoglio, the Obelisco and other wonders such as the Castel Sant'Angelo, Trinitá dei Monti and the Trevi Fountain with its sparkling clear water jets. I did not have a chance to toss the ritual coin into it, but I felt that I would return to Rome someday and then for sure I would throw a lucky wish coin in the fountain.

That evening, Myra took me out for dinner to a Hungarian restaurant. The ambiance was typical, with violins playing czardas and other gypsy arias and the aroma of paprikás and Tokai wine lingering in the air. I got very emotional. So many wonderful things happened to me, and all in a day's work. I could not stop the tears from flooding my eyes. Myra became emotional as well and hummed along with the violins. The two of us had great food and great wine. For me, it turned out to be an unforgettable day.

Back in the hotel, once we had changed into our pyjamas and settled in our respective beds, we chatted until the early hours in the morning about philosophy and religion. Myra was extremely happy to have a listener who understood the way she felt and it did not matter that there were twenty years of difference between us. For a moment, I thought of Lilly, my first boss. Myra was just as generous. I whispered a prayer for both and fell asleep.

The next morning, shortly after breakfast, the American client knocked at the door and surprisingly, so did Sarah who, once more, could not resist the temptation to show off. Since the client was pressed for time, both Sarah and I modeled for him. He had very clear ideas about what he wanted to order and so he asked that only those outfits he intended to buy were modeled. Later on, he mentioned the possibility of presenting the collection in New York and Myra promised to send over Sarah to do the modeling. The client sized Sarah from head to toe and did not seem too impressed but thanked Myra nonetheless. Sarah was obviously overjoyed with the prospective of a trip to the United States. As soon as the client left, Sarah also conveniently disappeared, leaving Myra and me to fold and pack away the outfits and clean up the mess. While Myra commented about the business meeting, I allowed myself a quick observation.

"Why, instead of Sarah, don't you send your own daughter to New York? Not only does she speak fluent English, but she is also very pretty."

Myra's eyes lit up like Christmas lights.

"Why yes. You are right. How stupid I am sometimes. My daughter would love to take a trip to the United States, and as you say, she is cute, too. She certainly has a better presence than that slut Sarah."

After packing the luggage, we took off, back to Milano. Sarah remained in Rome with her friend over the weekend. Myra's happiness and satisfaction were contagious and we had a pleasant trip back home.

Nothing had changed at work except that I had now been invited to participate in the confidential meetings with Myra and David. I went only when expressly requested. I had now plenty of work and did not care much for the privilege of listening to their conversation, which never changed in substance, while the problems seemed to remain unscathed. Besides, after every such meeting, Sarah would drill me to find out about the details, whether her name had been mentioned and if the things they said about her were good or bad. She would then often play the desperate victim, sobbing, because she thought that everybody was against her and hated her. Myra and David would indeed speak about her quite often, but I disliked office politics and the darn gossip, so I simply reassured her that everything was fine and that she did not have to worry.

Meanwhile, Sarah's spending habits had not changed. More expensive fabrics were purchased and she continued arriving well after nine in the morning with the excuse that being a partner she was allowed to establish her own convenient schedules. She still talked on the phone for hours, not necessarily matters related to the business, and she still interfered with the production schedule—but all that was definitely none of my business. Only Myra and her genius consultant could tackle that problem. The company's finances also continued to deteriorate. Something had to be done, fast. Myra decided to sell anything sellable and to reduce personnel to the essential.

One Saturday afternoon, Myra showed up at my doorstep. Surprised with the unexpected visit, I felt a little uptight, mainly because I had not been feeling too well since Friday. I had a temperature, a runny nose and watery eyes, yet Myra did not hesitate to ask me to join our sales rep in Bari for a promotional tour of two weeks. I was surprised with the unusual request as it had always been Sarah's job to travel when a modeling job came along. Before I could even blink, Myra handed me a train ticket.

"You have to help me out here, Isabel. You know how much we need the sales," she begged. I agreed, hoping that my intervention would really be of help to the company. Only when I arrived at the train station did I realize that the ticket I had was not even a first class ticket. No wonder Sarah refused to travel in those conditions.

The trip was not a pleasant one. The compartment I was assigned to was crowded with women, men and little children, some crying, others screaming. There were demijohns of wine, big bags and luggage of all sorts cramping the space. It was also very warm inside, which intensified the acrid smell of body and used diaper odors. I decided to hang out in the corridor, watching the sun go down while the shadows of the evening slowly swallowed every remaining speck of light. When things finally quieted down in the compartment, I tried to take over my seat, but by then, it had been taken by another person. I did not feel like arguing; neither was I tempted to offend my nostrils with the foul smells, so I decided to continue hanging out in the corridor. Towards the early morning hours, however, I was tired and longed to give my body a rest. I got hold of the conductor and after I showed him the ticket and the crowded compartment, he escorted me to the far end of the coach and invited me to join him in his little cubicle. He was a great chatterbox and definitely considered himself a God-given gift to women. He bombarded me with questions and became more daring once he learned that I was traveling alone. Annoyed with his impertinence, I respectfully and firmly requested a regular seat or bunk bed. My tone must have come across serious and a little too loud, and as the man did not want to get into trouble, he rushed to find me a last available bunk bed in one coach. It was dark inside, people were sleeping and from the snoring noises I could tell they were all men. Reluctantly, I took the place. I was so tired that I did not really care who was in there and rapidly dozed off.

Marco Soriani, the company's rep was expecting me at the train station. He was a very charming man in his late thirties with a noticeable bald spot among his otherwise wavy brown hair. He drove me to the hotel he had booked and waited for me to take a shower and get ready for the day. The trip had taken about seven hours and a nice, warm shower was exactly what I needed. We then drove to his small office in downtown Bari, and worked on the sales program for the next week or so. The new collection of outfits arrived two days later and both, Marco and I, started our sales program with great enthusiasm and high hopes.

Unfortunately, the first few visits were extremely disappointing. Our prices were too high compared to identical products by competitors who had identical fabrics and even more elaborate models. There was no other alternative but to call Myra in Milano and point out the difficulties. Myra, too, was very disappointed and it was no easy task convincing her to allow for a better discount.

"Ok then, but make sure you do not go over 10 percent. We simply can't afford giving a bigger discount," she said after much ado.

The prices were now slightly below the competition, and Marco and I raked in a fair amount of orders. I returned home happy and satisfied with the positive results of the tiring trip. Even Myra at first seemed very happy with the orders, even though they were not enough to heal the company's financial troubles, and immediately ordered the necessary materials. A few days later, however, for some unknown reason at the time, Myra reconsidered her decision.

"No," she said without addressing anyone in particular. "I simply cannot give them this discount. I would not make a penny. Are we getting crazy or something? No. Just cannot do it. I'm canceling everything and that's that."

I was surprised as well as upset with Myra's reaction. I simply could not figure out why that sudden change of heart, especially after having purchased all the necessary materials. Myra must have been influenced by Sarah or even by her consultant. I was unable to imagine how Myra or I could call up any of the customers and tell them that on second thought, the 10 percent discount was withdrawn. Besides, that was not even my job. That is why the company had a rep, to deal with sales issues and Myra should have yelled at him, if at all. Bosses have the privilege to act silly, contradictory or be wrong. After all, the darn company is theirs. Right or wrong, they will always be right, I thought.

Sarah then added more fuel to the flaming situation.

"Just so you know, Myra has been bad-mouthing you while you were away," she whispered in a tone of confidentiality, but did not get into specifics. Considering Myra's hostile behavior in the last few weeks, I couldn't but believe Sarah. Poor Myra, by now she was so terribly confused that she was unable to distinguish between friend and foe. She saw spies in everyone and everywhere. Her emotional instability became more apparent as she would take out all her anxieties and frustrations on the seamstresses. There were feisty arguments, tears and dismissals, and if all that was not enough, Sarah succeeded, with her innate ingenuity, to convince some of the employees that the culprit for all that upheaval was my negative influence on Myra. I learned about this incident only a few years later, after I had left the company. How totally unfair all that was and how ridiculous to think, even jokingly, that I had any influence on Myra's thought pattern.

At that point my interest and enthusiasm had suffered a major setback and I simply retreated into my own shell. I had neither the energy nor the will to fight back or defend myself. Myra and Sarah meanwhile seemed to have strengthened their old relationship and acted chummy again. Perhaps it had something to do with a line of credit Sarah obtained through a loan officer friend at the bank.

Myra certainly noticed my apathy but did not dare confront me. She sent David instead. With a large smile, he paternally placed a hand on my shoulder and invited me for a chat. To underline even more the importance and confidentiality of the matter, he spoke to me in Hungarian. He began by asking me questions about my work in general. Then slowly, he approached the true subject matter and that was the inability of the company at that time to grant me an increase but that within the next three or four months, the situation would improve and then I would get an increase because I deserved it.

It was the same good old story I would hear many times in the years to come. At that point, however, I did not even expect a raise because I was aware of the company's struggle.

"Look David," I said. "Tell Myra not to worry about my increase, even though a little more always comes in handy and pleases one's morale."

"That's awfully considerate of you, Isabel, but there must be something bothering you lately. You are not the same happy, smiling Isabel as before. Everybody notices it."

"Neither are the things here the same as before," I replied.

"I know. The company is facing some real tough moments and that can also be very frustrating to all."

"Yes, on top of all the gossiping, the endless yelling and threatening, the constant innovation plans and rules and then, nothing is ever accomplished."

"You are right, my dear. You are right." David shook his head from side to side.

"Besides, I really feel very uncomfortable in having two bosses, especially when one doesn't know, or chooses not to know what the other one does."

"What do you mean by that, two bosses?"

"I mean Myra and Sarah. Are they not partners?"

"That is not quite so," David said, calmly. "The only boss, owner in here is Myra. Sarah's power and participation is minimal. Actually, I dare say almost nil."

"Well, but Sarah maintains the contrary," I said.

"Sarah is wrong, and what is more, she lies. She lies a lot."

"It may well be so, but in the meantime she is still purchasing expensive fabric without consulting Myra who, as far as I know, never really dared to intervene. Why?"

"Well, you see Isabel, you also have to understand Myra's position, which is not at all that simple," David said.

"Oh, I know. Sarah is an uncomfortable, embarrassing character yet very useful when it comes to the money part. So far she has been the only one to find willing donors to lend her money for the company. This is why I say that I have two bosses and it is extremely difficult, and at times even impossible, to please both on a same subject when both have different views about it and neither wants to let go from their stubborn viewpoint. And then I feel sandwiched between them while they ping-pong their opinions to each other through my voice."

David smoked incessantly and was somewhat surprised, not only with my awareness of certain aspects of the business, but also for my emotional outburst.

"I want you all to understand that I have nothing against Myra or Sarah personally," I said. "I would only like to be left out of their personal conflicts. Not having any decision powers within the company, I should also not be put in a position of selecting which of the two is right or wrong. Do you understand what I mean?"

"Of course I understand my dear. So how can we help you in this?"

"As I said, leave me out of the quarrels and let me do my work in peace, if you like what I do. Let me know if you want anything changed, but only one should speak to give me directions. That would be a lot better for all concerned."

"You are perfectly right, Isabel, and I do agree with all that you said and I will talk to Myra about it. Just be patient a little longer and everything will fall into place, you'll see. We understand each other, do we not?" He winked while gently tapping on my shoulder.

"I truly hope so, David."

David left me alone with my thoughts. He had asked me to be patient but I noticed that I was no longer as patient as I used to be just a few years back. Mentally, I summed up my abilities and skills and realized that during my time with Teenstyle, I had definitely learned new things and definitely improved my Italian vocabulary. I was already able to write my own letters and memos to customers and suppliers. I had also become very comfortable with the phones and dealing with people in general. Perhaps it was time to move on to something better, a real secretarial job. No harm in trying, I thought. The worse that could happen was to be fired in case I did not stand up to the company's expectations. From that moment on, the idea of quitting became always more persistent.

David's promises and assurances never materialized. Nothing changed, while time was passing fast and the old problems resurfaced. Even the words were the same and always conjugated in the future tense. From the little experience I had so far, that future was a very distant and possibly, uncertain one. Sarah kept interfering with my work by constantly changing recording methods whereas Myra preferred my system and exhorted me to ignore Sarah's instructions.

Fed up with the entire circus, I decided that it was time to move on. Considering that I spent most of my daily existence at a place of work, I might as well choose a job that proved more gratifying. A place of work should not be a source of tears or grief. I did not want to end up like Mariuccia, one of the seamstresses, who suffered and cried almost every day in exchange for maintaining her seniority within the company, and the more she suffered, the more nervous she'd become and the more mistakes she'd make.

Myra was shocked when I submitted my resignation. She had certainly not expected that reaction from me, who had always shown much patience, always smiling and accommodating. Myra tried to dissuade me with the most incredible excuses, but once I made up my mind about something, I would hardly ever turn back on my decision. Throughout the two weeks notice period, Myra pestered me with new promises and assurances, but I was determined not to give in. I had foreseen Myra's reaction and hoped that blaming Mefisto and his fictitious new job in another town altogether would deter Myra from pursuing her plan.

"Listen, Cremona is not that far." Myra said. "You could take the train back and forth. Actually, you could come and live in my house and go home on the weekends."

Not only would Mefisto disapprove of such a plan, but neither would I agree with such a ridiculous arrangement. The more Myra begged, the more I wanted to leave. I always ran from possessive and overpowering individuals.

Myra and I hugged on my last day of work and she did not bother to wipe the two big tears rolling down her cheeks. We promised to keep in touch. In my heart, I always kept a little space for the friend I had found in Rome.

12

Orion Equipment

…Large German earth-moving equipment company requires bi-lingual secretary, well groomed, with perfect typing and short-hand skills. Send résumé with salary expectations to…

I re-typed my old résumé, adding my last experience as model/secretary and mailed it. One week later I received a letter inviting me for an interview. I was introduced to a man in his late thirties, medium height, blue eyes, red hair and a face speckled with many happy freckles. Dr. Midas was addressed as "Doctor" because he had a degree in accounting. He was the company's main asset. He was also personnel manager and had arranged for my interview. He showed me to his office and invited me to sit in the chair across from his desk. He read my résumé twice and asked questions about the previous positions I had filled. He also asked me to fill in an extensive questionnaire in the German language. When I was finished, he escorted me to see the directors of the company.

Herr Hilsberg was the general director. Blue-eyed, blond, medium height, he wore heavy rimmed eyeglasses that kept sliding down his pointed nose. His lips were thin and he spoke in a very calm manner, asking questions already answered in the questionnaire. It was clear that he preferred to hear the answers straight from the horse's mouth, and to get a feeling for the person he was going to hire. As the interview progressed, I had the impression that Herr Hilsberg was quite satisfied with me because he personally introduced me to his colleague, Herr Kassler, who acted as vice-director.

Herr Kassler was also German, tall, heavyset body, blond and blue-eyed, with a potato nose and puffy lips. He was the total opposite of Herr Hilsberg. He had an extremely vivacious personality, very friendly, always smiling and very interested in my résumé. He stopped at length at my Brazilian experiences and it was then that I revealed having also been a lady crooner for a jazz band.

"Oh and how come you didn't mention it in your résumé here?" he asked with genuine enthusiasm.

"I didn't think it was important and worth mentioning it," I replied.

"Well, I think it is important," he said almost with fervor. "All that we are capable of doing is important. If I were you, I would put it in my résumé. We should never hide our talents. You should rather be very proud of all the wonderful things you did in your life. I feel that you are a very exceptional person."

I blushed and thanked him for the compliment, even though I didn't think of myself as a special being.

"There is one thing I'd like to point out. My shorthand is rather rusty. I haven't used it in quite a while." I suddenly remembered and thought it was the honest thing to do in pointing it out to the new boss.

"I don't think that will create a problem. I read in your résumé that you compose your own letters. Besides, our letters are mostly the same. There will be very little dictating here."

He then explained that I was to be in charge of their import-export department and that I had to try running things in the smoothest possible way. Working hours were from 8:30 a.m. to 6:00 p.m. with one hour and a half for lunch. The salary was also more than I had expected. They had practically hired me on the spot.

I started work the following Monday and was surprised to find an older gentleman in my office, eagerly awaiting his "new assistant." I must have misunderstood when told that I would be in charge, and try to run the department as smoothly as possible. Obviously there was a rat somewhere along the line. Whatever it was, I would certainly soon find out.

Mr. Balderi was a tall, slim man in his late sixties. He had grey hair and big brown begging eyes. His face was an expanse of deep wrinkles and he stuttered quite a bit while speaking. He had been with the company for a little more than twenty years and definitely did not sound like a retirement candidate.

"How good, you are finally here. If you just knew how much work we have to do," were his first words. "Oh don't be scared. Slowly, we will take care of everything." He pointed to what was to become my working area.

The office was large, even though it was cramped with shelving, filing cabinets and other furniture disorderly crowded with magazines, catalogs, price lists, document folders and forms of all kinds. Mr. Balderi was right about the "much work" part.

During the first few orientation days, I studied the environment, the people and mainly the contents of the filing cabinets. As in previous occasions, this would help me understand the type of correspondence being used by the company and their filing system. I always wondered why companies did not adopt a standard writing system. Each company I had worked for thus far had its own individual format for their heading, date, reference, margins, signature, let alone the wording. Some were almost poetic, obsequious. Other forms were concise, straight to the matter, mechanical. The greeting format seemed to have a particular significance to certain individuals. Some preferred using *truly yours*, others, *yours truly*. Some insisted in a warm *cordially yours*, others chose a simple *sincerely*, and then there were the inspired ones who loved to get carried away with words, *thanking you in advance for your generous attention to this matter, we remain with very best wishes, yours truly*.

I found it strange that whenever I tried to study the files, for the purpose of memorizing the location of the individual folders for quick retrieval, Mr. Balderi would appear from practically nowhere with an urgent letter to be typed immediately. Invariably, the letter would then sit on his desk for a few days "collecting urgent dust." Maybe he disliked my eagerness to learn. Whatever his reasons, for some time, I simply followed his orders: write letters, file order confirmations and requisitions for spare parts, send telex messages, etc.

As Orion Equipments did not have a manual of operations, whenever possible, I took notes on how many things were carried out by the different individuals, how people interacted between the different departments and so forth. For some mysterious reason, even those notes seemed to bother Mr. Balderi and my workload suddenly increased. I noticed that some of that work originated from a folder sitting on Mr. Balderi's desk. It was a very thick folder containing dozens of Invoices to be approved or checked, correspondence to be answered, phone messages that needed to be dealt with, and many other tasks which for a reason or another, he kept accumulating and procrastinating. No one was ever to touch that folder. He normally kept it locked away in his desk whenever he stepped out of the office.

I was still puzzled about my position in that office but I did not feel like discussing the matter with Mr. Balderi. I decided to give myself more time and experience in the field before reminding my superiors about the position I had been hired to fill. In the meantime, work kept increasing. From ten to twelve invoices daily, they had jumped to double the amount. The more work I did, the more work I was given, and not always everything ran smoothly. Often, the field technicians would send in a telex requesting spare parts. They rarely used the proper part number or description and used their own personal expressions instead, to describe a given part. The German headquarters would then simply reject the requested "unknown part" requisition. I then had to waste time by trying to get hold of the technician and argue about the matter. Sometimes, shouting would also become a communication tool as Mr. Balderi would finally intervene, shout some more, look into a catalog, jot down a code number with corresponding description and then pass it on to me with some mumbled apology. Many times the technicians would send in an order with a correct code number but an incorrect description. The headquarters would then send back the requisition or simply ship the wrong part with consequent wasting of time and money.

I pointed out this problem to Mr. Balderi numerous times but he invariably shook his shoulders, "I know, I know, what can I do?" he would say. Another of his favorite action words were, "I'll take care of it. I'll take care of it," but he rarely did what he said he would do.

The lack of patience in elderly and younger people is notorious, and I was no exception. I strongly disliked people who would drag out a given task and Mr. Balderi was a true champion in the field. I decided to have a talk with one of the directors. I approached Herr Kassler because Herr Hilsberg was always extremely busy. I explained to him the problems encountered in my department and suggested some changes. Herr Kassler seemed enthused with my ideas and asked me to prepare a draft, listing each problem along with the corresponding suggested changes, especially the one concerning the ordering of spare parts. I typed up a new work program with copies to everyone involved in the operation. Both Herr Hilsberg and Herr Kassler were very impressed and endorsed my initiative with enthusiasm.

Everything seemed to work perfectly the first three weeks and then gradually, as work and orders increased, the new system was ignored; nobody cared and chaos and waste returned rampantly. Meanwhile, orders and the typing of corresponding invoices had increased and I often sacrificed many of my lunch breaks to catch up with my work. Soon, however, not even my sacrifice was enough to keep up with the volume of work generated by a particularly favorable sales period.

One of my suggestions to Mr. Balderi was to consolidate orders, whenever possible, to save on labor and shipping costs. I also suggested the introduction of pre-printed forms to avoid having to type similar texts over and over again.

Even though Mr. Balderi praised most of my ideas, I was not quite sure whether he meant it or not. He never approached the bosses to discuss any of those ideas.

"I don't think tha...tha...that is such a good idea," he would say each time. "The...the management would no...no...not understand, a...agree or a...approve."

Because work was increasing, I suggested that he ask the bosses to get us additional help for the clerical work. That would allow Mr. Balderi and me to dedicate more time to source replacement parts and other materials on the local market, avoiding large amounts spent on imported goods. I also mentioned to him that I was tiring of the mechanical typing work and all the repetitive, boring tasks pertaining to my position.

"Leave it u…u…up to me," he said in a paternal tone. "I…I…I'll talk to them."

As on previous occasions, however, Mr. Balderi failed to take action. Was he simply timid or was he a coward, I wondered. All he had to do was to submit an idea, exchange views, but his spirit of subservience was so deeply rooted within his character, that the basic thought of communicating with his superiors, even after twenty years, terrorized him.

Somehow, I felt that the bosses were aware of Mr. Balderi's weaknesses and inability to cope with all the responsibilities of his position. Neither was I surprised when unexpectedly, one or the other would storm into the office and yell at him as if he were a little kid who had just committed a misdemeanor. Their anger was triggered mainly by Mr. Balderi's failure or forgetfulness in ordering or delivering a given material on time. Mr. Balderi's face would turn pale but there was never any reaction such as an explanation or justification for his errors. Even though I felt pity for the old fool, his inability to defend himself irritated me a fair bit. Maybe it was his fatalistic resignation, or years of fatigue that made him bend like a willow tree and triggered in me feelings of compassion. I wanted to help him and heaven only knew how often and how much I tried, but Mr. Balderi worked against himself, supported by his own stubborn jealousies and pride, rejecting any help I would offer.

I would often jump up in my chair when an irate Herr Hilsberg would bark through Mr. Balderi's intercom requesting his presence p.d.q. (pretty damn quick) in his office. That meant that I had to drop whatever I was doing to help Mr. Balderi, visibly shaken, to put together the documentation of whatever Herr Hilsberg was asking for. It was not easy to please Herr Hilsberg, who expected the well-known German precision, cleanliness and punctuality from everybody, especially when coming from Mr. Balderi's department.

Herr Kassler was a more tolerant type instead. In a good mood most days and almost always smiling, he hardly ever raised his voice and was always ready to explain everything to everybody. He took pride in being knowledgeable, especially when it came to replacing a German word that had been used incorrectly in a sentence. He definitely did not bother with typos and whenever he came across one, he would tell me to simply ignore such a minor thing and not waste precious time with corrections.

"Only an idiot, who has time to waste, would notice and fuss around small typing mistakes," Herr Kassler declared solemnly.

There were occasions, however, when Herr Kassler did not know the answer to a particular question but was too proud to admit it and played cleverly around the situation. There was an instance when I needed information regarding special customs papers with which I was not familiar at the time and as both, Herr Hilsberg and Mr. Balderi were absent that day, I had to resort to Herr Kassler's help.

"You know something?" he said with a big, bubbly smile, while adjusting himself in his high backed swivel chair, "I won't tell you a thing. It is not because I don't know it, I just want you to call our brokerage agent and find out by yourself."

I got the drift and left his office with an imperceptible thank you. In a way he was right. The best method to learn anything was to work your way through the process and that is exactly what I had been doing all along even though I could have used a little shortcut in this particular instance considering the extreme urgency of the special shipment. Luckily, I was not the type to avoid obstacles or challenges; the worthy ones, anyway. I called the broker, explained the situation and followed his instructions carefully. Once the papers were filled in, I returned to Herr Kassler who, once again, adjusted himself in the chair, fixed his glasses on the bridge of the nose, then crossed his arms and with a quick movement of one foot, caused the swivel chair to roll a little backwards.

"So Fräulein let us hear exactly what you learned."

Ignoring his Oscar-winning act, I explained in detail what Luigi Brambilla, the broker, had told me to do. I even went to the extent of showing him every detail of the form I had to fill in.

"Exactly, that is exactly what I would have told you, too. I'm really glad you got this one straightened out. Now go and have it signed by Hilsberg when he comes back."

I felt a sudden impulse to laugh and cry at the same time. He really thought he could fool me. Meanwhile, we both learned something new that day; myself dressed in pure ignorance and Herr Kassler in semi-ignorance masked in knowledge. For a moment I was overcome by anger, but then looking into those innocent blue eyes, the pouting lips and squeezable pink cheeks, I felt compassion and simply crossed out his silly behavior. In the meantime, Herr Hilsberg had returned to the office and I went to see him to get his signature. He read through the documents and smiled slightly.

"Who told you to fill in the form this way?" he asked.

Even though Herr Kassler hadn't been too nice to me and acted like a jerk earlier, I did not believe in revenge and thought of doing a good thing by praising Herr Kassler's knowledge and competence in the matter.

"Herr Kassler was kind enough to help me with it since I was not familiar with this type of special customs procedure," I said.

Herr Hilsberg's face turned red. He grabbed all the papers and threw them violently across his desk while screaming that everything was wrong and that Kassler did not know much about anything.

"Just go and tell him that," Herr Hilsberg told me, banging his fist on the desk. "I'm not going to sign diese Scheisse (this shit)."

Poor Herr Kassler, unwillingly, I put him in an embarrassing position and so I quickly tried to correct the situation.

"Actually, we did also call the broker, Mr. Brambilla," I said. "It was him who suggested filling the form this way."

"In that case, both Kassler and the broker don't know a thing about import procedures," Herr Hilsberg snapped.

I disliked Herr Hilsberg's rude manners and the fact that he never bothered to indicate what it was that displeased him or was wrong with whatever he was bitching and ranting about at the time. At any rate, I went to see Herr Kassler and delivered Herr Hilsberg's message, leaving out the vulgarities. I wondered why females were always expected to use proper terminology and be at their best behavior, while males could curse and use all available four-letter words. Herr Kassler listened while blushing. He narrowed his eyelids to a slit, his lips curled and his breathing became heavier. He looked at the papers, shuffled them back and forth in his hands, and then gave them back to me.

"You just go back to my colleague and tell him that these forms are filled correctly. This is not my first time to deal with import papers." Just like Herr Hilsberg, he punched the top of his desk with his fist.

I wondered why he did not simply lift the intercom to tell Herr Hilsberg directly about his personal opinion instead of using me as a shield or a ping-pong messenger. I delivered the message and again put up with an angry reaction from Herr Hilsberg. Then once more, I returned to Herr Kassler to deliver yet another nasty dispatch. Herr Kassler's anger was evident as he swung his chair backwards with such energy that he bounced back from the wall. With the same speed and violence he then propelled himself forward towards his desk, grabbed the intercom, pushed his eyeglasses back onto his nose bridge and pressed Herr Hilsberg's extension.

"Listen here, Hilsberg. What is your problem with these import papers? You should know better that this is the right way to do it."

"Ja, das ist klar, that I know it better than you," Mr. Hillsberg barked from the other end of the line. "I wouldn't have asked the girl to do something that stupid."

Herr Kassler's face turned red as a hothouse tomato, while trying very hard to conceal his embarrassment. He simply pressed the intercom button to end the conversation. He quickly composed himself and acted as if nothing had happened.

"Just leave everything with me," he said with an air of superiority. "I will take care of it myself. That would be all."

One hour later, he showed up in my office, happily waving the documents in the air.

"We solved the problem. Actually, there was no problem whatsoever. It is signed and everything and you now can courier it to the broker."

He then left the office with a little more than a triumphant smile on his face while I had to fight back the urge to giggle. So much fuss and puff over totally nothing.

Aside from my workload, I tried to interact with the other co-workers. It proved to be very difficult to convince certain individuals that I was not the enemy but a friendly person, trying to help. I always had a fertile, restless mind, and was always thinking of ways to ease repetitive, boring tasks. Unlike many of my colleagues, I was always willing to share my ideas and experiences with others. Most of the time, however, my generosity was misinterpreted. "Who does she think she is? Einstein?" I once overheard one of the secretaries saying. Day after day, I learned new lessons. It was difficult, if at all possible, to be likeable and efficient at the same time. Some superiors wished I was capable, but not too much either. Or, some of colleagues found me likeable but frowned about my efficiency. As long as I merely exposed a new idea, I was looked upon as an intelligent, cultured individual. As soon as there was the real threat of that new idea being introduced, I became a presumptuous intruder.

One day, Herr Hilsberg's German-speaking secretary, Brigitte, asked me to help type a very important and urgent report that had to be ready that same afternoon. As I was the only other German-speaking secretary, Herr Hilsberg thought it to be a good idea that I pitched in with the typing. We both had about fifteen pages each to type. I was fast, mainly because I did not want to fall behind with my own work. When Brigitte noticed that I was at my last page whereas she still had two more to go, she begged me to slow down.

"I'd be really very grateful if you held back just a little. You know, I don't want the boss to think that I am not fast enough."

I was shocked. The girl who thought so highly of herself was begging me to fake a lower typing speed.

"I'll do what I can, Brigitte. I usually make mistakes when I slow down too much." I was teasing and continued typing away to the end. I then placed all the pages on Brigitte's desk and walked straight back to my office and to my own work. The environment obviously was not geared towards teamwork.

After this and other similar petty episodes, I decided to keep to myself and no longer volunteered for anything. To alleviate the monotony of my day-to-day activities, I decided to challenge myself on the amount of invoices, orders or letters I was able to type in one particular day. Often, I got so carried away with that little game, that I even skipped lunch outside the office and continued working while nibbling on a bun filled with Swiss cheese and Mortadella. On many occasions I even stayed after hours to finish a particular job. As I belonged to the privileged category of "Executive Secretaries," I was not entitled to any overtime retribution. I never understood the logic behind such a poor money-saving scheme. Maybe it was related to some sort of hierarchical principle. After a few months, finally, part of my typing load was distributed to Marietta, the receptionist who seemed to have enough time to absorb some of it.

Sometime in June, the company had programmed meetings with some of the parts suppliers from Germany and England and I was invited to participate in the various meetings, visits to the warehouse, dinner parties and act as interpreter between the different groups.

Dr. Roberto Valli, one of Orion's engineers, had made dinner reservations in one of the better restaurants in Monza. At first, I felt uneasy accepting the invitation, being the only female among nine guys, but later in the day, I made up my mind and accepted after all. The group discussed their product lines, sales targets, pricing structures, etc. After dinner, and as the wine consumption increased, the talk about business was replaced with jokes. There were instances when I had trouble translating a particular joke and finding a proper expression, because what might have been funny in Italian wasn't in English or German and vice versa. Yet everybody laughed just the same.

Towards 10 p.m., some of the technicians had had a few too many goblets under their belt and at that point, I felt tired also. It simply wasn't easy to act as interpreter for so many people and for so many hours. I was also worried to let any of those guys drive me home while under the influence. Not that there was a particular law enforcement against drinking and driving in those days, especially in Italy; what counted was good judgment. Luckily, Mefisto was home when I called and came to my rescue. We also drove a couple of grateful guests to their respective hotels as they seemed unable to deal with the laws of gravity at the time.

The following day everything was back to normal. Mr. Balderi was busy running around with an armful of folders. He looked very tired and the wrinkles on his face appeared even deeper. Later that afternoon, to my surprise, he expressed the need to confide in me. Mr. Balderi was an extremely private person and was not known to share his problems with just anyone. Even though most of the time he behaved as a stubborn, old mule, I felt sorry for those puppy eyes, begging understanding. There had been many rumors about Mr. Balderi among the co-workers and it was through that grapevine information that I learned about the management's intentions. They simply wanted to get rid of Mr. Balderi but had no guts to confront him directly and fire him. They hoped that I could take over his place while slowly pushing him off the bench. I was horrified at the prospect of harming a co-worker. To deserve a position was one thing, but to encroach someone else's was another, and totally incompatible with my character and principles.

August is holiday month in Italy. Many businesses and manufacturing plants shut down completely for two weeks, some even more. At Orion Equipments, the personnel took holidays at different times so that the offices and the field service departments were never totally closed for the clients. Mr. Balderi went to spend two weeks at the seaside with his family. Before leaving, he gave me some of his precious file folders with corresponding instructions regarding their contents. What he did not leave with me, however, were the keys to his desk drawers. I did not think much of it; neither did I interpret it as a lack of trust. I knew how very jealous he was of all his belongings. After all, I wouldn't appreciate it either if someone went rummaging through my stuff, even though I never locked my drawers or kept any particular secrets in them. Actually, to facilitate anyone who needed anything for whatever reason during my absence, I made up a detailed list of the contents of drawers in my desk as well as the contents of each numbered filing cabinet. The only thing I requested from anyone taking a document was to leave a note on my desk stating so. Mr. Balderi obviously did not share my view in the matter.

One morning, Herr Hilsberg walked into my office with an unusually friendly smile on his face and went straight to the filing cabinets, pulling out various folders and studying their content. I offered to help. He was searching for a letter sent to Orion some time back, which contained a very important reference number. The letter could not be found in the folders where it should have been filed. The only other possibility was that it had been misfiled, got accidentally attached to a paperclip of another document and ended up in a totally different file.

"I have to attend a meeting now, so please continue looking, Isabel," Herr Hilsberg said and left the room.

I spent at least two hours searching the cabinets. Never before did I have the opportunity to learn so much about the paperwork in that department as in those two interminable hours, but the letter Herr Hilsberg was looking for had vanished and I went to tell him that.

"This is absolutely impossible. I know for a fact that the letter was received as I had seen it personally. It contained some technical description and a very important reference number." He sounded visibly irritated. "Just go and try to look for it again." He dismissed me with a wave of his hand and turned his attention back to his customer.

I returned to my office discouraged and angry. How much more could I look and leaf through hundreds upon hundreds of paper pieces? Being myself a temperamental Hungarian with hot paprika flowing in my veins, I couldn't resist throwing the dusty piles of catalogs, old folders and papers onto the floor. I checked the items one-by-one and again ran through the filing cabinets' folders that had absolutely nothing to do with that type of paper work. There was no trace of that letter to be found anywhere. Tired of searching, I buzzed Herr Hilsberg telling him about the failed search.

"Sorry. I can't find the letter."

"Ok. Don't worry; I'll be over there as soon as I can," he said quickly and turned off the intercom.

About twenty minutes later, Herr Hilsberg walked into my office, this time without a smile on his face.

"So, shall we both search for this darn letter?" he asked.

He told me to pull out a number of files, which I did. In the process he noticed the neatness of the nicely labeled folders and expressed his satisfaction. I felt really good about it. Appreciation can be shown and felt in many ways, besides money. We kept leafing through more files when suddenly Herr Hilsberg glanced at Mr. Balderi's desk. He leafed through the documents lying in his in and out boxes. Then he tried to open the drawers.

"Do you have the keys to this?" he asked.

"If it is not in his pencil cup, then I don't know," I said. "He must have taken it with him."   After a long pause, all hell broke loose. Herr Hilsberg was taken over by an authentic temper tantrum.

"This is totally inadmissible," he screamed. "The keys are the property of the company and no employee has the right to take them home." He banged his fist on the desk. He then called in Cesare from the mailroom and ordered him to break open the desk lock. Needless to say, Herr Hilsberg found not only the famous letter, but many other documents long expired or in need of some sort of action. It was the end of the world and also the end of Mr. Balderi.

As soon as Mr. Balderi returned from his vacation, I rushed to inform him about the events that had taken place in his absence so that he could prepare himself for whatever was coming his way. Unfortunately, he had not much of a defence against all the evidence found by Herr Hilsberg. Mr. Balderi confessed that sometimes he would hide the letters with contents he could not understand because he did not want the bosses to find out about it. He was ashamed of the fact and hoped that soon someone would be hired to deal with the problem and translate it all for him. He did in fact call upon me numerous times to translate letters and documents but he invariably kept forgetting to show me the old ones he had been sitting on for months.

That same morning he was called in for a meeting. As much as I felt sorry for him, I could not avoid understanding the management's position as well. When Mr. Balderi returned to the office, he appeared visibly disturbed. His ears were red and his eyes were watery. Yet his pride prevailed above all. With a grave tone he declared he had submitted his resignation.

"You understand me, Signora," he said. "It has been more than twenty years that I have worked for this company and I know my job very well, but I don't like to be treated as a child. If I wanted, I could find myself a new job tomorrow. I've got many friends, I have."

I was quite impressed with Mr. Balderi's confidence and surprised with the fact that it had taken him that many years to wake up and react.

Screaming and yelling was almost a daily event at Orion Equipments. The controller and personnel administrator, Dr. Midas, was having a heated discussion with an employee who became a little more than just verbal by threatening Midas with a fist. In turn, Midas screamed at him to the point of almost suffocating from the effort. Midas had the reputation of being a tough guy and no one dared confide anything to him because it was known that he would immediately spill the news to the bosses. He always had the right answer at the right time. His favorite weapon was sarcasm, which he used freely and frequently with all employees. Whenever he stopped by any office, smiles would disappear, heads would bend over paperwork and the whole atmosphere would suddenly be wrapped in an unpleasant sensation of discomfort and tension. He seemed to enjoy his power over his underlings very much. Yet there was quite a difference between how he treated the others and how he treated me. While rushing from his office to one of the directors, he would often stick his head into my door.

"And how are you today, my dear?" he would say with a great smile and a soft tone of voice.

Sometimes, on my way out, I would briefly stop at his door to say goodnight or for a quick chitchat, which he seemed to enjoy very much. He was always very curious and fascinated with my descriptions of Brazil. I never had reasons to complain about Midas' behavior until one Friday evening, when he offered to give me a ride home.

"I actually live in that area also, so it is not a problem for me to drop you off," he said with a smile.

Being particularly tired that evening and not looking forward to standing in line, waiting for a packed streetcar, I accepted the offer. The family car was mainly used by Mefisto for his field trips and our budget did not allow for a second vehicle. Moreover, it would not have been practical anyway as parking in Milano was nothing but a headache and so was traffic, especially during peak hours. I noticed that Midas was deviating from the regular route I used to follow when travelling by cab or car and pointed it out to him as he slowed down and then came to a stop on a small parking lot behind an old, semi-deserted factory. Before I even realized what was happening, Midas was all over me.

"What in the world are you doing?" I shouted. "Will you please stop this?"

"I'm not doing anything bad," he said, hugging me tight and pressing his face against my cheek. "All I want is to give you a little kiss. It's that simple."

"You are going to be in big trouble if I tell my husband about what you have done. I don't want to be kissed, so please let me go."

"Oh, you dummy," he whispered with his eyes half closed. "A little kiss won't harm you and your husband will still have you all in one piece."

"I don't like your line of conduct. Just forget about the ride. I'll proceed on foot from here." I attempted to leave the car.

"Ok, ok, stay calm," he said, sitting back into his seat. "I'll never understand you females. First you tease us and when we fall for you, you suddenly retract in your shells and play innocent victims."

"Well, there are types like that around who, like men, can be stupid. I'm not one of them. I really don't remember having ever given you reason to take certain liberties."

"I still can't figure out women," he insisted.

"Neither can I figure out men."

"Why? What's wrong with men now?"

"The fact that as soon as you look into their eyes for more than ten seconds or try to be socially friendly, they immediately translate it into a sexual language."

"And that is all the female's fault. You people are the sexy vixen, the ones that dress in tight sweaters, skirts, wear attractive make-up, all just to drive a guy nut."

"Why, am I doing that to you?" I asked, slowly losing my patience.

"You better believe it. You're pretty, outgoing and very sexy."

"And according to you, that would give you the right to confine me in your car and to steal a kiss?" I asked.

"Perhaps not, but I don't want to argue with you anymore; I don't want to spoil our friendship," Midas said, looking at me sideways while adjusting himself in the driver's seat.

"So, in the name of friendship, why don't you take me home right now, or drop me off at the nearest bus station, please," I said with firmness.

I took a deep breath of relief when he finally dropped me off in front of my apartment building. From that day onwards, I avoided as much contact as possible with Midas who, however, continued persistently in his pursuit. He was unable to accept rejection. Even though flattering to an extent, Midas' impudent, oppressive behavior was beginning to disturb and annoy me. Yet I would have to juggle the situation for sometime, at least till I found another job somewhere else.

Mr. Balderi's three months' notice was coming to an end. It had been a very difficult and unpleasant time for both Mr. Balderi and me. Yelling and cursing occurred almost every day. The words used by Herr Hilsberg were in total contrast with his otherwise calm and refined manners. The atmosphere had become that of constant tension and to escape some of that kerfuffle, I liked to hide out in the sales office. The company's sales force was made up of five good-looking young men and two secretaries. They had established a harmonious, efficient teamwork. They worked hard and still had enough time for niceties and the occasional joke that would tickle everybody's funny bone. From one room to another, it was like visiting a different company. I wondered why the other departments could not also work in the same, relaxed manner. Maybe Luigi, the happiest and funniest of the team, should teach them a thing or two, I thought. Luigi was twenty-eight years of age, tall and athletic. He had chestnut brown hair and intense blue eyes. He was always dressed in designer suits and Gucci loafers and was the very best sales person of the company. He would say so himself, in case somebody had not noticed it yet. A little conceited but who cared, he sold well. Aside from a nasty little secret habit—he loved porn and kept his drawers well furnished with all sorts of magazines—Luigi was a good guy. He loved to embarrass the secretaries in his department by "accidentally" leaving an explicit page open on their desk. Sometimes the girls would blush and call him a pig; other times they would leaf through the pages with curiosity and joyful giggles. Luigi was never reprimanded by any of the superiors.

Herr Kassler's office was also a good place to be when Herr Hilsberg was in a bad mood, ranting and raving about anything and everything. Herr Kassler always welcomed me for a brief chat and each time, begged me to speak in the Bavarian dialect, which always triggered in him a hearty laughter.

He often asked me to repeat a particularly funny expression for which he would then laugh so hard, that his belly would jiggle like Jell-O and his eyes would fill with tears. Laughter was contagious and most of the time, we both kept laughing at each other.

Unfortunately, those peaceful moments did not last too long. I had to return to my office and lend an ear to Mr. Balderi's confidential news. One morning, he told me that he had found another job with an even better pay. I congratulated him and wished him all the best. Deep down, he was a good man, unable to say "no" to anyone. He was only guilty of having always been very obstinate, a trademark quite common among older folks.

With Mr. Balderi's departure, I became the person in charge and for a while, I seemed to cope well with the hectic work schedule. Soon, however, I pointed it out to both Herr Hilsberg and Herr Kassler, that if I had to carry on with all the responsibilities that the position required, I would need a helper for the clerical tasks. They promised to study the situation with the utmost urgency. As usual, they were dragging their feet while my patience was running thin. One month later, I was called into Mr. Hilsberg's office. Herr Kassler and Midas were also present at the meeting.

"We have finally found a replacement for Mr. Balderi," Herr Hilsberg said without much ado.

"Oh? And what will I be doing then in that department?" I asked, rather surprised.

"You'll be doing a good job, just as you have been doing till now," said Herr Hilsberg, slightly blushing. "He is a very nice person and very knowledgeable in the field and besides, it is better to have a man to deal with brokers, shippers and suppliers, don't you think?" he added.

"Perhaps you are right, even though I feel that I could have managed the position pretty well, with the help of a secretary, of course," I remarked.

"No doubt that you are a very capable person, but we always had a man heading our import/export department. Besides, you cannot always tell a woman what you feel like telling a guy," said Herr Hilsberg, certainly referring to the cursing part of the job.

I did not insist since it was clear that they had already made up their minds and would not admit that a female could perform just as well as her male counterpart. Once again, prejudice and discrimination were determining factors in the choice of male over female. As the days dwindled down, enthusiasm and interest in my work slowly vanished. I performed like a robot, mechanically. It had become nothing more than a simple exchange of services. I worked and the company paid for it. Yet I had a hard time in working without any motivation, incentive or interest in what I was doing and, therefore, decided to submit my resignation.

Both directors were greatly annoyed with my decision even though they tried to convince me to stay, but once I made up my mind, I would not go back on my decision and even lied by saying I had to move to another town. Only then, they stopped insisting. Herr Kassler felt that there were other underlying causes for my decision and questioned me privately in his office. His interest, however appreciated, had come a little too late. Moreover, I was aware of his limited authority within the company and that he had no powers to change not even an iota in the company's policies, let alone in decision-makings such as personnel assignments. I left without regrets and without hard feelings towards anyone. The world of business was like that and one had to adapt to a given employer and make the best out of it or simply move on, and that is what I did.

After a brief intermission, I decided to place an ad in the classified section of a newspaper. A couple of weeks later, letters and phone calls started pouring in from various parts of Northern Italy and as far as Switzerland. Some companies offered extremely attractive wage packages making my choice that much more difficult. For residence and travel purposes, I excluded jobs that were located outside Milano. My attention was ultimately captured by a newly established electronics company in downtown Milano.

13

DEC Data Processing -
Phase I - Milano

…Electronic company seeking self-motivated, outgoing, experienced secretary with good typing skills, fluent English and Italian a must. Excellent salary with benefits…

I immediately called the telephone number shown in the ad and was given an appointment for the next day. With a copy of my résumé, I showed up at the address given to me over the phone. I was received by a very friendly young lady named Layla. Her pitch-black curly hair accentuated the beauty of her impeccable white skin. Her classic profile recalled the features of an Egyptian goddess. I followed her into a small room crowded with desks and filing cabinets. Every corner was cramped with books, catalogs and document folders. Noticing my inquisitive stares, Layla quickly stressed the fact that those were temporary accommodations and that soon they would move into larger premises. The apartment served also as residence to the company's director, engineer Noah Binda.

Layla explained that DEC Data processing built computers and was slowly establishing itself in Europe, with headquarters in Paris, and that it had become necessary to open a branch in Italy. The plan was to improve customer service for those who had already purchased their computers, and to expand the overall sales force on the Italian market. Layla then switched the conversation from Italian into English to test my knowledge of that language.

"Ok, ok. I see you speak it well. Better than myself I must say. My French instead is a lot better though." Layla giggled, while dragging on her cigarette.

I was surprised that I had not been submitted to further tests such as typing, composition, shorthand, etc. Layla seemed satisfied with the preliminary interview and introduced me to Engineer Binda. He was short, slim, black hair with speckles of gray, dark brown eyes and a well-kept goatee. He shook my hand and offered me a chair. Layla handed him my résumé and then left the room. Engineer Binda examined the typed pages very carefully.

"I noticed that under salary expectations you did not change the amount from your previous earnings," he said with a calm, gentle voice. "Are you sure you do not wish to change that?"

I was surprised with his question and generosity.

"I am satisfied with that amount, at least for now. Let me first show you what I can do and then, if your offer still stands, I will gratefully accept an improvement."

Engineer Binda was surprised with my reply and approach to employment.

"Tell me, Isabel, any particular reason for which you left your previous job?"

"Let me tell you what I am looking for instead: a company that, once given me a task, will allow me to carry out my job peacefully and make good use of all my skills and accept the enthusiasm I bring with it. I like to work and take pride in what I do."

"Well, then I think you just found that company. You will be in charge of organizing and taking care of our Field Service department. You will naturally be trained for the part. Layla will help you with all that. Would you like to give it a shot?"

"I certainly would," I replied eagerly. "As you can see from my résumé, I did work for a computer manufacturer once before, in their software division. I am sure that I will master whatever there is to know pretty fast."

"Excellent. When can you start?"

"Right away," I said.

Engineer Binda seemed very satisfied with the interview. As it was close to a long weekend and they still had to organize a few things, Layla would call me on Monday to confirm the exact starting date. Engineer Binda shook my hand while walking me to the door. I was very happy with the outcome of my interview and had a general good feeling about both, Layla and Engineer Binda. They were both down to earth, straight forward, friendly people.

The next Monday, I received the promised phone call.

"Congratulations and welcome on board," said Layla in a happy tone. "When can you leave for Paris?"

"Leave for Paris? Why Paris?" I asked, flabbergasted. The news had caught me totally unprepared.

"Well, it is just for a couple of weeks. At our Paris headquarters they will introduce you to the organizational aspects of the work you will be carrying out here. They will go through the various service manuals, and so forth. You will also get to know a little more about the general environment and the politics of the company."

For a moment, I did not know what to say. How could I go to Paris all by myself? It wasn't that I had never traveled alone before, but Paris seemed so far away, even though the real distance was only one hour by plane. I had to talk it over with Mefisto who did not seem to have a problem with the good news. That same afternoon, I called back Layla confirming my trip to Paris. Three days later, I went to pick up my air ticket and some money for my expenses. Mefisto's encouragement lifted in part the fears and doubts about my abilities, which inevitably resurfaced at the beginning of every new experience. Once I was on the plane, however, everything seemed to be much easier and I chased from my mind any residue of negative thoughts. It was nothing but a new challenge, no big deal.

At Orly Airport, I took a cab to the Paris DEC branch. After a short wait at the reception, I was greeted by a jovial brunette named Marie Josée. After the usual preliminaries, Marie Josée introduced me to a bunch of smiling co-workers as the Italian Field Service representative. She then offered me a coffee and began telling me about the company. There was a fair bit of information to be digested and so I pulled out pen and notebook to write down as much data as possible. Marie Josée's instructions were so clear and precise, that after only a couple of hours, I had formed a pretty good idea on the company's operations and procedures.

After a quick lunch at a local Rotisserie, I was introduced to Claude Dessin, general director for the Parisian branch and up until then, also responsible for the Italian Field Service operations. Claude was a man in his early fifties, with blond curly hair, medium height and very soft-spoken. His clear blue eyes were always wide open, giving his face the expression of constant surprise.

"So Isabel, how much have you learned today?" he asked me with that unmistakable French accent.

"A whole lot actually. Marie Josée has been very kind and helpful."

"I see you have made a lot of notes on that pad of yours," he said with a charming smile. "Yes, there is a fair bit of information to absorb. Of course, you cannot do all that in one day. But one day at a time, and please do not hesitate to ask when in doubt. We are all here to help you."

For a while he explained about details pertaining to the company's policies. Interrupted by the arrival of a customer, I left Claude to join Marie Josée in her office where, sitting beside her desk, I observed how the various customer calls were dealt with and how the various service call forms were filled in. After work, while accompanying me back to my hotel, we also spoke about ourselves and naturally, about Paris.

After having settled in my room and taken a shower, I decided to find a place to have some dinner. There were a few fancy restaurants in the area but they seemed fully booked and I wasn't that hungry after all. I would try those some other day. The company had given me plenty of money and told me that I could ask for more if needed, but I was not the type to take advantage because I knew how hard it was to make money. I settled for a nearby Rotisserie. There was an abundance of shellfish and all sorts of seafood salads as well as roasted meats and other delicacies.

The next morning, Marie Josée was already waiting at the hotel's reception desk to escort me to the office. There was a whole lot to read, to learn and both, Marie Josée and Claude did their utmost best to ease me into my new position. The atmosphere in that office was a relaxed one and of extreme cordiality. Everybody was eager to pitch in with something.

"I will help you with those photocopies, Isabel," said Josephine, one of the secretaries. "Mireille will help with the catalogs and later on you could join us for lunch, ok?"

They were all ready to make me feel welcome. Some offered information on the best way to visit some of the most noteworthy sights while in Paris and taught me how to get there *avec le metro*. I felt immensely pleased and grateful for all those demonstrations of friendship, which only fueled my enthusiasm even more.

Once I had overcome the initial fear and hesitation, I decided to adventure in the discovery of the fun-loving Ville Lumiére and its beauties. Incredulous and mesmerized, I enjoyed strolling along the Champs-Élysées; the Quartier Latin and Saint-Germain-des-Pres. Goose bumps ran over my back as my eyes gazed over the magnificent Notre-Dame Cathedral, the Tour Eiffel, the Louvre and the Opera. On the streets of Montmartre, I even eluded a rather persistent local Romeo. Vive l'amour, et vive Paris. Later, the Moulin Rouge triggered memories of Toulouse-Lautrec's paintings; happy folks and lovers stealing kisses by candlelight, crowded small sidewalk cafés, with tables covered with red and white checkered tablecloths, while sounds of Edit Piaf and accordions echoed all around.

Mefisto joined me for one weekend and after having had a fabulous *Coq-au-Vin* in one of those fancy restaurants, we went to visit the top of the Eiffel Tower. I was overcome by emotion as I embraced Paris with my incredulous eyes. I would have never imagined, years back, while working for Father Anthony in Brazil, that one day I would return to Europe and personally see all those places, which until then had been nothing but unattainable dreams. I often wondered what forces stood behind my destiny.

After less than two weeks training, I felt it was time to return to Milano and initiate the work that had been planned for me. I packed my luggage and for a moment paused in front of my room's window to bid farewell to France's beautiful pulsing heart. I poured myself a last shot of Remy Martin toasting to la Ville Lumiére. The cognac traveled smooth down my throat. The trip to the airport was a happy one, chatting with the cab driver in the scholastic French I had learned in school many years back. I must have done well because the cabbie enjoyed the chatter a lot. I had the feeling that Remy Martin had something to do with it.

Back in Milano, I found out that Layla had moved back to Paris and so there were only two secretaries left, myself and Elly, who was my same age. Timid and emotional at times, Elly was a pretty girl, with big chestnut brown eyes peeking from a minute, delicate face framed by long, silky brown hair. She was Engineer Binda's personal secretary but also assisted two sales people, both electronic engineers. Aldo was the lonesome bachelor in his late thirties. He had grayish hair and blue-gray bedroom eyes. He was a very quiet fellow who kept to himself and hardly ever bothered anyone. The other one was Gary: tall, slim, with brown hair and brown eyes, he always sported a smile on his face.

Then there was Danny, an American computer expert who was one of the very first ones to join the company. Short and lean, he had dark brown hair and two big, magnetic black eyes. Also Danny was the withdrawn type, yet very efficient and knowledgeable in his field. The serious expression on his face was soon replaced by a vague smile when he learned that I spoke English.

"At last, someone I can talk to normally," he commented.

He was to work closely with me in the Field Service department.

A few weeks later the company finally moved into an office building with plenty of rooms for the various departments. The Field Service alone had three rooms: the office, which had two desks, one for me and the other for Danny, two filing cabinets and shelving. The second room was large and was used as diagnostics and repair shop and the third room was designated for spare parts. Elly and I took care of the purchasing of office furniture and equipment. It was a lot of work, but everybody was willing to pitch in somehow to get things done as fast as possible. In the meantime, Engineer Binda had selected the person who would become the sacred icon of the company—the Controller. Carlo Dalla was a tall, very jovial fellow, who would soon reveal additional traits to his personality such as excessive curiosity and stinginess, so characteristic of the trade. His co-workers would often tease him because of that and also because of his excessive groveling when it came to his relations with any superior. Whenever Engineer Binda popped into his office, Carlo would immediately jump to his feet, arms pressed against the sides of his body while slightly bowing forward in a respectful greeting motion. He must have learned that from the Japanese, I thought. He would pull a chair for the boss to sit in and without even asking, also order a coffee for him. Often, Engineer Binda had to repress the urgency of a giggle, to spare Carlo an embarrassment. To avoid problems of hierarchical nature, Binda invited every one to refer to each other by their first names, leaving out the cherished titles of Doctor, Engineer, Ragioniere (Controller), etc. And so, with the exception of Carlo, everybody called Engineer Binda by his first name: Noah.

The general atmosphere in the office was a relaxed one. Everybody was friendly and gossip was rare. Noah was well-liked by everybody, especially by Elly and me, who admired him for his intelligence, his sensitivity and the human warmth he spread around himself. He was of great help to me during the initial stages of my work, especially in the technical areas. He would never inspect or control my activities, but greatly appreciated it when I reported on particular problems and their solutions. Very rarely did he ask me to change the sentence in a letter or report and even when he did, he requested it in such a polite and gentle manner, that I would not hesitate to re-write the same material a hundred times. Noah never raised his voice nor did he ever curse or use bad language. "Maybe we should re-write this paragraph to better reflect our ideas, don't you think?" was Noah's typical approach when he wanted to change something. The girls loved him for always being considerate and did not spare efforts in helping and pleasing him in every way possible.

As usual, good things always come to an end too soon. Noah was asked to take over a research position at their U.S. headquarters. When I learned about his transfer, I was extremely disappointed. Now that everything was well-organized and running smoothly, we were losing a great boss and even greater person. Both Elly and I felt like we had known him for many years and more than a boss, he had become a friend, a generous, sensitive friend. In time, I would learn that the business world preferred pugnacity, ambition and shrewdness instead of sensitivity and generosity. Business was business.

Noah was replaced by pensive Aldo, whose manners weren't as smooth as Noah's and often used irony or sarcasm as his favorite weapon to extort whatever he needed. Elly was the one who mainly suffered with that, she who became his executive secretary. Despite his abruptness, Aldo was well-liked by most people—maybe the little wisp of hair casually falling onto his forehead to mask his balding crown, had something to do with his charisma. He was only thirty-six years old and already his hair was mostly gray and his posture and arched shoulders, made him appear even older.

The growth of the company required the hiring of additional personnel, and consequently, the close-knit family atmosphere suffered, even though Elly and I worked hard to maintain the original, warm and harmonious environment. Also my department had to hire more technicians. Gerald, a tall, slim Dutchman; Giovanni, a.k.a. *Ciccio* (fatty) because of his overall generous stoutness and Caesar, a fairly good-looking young man with a perennial furrowed forehead that made him appear as if he were angry all the time.

Not having had formal technical training in electronics, I found myself in occasional difficult situations when trying to help a customer who urgently needed help over the phone. Danny had been chosen to act as the company's resident trouble-shooter and problem solver. He was definitely not enthused about the idea of hugging an office desk, surrounded by piles of paperwork, files and endlessly ringing telephones. He thought of himself as an action man, who preferred to hear the monotonous sounds of magnetic tapes, watch the flashing console lights or dive into the electronic entrails of one of the computer models.

Danny was not one to waste a smile. Those who did not know him would easily assume that the man was angry, and most of the time, he was pissed off. He had a few great passions in life aside from electronics and those were airplanes, stereophonic systems and fish. He owned a most beautiful aquarium which he cared for with special affection. One day, he had invited Mefisto and me for a drink at his flat. He introduced us to his wife, Diane, a petite 5'3" blond beauty with intense sky blue eyes. She loved good conversation and immediately revealed that one of the best things in Italy was the good wine, an opinion shared also by Mefisto and me. She happily sipped away from her glass and proved to be a true connoisseur of her vast wine collection.

Danny proudly showed off his stereo set and naturally, also his aquarium. He stood there in quiet contemplation.

"Just look at him," Diane commented with slight irony. "He is totally entranced by his fish. He would take them to bed if he could. I just can't understand how someone can love such cold blooded creatures." She then exploded in hearty laughter.

"If you don't understand, let me explain," Danny said dead serious. As usual, his voice was calm and clear while his face did not betray any form of emotion. "When you are hungry, you get up and go to the kitchen to get some food. The fish can't do that in their artificial environment. They need help, like any other house pet," he added while turning his attention back to the fish, lovingly sprinkling some food into the water. "Also the fish want to communicate, to feel loved and protected. Just like you do. You go to the person who can understand and give you a hug. Fish can't walk or talk. That's what I am here for." Danny then sat in front of the Aquarium to initiate a mute conversation with his aquatic friends.

Perhaps Danny was right about his fish because they instantly collected at the position where Danny's face could be seen through the glass. Danny was certainly not a chatterbox because his mind was immersed in deeper matters.

To avoid getting constantly stuck in the office, Danny made an extra effort to teach me some of the basic technical notions to help me in becoming more efficient when dealing with customer telephone enquiries. Only in cases of total breakdown was I supposed to disturb him at whatever location he was scheduled to be at the time. The causes of a breakdown could be several. They could be complex or they could also be extremely simple. Normally, I would collect as much information as possible about the client's technical problem and then pass it on to Danny, who would in turn contact the customer with instructions or pass the task on to one of the other technicians.

As the sales of computers increased, also the Field Service department became busier and not always could trace Danny because he had already left or was on his way to yet another destination. In order to keep Danny and the other technicians updated on the Field Service activities, I introduced a bi-weekly report, describing the different types of service calls received and the corresponding solutions to the various problems. A copy of such report was also sent to Claude in Paris who was not only impressed, considering it a good idea, but grateful as well because it saved him from making a trip to Milano. Moreover, it proved to be very useful as a communication tool among the various technicians who could learn from each other about the different problems and repair methods.

My task not only consisted in facilitating the technician's work by relaying as much information as possible, but I also acted as moral support when one of them felt defeated by a particularly difficult problem. I would then consult with Claude in Paris and check whether they had come across a similar problem in the past. If the team in Paris were unable to help, I would send a telefax to the American headquarters and then share the eventual solution with Paris also.

Sometimes, due to heavy service schedules, my boys would react abruptly and even more so when they encountered problems not listed in the *Service Manual*. To alleviate the tension, I would try to cheer them by calling them on site to find out how they were doing or if they needed anything. A few words of encouragement and even a little flattery would go a long way and keep their morale balanced. Each time one of them returned to the office after having successfully solved a particularly difficult problem, he was received as a hero. Caesar, the youngest of the team, was capable of shedding tears of joy while narrating in detail his great adventure.

Clients were another delicate area to deal with. Often impatient and unreasonable in their expectations, they did not always accept my explanations or assurances and nerves would tense like violin chords.

One particular incident literally terrified me when a customer called reporting a problem with his unit but was unwilling, or unable, to produce specifics.

"I need to speak to a technician right now," he barked into the telephone.

"I'm sorry, I don't have a technician available right now but I will try and trace one for you and have him return your call as quickly as possible," I said.

"That is not good enough. I need an answer to my problem now, goddamn it."

"Could you please describe what the problem is? What is it that your unit is doing or

not doing?" I tried to keep my cool.

"The unit is not working. It's as simple as that."

"Do you mean to say that there is no response whatsoever?" I attempted to gather

some sort of information for the technicians.

"Listen, Signorina, just pass me the manager, right now," he yelled so that I had to remove the receiver from my ear.

I could have easily hung up on him as there was no law in the country requiring me to accept insults or rude behavior from strangers. I remembered Claude's rules, however, that the customer was always right.

Even though I hated to disturb Aldo, I could not avoid transferring the call to him.

"Don't worry, Isabel, I'll take care of this chap," he said with a calm smile.

He then told the caller the exact same things I had relayed to him just moments before. A total shutdown could not be diagnosed over the phone. The customer had to be patient until we could get hold of one of the servicemen. To that particular customer, coming from a male voice, rather than from a female voice, the explanation sounded more reassuring and acceptable. Old prejudices that had built up for centuries could not be swept away so easily. I took a deep breath of relief when Danny finally called in for messages. There were no cell phones in Milano in the late '60s. I briefed him on the irate customer, leaving out my own emotional drama.

"He has to wait like everybody else," Danny said curtly.

What do I do now, as Danny could not split himself in two and be at two different places at the same time? He did not care much about the social status of a given customer either. Calls were taken care in order of arrival. The status of top priority was given only to units installed in hospitals or big corporations with assembly lines. One hour later, Danny returned to the office.

"So, what's new around here?" he asked impassibly.

I reminded him of the irate customer, but Danny was not easily intimidated nor taken over by panic. He was a little pissed off, however, at the fact that, neither Aldo nor I could give him more details on the nature of the customer's breakdown. For a few minutes there was a deadly silence in the office.

"Get me the client on the phone, please," he told me.

I dialled the number and handed the phone over to Danny, who listened attentively, holding the receiver far from the ear, probably to save his eardrums from the yelling on the other end. His several attempts to cut into the customer's soliloquy failed. Annoyed with the situation, Danny simply hung up.

"You can't win with ignorance," Danny said. "Anyway, we will not go there until he gives us adequate info on his problem and in a civilized manner. We cannot carry the whole lab with us." He then walked away to the parts room.

About an hour later, that same customer called back. Again, Danny listened with admirable self-control. After a few minutes, a smile materialized on his face.

"I would suggest you check all the wires and make sure the machine is properly plugged in. Then call me back," Danny told the customer and hung up without another word.

The customer never called back and during a courtesy call to the site a few days later, Danny found out that accidentally, their cleaning crew must have tripped over a cable and unplugged the unit. That is why the machine wasn't "humming." Luckily, such cases were extremely rare. To avoid similar incidents in the future, the company introduced a free seminar for all their end-users, training them to identify the different types of breakdowns and respective basic solutions.

Aside from the occasional more serious troubles, I still loved my job for its variety and the challenges it involved. I organized myself in such a manner that I could still keep up my weekly visits to the other departments to simply keep the human contact alive and reinforce the spirit of collaboration. I always reserved a little time to chat with Aldo, mainly to bring him up to date with the field service situation for which he was always very grateful. The information received was useful to his sales agents who could direct the customers towards more expensive and efficient equipment. Aldo also enjoyed chatting with me and was sensitive to my little flatteries.

"My dear friend, Isabel, you are the only one to pay attention to this old man," he used to say.

There was a great sense of camaraderie among employees and superiors alike. I was well liked, respected, and often invited for lunch, a drink or dinner. A small bunch of flowers would also materialize on my desk once in a while.

One day, Carlo the controller, invited me and Mefisto to spend a weekend in a small seaside villa he had rented in Bonassola, a small township in the Gulf of Genova. His wife and two-year-old daughter had travelled ahead by a few days. Carlo decided that it was best to use Mefisto's Renault because the car had enough room to house all his luggage and fishing gear. Carlo sat in the front passenger seat and throughout the entire trip, Milano-Bonassola, entertained us with jokes and tales of life experiences. I did not mind his chatter because it gave me time to relax in the back seat while enjoying the beautiful scenery along the way.

I hoped to spend a relaxing weekend without the nuisance of dirty pots, pans and dishes. Mefisto and I suggested taking out Carlo, his wife and daughter to a typical seafood restaurant of the area but Carlo was unyielding.

"For heaven's sake, don't even think about it," Carlo said. "Imagine letting you guys spend money for nothing. And besides, I don't trust the restaurants. Who knows what they put into your food. It's a lot cheaper and more hygienic to eat at home, believe me."

I felt tempted to break the conventional principles of good behavior and social etiquette, and simply go and enjoy the appetizing dishes of the various local *Trattorias* (eateries), but we were guests and had to abide by the rules of the hosts.

Aside from the endless chatter, mainly by Carlo, we went for long walks in the village, into the surrounding woods and along a small river where Carlo described in elaborate detail, his various fishing techniques. Only Sunday, was I finally able to approach the longed-for beach and jump into the cooling waters of the Ligurian Sea. Unfortunately, the sun was weak by the time they dragged themselves to the beach because Carlo and his wife meticulously observed digestion times before stepping into the water. I was a little disappointed and surprised with such rules as I had never had to face such dilemmas while living in Rio or while vacationing elsewhere in Italy such as Rimini, Riccione, and Porto Recanati on the Adriatic coast. Anyway, everybody was entitled to their own idiosyncrasies and it was not my job, nor intention, to change them. For a moment, I was overcome by *saudade* (nostalgia) for the beautiful beaches of Rio and the greater freedom I enjoyed in those far away days.

Returning to the villa that evening, we passed in front of a fruit stand and

Carlo could not resist buying some juicy, red strawberries. He picked up a couple of baskets, not without arguing about the price, however. Back at the villa, while Carlo's wife proceeded into the house with the little girl, he sat down at the front steps and began massaging his feet and cleaning out the sand from between his toes. He then walked to the back of the courtyard to check on the available charcoal for the steaks he was to grill that evening. From there he walked into the house and into the kitchen where he carefully washed each one of those beautiful strawberries. The only thing they would have done differently at the restaurant perhaps, would have been to wash their hands after having rubbed their toes, I thought. Later that evening, Mefisto and I returned to Milano. Carlo would return one day later. For me, it had been a different weekend, a new experience.

With enthusiasm, I started the week filled with different problems and just as many satisfactions. One of these was finding out I was pregnant. After having given up hope due to an earlier salpingectomy—removal of my left fallopian tube and ovary because of a fallopian tube pregnancy—it happened after all. I notified management and with the exception of Danny, everyone seemed happy with the news. Danny wasn't displeased with the news itself, but with the changes that the situation would create, in addition to the rapid development of the company over the entire Italian territory. The field service department had to hire additional personnel: technicians as well as a permanent manager. Initially, they had planned to assign that position to Danny, but Paris viewed him as being a little too abrupt. Besides, Danny himself agreed that he was not the desk type of guy, having to deal with dumb customers day in and day out. Therefore, the management decided to put an ad in the papers. The person they were looking for had to have a diploma in electronics, be Italian and capable of dealing with a large number of customers of different levels.

Hundreds of applications were received. The most promising candidates were invited for an interview at an elegant downtown hotel in Milano. Also Claude arrived from Paris to participate in the selection of candidates. My job was to receive them and have them fill in the application form. Then, one by one they were submitted to tests in electronics. I found it a little awkward to assist in the selection of my future boss, sitting in front of an examiner, like a student in front of his teacher, scrambling to come up with the right answer. Some of the candidates appeared insecure, shy, while others were arrogant, with an attitude of, "How do you dare ask me stupid questions?" Or "Don't you see I know it all?" A bunch of them was so shy and scared that they left even before being interviewed. After endless consultations, the management selected Engineer Carlo Piotti. Tall, with brown eyes, a balding brown crown, a boxer's nose and fleshy lips, he was my same age, twenty-eight. I could only hope that it was the best choice for the position.

In the meantime, I had to worry about finding a replacement for when I went on maternity leave. I placed an ad in the papers and received a considerable number of replies. Many came equipped with diplomas and certificates. Some asked for exorbitant salaries, added to a list of personal requirements. While some accepted the typing or translations challenge as natural, others reacted with a fair amount of irony. An irony that slowly vanished as I underlined in red ink, the many spelling and typing mistakes made, just like Father Anthony had done to me many years ago.

I was not looking for a genius but simply for a person who spoke good English, who was able to write/compose her own letters and to make a close enough translation from English to Italian and vice-versa. Needless to say, good typing was essential, not as much for speed as for accuracy. I seemed to have found those qualifications in Angie Coles.

Once the bureaucratic aspect of the hiring was overcome, I began teaching Angie Coles all the things she was expected to know and do during my absence. Luckily, Angie was a fast learner and I did not have to waste time in repeating explanations. It never occurred to me that my generosity could someday backfire and harm my own position within the company. I figured that just as I had received help in the past, why not, likewise, help this young girl. I ignored any feelings of professional jealousy. At the beginning, not everybody liked Angie, but the girl did not seem to be affected by some of the hostility. With the typical British aplomb, she observed how I prepared reports, handled customers and recorded the service calls.

Angie was a tall, slim girl, with short dark brown straight hair, a round face with high, pink cheekbones and two magnificent, bright, brown eyes. She had nicely outlined full lips that did not require lipstick as they were naturally red. Her fingers were long and thin and the nails revealed that she was a nail biter, which betrayed a timid, nervous personality. Yet she beautifully masked any possible turmoil with an apparent happy serenity. She moved in slow motion and her talk was almost a whisper. All that contrasted with the rapidity with which she executed any given task. Sometimes appearances can fool one's perception, I thought.

Another change was Danny's assignment to a new position in Geneva. He was preparing for the transfer and the moving expenses were supposed to be charged to the company. Danny therefore asked Carlo to take care of the payment. Carlo refused with the excuse that Danny had chosen a moving company that was far too expensive. As a result, a squabble took place between the two men.

"I don't understand why, among all the movers we have in town, you had to choose one of the most expensive ones," said Carlo.

"And I don't understand why you are getting so uptight," replied Danny, "as if the money came out of your own pocket."

"If it was mine, I would give you not even half of the amount," said Carlo, excited and flushed in the face.

"I know that you are rather stingy but in this case it shouldn't really concern you. The company asked me to move. I asked you to take care of the details. You farted around too long, so I had to take charge myself. And so I have chosen, what for us Americans seemed to be a decent moving company. Personally, you may even use a cart pulled by a donkey, certainly more befitting your mentality."

Carlo did not seem to yield and so Danny returned to his office and called up Geneva

to let them know about the bureaucratic difficulties encountered in the Milano office. Mr. Benoit, who was the general manager for the European Division, asked to talk to Carlo. Danny looked at me.

"Go get the bastard," he said.

I went to fetch Carlo who took the request of talking to the big boss in Geneva as an enormous privilege. In his broken English, he tried to explain his refusal to pay for Danny's moving expenses, but he was interrupted halfway through and remained silent, listening. With one hand he loosened his necktie and from a back pocket he pulled out a large, crumpled handkerchief to wipe the rivulets of sweat that suddenly appeared on his forehead.

"Si Signore. Yes Sir. Yes. Si, me understand, Sir. Yes Sir, yes," were the only words he could articulate while following every yes word with a slight bow.

Danny watched the scene impassively. His facial expression was so serious that he resembled a figure carved in stone. Meanwhile Angie and I were fighting back giggles for the scene was more pitiful than comic. Once finished the conversation, Carlo replaced the receiver with great delicacy, as if an abrupt motion would materialize the general director through it. He then looked at Danny, with a great smile on his face.

"I'm glad," he said. "The director gave me permission to pay the moving bill." He then walked back to his office, followed by Danny. Carlo Dalla would have loved to pursue the argument on how easily Americans throw their precious money out the window but Danny did not give him that chance.

Two weeks later, Carlo Piotti took over as official Field Service Manager for Italy and now Claude ceased to visit Milano, but continued to maintain contact with me on a personal basis. I explained to Carlo Piotti the procedures followed by our department, the contents of the various filing cabinets, the recording procedures and the bi-weekly reports. I also introduced him to the various technicians as well as the lab and parts departments. I tried to help him in every way possible to ease him into the new position.

Weeks later, Carlo Piotti left for a period of training in the United States. He left behind a list of things to be done for his return such as statistics on service calls, categories of computers with the greatest amount of problems, description of the most common problems, most popular models sold and installed, profits on service calls on equipment no longer under warranty, and on and on ad infinitum. That assignment alone would keep me busy for several days—like Angie and I needed the additional workload!

At home, I was absorbed in preparing for the arrival of our first child. We purchased a wonderful crib lined with bright red upholstery, pillow and sheets, the various toiletries, milk bottles with corresponding sterilizing kit, bibs, clothes, blankets and whatever else was necessary. One Friday evening my water broke. I was not sure what to do and so, around 11 p.m., I called my friend Mariuccia who told me to head immediately to the hospital. Mefisto drove me to the Niguarda training hospital on the other end of town—a real citadel on its own. In those days, labor and childbirth was a business pertaining entirely to the female gender. Aside from the doctor or surgeon, no other male figure was allowed into the labor area. Different times, places, mentality. At about 6:15 in the morning of February seventh, 1970, little Peter was born with the help of a suction pad. When I laid eyes on the little boy, I forgot about the labor pain, the nurse's elbows pressing against my stomach, leaving me breathless —procedure used to help push out the baby, the nurse explained. I also forgave her for slapping my hand because, in the absence of a handgrip, I had squeezed the next nearest object on my left which was the nurse's hip. Somehow, I even forgave the almighty doctor— who was not even my regular obstetrician because mine was away on holidays—for criticizing my moans while invoking my mother's name and finally, the six stitches the doctor gave me without anaesthetics because he said "it's not worth it, we are almost done." I was kept in the hospital for about five days, in a large common room with other ten or fifteen new mothers. The nurses were all very busy, running around, some reprimanding the new mothers when too weak or in pain to walk as far as the nursery to have a peek at their newborn.

"Get up you lazy bunch," one of the nurses said rudely. "Go see your babies in the nursery and stop whining."

Not used to the regimented, sterile and hostile environment, I was on the verge of desperation and begged Mefisto to take me away from that hospital. However, they would not release me ahead of time, nor was it advisable to complain, as it would have made things only worse. I had to muster all the strength and courage to endure a few more days of in-hospitable surroundings.

Finally, the day came when the three of us returned home as a family unit. Relatives, friends and colleagues came to visit, bringing gifts and flowers. It was a time of intense learning: how to become a good mother, how to cope with a new lifestyle and learning new routines. For three months, I was absorbed with pampers, sterilized milk bottles, tears, tummy aches, fever, and weight measurements. The slightest whimper would make me jump to my feet and run to check on the little one. Then there were the weekly pediatric visits. Such visits would take place at the nearest ONMI center for mother and childcare. Two separate unpleasant incidents bothered me a fair bit.

One occurred when taking Peter for his first immunization shots. It was raining and I had a little trouble juggling Peter and the umbrella, at least until I got inside the building where the long line-up continued. There were dozens of new mothers with their crying babies, but just a few chairs and no benches. After a while, the tiny baby became a heavy bundle and I was afraid I could no longer hold on to him. There was only one doctor in the building for that entire crowd. Sitting on a high chair behind the examining table, the middle-aged man enjoyed his glorious status of powerful physician. One after the other, the mothers placed the babies on the table in front of him to receive the shots. When it was my turn, while lowering Peter's jumpsuit to expose his butt to the doctor's infamous needle, I accidentally brushed against the doctor's hand with the nails of my right hand. He reacted in a rather dramatic way by shaking his hand in the air.

"My God, look at those nails," he said. "You really should cut them as they could seriously injure somebody."

I apologized even though I had barely touched his hand. I had indeed nicely manicured, medium length nails. It must have been more the red color of the nail polish to intimidate the poor soul of a doctor, whose reproaching stare followed me to the exit door.

Another scary encounter, with the same doctor, happened a month later when after a likewise long wait and to expedite things, I had lowered Peter's pants when my number was called.

"Who told you to lower the child's pants?" he yelled almost out of breath. "I did not ask you to lower his pants. You go outside now and wait till I call you back."

I was stunned and so were the other women who witnessed the uncalled for incident. The assistant nurse apologized for the doctor's rudeness and helped me to get back in line. I was close to tears and could not understand why some of those public servants placed themselves on such high pedestals, acting like despicable, ignorant jerks. I left the building vilified, angry and in tears. I only wished Mefisto had been there to help in such difficult situations, but he was busy, taking care of business, as usual.

The three months maternity leave ended very quickly and more than ever a second pay check was indispensable because Mefisto's income alone was not enough to make ends meet. Health care would not extend maternity benefits beyond the regular three months. After having unsuccessfully searched for an affordable nanny, I succeeded to place Peter in a nursery daycare. It was a lengthy, bureaucratic process because it was a government institution.

I had to leave two hours earlier from work to make it in time to pick up the baby by the 4:30 p.m. closing time. As most new mothers around the world, also I had a hard time at the beginning juggling work, the new baby and the house chores and with Mefisto on continuous sales calls, it turned out to be a little more than a challenge.

By reducing my work hours, my workload increased. Angie, who had replaced me during my absence, was assigned to the position of receptionist because everybody learned to like and respect her and management did not have the heart to dismiss her just because I was back. Angie, however, did not like to play the receptionist because she considered it a monotonous, dreary task. I exhorted her to hang in there because, eventually, an interesting opening might just come up for her.

In the meantime, Carlo Piotti, who months before had returned from his training stage in the United States, was still filled with enthusiasm and a mountain of new ideas, which he was eager to unload on me. I had hardly finished one task and already he was changing or replacing it with an even better and bigger one. In addition to all that commotion, there were also my personal problems to contend with, which were just as important and deserving the number one priority treatment.

On occasion, the daycare employees decided to declare a strike so that I had to scramble, trying to find an acquaintance willing to take care of the little one for a few hours or when unable to do so, stay home completely. The same applied for when Peter suddenly developed fever and the daycare would call and ask me to immediately pick up the child and then run to the doctor to check on the origins of such fever. The tension and the anxiety were slowly building up and my nerves were constantly put to the test of endurance. Especially when reminded, even though tactfully, that my personal problems should not interfere with the smooth operations of the company. It was then that I fully realized how difficult it was to be not only a mother, but a full time employee at the same time. It certainly required a lot of will power and a well-balanced physical and psychological conditioning.

Had my work been merely mechanical, not requiring a particular assiduity and precision, the management probably would not have bothered, but part of my job was to coordinate prompt action for those calls that involved breakdowns on equipment installed in hospitals and assembly lines. Sometimes I had to trace a technician right away, re-route him to another location, and even meet him halfway with a particular spare part. The daycare management, however, could care less about those details. I had to reorganize my life. To maintain my job and make sure that little Peter was well taken care of, we decided to leave him, at least temporarily, with Iolanda, Mefisto's sister, in a town named Bergamo, some 30 km north of Milano. Mefisto and I would then spend Saturday nights and part of Sundays with Peter. Needless to say, how distraught I felt after every weekend and how often I asked myself: "Live for what: Work or family?" To live for work alone had never been my life philosophy and having to be separated from my baby was at times unbearable. I often wished Mefisto had a better income and did not have to rely on my contribution, so that I could look after our offspring during the most important formative years. My parents had suffered hunger during the war and again during their first few years in Brazil as immigrants, but they never considered, not even remotely, entrusting their children to anybody else. My father provided, proudly, even if sometimes the loaf of bread was not as big as he wished it would be. So why, I thought, could it not be done in a modern European city such as Milano? Something had to be changed and quickly, but what? To hire a person to watch over the baby at home was impractical because nannies in Milano cost just as much as the salary I was earning. To leave the child permanently with the relatives was unthinkable. Why then had we brought a child into this world? The reply came through a serendipitous long distance call from my father. After Uncle George's tragic death (he committed suicide), my father had become the owner of a small metal shop and offered us shares in the company in exchange for our collaboration. "Do not despair. God and good luck have never abandoned us. On the darkest day, there was always a light at the end of the tunnel," words my father used to say when things got tough.

It was not easy for me to notify the management of my intentions, but I had to do it. Even though just verbally, most everyone offered their help just so I would not leave the company. The news traveled as far as Paris, Geneva and overseas. I felt flattered by the commotion my situation had triggered everywhere, but my problem could not have been solved easily. Not even a generous increase in my salary could have helped, firstly, because it would have created an unprecedented incident in the company's hierarchical and budget level and secondly, because at that point, my thoughts and heart were settled on our return to Brazil and my parents.

One last item on the agenda, therefore, was my replacement. I convinced Carlo Piotti to keep Angie as she already had experience in the different problem-solving techniques of the field service department. She had after all done a good job in my absence.

I remained to fill my position for the required contractual two week-notice and did my best to organize my personal agenda in such manner, as not to interfere with the company's normal, smooth operations.

On my last day at the DEC Corporation, they had prepared a surprise party for me. Carlo Piotti and Aldo had prepared speeches in which praise and credit given to my work history bordered on pure adulation. Gary read a message received from the general manager in the U.S. through which he thanked me for the great job I had done for the Italian branch. He also mentioned that, should an opening come up in the newly planned Brazilian branch in São Paulo, I was more than welcome to apply for a position within the company. I was ultimately showered with gifts and good wishes and many of my colleagues could not refrain from shedding a tear or two.

To avoid dragging on the emotional tensions, I bid farewell and rushed out of the office with my gifts and the envelope someone had placed on my former desk. Before calling a cab, I opened the envelope. It was a long letter, reiterating what Carlo and Aldo had already said in their speech and it was signed by every one of the superiors and employees. It was the most beautiful letter I had ever received from strangers. It was then that I could no longer hold back the rollercoaster of emotions and broke down in sobs. One more chapter had ended and a new one was soon to begin.

14

Olá, São Paulo

Relatives and friends escorted us to the port city of Genova, where the *Eugenio C* ocean liner had already docked, ready to receive its passengers. There were hugs and kisses and smiles mixed with tears as we said goodbye. We boarded the ship, found our cabin, dropped off the luggage and then went up on deck where we enjoyed a wonderful view of the busy port and the surrounding landscape.

After almost two hours, the boarding procedure had finished. Ropes were released, the anchor was lifted, and on the third whistle, the vessel started to slowly move away from the quay. For a long time we waved to our relatives and friends who had remained until our departure. For a moment, I felt a pang of sadness in my heart. I wasn't quite sure if that was what I really wanted; leave Italy to return to Brazil. But then the thought of embracing my folks again, introducing them to their first grandchild, erased any gloom or doubt from my heart and mind.

Eugenio C of the Costa Lines was a beautiful and comfortable ocean liner with all the amenities that turned our voyage into an unforgettable experience. Problems simply disappeared aboard that vessel, so grand and yet so tiny if compared to the vastness of the Atlantic Ocean. We had now plenty of time to relax and finally enjoy our little nine-month old, Peter, who constantly smiled to show off the tiny teeth that would pop up always more frequently. He was the sensation on deck, with the chubby padding in all the right places, running at full speed ahead with the aid of a circular walker, along the deck's long promenade. At lunch or dinner time, he attracted the attention of neighboring tables because of his healthy appetite. He simply loved to eat, anything and everything.

Ten days later we disembarked at the port of Santos where my mother and father were impatiently waiting for the great reunion. After countless hugs and kisses, their attention was entirely captured by little Peter who expressed his happiness for all the attention he was getting, by giggling and clapping his hands. We then took a cab and drove home where my Grandmother Nani and Aunt Mary were anxiously waiting to embrace me and the baby. Tears of happiness scored their faces. Only my grandfather was missing as he had passed away two years earlier, and my brother Frank, who due to the bureaucratic difficulties in getting a scholarship for nuclear physics at the local university, decided to apply, and successfully obtained, the help he needed from the Canadian government instead.

After having exhausted the news report, the family gathered to discuss business. The financial situation of the little metal shop was not the best. To reactivate the business after a big fire had destroyed the main building required a considerable infusion of money. My father had taken out a bank loan, which he did not seem to be able to repay. The salary he could afford to pay Mefisto was definitely not enough to survive in a mega city such as São Paulo. To save everybody some money, we had all decided to live under the same roof, at least for some time, reason for which father had rented a three-bedroom apartment. There was one room for my parents, one for Grandma Nani and one for us and the baby. There was a nice living and dining room, a large bathroom and a likewise large kitchen with an eat-in area entirely tiled—floor and walls.

Soon enough, Mefisto and I realized that once deducting our portion of rent, food and utilities, there was just barely enough left for the cigarettes and the occasional movie. Even so, we offered my father most of the money we had brought from Italy, hoping that he could at least partially get rid of some of his debts and give us all a chance to restart with a brighter outlook to the future.

I spent most of the morning hours cleaning the house and scrubbing the kitchen floor to mother's specification because little Peter was crawling everywhere and touching everything and disinfection was a primary concern of hers. I was a little less obsessed with germs and could not imagine the rest of my life spent cleaning, scrubbing, sterilizing and cooking on command. Besides, there was not much space for our belongings in the apartment. The bedroom furniture father had purchased for us was too cumbersome and it was even difficult to make up the beds in the morning. Mefisto definitely longed for his own space, where if he wanted, he could walk around in his underwear, watch the TV programs he liked best and eat foods of his choice.

I began to check the newspapers. Endless pages of classified ads, which aside from the regular job description, also gave the location of the company as well as the salary offered. I started by considering the companies closest to my residence, and applied to several. Everywhere I encountered long waiting times as countless candidates had applied for the same position. Not always did they have air conditioning in the crowded waiting rooms. Sitting side-by-side, some sweating profusely, others sending off the pungent smell of a cheap perfume, the candidates were requested to fill in long application forms. Then one at a time, the girls were called in for a brief interview and were told that a decision would soon be made and the selected person would be notified accordingly.

To avoid wasting any more time, I decided to visit one of the best employment agencies in town. They were well organized and the waiting times were reduced to a minimum. I was interviewed by a young lady who, after quickly reading my résumé, asked me a few additional questions and then showed me to a bright, pleasant waiting room. Some twenty minutes later, she returned with a large envelope and the address of a company where I was to show up that same day at 2 p.m. After having wished me good luck, she stressed the fact that punctuality was necessary and suggested that I do not ask more than two thousand new cruzeiros as a starting salary.

15

GEM-AIR S.A.

At two o'clock sharp, I was reporting to Mr. Staetler, Administrative Director and Treasurer of a company specializing in the manufacturing of anti-pollution equipment. His friendly and jovial face revealed sincerity and a happy disposition. His words were calm and composed. He carefully examined my résumé and asked me when I could start working. I explained that in view of our move to a new address, I would be available in two week's time. Mr. Staetler did not seem overly concerned with such a minor problem and sent me over to the personnel department for a small test. He wanted me to write a commercial letter in all the languages I knew. I chose the ones I knew best: Portuguese, Italian, German and English. Although I read and spoke Hungarian, I was not able to write a commercial letter. I also spoke some Spanish, read it well, but was unable to write a commercial letter. Then there was French. I could read it, but aside from the very scholastic basics, I could not write or speak it too well. *Except perhaps after a Remy Martin*, I thought playfully.

Dario, a very friendly individual, was the personnel manager. He showed me to the nearest available typewriter. When I finished with the typing, Dario asked me to fill in the company's application form, which upon completion, he attached to my résumé and then returned to Mr. Staetler.

"Very good, Isabel," Mr. Staetler said after reading through the letters. "I must admit that I am pleasantly surprised, especially with your knowledge of the German language," he added, with a big smile.

I was extremely happy because apart from two years elementary school in Germany, I had no formal training in the German language. The German spoken at home was mainly a Bavarian dialect. Any additional knowledge I

160

acquired from reading books and magazines and later working for German-speaking companies such as Orion Equipment in Milano.

"So when can you start?" he asked again.

"I wish to remind you of our moving problem," I replied. "Not more than two weeks, maybe even sooner."

"Very well then, I'm willing to wait as long as you keep me updated," he said very seriously.

Perhaps he was afraid that I would change my mind.

"Don't worry. I will call you every two days," I said.

"That will be fine. In the meantime, for your information, you will start with a salary of 2,000 new cruzeiros," (US 415.00 approx. in 1971) he added.

We shook hands and I returned home with my heart singing joyful songs of contentment. A fantastic salary—four times the amount Mefisto was making through my father's company—full health benefits for the entire family, and company transportation to and from the office.

In the meantime, we found a beautiful two-bedroom, bath, kitchen, living and dining room on the fifth floor of a building located half way between my parent's apartment and the metal shop. Despite the protests of my parents, who were now stuck with the entire rent of the large apartment, the move proved to be necessary to maintain the peace and harmony between the two families. To live with one's in-laws had always been statistically, a recipe for disaster, especially when both sides were strong-willed, obstinate and opinionated. As usual, once again, it was me who got stuck between a wall and a hard rock as I hated to hurt either side, yet I ultimately decided to follow Mefisto to the new home. Through my Aunt Mary, I got hold of a wonderful nanny named Casé, to look after little Peter whom she affectionately called "Pedrinho, o gordinho" (little Peter, the fatty) because of his chubbiness. She was also to keep the house in order and do some simple cooking but her main task was that of taking good care of Peter. Because there were no Pampers in São Paulo at the time, I purchased tons of cotton rolls which I cut in long strips and used those instead. They needed to be changed more often to avoid skin rashes. There were, of course, regular diaper services, which not only were more expensive but just as un-hygienic. At least I could toss out the cotton balls along with the garbage.

Interestingly enough, Mefisto and I approached the local Johnson & Johnson office one day, to find out why they had not come up with Pampers yet, like in Europe. The explanation that particular customer service representative gave us was that the majority used regular diapers because they had nannies and maids to do the cleaning. Besides, not only would the Pampers prove to be more expensive, but would also jeopardize the employment of countless nannies. There was no point, therefore, to introduce Pampers onto the market. These were the early seventies in São Paulo, Brazil. Nanny Casé certainly liked the idea of the makeshift cotton roll. It allowed her to stay out longer with Peter at the local playground, just across from the building. She spent most of the day playing with him.

Two weeks later I showed up for work. I was introduced to Betty, who was executive secretary to the director general and owner of the company, Mr. Kunz; to the sales manager, Mr. Almir, and partly, secretary to Mr. Staetler as well. Poor Betty overwhelmed with work, hoping to be soon relieved from at least one of the bosses. The office was very small, breathing was difficult and to work in it was even worse, but Mr. Staetler reassured me that we were to move to larger premises soon.

During the first few days, I devoted my time to reading the correspondence that Betty kept producing, and studying the contents of the various filing cabinets. Betty got very upset when Mr. Staetler gave orders that I was not to be disturbed while reading company material.

"Even more so, because she is a secretary at international level, she should show her abilities and dig in, helping me with the work overload here," Betty said.

In order to keep himself on Betty's good side, Mr. Staetler began dictating letters to me. I also had to keep a list of all the phone calls received for Mr. Staetler, specifying dates, subjects and actions required and taken.

A few days later, Betty introduced me to the various departments. She started with my closest co-workers, Alfio the accountant, Nerone the cashier, and Dario whom I had already met. The sales department was made up of twenty different area managers and their respective secretaries. The technical division was formed by eighty individuals among which engineers, designers and technicians, directed by Engineer Weiler, also technical director and son of the owner. His secretary, Tammy, gave me a healthy handshake, and a detached "welcome aboard" with a faint smile. To me, she came across as a snob with a well-rooted superiority complex—someone you would not want to rub on the wrong side. Mistrust, unfortunately, is a barrier that only time can overthrow.

We visited the room where they kept office supplies and reproduction equipment. Another office was filled with technical supplies, managed by Nino, an eccentric yet very friendly man. Although his salary was modest, he always dressed in the most fashionable outfits and drove an American luxury car, second only to the owner's black Mercedes Benz. He was also not shy to reveal his Casanova tendencies and would hardly ever lose a "good occasion," I was told. The manufacturing plant occupied an area of 13,500 square meters and employed 256 specialized workers.

Finally, I was introduced to the general director and owner, Mr. Kunz. He was in his early seventies but still very active and on the ball. His face revealed a good heart and he never bothered anyone as long as his office was kept in good order and the work was executed to perfection. His questions were limited to the strictly indispensable and he expected that also the replies were just as clear and concise. He was always very busy and had no time to waste nor the necessary patience to listen to a "because." To get along with him was very easy, remarked Betty. "All you have to do is always say yes." It was useless to think about anything new he had already thought of, but not expressed in words earlier.

A few weeks later, along with the accounting and personnel departments, we moved to a small building attached to the main office. Betty was relieved as she now had more space available and a lot less work to worry about. My office turned out to be much larger than that of Mr. Staetler because of the various filing cabinets. Days later Mr. Staetler hired an office boy to help us with small tasks such as run errands, pick up or deliver mail or messages, take telephone calls, forward messages and many other minor things which according to Mr. Staetler, would cause me to waste precious time from other more important tasks.

Mr. Staetler disliked shorthand. He considered it a double waste of time, both for the secretary and the boss. He preferred to use a recording device best known as a "Dictaphone" and carried one with him everywhere he went. He would start every dictation with proper instructions, whether the document was a letter or a report, if it was to be typed as a final copy or just a draft to be re-edited. In that manner, while he was re-reading and changing one item, I was free to do something else. His method was very functional and I liked it. Every Monday morning, I found my desk littered with the small cassettes.

After the first month of work, Mr. Staetler called me into his office to tell me that he decided to increase my salary to 2,300 new cruzeiros.

"Are you sure you really want to do that?" I asked pleasantly surprised. "After just one month?"

"I'm sure, Isabel," he said with a chuckle. "You proved yourself very well."

His gesture triggered even more enthusiasm in me so that I worked even harder to keep him satisfied.

Aside from his position as treasurer, Mr. Staetler also headed the personnel department and was responsible for the internal discipline and all administrative rules and regulations. For that purpose, he had introduced a Manual of Operations that contained information on most anything relative to the company's activities. It was updated on a regular basis for subjects such as the outcome on particular meetings of general interest, change of suppliers or personnel, new public relations methods, even information on the increase in the cost of living. Mr. Staetler was meticulous about his manual and it was my job to make sure that it was regularly updated and that every department had a copy in perfect chronological and logical order.

Mr. Staetler was, without a doubt, a perfectionist. He loved order and precision and like some of my previous superiors, had a great interest in his filing cabinets. Occasionally, he would come up with a new and more efficient system and I had to re-organize the files accordingly. The administration folders with the green labels became folders with white labels. The legal folders changed from red to yellow labels, and so forth.

Initially, I had fun in getting involved with that type of work, but as the contents of the cabinets increased and reached some 400 pieces, I began to have a lot less fun. Aside from the perfect maintenance of the cabinets, Mr. Staetler required a detailed, typed list of their contents to be kept in the first folder of each drawer. Furthermore, these lists were to be updated each time a new file was opened or the boss decided to change yet again, the grouping of the files or the color of the labels. It was definitely an elaborate system but extremely handy for whomever needed to retrieve a document without my assistance.

Mr. Staetler's meticulous obsessions went as far as recording any correspondence, telegram, import paper, legal document, insurance paper, arriving or leaving the office, into a designated book. It even showed the time of day a given document was sent or delivered to a certain person. Such precision work turned out to come in very handy because in minutes, one could find out when and where a particular letter was sent, its subject, description of the enclosures, if any, copies sent to other recipients, if a reply was received and on which date, and finally, where it all had been filed. Marianne would have certainly relished every bit of that efficiency. Who knows, maybe Mr. Staetler and Marianne had gone to school together. I giggled to myself while remembering Marianne's wonderfully organized filing system.

The hectic activity that ploughed into Mr. Staetler's office did not leave much time to think. Being a capable, very dynamic person, Mr. Staetler happily took upon himself new jobs and responsibilities. The privilege of their execution however, always fell into my lap, naturally. His dedication to the company's interests was touching and his energy admirable. For the weekend, he would pack his executive briefcase with paperwork to spend the happy family hours working for the company, or so he said. Monday mornings he would always show up re-charged and smilingly unload the fruit of his weekend labor on my desk. I had barely turned around to plug in the recorder and start to type the first letter and already Mr. Staetler peek-a-booed from his office door to find out if I had finished a particular document. Upon hearing a

"Not yet", his face would clearly show disappointment and he would quickly slam his door shut.

I must have spoiled him with my efficiency because he often ignored the fact that I had only two hands and had not yet trained my lower extremities to perform just as well. His obsession with perfection, speed and efficiency was often frowned upon by the other employees. On one occasion, he candidly confessed that he had always had a hard time finding the proper secretary. Geez, I wondered why!

One day, I decided to confront him about all the work matters.

"Mr. Staetler, you must have certainly noticed my good will and the effort I put into my work," I said. "You must have also noticed that I do not waste time chitchatting around but I'm beginning to think that I am not the right person for you after all."

"What do you mean?" he replied. "I don't understand."

"Well, there is always so much work, so much rush and time is always so limited. I do not seem to be able to keep up with our schedule anymore. That is why I am saying that maybe you should look for someone else."

"What are you saying, Isabel? Very much to the contrary, I am extremely satisfied with your work. You are like us Germans. You really take things to heart and do not stop till you're finished. But you have to learn to take things a little easier, and everything will fall into place, just be patient." Mr. Staetler smiled with encouragement.

I felt tempted to ask him why, if he was so satisfied with my performance, he slammed the door in my face whenever I was unable to finish a letter or a report before the established time schedule. I decided against it as I considered Mr. Staetler to be an intelligent man who understood what I had said earlier. Meanwhile the plant's siren signalled that another day had come to the end and Mr. Staetler exhorted me to go home and have a "well deserved rest." He was meticulous with punctuality. It was of utmost importance that arrival and departure times were observed. "You came early, worked hard, you deserve to leave on time," he used to say. Overtime was entirely his privilege, even if perhaps, useless.

The next day, Mr. Staetler arrived in a good mood and with a loud entrance.

"Here," he said, dropping a small, wrapped package on my desk, "to sweeten your bitter moments." He walked away with a smile of satisfaction.

Despite his occasional bouts of anger and impatience, Mr. Staetler knew how to be kind and caring. He was also aware of the fact that a box of chocolates was not going to erase the meaning of a rude word or a poorly pondered observation. At the end of that month, Mr. Staetler decided to give me yet another increase, bringing my salary up to 2,500 new cruzeiros, an excellent salary for a secretary in those days.

On secretary's day, he gave me a beautiful bunch of orchids and because his thoughtful gesture had been totally unexpected, I jumped up from my chair and impulsively smacked a kiss on his cheek. Mr. Staetler blushed to a bright red and with great embarrassment sought refuge in his office. That day the management also offered a special lunch in a fancy downtown restaurant to all the secretaries. Each secretary was escorted by her respective boss. Among all the other men, Mr. Staetler was the only one standing out from the otherwise happy crowd. In spite of his apparent self-confidence and authority, he was nothing short of being an incredibly shy person. He did not seem at all comfortable amidst that crowd, and the commonplace conversation he carried on, just proved it.

"So, today is secretary's day," he said. "Do you celebrate such an event also in Italy?"

"Oh yes, I think it is a date observed all over the world."

"Interesting, isn't it?"

"I guess, it is," I said.

"And it turned out to be a nice day after all that rain," he commented after a long pause. I could tell he was more comfortable while eating and more so after we all left the restaurant.

A few weeks later, Betty, after having had a major disagreement with Mr. Kunz, resigned her position. She had had enough and for a while, there was a filing in and out of new candidates to replace her. The old man was not happy and one afternoon, showed up at Mr. Staetler's office.

"Hello, Isabel," he said with a friendly smile. "How are you dear?"

From inside closed doors, Mr. Staetler recognized Mr. Kunz's voice and stormed out from his office.

"I need to borrow your secretary," Mr. Kunz said curtly. "I am at a loss with all the "dumme Gänse" (dumb geese) you keep sending over to my office." He sounded impatient.

Mr. Staetler did not like what he was hearing and denied lending me to him.

"Then at least let her teach the new girl how I like things done over there,"

Mr. Kunz insisted.

"All right, but just for a few days and just a few hours each day," Mr. Staetler said.

I failed to understand why Mr. Kunz had chosen me to teach his new secretary as I did not have a clue on how his office operated. Why he could not explain to the newcomer directly about how he wanted things done in his office, I wondered. In a way it was flattering; on the other hand it would interfere with my own workload. I did the best I could under the circumstances.

In the meantime, Mr. Staetler, having obviously forgotten about my concerns regarding my inability to cope with the increasing workload and the rush that was required each time, gave me yet another important job to take care of. He appointed me the company librarian. I was to prepare a detailed list of every piece of technical books existing in the company and monitor their location at any given time.

With very little enthusiasm, I began to collect the many dust-covered books lying around everywhere. Some were dated 1928 and a couple went as far back as 1800. There were a few well-preserved books, but most were soiled and some had even the covers missing. It took me a few days to organize everything and record them in a book indicating title, author, subject and location of the volume within the premises.

Soon I realized how difficult it was to keep track of the books as the library was located at the other end of the main building and engineers and technicians had free access to them at any time. Mr. Staetler, however, simply brushed aside such insignificant technicalities.

"I just fail to understand what can be so difficult in a task that is so pleasant and most importantly, instructive?" he asked while smiling and shaking his head in disbelief.

It was me instead, who could not understand his refusal in comprehending my problem, but maybe he was right. What were, after all, 300 miserable books!

Loyal to his image of ambitious, dynamic executive, Mr. Staetler decided to grant me the privilege of taking care of his private correspondence and affairs such as keeping track of his dental appointments, the sending of flowers for a birthday or a sympathy card to the relatives of a soul passed on. When he discovered that instead of joining the rest of the girls for lunch, I preferred hanging out in the company's recreation club to play billiards with some of the plant employees, he suggested to the management that I be appointed Counsellor of the Female Committee of the Sports Association. He was evidently not counting on the consequences of such an appointment, which often required meetings during regular working hours. As a matter of fact, he would reluctantly release me from office duties the first two or three times and then just cut off those privileges for any subsequent events. One month later, convinced of the impracticality of such activity and with Mr. Staetler's enthusiastic support, I resigned my position from the committee.

The stress generated by work was slowly sneaking into my private life. I was often tired and flustered and perhaps it was due to one of those moments of distraction that I missed one dose of Ovulen and got pregnant again. We had not planned a second baby so soon and I wondered how the company would take my good news. At first there was fear and hesitation because employers were known to avoid anything that hindered the smooth running of their operations, and one of those things was the female pregnancy. Surprisingly, Mr. Staetler did not make a big issue out of the news and minimized my worries and embarrassment with words of encouragement.

"It is the most beautiful thing one can do in life and I congratulate you," he said with a bright smile.

Mr. Staetler was himself a father of five children and therefore his remark sounded credible and sincere. Whether he fully realized the implications of my pregnancy were an entirely different story, that only time would tell. Anyhow, I was one of the few lucky ones; I was not dismissed.

Nothing, however, had changed on planet work. It actually got worse, the hectic work schedule that is, and I often ended up in tears from exhaustion. On the other hand, my new salary of 3,000 new cruzeiros proved to be extremely useful under the new circumstances and also because Mefisto's income from the metal shop was so low that he had to take on a second job, that of English teacher at a local foreign languages institute.

When I reached my fourth month of pregnancy, Mr. Staetler invited me for a chat in his office. He initiated by asking me about how I was feeling and if I was being regularly checked. After that, his face lit up like a TV commercial and he began to ramble about dos and don'ts. One of the don'ts referred to the people who do not work, obviously, do not get paid either. He paused for a minute. Then before continuing his arguments, he wanted me to agree with his principle of "Keine Arbeit, kein Geld" (no work, no pay).

"See, Isabel, now that you will soon be leaving us for maternity reasons, you will not be able to work and as I said before, who does not work, does not get paid. Now, however, since I know what a fine employee you are, and instead of not paying you at all, I was thinking that maybe I could give you one third of your salary and why not, even send you some work to do at home. What do you think?" He smiled generously.

Not being familiar with the labor laws of the country at that time, I refrained from giving him an immediate answer. Noticing my hesitation, Mr. Staetler hurriedly added, "Of course, you do not have to give me an answer right now. Just think about it and let me know your decision."

That evening, while being driven home with the company's mini-bus, I mentioned Mr. Staetler's offer to Tammy who happened to travel on the same route. Tammy and I had become good friends after all. While in my company, she totally dropped her snobbish behavior.

"You must be kidding, right?" Tammy said with a hearty giggle.

"No. I am not. Unless I misunderstood the whole thing, those were his exact words."

"Well, I would ask him to clarify things again. Just to be on the safe side. There is something not quite right there," Tammy sounded more serious. "By law he cannot deny paying you for the three month's maternity leave."

Later that evening, Mefisto also agreed with Tammy's advice and attributed my misunderstanding to stress and tiredness.

Early next morning, I went to see Dario in the personnel department to ask for information on maternity leave issues, without mentioning any of Mr. Staetler's interpretations. Dario's information confirmed Tammy's input and both, strongly contrasted with Mr. Staetler's version on the issue. I thanked Dario and walked up to my office. Mr. Staetler arrived shortly after, mumbling a quick "Good morning" and rushing into his office. I allowed him to get settled before knocking on his door. Clearly embarrassed, I asked him to repeat his proposal, as I seemed to have misunderstood what he had said the day before. Surprised at first, Mr. Staetler repeated his offer visibly annoyed.

"And which part of my proposal you did not understand?" he asked.

"About paying me for one third of my salary; would that be on top of my regular salary?" I asked.

"Why? Do they give you the full wages in Italy?" he asked between amazed and amused; maybe just faking both.

Anyway, I nodded affirmatively. After a long pause, Mr. Staetler promised to look into the matter and perhaps even review everything.

I returned to my desk and answered a phone call from Tammy who asked me to bring over copy of a given memo. Tammy did not really need the document; it was only an excuse to find out about the outcome of my conversation with Mr. Staetler.

"I did understand exactly what he said yesterday and nothing changed about it today, except that he promised to review his offer and then get back to me," I told her.

Nonetheless, Tammy escorted me to Engineer Weiler's office who exhorted me to repeat the whole story. He too, seemed to have a hard time in believing what he had just heard and I felt extremely embarrassed. The incident threatened to assume unexpected proportions and I almost regretted having confided in Tammy, but Engineer Weiler promised to deal with the issue very discreetly. Two days later, he told me that the matter had been settled and that I should not worry. Later that same evening on the mini-bus, Tammy told me about the details because she was present at the board meeting taking notes.

"We were all waiting for your boss who as usual, came running with an armload of files and folders. The meeting was proceeding well and lively as usual when at a certain point, he decided to inform everyone on the physical status of his secretary—as if nobody had noticed the bulge you have sported for sometime now." Tammy chuckled. "He then told the others about the economic proposal he had offered you and the money he was going to save the company."

"And what did the others say to that?" I asked.

"Well, my boss said to him: 'And did she not tell you where to go?' They all laughed except for Mr. Kunz."

"What did Mr. Kunz have to say?" I asked

"He punched the table with his fist and said: 'Oh, let's stop all this nonsense. You wouldn't want us to get into trouble with the Ministry of Labor or worse, lose the girl,' he said addressing your boss, who at that point was definitely disappointed for not having received the expected approval and applause for his brilliant initiative."

When Tammy finished her story, I told her about what happened on the other side of the building, when Mr. Staetler returned from that famous meeting. He called me into his office, paused briefly while mentally building up his speech and then with a big, bright smile gave me the good news.

"I have good news for you, Isabel. I succeeded to obtain the full payment of your wages while you are on maternity leave. So, please forget my earlier proposal." He sighed with relief.

While I felt more tired as time progressed, work seemed to increase further and so did Mr. Staetler's temper and impatience. I thought that skipping a day or two occasionally would give him a taste of what it would feel like, if he had to do things on his own. The strategy worked for two or three days, then everything returned to the old routine, although Mr. Staetler insisted in saying that he could have easily managed all by himself. He proved he could type a letter by picking the keyboard with his two index fingers.

Everything quickly goes and quickly comes and so did the holidays. I was entrusted with yet another important task. I had to prepare the Christmas list and the gifts to be sent to our most important customers and some close friends of the company. There were large baskets of dried fruits, fine wines, and agendas in real leather with delicate inscriptions in gold, and so forth. Mr. Staetler constantly checked on the quality of the packaging. Only first class wrapping paper was to be used and the package had to look like it had been done by professional wrappers. Then every Christmas card was to be signed by each of the directors, attached to the package and delivered in person to the recipients. The entire operation was meticulously recorded: name of recipient, address, type of gift, date and time of delivery and name of the person signing for it.

To the employees under his direct supervision, Mr. Staetler gave cute little red booties filled with candy, cookies, chocolate and walnuts. The boot was tied with a red silk bow, along with a small evergreen branch. For the plant workers he organized a party at the Recreation Club with beer, sausages and large slices of roast. A Santa Claus was also present, distributing toys to all the kids.

Unfortunately, the beautiful holiday celebrations ended too soon while the New Year brought along new situations and new problems. For disciplinary reasons, Mr. Staetler's office boy was transferred to a different department and I was given a young girl who seemed to have considerable difficulty in becoming part of an efficient teamwork. She had no previous office work experience and her typing was pitiful. Moreover, she disliked being given orders or instructions. She preferred doing things her own way, even though she had no idea of what she was doing. Her incompetence clearly disrupted the otherwise smooth operation of my work schedule. To make things worse, she would often burst into tears whenever I would ask her to re-type a letter bearing mistakes. She would spend considerable time in the washroom touching up her make-up or chatting with other girls her age, while her work would pile up on her desk and in her drawers. Even with all the labels and indexes glued onto each drawer of the filing cabinets, sleeping beauty Marisa would still be misfiling letters and documents. The situation was getting out of hand, because Mr. Staetler blamed me and not Marisa for the many mishaps. So one day, I decided to have a talk with her.

"If you are seriously considering learning this trade, I am more than willing to help you, but you need to show me your true interest and willingness to learn," I said. "You need to listen, open your ears and eyes and learn, because contrary to your own opinion, you know very little, if at all, what a secretary is really all about."

Marisa broke down in a hysterical sob. I tried my best to calm her down, patting her shoulder. Then suddenly, she revealed her great dark secret. She had fallen in love with the boss, but instead of working more and better to prove her love for him, she simply sought refuge in her little world of dreams and fantasies, so typical of most teenagers in love. She promised me that she would work harder and better, and so she did, for almost a whole, entire week. After that, she fell back into her old, disruptive routine.

I felt the need to clarify things with Mr. Staetler. I told him that I had plenty of work to keep me busy all day and could not worry about Marisa's unfinished tasks, too. Mr. Staetler recognized the seriousness of the situation and decided to have a heart-to-heart himself with his ardent admirer. His conversation with her finally put an end to her illusion, broke her heart, and brought her back to planet earth.

Another problem that had to be tackled as quickly as possible was my replacement, but Mr. Staetler did not seem overly concerned and was almost annoyed at being reminded of it. He did wake up, however, three weeks before my departure. An incessant parade of possible secretaries followed, but none seemed to be good enough for the boss. He ended up choosing a middle-aged lady, suffering a number of complexes and insecurities. Already one week after having been hired, she complained, among tears, how difficult it was to work for Mr. Staetler. I minimized her apprehensions and taught her as fast and as much as possible in the little time available. Mr. Staetler seemed satisfied with the results, but had me promise to pop in a couple of times before going to the Clinic.

I often wondered if the baby had the ability to feel the constant stress that his or her mother was living under. Perhaps that was one of the reasons why little Nakina decided to become an earthling two weeks earlier, on June 21, 1972. I received countless congratulatory cards and presents and big baskets of flowers. Even Mr. Staetler's wife showed up in person, bringing their best wishes along with gifts for the little girl.

Nakina's birth experience was a pleasant one for me. I had a private room; the food, served on porcelain dishes with silver cutlery, was abundant and tasty. Nurses and doctor alike treated me with much respect and affection. The nurse did not knead my stomach with her elbows but gently massaged my belly while exhorting me to push. Even the doctor, once finished, bent over my face, congratulating me for the beautiful doll I just had and gave me a gentle peck on the forehead. What a difference from the Milano experience two years before. And they dared call Brazil a third world country!

Four days later, I returned home, very happy and very tired. Nanny Casé had asked permission to take off a few days to visit relatives in the interior of São Paulo to which I agreed not knowing that Nakina was to show up that much earlier than the time scheduled by my doctor. I was all by myself, taking care of both children and the household. Stress and happiness seemed to always go hand in hand and so did sadness. While the Almighty brought me baby Nakina, he took away Granny Nani. One soul had come, while another one was gone.

It had hardly been a month since the baby's birth and already Mr. Staetler had sent over Dario to find out if I could return to the office sooner.

"He would even give you one extra free week," Dario said, without noticing the blunder. What for an extra free week I thought, if I still had two months coming to me anyway?

"Oh, Dario, of all the people, you should know best what a maternity leave entails," I said.

"He would even be willing to send you a typewriter and all the necessary materials, so you could work at home," Dario said, ignoring what I had just said.

"I know that it is difficult for him, as a male, to understand what happens with a person after childbirth. I am tired; my Nanny is away on holidays and I am busy taking care of two little ones," I tried to explain, clearly annoyed while anger was beginning to build up.

Besides, little Peter was becoming a handful, always running and exploring things and sometimes stumbling and hitting a hand, a knee or his head against an obstacle—not always the softest one—to end up in tears. For me it was a new reality to master, but not on command, like the people around me expected me to do. Dario seemed very disappointed with the outcome of his mediation, and left. Mr. Staetler had definitely no clue on what it meant to look after a two-year-old vivacious little boy and a new born baby. I had plenty of homework and did not need additional work from the office to keep me occupied.

In the meantime, serious family problems threatened the little family unit. Mefisto was slowly tiring of the many unkept promises, having to keep two jobs and the hurt to his pride for being unable to bring home a pay check at least as good as mine. The seed of returning to Italy was slowly germinating in his mind and growing stronger every day. He did not wish to remain in São Paulo or to look for a job in another town, far from my parents. He was of the opinion, that the situation required a clear-cut from everything and everybody. I was not happy with his plan. I had a good job, an excellent salary; we could afford a wonderful nanny and be together, building a future. for ourselves and the kids. I rejected the idea of returning to Italy, mainly, because I could foresee the difficulties in finding proper childcare and the idea of having to leave them once again with relatives, disturbed me deeply.

Even though we did not always see eye-to-eye with my parents, I hated the idea of having to leave them once more. Besides, I felt comfortable in the country I loved so much and grew up in, but Mefisto was unrelenting in his decision and even threatened to leave without me. The pressure was intense from all sides. Would I overcome one more endurance test? There were my parents trying to dissuade us from returning to Italy. My mother often came by the apartment to beg me to reconsider our decision. She often cried because business was bad and my father was so desperate, that he seriously considered committing suicide. It broke my heart, as did the fact that Mefisto was not only unable or unwilling to accommodate me by finding another position, perhaps even in another city, but came to the point of playing with my emotions by threatening to abduct little Peter. My pillow absorbed the tears I would shed after everyone was asleep. I was terribly hurt and angry. Nobody would harm my babies, not even Mefisto—I would definitely see to that.

Mefisto finally noticed my distress and had a change of heart by promising, that he would provide for everything once back in Milano, including a reliable nanny, so that I could return to work peacefully. Comforted by Mefisto's assurances, I slowly accepted the idea of returning to Italy. Yet something in my heart had been irreparably damaged. Once again, we would have to sell our belongings at a total loss, or simply give most of it away and start from ground zero.

A while later, Mefisto paid a visit to Mr. Staetler, who was very disturbed by the news that I would no longer return on a permanent basis. He most probably thought of me as ungrateful, after all he had done for me, but, "no one is totally indispensable," was one of his favorite expressions. It was for that reason I was not overly concerned with his reactions. I returned to the office some time later to fill my two-week resignation obligations. A real hunt then began to find a replacement. The fact that Mr. Staetler had a hard time in finding the "right person," flattered me a fair bit. If not at all "indispensable," at least I was "not easily replaceable," and that was a good enough compliment.

Mr. Staetler finally chose a lady in her late forties who had also worked as a librarian. It was clear that his first thought was directed to the company's library and not to the ever-increasing pile of clerical work building up on my desk. Tereza, the new secretary, was not a quick learner and was extremely sensitive to remarks. A strong word caused her to break out in tears. She also continued saying that she would not be able to handle all that pressure much longer—and she had just started. What I had feared all along came through. Mr. Staetler fired Tereza and hired Margarida, a much younger person, who happened to be just as slow and emotionally unstable. I had to start all over again, teaching as much and as fast as possible. Mr. Staetler did not seem too concerned about whether Margarida was learning anything because he asked me to re-organize the filing cabinets for one last time.

"But Margarida still needs directions," I said.

"Well, look at it this way," Mr Staetler replied. "You had to master things on your own when you got here. It is actually the best way to learn, believe me. Just let her be. If she is as good as her résumé describes, then she should not have any difficulties. It will only be a matter of time." I had to agree.

One morning, Mr. Staetler submitted Margarida to a number of tests including the typing of the last board meeting's minutes. It was about three pages long with five carbon copies. Margarida seemed very nervous that day, as she had to re-type everything at least four times. Mr. Staetler's complaints about the many errors also did not contribute to her fragile emotional state of mind. She tried one more time and once again, she failed and broke out in sobs. Mr. Staetler noticed the scene as he walked out from his office but ignored it and simply asked if the report had been typed already. Only his face got red when Margarida told him that she had not finished yet. He then turned to me.

"Do me a favor, will you? Type me this one page and bring it over to the boardroom. You have five minutes." He handed me a hand-written page and then left the office slamming the door behind him.

It took me more than five minutes instead, between typing, the phone and Margarida's lamentations. I then rushed over to the boardroom and handed the typed page over to Mr. Staetler who, without lifting his eyes from his paperwork, mumbled a quick "thank you."

In the next few days, I used all my persuasion power to convince Margarida to stay, be patient and calm down more. Mr. Staetler hardly noticed that my final day had come. I toured the various offices to bid farewell to managers and colleagues. The last one to shake my hand was Mr. Staetler. He presented me with a beautiful lithography of the Brazilian 1800s, wishing me all the best and thanking me for the precious collaboration. Should I ever return to São Paulo, he would make sure that I was offered a position within the company. Those words were flattering but useless because deep down, Mr. Staetler must have known that I would never return.

16

DEC - Phase II - Milano

Two things comforted me in our move back to Milano. Mefisto had promised that at no time would I have to be separated from the children and Carlo Piotti, when informed about our return to Italy, wanted me to return to work for him. This all helped take some of the edge off my feelings of failure as we yet again had to prepare for a humble beginning.

We were lucky to find a small one bedroom, living room, bathroom and kitchen apartment in a century old building in the Porta Romana area. Since we had very little money left for furnishings, Mefisto's brother, Gian, arranged for a gas stove, beds for the children, an old wardrobe for the clothing and other miscellaneous furnishings he had received from friends and acquaintances. There was no time to be fussy or to regret the loss of the beautiful furniture we had left in São Paulo as well as all the other comforts we would not be able to afford for quite a while. It was time again to roll up the sleeves, and with humility, walk a stretch of road that had already been walked on but this time, plagued by obstacles and difficulties.

A few days after our arrival in town, I decided to pay a visit to the old office. Aldo gave me a warm reception, a big hug and a peck on my cheeks. To celebrate my return he immediately ordered some champagne and pastries from the bar in the lobby. We chatted for quite a while before visiting all the other departments, beginning with Elly with whom I had always been best friends. As expected, the company had expanded. New departments were created and more people had been hired. Carlo Piotti now had a very large, bright and modern office. I was pleased to learn that Angie had remained with the company and was acting as secretary assistant to Carlo. They all appeared very happy at the prospect of my return.

"So, when can you start?" Carlo Piotti asked.

"As soon as I can make proper arrangements for the children," I replied.

In the following days, I began the search for a nanny, but all the candidates not only had a handful of conditions and demands, but also required a salary far superior to what we could afford at that point in time.

After countless visits to various daycare agencies, I succeeded in placing at least Peter in a government-run daycare. Mefisto's sister, Iolanda, offered to take care of Nakina instead, as there was a long waiting list for her age group. That meant that we would see the little girl only on weekends up in Bergamo. As much as I felt betrayed once more by Mefisto's broken promise of keeping the children together, the situation was critical and required my full cooperation, patience and understanding. The only consolation was that Iolanda was family, and would treat Nakina like her own three children.

I started working no longer in charge of a given department, but as assistant to Angie, who by then knew more about what was going on in the company. Carlo told me about all the changes that had taken place during my absence and found it important to underline the fact that due to the considerable increase of personnel, the past family atmosphere had ceased to exist. It was hard for me to believe it, absorbed as I was in memories of the past. It was nice to see old friends again and work with them as it was satisfying to open files that still contained documents in my handwriting.

I was a little disappointed, however, when Carlo offered me the same salary as two years back. The cost of living in Milano had since taken giant leaps, while the standard salary for a secretary, so they said, remained at the same level. After Mr. Staetler's generous figures, the new ones felt almost like an insult, but losers can't be choosers so I accepted the offer hoping that it would improve in the months ahead. I was definitely not ready psychologically to face new challenges with an entirely new company.

Under Angie's direction, I began to work and soon noticed that everything seemed more difficult than what I had imagined. The silent, timid girl that I had hired to replace myself during the maternity leave had become a strong, confident and demanding woman. She was passionate about her ideas and used persuasion in having those ideas accepted and followed even by her superiors.

Slowly, I began to understand Carlo's earlier observation on how things had changed within the company. I began to notice the existing tensions and misunderstandings and even resentments among employees and superiors alike. There were those who complained about being overworked and underpaid compared to a colleague who was laboring half as much and was making more money. The others complained about not having a secretary like the other guys, or resenting a missing promotion. The spirit of teamwork and cooperation seemed to have vanished and remarks such as "this is not part of my job description," became almost a slogan. I began to feel uneasy, as if I had been hired by a new company entirely. I would have to set aside old memories and start all over again. I resigned myself to take the good with the bad and make the best out of it, by even accepting tasks that hardly triggered my interest or enthusiasm.

Angie would often put me ill at ease, which angered me because after all, I had never been nasty to her in the past. I tried to point it out to Angie who then used the evasive tactic by immediately switching topics. Once she realized she had gone overboard and wanted to be forgiven, she would appear with a little gift for me or the children. Responsibility and stress can trigger different reactions in different people.

Carlo was a *moto perpetuo*, continuously interrupting with requests of information that had already been placed on his desk or in his "personal files." He would ask us to make urgent phone calls and expect an even more important letter to be typed at the same time while he was breathing down our necks. I noticed that some of those extremely urgent letters or reports would linger a few days on his desk, collecting dust. It was practically impossible to finish a given task from A to Z without at least two or three interruptions, which most of the time would be greeted with a quick roll of the eyes or a whispered curse word.

"I really don't understand you secretaries, always complaining. We make an effort to give you work and all we get for it is ugly faces. After all, this is all part of your jobs and you should be used to it by now," was Carlo's favorite remark.

After some time, Carlo put me in charge of the Parts and Logistics department, which initially seemed too complicated and therefore too boring for me. The more I got to familiarize myself with the new task, however, the more I began to like it and the old enthusiasm soon re-appeared. I began checking the inventory and updating each inventory card accordingly. This helped me to get better acquainted with the piece itself and its electronic characteristics. I also found that several pieces had been recorded incorrectly and so I issued a new card. I checked all 1500 cards, which in Angie's opinion were not even functional, but Carlo had put me in charge and therefore I was free to organize as I saw fit.

My task, therefore, was that of ordering in spare parts from overseas, following the import procedures, checking the parts on arrival, recording each item on the individual card, placing the item on the warehouse shelves in alphabetical order, shipping out spare parts orders to customers and other DEC branches located, by then, in all major Italian cities. The task kept me busy all day long and I could not understand why Carlo insisted on saying that such work would not take more than an hour per day, leaving me enough time to help Angie with some of the other work. The chaos that I found in the warehouse before I put things back in order just proved that Angie was unable to keep everything under control.

Patiently and persistently, I pointed out to Carlo that an efficient and well-supplied spare parts warehouse was a must to satisfy the needs of both customers and technicians. Carlo was of the opinion that many of the defective items could easily be repaired in house, without having to waste money in importing new ones. The only problem with his logic was that the defectives' box was overflowing and no one had ever time enough to repair them. "We'll take care of it," was the most popular expression and the most ineffective one as well.

I took my job very seriously, and worked hard to keep the warehouse in order and updated, and at the same time, tried to please Angie, who kept giving me tasks she considered more important. With time, I noticed that the warehouse, my main responsibility, was falling back into chaos. By carrying out different tasks for Angie and Carlo, I could not always be in the warehouse when one of the technicians picked parts. They didn't always remember to record the items taken either, let alone dates and quantities. For this reason, I found myself in trouble with customers and other technicians. For example, the inventory card called for a certain amount of integrated circuits, whereas the physical count resulted in only half the amount. Anger and frustration slowly cancelled out the initial enthusiasm.

Soon family problems were added to those at work. Peter had developed mumps. The daycare Pediatrician ordered a fifteen-day sick leave for Peter, which meant that I was unable to go to work. I spent two weeks nursing Peter back to health, with visits to the family doctor and updates to the daycare.

When I returned to the office two weeks later, I encountered much tension, almost hostility. The warehouse was a mess again and I had to re-check the inventory. Angie complained about the ever-increasing workload while blaming me for spending too much time among the spare parts. I tried to ignore her often-ironic remarks and just execute what was requested of me. A few weeks later, I had to stay home again because the daycare employees had decided to go on strike. It seemed that strikes were the preferred course of action of most Italian laborers. Of course, the boss was not happy and I was not happy, but we could not fight the unions, who's right to strike was detrimental and unjust to other workers not involved in the same dispute. My emotional balance was slowly faltering. It was definitely very hard to be a mother, hold on to a full-time job, run errands, take care of the household, and hope to keep my sanity. Regretfully, Mefisto was mostly on the road, still taking care of business.

A few days later, Carlo invited me to accompany him to the airport. I did not know about the reasons for such an unusual request, especially knowing how busy Angie and I were. Once inside the cab, Carlo stormed me with questions.

"I'd like to know what's going on with you," he said. "What is it that troubles you? You're no longer that smiling, happy girl of one time. You know, everybody noticed your change."

"Well, many things changed since I left for Brazil," I replied. "I think it is all part of life, of living; new experiences, ups and downs, the whole bit."

"Some of the girls are also complaining about you leaving early every day," Carlo said.

"I thought I had made that clear at the time you hired me, that because of the daycare hours, I would have to leave early to pick up my son."

"Well, excuse me; can you guys not hire a woman or something, to pick him up from daycare?"

"That is easier said than done. To hire a nanny in Milano you have to be rich. I might as well stay home then, since my salary would go straight into her pocket." I repressed my anger and frustration.

Obviously, those who do not have such problems cannot imagine how hard it is to earn just enough to make ends meet. Carlo then touched the work subject.

"So what do you think of your job? Are you satisfied?"

"Not really. You put me in charge of the warehouse and I think I'm doing a good job. I only don't know how I could do all that in just one hour per day as you suggested some time ago. Maybe you could show me?"

"And how is your relationship with Angie?" said Carlo, brushing aside my last remark. "Sometimes I feel that there is a certain degree of incompatibility between the two of you."

"Oh, I don't mind helping Angie, but I find it useless that both of us are doing the same task split in half. Besides, we do need a second typewriter. It is just so ridiculous having to wait in line to type a letter or whatever."

"Besides that, what would you suggest to better organize our department?"

"Better coordination, more action and less chatter," I replied.

When we reached the airport, Carlo promised that he would study a better distribution of tasks between Angie and me.

"While I'm away, I'd like you to prepare a layout of all the tasks you are both in charge of and how much time each of you spends on them," he said. "Based on this info, I'll study both your cases."

Carlo checked in at the boarding desk.

"What is most important, however, is your family situation. I wish you could settle it as soon as possible because I need you to dedicate yourself fully to your job. We have a lot of work to do and it is necessary that we all do a little of everything, like multi-tasking, fast, well and possibly all at the same time."

I refrained from commenting and just smiled, while walking with him to the departures gate.

"You know, I wish people would stop gossiping about your early leaves and absences. We wouldn't want to create a precedent. Do you think you could do something about this situation, possibly by the end of the year?"

"I'll do what I can," I said almost inaudibly.

We then shook hands and while Carlo disappeared behind the gate,

I took a cab back to the office. Somehow, I envied Mefisto who did not have to put up with all the practical parenting issues and could work peacefully, without the nuisance of a reprimand for being a parent.

Once back in the office, I recalled the conversation I just had with Carlo and tried to analyze my situation. I had left the company two years earlier on my own accord. Returning two years later, they re-hired me happily because I was familiar with the company's policies and because they needed additional personnel anyway. Carlo entrusted me with the responsibility of the warehouse, and yet I was somehow restricted in my activity by having to share the load of another secretary. At the time of hiring, Carlo had been well aware of the problem "bambini" and did not seem concerned when told that I had to leave earlier because of specific daycare hours. Suddenly, everything seemed to have changed. My schedules were creating a disciplinary problem and there was no room for precedents.

Placing myself briefly on the other side of the fence, I understood the company's problem. They paid me to work, not to miss days of work due to strikes or children's illnesses. That was not their problem. Whose fault was it then? There were mothers with the right to strike, but there were no rights for the mothers who needed to work!

"How come Carlo invited you to accompany him to the airport?" Angie suddenly asked, interrupting my thinking.

I decided to tell her the whole story. Angie listened carefully, her face turning red as if taken over by anger.

"You know, you shouldn't take it so hard. Carlo really has no idea about other people's hardships. He's nothing but a peasant who had the good fortune of finding a comfortable easy chair, and very well paid, too. He should really not be talking about dedication. Oh, give me a break." Angie was all riled up.

I did not know what exactly Angie was referring to since Carlo had always proved to be a hard worker and never refused to pitch in, not even on Sundays or holidays, if necessary. Angie noticed my surprise and continued, with more excitement in her voice.

"Did you know that his wife works for a government office and do you know what she does? She shows up only a few weeks throughout the year, just so she doesn't lose her seniority. The rest of the time, she calls in sick yet gets paid the same. That's why I think that he is in no position to preach." she said.

I was not aware of these details concerning the boss' wife, who, thanks to lax government working rules, did not hesitate to milk the cow as much as possible. For a moment, I questioned the validity of principles such as honesty and loyalty. Was it all really worth it?

"What do you intend to do now?" Angie asked, after a long silence.

"What do you think I should do? There are only two alternatives. Follow the flow and don't give a damn about anything and anybody or, I quit and close another chapter in my life," I sighed with resignation.

Angie looked at me, slightly shocked and began asking questions similar to those Carlo had asked me on our way to the airport. Patiently, I answered, but Angie could still not understand why I was unable to hire a nanny and once again, I had to explain the various reasons, including the financial obstacles. I hated when people became pushy and too nosy, reaching into my pocket to calculate possible solutions to what I already knew were non-existent, at least at that point in time. To avoid dragging out the conversation, I told Angie about what Carlo expected us to do in his absence.

"Keep track on our activities and write down how much time we spend on each task. After that, Carlo will decide about the best way to divide our work load."

"Ridiculous, and idiotic at best; what about writing down the time we will waste in writing down the time wasted in doing so?" Angie remarked with sarcasm.

At any rate, Angie respected the instructions received and kept notes on everything she did and the time wasted in doing so.

In the meantime, Peter was transferred from daycare to nursery school or better known as kindergarten, and so I convinced my sister-in-law, Gina, who lived on the fifth floor of the same apartment complex, to pick him up in the afternoon. By a fortunate coincidence, Gina had given up her full-time occupation for a part-time activity and did not mind to help out with the pick-up.

For the peace of mind of all concerned and the general happiness of the company's gossipers, I was now free to remain in the office until the official five o'clock closure time. Carlo then permanently assigned me to the logistics department, recognizing that it required full time attention if the work was to be carried out accurately and responsibly.

There came a time when it became necessary to lock the door to the parts room to avoid the quick self-serving technicians from withdrawing items without notice. I kept the key in a special drawer, known only to Angie and Carlo and so the technicians had to ask for help whenever they needed parts. All in all, work was running smooth again, at least for some time.

A few months later, Carlo was appointed regional manager for the Field Service division and transferred to Geneva. He would remain, however, in charge of the Italian branch until a new Italian manager was elected. After weeks of interviews and tests, the selected candidate to replace Carlo's position in Milano, was invited to show up in Geneva for the final approval. Once he had overcome that final bureaucratic obstacle, he would leave for the United States for the usual training period.

Gil, short for Gilberto, obtained the approval of superiors and electronic testing experts but also, and mainly, of his co-workers. Angie and some of the other girls found him to be very pleasant and very handsome. A modest career was ahead of him initially, but with the possibility of future developments and the possible promotion to more important positions. Capable subjects had no difficulty in climbing the corporate ladder in a relatively short period of time—a privilege reserved entirely to the male gender and unthinkable for simple secretaries. Especially those in their childbearing years, or already tangled up in raising the children who would eventually become the executives of the future. All those poor bosses, what would they do without the efficient help of a good secretary, I thought, jokingly.

I remembered some of the meetings held with a group of top-notch executives. They came from the various technical divisions of France, Holland, England, Belgium, etc. They would always arrive in happy, boisterous groups with big, happy smiles plastered over their faces. They were all dressed to the latest fashion: impeccable white starched shirt collars, gold Cartier cufflinks, light colored raincoats and the unmistakable "executive lunch box" (a term I coined myself, meaning briefcase). Most were naturally happy and pleasant, while some were serious, immersed in their own thoughts and problems.

In those occasions, it was my job to help out Angie from the probability of a nervous breakdown. We had to order drinks, sandwiches, prepare hot coffee, place intercontinental (long distance) calls, send extremely urgent telex messages, book airplane or train tickets and notify their respective secretaries of their departure and arrival times. There were also postcards to be sent to their wives or girlfriends. We were also to book hotel rooms, preferably first class sound-proof rooms, restaurant tables in pre-selected eateries, check flight schedules, book train tickets with sleeping accommodations, and then cancel everything a half hour later just to re-book everything with an alternate itinerary.

As irritating as these meetings could be, in retrospect, I enjoyed the entertaining side of it all. Asked to place a long distance call for one of the visitors, I would notify the caller in the boardroom that his party was on the line. Many times the caller then played dumb by faking surprise and saying, "Who the heck is calling me now? I'm in a meeting here guys." Most of the time the conversation that followed was not of an important nature and usually had the purpose of showing off by telling someone that the caller was presiding at a very important business meeting in Milano.

Sometimes the atmosphere in the boardroom would get really heated. Voices would get louder and a punch or two on the desk could also be heard. One or the other would get up and walk nervously back and forth while someone else would torture his jaws by furiously chewing gum. One at a time, the men would each take his place in front of a wall covered with charts and statistics where they pointed to their respective figures with a long stick lit at its tip. It reminded me of the many old American war films where a colonel or general would invariably use a similar stick to indicate strategic positions and attack plans. Ever-present Hollywood was at work again.

Towards one o'clock in the afternoon, they would pause for lunch, ordering sandwiches, beer, Coca-Cola or mineral water. They then continued their agenda till about four o'clock when suddenly, they all remembered their flights or train departures. They would leave with hurried steps through the heavy glass door. Dense clouds of smoke followed them. Sweating, hoarse voices, reddened eyes and loose ties, also were part of their departure. Some even exited without shoes, hopping on one leg while trying to slip into them. They were, or just looked, exhausted from their heroic executive battle and decision-making ordeal. There was one who hurriedly grabbed the wrong raincoat; the coats were all the same, almost. There was one who couldn't find his briefcase and another who checked his air ticket without reading the imprints. It was time to call the cabs, hoping that no one forgot to leave one last important recommendation or jot down somebody's address for a possible future use.

The most important activity had reached its conclusion. Now came the secretary's turn to clean up. Wipe the spills from the board table, keep or toss bits and pieces of scribbled paper, empty ashtrays with cigarette butts and chewing gum and then disinfect the room with a good deodorant. At the end, both Angie and I had piles of notes to type, with copies to each of the participants to the meeting. Hardly did they all agree on the various points discussed, making it necessary to call a new meeting with the "big boys," and so forth. More words, different statistics, more sandwiches, typed reports and deodorants.

In the meantime, Gil was taking his first steps as Field Service Manager. Despite his training in the United States, he seemed insecure. Not yet experienced in the ways of the "big boys," he was too soft with everybody, which was nice for the employees' sake but definitely not for himself. I hoped that he would toughen up with time, because I liked his straightforward, honest and very human approach to everything and everybody and wouldn't want to see him replaced. Regrettably, not everyone shared my opinion. Angie for example, even though she found him to be handsome, thought of him as not being a real man. By that, she meant that he wasn't the type she would consider to hop in the hay with. She preferred the more virile, aggressive types. Gil was the total opposite. Of medium height, brown hair and expressive chestnut brown eyes, he always displayed a friendly smile. He was also very timid and blushed very easily.

In the meantime, the parts department acquired a more important status within the organization. Now the U.S. Headquarters required periodical inventory controls and I was happy to be in charge and do a good job. Things, however, could possibly not run without an obstacle for too long.

The smooth sailing at work was interrupted by Peter's flu. Several of his little schoolmates had the same problem and that meant that the mothers had to stay home and nurse the little ones back to health. During my absence, Angie would help out with mostly the urgent cases. The only problem was that she would do things her own way, ignoring what the Manual of Operations specified. She figured that there was no time to waste with insignificant minor details. One item, more or less, couldn't make that much of a difference. Besides, she had enough on her own plate. Two tasks can always be done well, almost simultaneously. More than two, always turned out to be a mess, no matter how young, how bright and how efficient a multi-tasker was.

Once the parts department was again totally re-organized, and I had time to spare, I offered a hand to Angie with the typing and other clerical work that was piling up. No matter how fast we both worked, however, Angie's work seemed to increase more every day. While the number of technicians and the consequent clerical workload increased almost three times, the number of secretaries remained the same and so was the excuse: "The available budget did not foresee any new hiring for the next two years." We girls couldn't but put our hearts at rest and pitch in with renewed energy. Not even Gil was in the position of doing something about it as any major decision was to be submitted to Carlo in Geneva, who evidently denied the request. It was expected.

Luckily, Gil was made of a different clay altogether. He understood when Angie and I were swamped, and took upon himself the task of taking phone calls or making his own. After all, it did not take an engineer's degree to dial a number. Without disturbing us, he would also look for a given document on his own and then put back everything where it belonged. His behavior was soon noticed by many others and suddenly, he became everybody's favorite boss, deserving more attention and collaboration. Needless to say, jealousy on the part of his colleagues soon built up and he was often criticized for his excessive democratic ways of dealing with his underlings.

One day, Carlo Piotti paid an unexpected visit to the Milano office. Among other things, he seemed very interested in the parts department and of the new improved changes that had been introduced. When he noticed that no one else was around, he decided to share his ideas with me.

"I know that you are a very capable woman and I would like to turn you into a manager. Not only would you still be in charge of Logistics here in Milano, but you would also have to travel and check that all other parts departments of the various branches are well maintained. You would also have to participate at the various meetings, here and abroad and travel as far as the United States." His voice was very authoritative.

For a moment, I did not know what to think about his proposal and did my best not to betray any possible emotion.

"See, my colleagues can't see a woman filling that position because they don't find them reliable enough. But I told them that I would guarantee for you and I am sure that you would not let me down, right?"

I was still too surprised to say a word.

"Of course, it is entirely up to you to decide whether to accept it or not; to see if your family situation would allow you to take on such a great responsibility because it is obvious, that with all the traveling involved and pre-scheduled meetings, you cannot suddenly forfeit your obligations because the children are sick."

I briefly flirted with the idea of becoming a manager, of occupying an important position and having the privilege, like Mefisto, of travelling unhindered. It could well be a unique opportunity and I was certain of being more than capable in carrying out that task, but reality stopped my daydreaming. What would happen to the children? Who would take care of them? Besides, I did not want to be separated from them either. It was bad enough that I only had those few hours in the evening to play with them and thanks heaven, most of the weekends. No, I did not want to become a career woman, to climb the corporate ladder, not anymore. Besides, Carlo's mischievous beady eyes forced me to reflect even more carefully. How often throughout my working experiences, was I made to believe that I would achieve important positions if I just gave it enough time, patience and hard work? The irony of it all was that my salary would remain the same, not to create ill feelings among the other very competent co-workers. Carlo must have noticed my hesitation.

"At any rate, there is still time to think about it," he said. "I give you a couple of months to get organized and once you have reached a decision, we will sit down and iron out the details."

With the arrival of the year-end holidays, I managed to miraculously find a temporary daycare for little Nakina. It was a few blocks further down from the kindergarten, a little more walking in the morning and the evening. I also had to get up earlier to clean and feed both kids and then walk each one to their destination. Not only did our finances not foresee a second car, but neither was there enough parking in our neighborhood. I had to take a cab, a streetcar—mostly always packed as a cattle wagon—or use good old footwork. Tormented by the fear of being late to work, I often took a cab in the morning with obvious negative financial consequences at the end of the month. Then at the office, I was tormented by the thought of being called at any time by the kindergarten or the daycare, requesting that I pick up one or the other because of a fever, a tummy ache, a strike or a bomb threat at the school. At the end of the day, I was terrified at the thought of getting stuck in traffic and not being on time to pick up Nakina. Most daycare employees were courteous, very professional and likewise emotionally sterile. Punctuality in the pick up of the children was critical, if one was to avoid the annoyed, angry reaction of the supervisor.

With Nakina on my side, I would go pick up Peter from Gina's place and then it was back at home, getting ready for the second shift of my day. Prepare dinner, wash the kids and the darn white smocks the kids had to wear—I never understood the practicality of dressing little kids, who love dirt and paint, in white outfits—fix a ripped pocket or attach a missing button. Then finally sit down and have dinner, play or watch a little TV and away into the hay because the night was short and soon another full day of activities and anguish would knock on the door.

Worries seemed to be my daily companions, especially during the colder season when sniffles and bronchitis were a constant occurrence among the children, to be invariably treated with antibiotic suppositories. There were days when I just wished to stay home and take care of the kids, like my mother did, but Mefisto's income was still not enough to cover our expenses in a city like Milano and therefore, a second income was paramount. What a world, what a life. There was nothing but work, work, work, or so it appeared.

For a while, I followed a very irregular lifestyle. Skipping meals to make up for the times I had to leave earlier; smoking a full pack of cigarettes per day and during the cold winter days, enjoying an invigorating espresso laced with a good cognac before going up to the office in the morning. It would give me that necessary boost to get my energy and enthusiasm into proper gear, but I realized soon enough, that I would not be able to carry on for much longer and decided to confide in Gil by asking him to allow me to work part time for a few months. Since he would have to ask Carlo about this issue, I also asked him to inform Carlo that I would not be able to accept his generous managerial offer. Gil didn't bother to ask what that position was.

I also realized that the part-time arrangement was not a very good idea because the workload had not only doubled, but would create administrative problems and unnecessary precedents. Considering my past history with the company, however, they agreed, very exceptionally, to allow me to work part-time. Yet the problems never ceased to materialize. One of these were the school holidays and with it the question, what to do with the kids. The kindergarten actually had what was called a summer camp, within the school premises. They would build little tents to pretend they were camping somewhere. I registered both children but did not allow them to take day trips to any other destination. I was never comfortable with the idea of having them traveling with strangers.

The summer camp arrangement was a good one because no employer on earth would put up with a three-month absence by one of their key employees. In the meantime, work at the office increased and I felt more and more tired. I was physically and mentally close to a collapse. I often found myself sobbing for no particular reason. I mentioned the fact to our family doctor who was of the opinion that I was close to a nervous breakdown and needed some time out. Even Mefisto recognized that I should quit as soon as possible. We would have to tighten our belts for a while and hope that things would work out for the future.

I therefore submitted my resignation and throughout the notice period helped in the search for a replacement. I was told to possibly point to a male this time around as they had a lot less problems with working schedules than females with children. A few days later, I interviewed a young man who had placed an ad in the paper. He spoke good English and was familiar with the mysteries of spare parts. He had worked in the spare parts department of a large jewellery store, where he also repaired clocks and watches. Gil seemed to like him and found him to be intelligent and motivated, but the final decision in hiring Mario was not his. Other experts, including Carlo, did not consider him to be the right candidate for the position and more money was spent searching for the right candidate. At the end, the choice fell on Mario, after all.

I was happy for Mario. Carlo Piotti approached him with the same proposal he had offered me not long ago. The only difference was that Mario being a male was not offered the salary of a simple secretary!

I introduced Mario to the various details of the department. Luckily, not only was he a fast learner, but had the good habit of making notes and reading everything. In a few weeks, he would also travel to the United States to be trained in the American Logistics system and then implement it in Milano and all the other branches. With that, my task was ended. I left behind some good and a few bad memories, along with a wonderful bunch of people whose friendship I would cherish for many years to come.

In the meantime, I was supposed to take it easy and relax. Our family physician, Dr. Porta, had prescribed me Vitamin B12 injections, pills for a stomach ulcer, a tranquilizer and much rest. I followed the instructions carefully and was soon ready to open yet another chapter in my work experiences.

17

Recanati and Porto Recanati

"I have great news for you," Mefisto said one evening, very excited. "I received a job offer as sales rep for a new company in Castelfidardo. I've known the partners for some time now and they all seem to be serious, hard-working professionals. The pay is also a lot more than what I am earning now. I'll have to go down there to check things out."

"And whereabouts is this Castelfidardo?" I asked.

"It is a township near Ancona, half way down Italy's Adriatic coast. I'm sure you would love it there."

Mefisto then drove to Castelfidardo to complete his business negotiations and to find a suitable place for the entire family to live. His description of our new surroundings, in addition to his enthusiasm for the new job was so great, that I ended up relinquishing any reservations about the new relocation plan.

We moved to a three-bedroom apartment on the third and last floor of a fairly new building located in a small town named Recanati, with some 18,000 inhabitants at the time. The ancient city, founded around 1150, situated on the crest of a hill, was surrounded by undulating valleys, much of it used as farmland and vineyards. Cobblestoned narrow streets led up to the town's main piazza, the City Hall, schools, stores and to the house of one of Italy's favorite poets, the great Giacomo Leopardi.

From the front terrace of the apartment, I could see the Adriatic Ocean in the distance and the vast extension of the luxuriant countryside. Up until then, we had lived only in large cities. This small community town would be an entirely new experience. My first priority upon arrival was to place the kids in school and I was able to register both under the same roof, in the corresponding classes. Contrary to my apprehension, it did not take them long to make friends among their peers and also the teachers were extremely helpful in putting them at ease within the new environment. Initially, I would accompany them every morning and pick them up in the afternoon. While the kids were at school, I could peacefully unpack our belongings and organize everything so that the apartment would soon look and feel like a beautiful, cozy home again.

There were no large supermarkets in the area, but several medium-sized mini- markets that catered to the local gastronomic requirements. Fruits and vegetables were mostly local produce. Fish and seafood, in general, was always fresh and cheap. Baked goods were also produced locally. Wine and beer were available in all grocery stores. Food was never going to be a problem.

Job possibilities, however, were a totally different issue in that part of the country. I sent my résumé to a number of large companies in the city and seaport of Ancona. At the time, Ancona had an approximate population of 90,000 souls. The region is known worldwide for the Fabriano brand paper, manufactured in the township of Fabriano and used mainly in artwork. It is also famous for the manufacturing of fine musical instruments, a rooted tradition in the townships of Castelfidardo and Osimo. Not to neglect the good heart medicine, Ancona produced fine wines such as the *Rosso Conero*, a red jewel grown among the hills of Monte Conero and a white, *Verdicchio*, grown on the hillsides between the Adriatic sea and the Appenine chain.

Apparently, there was no need for a full-time secretary anywhere or perhaps they were afraid to pay a high salary for such an experienced individual and preferred to pass. I was frustrated and downhearted. Finally one day, through Mefisto's business connections, I came to know a manufacturer of fine pewter objects who was setting up a small office above the lab and design studio. Giorgio Miletti and his two artisan partners needed someone to act as secretary / receptionist, and welcomed the idea that I could write promotional letters in English and send them, with attached photographs of some of their articles, to possible clients abroad. The job site was at a discreet walking distance from home.

During the first months I was quite busy organizing the administrative aspect of the new office, collecting data, opening files and answering the phone. Once I had completed my main task, all I could do was hope to receive replies from at least some of the prospective customers. A much wider publicity campaign, with a professional brochure presentation, would have been a better promotional tool as well as a follow-up phone call or even a visit in person to the client, but there were financial restrictions to the owner's budget. Since there was barely anything else to do besides typing three or four invoices per day, work hours dwindled down to just a few.

I now had more time to play with the kids after they returned from school. Peter was always pretty fast in doing his homework. He spent considerable time drawing and painting his artwork before sitting in front of the TV or going down to play with his friends. Nakina instead, was an adorable slow poke, who had a hell of a time dealing with arithmetic problems. Her teacher, who adored her because of her friendly, generous character, justified her lagging behind by saying that "she is just a little late bloomer." After having finished their homework, both Peter and Nakina were allowed to go outside to play with their friends, mostly schoolmates who also lived in the surrounding areas. Once back upstairs, they would watch cartoons on TV, then have dinner, play some more in their bedroom, and finally prepare to hit the pillows.

Mefisto was very happy with his new job. He was earning well and travelled constantly to other European countries, to the Far and Middle East, Australia and Canada. It was during that point in time that I, taken over by an inspirational wave, began to write. I wrote poems and fictional stories of all kinds. I could not stop the outpouring of ideas and often worked till the wee hours in the morning, filling the third bedroom, which acted as my studio, with the bluish, acrid smoke of cigarettes.

Summertime had arrived; the kids were off school and I had my work time reduced to a couple of hours per week because the company had to downsize their activities. Their budget no longer allowed for a secretary. It would have been nice to take the car and drive down to the beach in Porto Recanati, but I had no driver's license and was unable to use the parked car in the garage. It was then, that at age thirty-seven, I finally decided to take driving lessons. When Mefisto returned from his trip, I asked him to give me some driving instructions, which he did. It was definitely not easy for me. I had serious trouble with the footwork on the clutch and the accelerator, especially when restarting on a hilltop with the stick-shifted Ford Fiesta. I feared the car would roll backwards and hit something or somebody or that the engine would just simply die on me, perhaps halfway up a steep hill, which was mostly the case in many old villages. In order to get an official permit, I had to go to an authorized driving school and attend at least ten lessons, both theory and road practice. My instructor wasn't the most understanding or patient person as he slapped my hand whenever I forgot an instruction or did an incorrect manoeuvre. Weeks later, with a pounding heart, I showed up at the testing appointment. I got a perfect score on my written test and fortunately, also passed the road test. I was jubilant. I had finally conquered the terror of driving and felt like a totally new person. I could now move around freely also in Mefisto's absence. The best part was driving down the winding road—lined on both sides by almond trees—towards Porto

Recanati and passing by the Villa of the great tenor Beniamino Gigli. It was an extremely pleasant drive and the kids were always excited in going to the beach to build sand castles, splish-splash in the water, eat a slice of foccaccia or get some gelato before driving back home.

Mefisto's return from a long business trip was always a great event. The kids were especially excited because he always brought them gifts and souvenirs and a beautiful dinner followed in one of the many fabulous restaurants along the beach promenade. Life was good, even if at times marred by a great emotional turmoil on both sides. I missed Mefisto who spent more time on the road than at home. He instead had troubles of his own, battling a period of physical and emotional instability for which he sought the help of a psychologist. It was entirely up to him, however, to fight whatever demons were at work in his mind and body. I couldn't but speculate about his behavior and certain reactions. Perhaps it was connected to his prostate and other related problems. Having always been a free-spirited, independent person, he certainly enjoyed the freedom while traveling all over the world. Maybe he had a fling somewhere—he always forgot to slip back the wedding band on his return. Maybe he was confused. It was hard to tell. I often wondered what my move would have been, had he decided to choose freedom and leave me and the kids behind. The only people I could count on, for whatever reason and at any time, were my parents. Time, however, is notorious for healing human afflictions and time came to our rescue once again.

"Why don't we move down to Porto Recanati, closer to the beach?" Mefisto suggested a year later.

"Oh, gosh, this would be our fourth move, you know? I'll have to pack again, hire movers, then unpack..." I mentally collected all of our belongings.

"Don't worry about it. Just think of the beach and the nice surroundings instead."

We found a beautiful three-bedroom, two bathroom apartment on the ground floor of a four-storey townhouse some 300 feet from the beach. Each bedroom, as well as the living room and the kitchen, had its own terrace. All floors had beautiful ceramic tiles. The kids were delighted, for each had a beautifully decorated, separate bedroom.

Porto Recanati is a holiday resort town with approximately 9 kilometres of beautiful, white sandy beaches. Grocery stores offered locally grown fresh produce, fruits and seafood. The cuisine of the Marche region is traditionally of peasant origin; therefore, much use is made of natural, wild ingredients such as mushrooms, especially the Porcini type, nuts, field herbs and the extremely loved and expensive truffles.

Whenever Mefisto was in town, we would eat out in one of the many fine restaurants of the area. *Il Brodetto* was one of our favorites and was famous for its hearty fish soup. Peter's favorite was a typical Sicilian restaurant named *Al Fico d'India* in the neighboring township of Civitanova Marche. He was especially fond of their rich buffet. He would start with a heaped plate of appetizers, followed by a generous portion of roasted rack of lamb, maybe even go back for seconds and finish with a nice slice of chocolate cake. Half an inch of red wine was also permitted to go with all that regal food. Both, Mefisto and I often wondered where that little, thin, eight-year-old stashed all that food. It was always a real pleasure to watch him enjoying every mouthful. Nakina did also enjoy good food but her eyes were always bigger than the capacity of her stomach and there were invariably many leftovers returned to the kitchen, for which she was always reprimanded. To finish the evening, we would stroll along the beach promenade and later drive up to Numana for an ice cream cone for the kids and a Petrus Boonekamp for the adults.

Once again, the kids did not seem to have had trouble adjusting to a new school and quickly built new friendships. Peter enrolled in a local soccer team and had dreams of becoming a future Juventus champion. Aside from the regular school curriculum, Peter also had to attend catechism lessons to be prepared to receive his first communion. He had skipped a couple of sessions and the priest in charge decided to reprimand both the child and the mother for their spiritual negligence. I did not make much of it as I had different ideas about the ritual but decided not to argue with the priest. I figured that Peter still had much growing up to do, intellectually and emotionally, before he would fully understand the communion ritual. From my viewpoint, it was nothing but a reason to throw a big party with nice outfits, lots of sweets and gifts. Most kids of their age did not really grasp the concept of "body of Christ" and the symbolism that involved blood, flesh and the tasty white wafer. It was a difficult concept even for grown-ups at times, let alone eight-year-olds who cared mainly about the goodies to eat and the presents to play with.

My parents, who had left Brazil years before and had moved back to the Black Forest area in Germany, visited often during summer holidays and so did my brother, Frank, who at the time lived in Montreal. He very much enjoyed his short stay in Porto Recanati but was even fonder of his new adoptive land, Canada. He constantly praised that country for giving him the opportunity to study and become a respected nuclear physicist. Whenever there was a chance, he would not fail in trying to convince us to follow his example. Mefisto, however, had other ideas germinating in his mind. His incorrigible wanderlust began to flirt with the possibility of moving to Germany, but far from my parents. The simple hint of yet another move terrified me. Ever since

I joined Mefisto, life had been a continuum of transitory episodes. Moving around like gypsies and losing much money in the process by having to leave behind possessions of minor and major entity. I had the gut feeling that he would not last long in Germany either.

"I do not understand why you do not want to move to Germany," Mefisto said. "Because you don't even speak the language, neither do the kids; it would be too much of a change for them. Besides, remember the clear distinction between the native German and "der Italiener.""

"Oh, you always make things worse than they are," he said.

I simply couldn't picture the restless, free-spirited man adapting to an extremely disciplined society. Yet the need for change in Mefisto's mind became ever more pressing. His heels were tickling again.

"If we have to move at all costs, then let's make it a big move, not just jumping into a neighboring country," I said one day. "Let's consider Australia or even Canada."

Even though I flirted with the possibility of moving back into a warm country, such as Australia, I had to consider the distances between that country and Germany or Canada. How would my relatives come visit that far or when, if ever, would I be able to visit them? Besides, in Australia they drove on the wrong side of the street. It would take me ages to adjust to that new system. What about Canada, at least there I had a contact person who could act as sponsor and eventually help us with a possible job. Mefisto considered my argument and decided that it was a good idea. We started gathering information and applied to the Canadian Embassy in Rome. Needless to say, my parents were saddened because they would have a lesser chance to see their grandchildren grow up. On the other hand, they were happy at the idea that the siblings, Frank and I, would be close to each other.

We were invited for an interview at the Canadian Embassy in Rome. We handed in our résumés, filled more forms and chatted with a very friendly interviewer who seemed pleased with our proficiency of the English language. Mefisto also spoke French fluently. In those days, it was expected that the applicants had a good working knowledge of at least one of the country's two official languages. It was also necessary to prove that one had a job lined up, or had a sponsor, or sufficient cash to take care of one's needs without burdening the Canadian welfare or social services systems. After all, to be accepted as an immigrant in any foreign country should be considered a privilege and the rules and requirements of the host country, respected and complied with and not the other way around. We received our Visas within three months.

Both Peter and Nakina were not too enthused about moving again. To leave their friends and familiar surroundings was almost traumatic. As usual, it was up to me to relieve such trauma by telling them about the many beautiful things they would experience in Canada. Knowing how much they enjoyed snow whenever we traveled through the Swiss Alps on the way to Germany to visit the grandparents, I told them how much more snow they would find in Canada because the winter was longer. I also told them about the beautiful, big white Polar Bears and their cubs and real Indian chiefs riding beautiful brown horses with white spots. Slowly, their interest grew stronger and I felt a little less guilty for uprooting them once again.

I spent time with the kids, trying to teach them some Basic English words and phrases. The lessons always started out very seriously and their attention span was superb for the initial fifteen to twenty minutes. Thereafter, their concentration degenerated into giggles and jokes, angering me because I knew how difficult it could be to fit into a new society without knowing at least the language.

"Oh, don't make such a big fuss out of it," Mefisto observed, minimizing my concerns. "They'll learn once they are over there."

He always accused me of exaggerating situations. Maybe he was right, it was never he who had to ultimately deal with the various issues.

All wheels, emotional and psychological, were set in motion on a way of no return. Consequently, I began ordering appropriate wooden crates and started packing as much as possible. Unfortunately, the cost to ship furniture, bicycles and the car would have been prohibitive and therefore such items as well as other chattel had to be sold below cost or simply given away because people in that area did not believe in second-hand merchandise. It broke my heart to see our wonderful dining set, bedroom set and living room furniture being hauled away, but Mefisto consoled me by saying that we would get much better things in Canada. Again, I believed and dried up my tears.

We took one last trip to the North and to Germany to say goodbye to parents and relatives, leaving behind rivers of tears and aching hearts masked by forced smiles of contentment.

The car was the last item to be delivered back to the dealership. A cab took us to the small train station. Tears blurred my eyes as the train slowly picked up speed, running through the familiar landscapes with destination Rome. From the Stazione Termini in Rome, we took a cab to our hotel. We enjoyed a last dinner in a good Roman Trattoria, had one more look at the Fontana di Trevi and tossed a coin into its waters for good luck, and then returned to the hotel for a good night's sleep. Early the next morning, a limousine took us to the Fiumicino Airport where we boarded an Alitalia jumbo jet with destination Montreal, Canada.

The flight had been a long, tiring yet pleasant one. We landed in Montreal on March 4, 1981. The politeness and warm welcome to Canada by a customs officer relieved all the tension and tiredness in having to wait in a long immigrant's lineup.

"And what do you folks have to declare?" the officer asked. I handed him neatly typed pages of our belongings, marked by the number shown on the crates that would arrive at a later date. The officer looked through the list, stamped it and kept it for his file. He seemed satisfied and dismissed us with a friendly, "Good luck."

We had finally made it. We took a cab to the hotel which Mefisto had booked ahead of time. We refreshed, stretched out on the beds for an hour, then changed our outfits and went strolling in the downtown core. Having left behind small cities, the kids and I were impressed by the many skyscrapers that towered over us, making us feel infinitely small.

Later that evening, we decided to treat ourselves to a nice dinner. While waiting in a lounge to be seated, the conversation fell onto music. Which music was whose favorite? There was the subdued sound of classical music in the background to which Peter observed loud and clear: "You know what? I still prefer Mozart. Mozart is my favorite and is the very best in my opinion." It was an unexpected remark coming from an eleven-year-old that made even the other waiting customers turn and smile with delight, even though he was speaking in Italian. Nakina, naturally, had to add her two cents to her brother's comment by saying, "And you know what? I love Mozart very much myself."

Soon after, the hostess came to escort us to our table. Once we had ordered drinks and chosen the meals, we sat back and relaxed. Peter's eyes darted in every direction and made his observations known to whoever was willing to listen.

"Papi, how come all these people are whispering?" he asked. Used to the loud, happy chatter of Italian restaurants, he wondered what was wrong with the one we had chosen to eat in.

"Well, in some places it is not polite to speak too loud," I said. "But I'm sure that if you went to an Italian restaurant or pizzeria here in Montreal, you would find lots of happy people who do not mind to share their happiness with others."

The appetizers were served and soon Peter's mouth became silent. Occasionally, during the course of his meal, he continued to point out a number of differences.

"I don't know why they are using candles in here," he said. "It is so hard to see what the food looks like."

"Maybe the bulbs are burnt out," Nakina suggested very matter-of-factly.

Darkness or not, they both cleaned up their plates to the last morsel and finished with a generous slice of chocolate cake. Before returning to the hotel, we walked a little bit around, checking out window shops.

The next day, Mefisto called upon a business contact he had in town and arranged a meeting to which he also took me and the kids. He used to sell them musical Instruments. They were pleased to meet with him and spent some time telling each other about news and changes in their business. Later that day, I called my brother in Vancouver, British Columbia, telling him about our arrival in Canada and the flight schedule to Vancouver. Frank was very excited and said that he could hardly wait to pick us up at the Vancouver airport.

18

Vancouver, British Columbia

The flight to Vancouver was pleasant and short in comparison to the one from Rome. Along with his longtime girlfriend, Therese, Frank was impatiently waiting at the gates. We hadn't seen each other for about two years. Hugs, kisses, and a few tears crowned the event. On our behalf, Frank had rented the only available apartment at the time in the same building he lived in and on the same second floor. He lived only two doors further down the hall. It was a one-bedroom, living-dining room; small kitchenette and bathroom apartment that had to suffice until such time the new immigrants could find something bigger and better. Therese had spent her weekends painting and cleaning the apartment. Frank and Therese purchased twin beds for us and a pair of flip-flop floor chair/beds for the kids. They also got us a round table and four chairs. As an extra gift, Frank gave me a ceramic coffee table lamp in the form of a pineapple with a cream colored hat. It all matched beautifully and I was grateful for the effort and thoughtfulness they had put into welcoming us. East 2nd Avenue was close to Commercial Drive, at the time populated by Italian nationals. It felt like we had never left Italy and it made the transition so much easier.

Once again, it was my priority to find a proper school for the kids. They were assigned one by the local school board. They were both placed in a special ESL (English as Secondary Language) classroom along with many other recent immigrants of various backgrounds. To reassure the kids with a familiar presence, one parent was allowed into the classroom, to stand or sit beside the kids and in my case, help translate what was said from teacher to student and vice-versa. It was a lot of pointing towards a figure on the blackboard and repeating the words clearly pronounced by the teacher. Two weeks later, I did not have to stay in the classroom any longer. I just dropped them off and then picked them up after school. One month later, they were confident enough to take the bus by themselves, back and forth. It was incredible how fast the kids picked up the English language and I was so proud of both.

On the weekends, Frank and Therese would drive us around to show us the many beautiful and noteworthy spots Vancouver had to offer. Snow-covered mountains, white sandy beaches and emerald-green lakes surrounded by luxuriant vegetation were truly the most beautiful British Columbia. What clashed with all the beautiful scenery, however, and shocked me quite a bit, was the sight of drunken natives, zigzagging across streets or sleeping in a puddle of their own excretions on a piece of lawn or sidewalk. What had happened to that proud, magnificent race of warriors? I wondered with sadness.

Contrary to Mefisto's expectations, Frank could not help us in the job search because he was unable to see how Mefisto could fit into his nuclear research facility, as they did not require sales people. Likewise, he was unable to find an opening for me in the secretarial field due to my lack of experience of the Canadian system. We were on our own. As usual, I not only sent out copies of my résumé, but also replied to countless ads in the local newspapers.

…Secretary required for major Import/Export Company. Must be outgoing, experienced, bi-lingual and capable of working with minimum supervision. $10.00/hr…

…order processing, clerical work, typing and most importantly customer contact along with scheduling and dispatch of Field Service Technicians. Tact and diplomacy to ensure effective customer relations…

…Cercasi segretaria bilingue, Inglese / Italiano. Per informazioni telefonare a …

…full-time position. Ability to correspond in German required. Good Salary…

Many employers would not even bother to reply. Probably because of the enormous quantity of mail received, but a handful of nice people took time in justifying their decisions.

"…your résumé will be reviewed in competition with others and given due consideration for present and future vacancies. Re-apply with new application if you have not been contacted for an interview during this time. Thank you for your interest in our company…"

"…after careful review of your background we have concluded that we will be unable to offer a position to you at this time. Our decision is based on a comparative review of several applicants and in no way reflects upon your experience or work record…"

"...*we have, unfortunately had to screen out a number of applicants immediately due to the large response received at this time. Your background and experience is excellent; however, we have decided to have a junior person and train them to meet our needs. However, we would be pleased to keep your resume' on file in the event, a more suitable position becomes available. In the meantime, we wish you luck in finding a suitable position and thank you for your interest in....*"

Some Human Resources managers took the time to personally give me a phone call to let me know that one of the reasons they had to pass my application was that I lacked Canadian experience. I could definitely not argue with that. I really had no practical experience in a typical Canadian environment but then again, how could I gain such experience if I was not offered the opportunity to do so?

I decided to place an ad in the paper for myself and Mefisto. A few days later, we received a phone call from a Roger Wilson, who immediately arranged for a business meeting between the parties. He showed up with his pretty girlfriend, Lisa, who was apparently an active partner in the enterprise. Roger did most of the talking and he was a smooth talker indeed. He described to us the many miraculous and high quality products we were to promote and distribute. We were not to disclose the name of the manufacturer till the very end of the presentation. I found it rather odd, but accepted it as perhaps a typical North American business strategy.

Roger and Lisa invited us to a special presentation in New Westminster. The show was indeed a masterpiece of modern marketing. While Roger illustrated, Lisa demonstrated the different products: soaps, detergents, vitamins, cosmetics, etc., and how they worked. We were deeply impressed with the participating crowd of witnesses of the successful enterprise by sharing with the newcomers their success stories and the apparent wealth they had accumulated. Most of them wore expensive designer clothes and shoes and drove typically showy American luxury cars. Cadillacs seemed to be the favorite to highlight their status quo.

Roger and Lisa convinced us to invest in a starter kit of an approximate value of $200. In the meantime, Mefisto began hearing contradictory statements about the company and decided to dedicate his time to a real job hunting expedition. Only I decided to continue for another little while and sold about $100 worth of materials thanks to the compassion of a handful of friends and neighbors. The products were far too expensive and the few people who were willing enough to listen to the sales pitch and the possibility of becoming rich by recruiting more people, preferred not to give up their day job for what they considered a somewhat shady pyramid operation. It was indeed a very popular business proposition in the mid-1980s.

It did not take us too long to realize that not only was it difficult, if at all possible, to make a living from that operation, especially being new to the country and lacking business contacts, but we could not even recuperate the money we had invested in phone bills, transportation expenses and promotional campaigns and materials. Roger and Lisa were deeply disappointed when also I finally called it quits.

Mefisto was the first one to come home one day with positive good news.

"Guess what? I just landed a job with a small ceramic tile distributor in downtown Vancouver. They are an Italian family and Nestore, the boss, was looking for a sales person."

"Well, congratulations," I said with a great sense of relief. "This calls for a toast."

"And guess what else, I told him about you, that you were job hunting, too, and he said to bring you along and he would see what he could do for you as well."

"Wow, this is more than a good reason for a double toast," I said, extremely happy and heading to the kitchen to pull out the wine glasses.

A new chapter was to begin and I was eagerly looking forward to it.

19

Tile Styles

Tile Styles was a family operation: wife, husband and two sons. Nestore was an Italian who, after many struggles, landed in Canada in the early 1970s and started distributing ceramic tiles, slowly developing a more custom-oriented product by creating specially designed patterns in custom colors, fired onto regular plain tiles.

Nestore was a tall man in his fifties, with some gray strands weaving through his hair. He had two bright, inquisitive brown eyes and a modest smile on his lips. His wife, Regina, about the same age, was of medium height, also showing a few greyish strands in her hair, and had the most gorgeous smiling blue eyes. She dressed elegantly and her manners revealed a refined background. Miki was their oldest son, very handsome with dark brown curly hair and brown eyes. Kyle was the younger son, very shy, quiet and serious. Then there was Vera, the loyal accountant/bookkeeper, also Italian, who had been with the company from its inception. Nestore and Regina gave me the tour of the premises, which were fairly big, especially the warehouse on the second floor where they had two large kilns and a small lab for the glaze mixing. A small enclosure served as office to their trusted installer, Romeo Costanzo. He had a permanent smile stamped on his face, even though his attention was totally absorbed by his job pricing calculations. Then there was a small section where the silk-screens were prepared and kept and where the actual silk-screening process took place. I was to learn all about this new line of activity as the company already had a secretary but could use additional help in the tile-printing department. I was hired that same day.

In the following weeks, I worked closely with Regina, who happened to be the artist behind the countless beautiful patterns that were created and printed onto ceramic tiles. Regina had extremely good taste for forms and colors and she was definitely proud of her accomplishments. She was very demanding of herself and also of those around her. A true perfectionist, she would toil with the colors till she obtained the exact color shade requested by her client. She loved challenges to the point of obsession and could become very fussy at times, which often created a little tension among the other co-workers.

The crates with our belongings had finally arrived, but their contents would not fit into that small apartment. We had to hustle and quickly find larger premises, which we did, not too far from East 2nd Avenue, in the above-ground basement of a two-storey wooden bungalow. Luckily, Mefisto's business arrangement with Nestore included a company car, a Toyota station wagon, and so the moving process became a little easier. He could also give a ride to the kids by driving them to school in the morning and whenever possible, pick them up in the afternoon. I took the bus to work. Unlike in Milano, people in Vancouver stood in neat lines and boarded the bus in orderly fashion, without pushing, pulling, shoving and cursing.

I was learning a whole lot of new things at work. Both Miki and Kyle taught me how to strip a silk screen from an old peeling pattern, clean it to perfection and then re-coat it for another pattern to be photographed onto it. Kyle showed me how the finished screen was fastened onto a framework with screw hinges, filled with glaze, which by means of a squeegee was pressed through the patterned screen onto the tile underneath. The printed tiles were placed into the slots of appropriate racks and then placed in the kiln to be fired at a given temperature. It was always a challenge at the beginning to figure out the correct temperature for the different bisques, to obtain a particular color to match exactly an existing Crane or American standard fixture. It was up to Regina and me to fiddle around with the measuring of glazes and repeat the experiment till Regina was totally satisfied. It was a tedious process and yet so gratifying when the designer or the client thanked profusely for a job well done.

I got to appreciate every nuance of my new, creative occupation and was always eager to go to work in the morning. Regina enjoyed seeing my bright, happy face and we both liked to chat about each other's life stories. It turned out that Regina and Nestore had also lived in Brazil for a number of years where they picked up the know-how of the tile-making business. Coincidentally, they had lived in the same part of town in São Paulo, Sumaré, where also my uncle had lived. Maybe we had even walked by each other back then, without knowing that perhaps one day, destiny would bring us together in Vancouver, Canada. Regina was also a polyglot and enjoyed chatting with me in the known languages, especially in Portuguese. Whoever once lived in Brazil was inevitably affected by what the Brazilians call *saudade* (longing for, missing something or everything, Brazilian). The sound of the spoken

Portuguese was like a caress to my memory bank of all things Brazilian. Miki, Kyle, as well as Nestore, also liked to speak to me in Portuguese or Italian.

The company grew constantly. Orders poured in and I had fun beating previous records of silk-screened piecework. At the time, it was all done manually because the company's budget did not yet allow for sophisticated machinery. There were times when for one reason or another, a certain color batch did not come out as expected. How did it happen? Was it due to an incorrect glaze mixture? One only tiny gram, more or less, of a given color could result in a variation and cause trouble or, it could have been an incorrect kiln temperature setting. Nestore then vented his anger at no one in particular, but the yelling seemed to alleviate his tension. There was unfortunately, nothing much anyone could do but restart the job and hope it came out correctly the second time around.

To facilitate the re-ordering process of a specified color, I created a recording system indicating the composition of each color in grams, the project it had been used for and on which type of tile it had been fired into. The different samples were stored in small jars with coded labels. The same code numbers were also applied to the various printed tile samples, which I kept in cardboard boxes in alphabetical order for easy reference. It was a time-consuming process that proved to be a good system in the long run.

There were days meant to be hectic, especially when all members of the family decided that their special order or project of the day deserved precedence over the others. Chaos normally followed. I had screens waiting to be repaired or prepped for a new pattern; sample tiles had to be printed and then fired by Kyle or Kenny—a newly hired ceramic artist —and urgent colors were to be mixed and tested. In those moments, I wished to have tentacles like a squid to be able to satisfy each of the bosses at the same time. Tension would often build up while smiles would hide behind grimaces of discontent. It was all part of the nature of that business. There was always a next day and another unexpected error to surface, as was the misspelling in a soup recipe printed on a promotional tile. Amazingly, even though inspected and read by several different people, including the artist who wrote each letter with china ink, the typo had not been noticed. Somebody had to be blamed for it. I took the rapper.

"Well, you are supposed to be a secretary. You should have detected the spelling error," I was told. Ouch!

Winter had come and the basement apartment where we lived was cold because the only thermostat in the house was controlled by the upstairs tenants. Mefisto had to complain several times to his Chinese landlord. For a few days, the heat seemed to kick in only to fail again a couple of days later. The upstairs tenants were three "ladies of the night," who slept during the day.

They loved to throw boisterous parties that would extend well over the kids' bedtime and the noise of their loudspeakers would reverberate throughout the walls and foundation of the house. Complaints and protests were of no avail. Frank suggested complaining to the Tenants' Bureau, which we did. A lady came out to inspect the premises and left shortly after having filled in pages of various forms. The end result was that we had to move again because that basement apartment was considered illegal. I did not mind moving after having noticed that mice were having a blast at night time.

Through searching in real estate papers and magazines, we located a nice three-bedroom bungalow on top of a hill in Burnaby. It had an unfinished in-ground basement and a huge backyard with a large willow and cherry tree. From the L-shaped dining area, we could enjoy the magnificent view of the Burrard Inlet. There was even a cozy fireplace. It was an old house, but Mefisto and I soon changed things around by re-painting the entire inside and outside. We added flower boxes to the front windows and flowerbeds to the front and to the backyard. Our new landlord, an Italian family, was happy with the caring new tenants and we were even happier that we had found a decent, spacious place to live. The kids were then transferred to a school nearby and they could even walk back and forth without having to take the bus.

As the house was not far from the PNE amusement park, we often went there for a stroll and a few rides on the weekends. Frank once took us on the giant boat. It was a scary experience, especially for me. There were no seatbelts, only a metal bar across the seats. I was afraid that the kids would fall over from the vertical position the boat had reached and extended my arm to hold them back while uttering a silent prayer. Luckily, the Guardian Angels were on the lookout and aside from a big empty hole in our stomachs, everybody landed safely.

Some other time we would prepare a picnic basket and head out into the country or to some beautiful park such as the Garibaldi Park. While lying on a manicured carpet of grass, my eyes swept the vast extension of a wonderful, cloudless blue sky, luxuriant vegetation all around, a peaceful emerald green lake and no other noises than the songs of birds. There was so much peace all around. The world's aches, pains and wars were so distant. What a beautiful, blessed country Canada was, I thought.

Life in town was a little less peaceful. Work continued with its ups and downs, some days better, other days worse. There were constant challenges to be overcome and each time, we hoped that the Lord would help us in crossing the many bridges and streams on the way. We finally came up with a sufficient down payment for a house of our own. We found an attractive Swiss-chalet type house in Coquitlam, a small community at the time, in the outskirts of Vancouver. We fell in love totally with the three-bedroom house that also had a carport, an unfinished above-ground basement, a small backyard with access to the forest and a small river with sparkling waters running through it. Occasionally, we would be greeted by a lost bear cub, which created havoc only among the grown-ups because the children did not seem to fear them. Yet wildlife rescuers were called in to re-direct the bigger teddies to the conservation areas. Reindeers, raccoons, skunks and countless squirrels would also visit the neighborhood. It was like living in a park, going to sleep and waking in the morning with the stupendous song of birds.

Once again, the new schools were close by and both kids could just walk over or ride their bikes to school. I loved the spacious living room above the carport, the fireplace and the thick woollen carpet throughout the entire house. Across from the living room were the spacious kitchen and a breakfast / dining area with a walkout to a front wooden terrace, offering a view of the surrounding mountains. We often took long walks up those mountains to view the breathtaking, still uncontaminated and unpopulated scenery from the very top.

Things were working out fine for us till Nakina came home one Saturday afternoon, crying from pain to her knee. There was no wound or bruising to be seen but she would scream at the lightest touch. The usual questions followed: What did you do? Did you fall? Did you hit it? Each time the answer was no. I thought to apply some ice but even that was unbearable to Nakina. We waited a few hours, hoping that the pain would subside, but it did not and so we decided to take her to the nearest Emergency. The X-Rays did not show anything and no treatment was recommended. She spent the rest of Saturday and all day Sunday in agony. I called our family doctor and pediatrician first thing Monday morning. Mefisto drove us to the doctor's office after having notified Nestore and Vera about the problem. The doctor was nice enough to see Nakina ahead of other patients and after having examined her, told me to take her immediately to the Children's Hospital. Mefisto drove us over there. With the doctor's referral, Nakina was admitted very quickly and they had to sedate her leg to allow them to proceed with the various tests that required touching and turning. What regular X-Rays could not detect on Saturday, the CT scan did. She had what they called a form of septic arthritis in the left proximal tibio-fibular joint and required immediate surgery. That meant that I would remain at the hospital for as long as necessary while Mefisto went back to the office. He returned home earlier that afternoon to take care of Peter for when he returned from school, and to inform him of what was going on. They had a bite to eat and then drove to the hospital where Nakina already had a bed assigned to her and was a little more comfortable due to the pain-numbing medicine she was given. Surgery would take place early morning. Nakina was very brave when they prepped her for surgery and inserted an

IV line in her hand. It was always very difficult to watch the kids when they were in pain, mainly because I felt unable to help them aside from holding hands, telling stories, and planning activities for when they'd be healed again. Nakina was kept in the hospital for a number of weeks and so I returned to work only on a part- time basis so that I could spend more time with her. During that entire ordeal, Peter behaved beautifully. He had become a smart, independent thirteen-year-old who made us extremely proud with his grades and the praises he received from teachers for his efforts and initiatives.

I realized that the company needed a full-time worker and could no longer depend on my complete cooperation. I hated to leave them because they had just developed a beautiful line of glass mosaics. They were the very first manufacturers of glass tiles in all of North America and I hoped to be part of that exciting program. But Nakina needed me, and so shortly after her return home from the hospital, I submitted my resignation. For a while, I just did what was expected of me: cooking, cleaning, gardening and shopping. Then during summer, my parents came from Germany for two weeks' visit. Everybody was happy with that reunion and there were many parties to celebrate the great family get-together. Nakina was also recovering fast, even though she had another two months worth of antibiotics to take before she returned to school.

I was ready to resume some sort of activity at that point, to contribute to the family income and found a part time job as sales lady in a small tile shop in Port Coquitlam, a fifteen-minute bike ride from home. The shop belonged to Romeo Costanzo, who months earlier had also been employed by Nestore and who, for personal reasons, quit the job and decided to open his own little contracting business. He spent a few hours at the shop teaching me those things I needed to run the store on my own. The best teacher, however, was practice, hands-on experience, trial and error—without much error, possibly!

I learned about tile setting compounds, grouts, spacers, trowels and measurements. Some days I was very busy with clients, other days not even one customer walked into the store. To fight boredom, I would re-arrange the displays or just simply dust them. Twice a month, sales reps from various tile manufacturers and distributors would come by the store to remove old sample boards or bring new materials for display. My favorite rep was Olympia's Maurice, a very pleasant, older gentleman who liked to chat with me about life in general. He was also in charge of collections for Olympia and was disappointed when there was no check to be picked up. He was not the only one. Romeo owed money to many other people and soon enough, even my hours were considerably reduced. On many occasions, Romeo himself or his wife would replace me at the store.

Somehow, Maurice happened to sense that something was wrong and started to show up on a weekly basis.

"So Isabel, do you have any good news for me this time?"

"I am afraid not. Romeo said he would be able to give you something next week." "Yeah, like all the previous weeks, which is nothing," he said with a chuckle.

"I am sorry, but I can't give you better news," I said a little embarrassed.

"It's not your fault, Isabel. But how are things going? Is he selling? Does he have orders?"

"All I can tell you is that business has been rather slow lately," I said without getting into details. After all, it was not my place to do so, even though it was no longer a secret that Romeo's business was in trouble.

One morning, Romeo entered in a hurry, grabbed a few items from the back of the store and then said, "From now on, come in only once a week, Isabel. I can no longer afford a full-time employee."

Coincidentally, Maurice stopped by the store that same day and I told him what had just happened.

"So why don't you come and work for me?" he asked.

"I'd love to. What do I have to do?" I said, enthused with the proposal.

"Come in next Monday," Maurice said. "Let's talk."

I remembered my father's words, that there had always been a light at the end of the tunnel for us. It was happening again. I left the store which closed weeks later.

20

Olympia

Monday afternoon, I showed up at Olympia, one of the largest tile distributors in town and at the time, in the country. One of the sales ladies showed me to Maurice's office,

"Hello, Isabel, how are you?" he said. "Please do have a seat. I am glad that you decided to come, so let's talk business. Basically, you will be working at the order desk with five other sales people and also help customers in the showroom."

"Is the showroom open only to the trade or also to the public?" I asked.

"It is open to both."

"And what are working hours?"

"Monday to Friday from 8 a.m. to 5 p.m., with half an hour for lunch," he said. "Come on; let me give you a tour of the premises." Maurice led the way.

Maurice, who was the sales manager for that branch, introduced me to the various departments and sales personnel. The newly renovated showroom was fairly large and displayed an incredible array of floor and wall tiles in countless shapes, sizes and colors. Next, we visited the enormous warehouse that housed endless rows of racks containing pallets of materials and employed a small army of employees and drivers. I liked what I saw, and the salary was also attractive. Needless to say, I accepted Maurice's offer without hesitation.

One week later, I started my new employment. Louise, who seemed to be the oldest among the girls, was the sales desk supervisor and took it upon herself to teach me about the many products, pricing and information related to my job. As often happens with large companies, it was difficult initially to fit in and please everyone. There were many friendly people though, willing to help and cooperate and others, who were rude and reacted with the typical "screw you" attitude.

It took me a little while to get used to taking orders over the phone. Unlike the other girls who immediately recognized the voice of a given client, I had to ask for their names. Some of the contractors were not the most understanding, polite people and reacted with impatient rudeness when I did not promptly recognize "who they were" or did not know whether we had 100 square feet of a given material on hand. I had to put them on hold and check with the warehouse where mostly Bob, the warehouse manager and human computer, had knowledge on a daily basis, of most of the available stock. Sometimes, I had to call the customer back a little later with that information because Bob himself was busy with more urgent matters. The public was also not always easy to deal with. Most required a whole lot of time while choosing the best shape and color for a kitchen backsplash or a tub surround, almost always involving my assurance of their choice of colors.

Noticing my artistic inclination, Maurice suggested that I create new boards for the showroom as they were constantly receiving new materials that had to be exhibited to the public. I loved the creative side of my job. The panels I had made up resulted in attractive three-dimensional artworks. They were concept combinations of floor tiles with matching or contrasting wall tiles to better illustrate to the customer the many ways the different products could be used in their homes.

My journey was smooth sailing had it not been for one particular young lady, who from the very beginning was always extremely rude to me. I could simply not figure out what Debbie, a fake blond in her mid-twenties, with her heavy eye make-up, her chain smoking and loud mouth, had against me. I decided to join her purposely during lunchtime on the well-kept lawn in front of the building. Initially, Debbie totally ignored me. A second time, I offered the girl a cigarette, which she took and even thanked for. Slowly, one day at a time, we initiated a conversation, and when a few days later, I did not show up at our usual lunch spot on the lawn, it was Debbie who came looking for me. Gradually, Debbie turned from bitchy into almost pleasant. I knew from past experiences, that there would always be that one person in a company to spoil the sense of peaceful coexistence most normal people looked for.

A few months into my job, Mefisto decided to take a trip to the east coast of Canada and the United States to explore business possibilities. Because for obvious reasons I could not go with him, he decided to take Peter who happened to be on holidays and was happy beyond belief with the traveling plan. They had spent a full week on the road, and to crown the event, Mefisto took Peter to a Blue Jays baseball game in Toronto. It was his favorite team and to be able to take a picture with some of his favorite players was like real icing on the cake.

The boys returned home full of enthusiasm and what I feared, came into being. Suddenly, Toronto was the city to be in, the roaring megalopolis and concrete jungle where the real action was. Back in the early 1980s, the construction industry had been slack in all of British Columbia. Sales were slow and low. Mefisto shared his views with Nestore who did not dissuade him from moving to Ontario, but rather encouraged him to extend the sales activity not only to that province, but to the entire east coast of Canada.

In the meantime, Frank and Therese had split up. With a broken heart, she returned to her beloved Belle Provence and settled in Montreal. The kids, who loved her as their real aunt, were deeply distraught with her departure and for a while were angry at Frank for letting her go. It just happened that Frank fell head over heels in love with a Hungarian brunette who had sparkling brown eyes and a happy giggle. She also had a handsome ten-year-old boy from her previous marriage. Magnolia was a very talented painter, poet and shared with me her interests in the paranormal and other mysteries of life on this planet. This new event in Frank's life minimized his shock in learning about Mefisto's intention in moving to Toronto.

I was not very enthused at the idea of having to sell our beautiful house, again get rid of our furniture, give up the job I was becoming fond of, leave friends and relatives and head towards heaven only knew what other surprises that were in store for us. The pressure was on. Unless we were blessed with a major windfall of some sorts, there was nothing I could have done to change what faith had already established for us. Being at the forefront of restlessness, Mefisto was the first one to leave, to find a job and a new home for the family. I was left behind with the kids, in charge of the sale of the house, the bank transactions, the packing and the shipping of the goods.

Maurice was very disappointed with my resignation as they were always displeased when losing a good worker, but he understood my situation and offered to recommend me to the Toronto headquarters, where they could always use another good sales person in their showroom. I was grateful and relieved. My last day at work was a pleasant one. I was given a farewell card, signed by superiors and employees, and a large, fine chocolate cake. Many had brought cameras to take pictures of the occasion. I was touched by the fuss around me. Tears spilled from my eyes while bidding goodbye to my co-workers. Another working chapter was closing and soon a new one would begin.

In the meantime, it seemed that Mefisto had found a place to live in the house of Italian landlords of Calabrese origin. Soon after, he asked Nakina to join him, which she did even though reluctantly, because she also loved Vancouver and hated to leave behind the many friends she had made.

I was very busy during my last few weeks in Vancouver. I had been successful in the sale of the house and used all available time to pack the crates, which we had saved from the Italian move. A few cardboard boxes were also filled. My good friends and neighbors, Kiyo and Wolfi purchased most of our furniture, sofas, bookshelves, tables and chairs. I also had to ship over the car we had purchased months earlier, via rail to Toronto, because Mefisto needed wheels to get around. For a short time, I had to resort to footwork, bus, cab or to good old Wolfi who never denied helping out when needed.

A very last party was thrown to celebrate the marriage between Frank and Magnolia who in the meantime had had a most beautiful baby girl named Lara. Again, I felt sad for having to give up the nearness of family and wondered how many more times our lives would be disrupted, emotionally and financially by an apparent better business opportunity excuse or, as in Mefisto's case, by simply giving in to the fatal attraction of new challenges. The party was the most condensed little wedding celebration ever. It had been Frank's request to hold the ceremony at my house, even though all we had at that point were the table, six chairs and two beds. He didn't care. There was no money for big restaurant bills and besides, no one else was supposed to know about that marriage. It was their secret and I wasn't the type to poke my nose into other people's affairs, even if that was my own brother.

I felt that they needed a little more than just crackers and booze and rushed to do some last-minute shopping. I picked up foil trays, cold cuts, cheese, fruit, bread, chicken and tuna salad, plastic cutlery and plates and some flowers to act as centrepiece. There was also plenty of wine and champagne, all served in plastic cups. All in all, the table looked quite festive once I finished with the final decoration. My best friends, Kiyo and Wolfi had also been invited. Finally the bride and groom arrived with their son and baby, followed soon after by the justice of the peace. Wolfi and I were witnesses. It was a simple ritual that left teardrops in Magnolia's eyes and I only hoped that those were tears of joy and not sadness for the extreme simplicity in which such a great moment, especially for a bride, was celebrated.

The TV was already gone. There was no radio or CD player. We talked; told each other stories and I played the harmonica. Whoever knew the lyrics, pitched in singing or simply humming. The wine helped animate the group who often broke out in hearty laughter. Even Peter was allowed to have a little champagne that evening. We all spent a couple of happy, unforgettable hours together.

Days later, the trucking company came to pick up the crates, the boxes and the bikes. Wolfi also came over to lend a hand. He tried to help the movers by pushing the crates up the little ramp and into the truck but his leather soles did not help much, causing him to slide backwards on the slippery driveway. It took him a few minutes to realize that he was not moving from the same spot. I thought it was a funny sight and Peter compared his effort with the Road Runner cartoon character, which rolled its feet real fast before finally taking off at full speed ahead. Yes, Wolfi was a funny man. He loved to laugh, to drink Vino and to help wherever he could. He was the type who could be disturbed in the middle of the night for whatever reason and be there for whomever, with a smile on his face, ready to take off. He was also a true aficionado of coupons. He always knew what was on special at Safeway.

One day, I just stepped off the bus and headed to the store to pick up a few items, when I encountered Wolfi. He was all dressed up with a serious briefcase in his hand. I thought that he had finally gotten a job but decided not to ask. We walked together into the store. I picked up the items I needed and then returned towards the cashier. Passing by Wolfi who had opened his briefcase on top of a pile of boxes, I noticed that the briefcase was filled with countless coupons. I smiled at him and he smiled back.

"Hey, if you need any coupons, just let me know," he said very matter-of-factly.

As if the events of the last two months weren't stressful enough, I also had to deal with my father's illness. According to mother, he was in his last hours. Unfortunately, at that point I was in no condition to simply take a plane and fly to Germany. I was traveling to Toronto with Peter and had a new job lined up when I arrived, so Frank decided to go instead, but asked me to pitch in with half the cost of the air ticket, which I did.

While staying at Wolfi and Kiyo's place for the last two nights in Coquitlam, Kiyo and her friend Carol, devout Buddhists, invited me to join them in prayer to alleviate my father's suffering by either healing or releasing him from earthly bondage. Frank called the next day from Germany saying that there was a considerable improvement in our father's situation. I wondered if it had been due to the prayers. I knew that prayers could be very powerful instruments and hoped that my father would recover entirely.

Finally, the day of departure came. Peter and I hugged, no longer able to hold back the tears, as we stood for one last time on the steps of our beautiful house while Wolfi took a picture. There was so much sadness in my heart. It was my ninth move since living with my wanderlustige husband. Later, Kiyo and Wolfi drove us to the Greyhound station. More teardrops made their way down cheeks, accompanied by sad smiles. It was late at night, dark and cool. Kiyo and Wolfi remained waving goodbye till the bus disappeared from their view. Both Peter and I dozed off after a while, to wake up hours later to the magnificent scenery of the Canadian Rocky Mountains bathed by the sun in patches of red and gold.

The bus trip that lasted three days and two nights was tiring, and at stretches, really monotonous, especially through the prairies where earth and sky constantly kissed at the horizon. It was, however, the best and only way to appreciate the full extension of the wonderful country we had adopted as our new homeland.

21

TORONTO

Peter and I were wide awake at about 5 a.m. as we were getting closer to our final destination. The myriad of pulsating city lights of the roaring city were a scene to behold. Swiftly snaking through the Toronto streets, the bus finally stopped at the Edward Street bus station where Nakina and Mefisto, even though ruffled up by the early wake-up call, were happy to see us. As soon as the luggage was transferred from the bus into our car, we drove off to destination home.

I was quite disappointed with what I saw as we reached our new living quarters. It was an in-ground basement apartment with one bedroom, shared by Mefisto and Peter; a kitchen-dining-living room shared by me and Nakina; a small bathroom and a large closet to store all our portable belongings. Noting my frustration, Mefisto quickly pointed out that it was only a temporary arrangement and, depending on our financial situation, we would soon move elsewhere.

Later on that morning, Mefisto introduced Peter and me to our landlord, Marietta, a middle-aged woman who, along with her son Gianni, lived on the upper level of the house. She welcomed us warmly and from that day onwards, always sent down some Calabrese specialty because she loved to cook and to please people. Her son, Gianni, was a handsome bachelor, working as a barber and hairstylist, who also welcomed us and always did his best to make our stay as pleasant as possible. For a few days after our arrival, Peter and I dozed on and off all day mainly because of the time lag between west and east, even though we experienced it at a more gradual rate than if we had flown over. A couple of days later I took the bus to visit Olympia's headquarters on the west side of town.

I walked into a magnificent place of business with an area entirely dedicated to skylights and luxurious tropical plants. The showroom itself was impressive for the quantity and quality of displays, shapes and colors. I hoped to get the job. Bob Stewart, who was the personnel manager, welcomed me to his office. Like Maurice, he was a very pleasant man in his forties who had already been notified of my visit by Maurice. For a while, we chatted about work and life in general. I gave me a company form to be filled out. I would start the next Monday, which gave me a few days to adjust to my new environment and study the best route to get to work. I would have to take two buses and a subway. I also explored our new neighborhood, schools, banks, shops, etc. Stuff the boys do not bother with because they take it for granted that "she" will take care of the details.

Before the week was over, I received a phone call announcing that my father had passed on. Even though I was aware of the fact that father was very ill, there was always hope that maybe he would somehow make it. Yet the inevitable happened and I was shocked just the same and disappointed and angry for I had not had a chance to see my father alive for one last time. Once again, my life was turned upside down and again, we were short of cash and life was not as romantic and beautiful as I hoped it would one day be. Well, I figured, if I could not see him alive, I would at least see him in his coffin. No one, not even our pitiful finances would rob me of this. My heart had too much anger and pain, but all I could do was cry, bitterly cry.

Mefisto took it upon himself to arrange for the air ticket to Germany, while I notified Bob Stewart about my unexpected traveling plans. He couldn't but understand and be patient.

The flight was long and boring, and so was the train trip from Frankfurt to Freiburg. Perhaps because I felt wrapped in a daze of sadness and was emotionally drained from the series of events of the last few months, the urge of breaking down in tears was almost overpowering, but I had to keep my cool, for mother's sake as well. Soon, however, we both broke down in heavy sobs. It was a small funeral, perhaps thirty people, if that. Only the closest friends participated. I caressed my father's hands and kissed his cold, lifeless forehead. Thousand thoughts and memories zoomed through my mind that instant. How little I knew about that man and yet I did love him and missed him. Regretfully, I could no longer tell him that in person. It was too late, as it always is when one finally realizes that things could have been different.

It was during that sad circumstance that I met mother's best friend, Senta, who in time would become my good friend, too. It was Senta who cared for mother during her hospital odyssey shortly after the funeral. Not only did she undergo surgery for colon tumours, but had also been mistakenly submitted to a hysterectomy. I only wished I could have stayed with her during those trying times, but unfortunately, I had to fly back home. The family needed me and I had to resume work to make ends meet. It was not cheap to live in Toronto either and only one pay check was not enough, especially if we planned to live in a better place than a dark, humid, basement apartment.

For many weeks, my mother and I kept in touch via quick phone calls, to and from the hospital. Frank and I then decided to alternate the calls to alleviate the financial onus of long distance telephone calls for both parties.

22

Olympia - Toronto

Even though I was not thrilled with my new working schedule, 9 a.m. to 5 p.m., Monday to Saturday, and on alternate Sundays, from 10 a.m. to 4 p.m., I had no other choice at the time but comply. The showroom was open to the trade as well as to the public and was a great place to meet a vast array of human beings of all backgrounds. It was interesting to listen to their plans, dreams and idiosyncrasies. It was not only a sales job but also a teaching job. Many customers were not aware of the basics of tiling and the differences in the various products. That is when my knowledge came into the picture as well as my diplomatic savoir-faire since no "Tiling for Dummies" had appeared on the market yet.

I quickly learned to avoid, or at least tried to avoid, those customers who at all costs forced me to decide for them on a particular type of color combination. The reason being, that there were plenty of those who would blame the sales people for an incorrect selection of colors just because once at home, and under a different lighting, the chosen one was not exactly what they had visualized at the showroom. Some had the ill-conceived notion that they could simply return the product after having already installed it, and get a replacement at no cost.

A few installers were also capable of causing trouble by blaming the sales people for incorrectly calculating the footage required of a certain product, based on figures and sketches supplied by the same installer who after all, should have known better how to calculate the necessary amounts required. There were squabbles at times about the choice of setting materials, which did not work well mainly because the installer neglected to check the bumpy substrate, or about grout shades, which did not result in a neutral color as suggested by the sales people. I faulted the installers because they were too chicken to select a shade themselves on behalf of their customer. It was during that time that I became acquainted with the term "passing the buck." Luckily, I was surrounded by a great team of co-workers who helped each other out in time of trouble.

All in all, it was pleasant to work for the company that belonged to clever, hard-working Hungarian Jewish brothers, even though the pay wasn't the greatest and did not offer much room for advancement either. Whoever wasn't satisfied with their earnings was free to leave and look somewhere else. Nobody was forced to linger and feel miserable.

I soon became well-liked by my co-workers and supervisors, alike and when needed, was also put in charge of handling the cash. Too bad the distance between work and home was so great, but I learned to appreciate the bus and subway rides because it gave me time to read or simply relax, while watching the behavioral patterns of other riders. It was less pleasant during bad weather when there was black ice early morning. I do not remember having experienced such weather extremes while in Italy. There were days when I had a hard time reaching the bus stop at Lawrence Avenue, while hanging on to any possible branch or fence on the way. I laughed at myself as I walked like a penguin, trying not to kiss the ground with my butt. Heavy rains were not that attractive either because they caused thousands of worms to surface, crawling all over the streets, filling the air with the smell of raw meat. I tried very hard not to step on any of those crawly beings like many did, bringing them into the buses with their shoes. Nothing could defeat Mother Nature. I had to make the best of it by getting used to the many new situations.

One Saturday, while visiting Marietta upstairs, Mefisto met with her son-in-law, Mr. Merdura. He was a middle-aged man, balding and very short-sighted. Like birds, he had the habit of tilting his head when bringing an item to be inspected as close as possible to his good eye. Talking about business in general, Mefisto mentioned some of the hardships he encountered while building up new business contacts.

"Why don't you take over my variety store?" he said. "It will cost you near to nothing."

"That cannot be," Mefisto replied. "You need money for anything these days, and I don't have any."

"You will need very little money in this case. Just enough to pay for the change of name and to purchase products you will need to sell."

"And whereabouts is this store?"

"On Danforth Road; I'll take you there," Mr. Merdura said. "I made good money with that store. I sold lots of cigarettes, and lots and lots of pop. Talk it over with your wife and then let me know."

One week later, Mefisto and I decided to visit the famous store. Mr. Merdura drove us over. I was disappointed in what I saw. The store was dark inside and very rundown. Too many shelves were covered in dust, leaving narrow passages between one and the other. The floor was old, dirty, squeaky hardwood. The walls were soiled and the front display was anything but inviting. It looked very much like a rat infested third world jungle store.

"All it really needs is a coat of paint and a good clean up and you're good to go," Mr. Merdura said in Italian so that the Chinese lady at the cashier would not understand what was said.

"What about that lady?" Mefisto asked, inquisitive. "Is she not renting now?"

"She is leasing the premises, which are my property, but she wants to sell the business, that is, the shelvings and the goods. But you don't worry about all that. Just follow my instructions and you will be all right. There is not even a goodwill value to this place the way it looks like now."

"Do you know how much she is asking for?"

"No, I don't. But whatever it is, just tell her that you don't need any of her crap on the shelves. Heaven knows how old those are anyway. Keep the shelving, the cooler and the cigarettes and you might just get away with a $2,000 – 3,000 investment."

Mr. Merdura was very convincing. It all sounded very simple and easy.

That evening we all sat down and seriously considered the possibility of taking over the store. We examined the monetary aspect needed to execute the necessary remodeling. The place had to be scrubbed thoroughly. The walls, ceiling and shelving had to be painted and the floor needed to be redone. The hours of operation would be demanding, seven days per week, fourteen hours per day. The entire family would be running it but mostly me because Mefisto had a full-time job and the kids were busy at school. We needed an additional $5,000 investment, which at the time was not available. We were rejected by a loan officer when we submitted a small business plan to the bank, because we had no collateral. Perhaps if we had claimed to be representatives of a third world country we would have obtained a nice figure. At Mefisto's suggestion, I tried to borrow money from my brother, but he was having financial problems himself. I then tried my mother who, reluctantly, gave me the money. Reluctantly, because she did not trust Mefisto's business acumen or dependability due to his constant moving around, hopping from one job to another and from one place to another in a short period of time. She had the feeling that he wouldn't last long with the store either and that the money would just get lost in the long run. It had been her intention to give that money to me so that I could buy myself a car to better move around, especially in bad weather. It was my decision to sacrifice my own convenience and pitch into a losing proposition, or maybe not.

In the meantime, I had to approach my supervisor and notify her about the new situation. The entire showroom personnel, co-workers from accounting, administration and warehouse were displeased with the news but nonetheless, wished me good luck, and threw me a beautiful farewell party at a Yorkdale restaurant. On behalf of the group, I received a gold-plated watch and many best wishes cards. Once more, I was touched by all the fuss people made about me and promised to keep in touch with them. I did, with some of the girls, for a short period of time.

There were always too many things happening at the same time. Multi-tasking was a constant necessity and so were nerves made of steel. Mefisto found a house to rent in the Victoria Park area and so once again, we packed our belongings, including the four crates still un-opened and stored in Marietta's garage, and moved to the new house. It had a large living-dining room, kitchen, bathroom and three bedrooms. The basement had a spacious bedroom, a small bathroom, a partial kitchen, a cold chamber to store wine and an unfinished area where the furnace stood. The house had a beautiful front terrace and a well-kept lawn with a flowerbed filled with roses. In the backyard, there were small vegetable beds, a grape plant and various fruit trees such as apple, pear and plums, all surrounded by a beautiful green lawn. I was happy. Finally, a decent house again and no more sleeping on a mattress on a humid basement floor or on sofa springs poking into my ribs, which kept me awake most of the night. Nakina was relieved as well, for the same reason. A new challenging chapter in our lives was soon to begin.

23

Papi's Smoke & Gifts

It was time to tackle the store and get it ready for a grand re-opening. Everybody was assigned a task. Peter did the painting and then helped with the floor setting. Mefisto purchased second-hand counters and a cash register. We had the Coca-Cola people deliver pop and Mr. Merdura showed us where to purchase goods at wholesale prices. I arranged the front window display with silk flowers, toys and other novelty items. We also had an ice cream chest brought in and lottery tickets but no machine because another store further down the road already had one installed. We were now ready for the grand opening, which we announced through a leaflet we had printed. Unfortunately, the leaflets were distributed to the wrong area of Scarborough by the advertising company, who adamantly refused to correct their error by reprinting the leaflets or at least, give us a partial refund. Others would have probably sued them.

The store looked beautiful: clean, bright, airy. We were all proud of our accomplishment and anxious to see the reaction of the people who used to visit the store before the renovation. Slowly, customers flocked in, first for curiosity and then to buy milk, cigarettes, candy, etc. Neighboring customers loved the store.

"You guys did a terrific job with this place. It is like night and day," said one Scottish lady who became our assiduous client and visitor.

Peter and Nakina pitched in after school and Mefisto, whenever possible, spent a couple of hours after his regular work hours. Those were tiring, long hours for everybody.

It was also during this time that my mother finally received her immigration papers and managed to fly over to her new homeland, Canada. As agreed with Frank, she would spend the first half of the year with him in

Vancouver, enjoying the nice weather, the beautiful surroundings and her little granddaughter, Lara. It was now easier for either side to phone whenever needed. She seemed so happy and enthused about everything. The only sad part up to that point was my father's final funeral. It had been his wish to be buried in British Columbia, a province he had fallen in love with. The urn with his ashes had been sent directly from Germany to the funeral house in Vancouver. Regretfully and for obvious reasons, I was unable to attend the service.

Then one day, all hell broke loose. I received a phone call from Frank begging me to accept mother over sooner than planned because of frictions that had developed between her and Magnolia. Life had become very unpleasant in Vancouver. Apparently Magnolia had given Frank the ultimatum: mother goes, or she goes. Frank did not want to lose Magnolia.

At first, I did not know how to handle that hot potato suddenly thrown into my lap, because Mefisto wasn't enamored of my mother either. What to do? I couldn't simply slam the door in my mother's face. Besides, she had nowhere else to go or turn to. I figured that in time Mefisto would get used to the idea of having her around the house. After all, when he suggested that I ask her for money, it had been Mefisto himself to hint to the possibility of getting her to help out at the store level because of her innate business acumen and financial management talent. She was like an ant, collecting and saving and saving. She had money stashed everywhere, in the bank and under the mattress, in drawers and apron pockets and was always proud to show it.

"Look how much I saved again," she would say with a big, bright smile.

Frank and Wolfi drove her over from Vancouver. It was a long, tiring trip but the scenery was worth every mile, she said. Both Frank and Wolfi spent a couple of days visiting before returning to the west. Peter and Nakina were happy in having Oma (grandma in German) around. Nakina surrendered her room to her and moved into the large basement bedroom.

Because of her handicap—she had had polio at an early age and in later years developed scoliosis of the spine—mother was unable to help with the house chores but she could cook. Sitting on a stool, she figured out the best way to chop her onions and prepare a scrumptious chicken paprikás. She walked with the aid of a cane and needed help going up and down stairs or when going out on the street or shopping. My schedules became even more hectic. I helped mother open a bank account and invest in some Canada Bonds. I also combed Scarborough in search of a German-speaking physician, which I found. The only problem was that his office was situated on a second floor and the flight of stairs for mother's bad leg was no laughing matter. One would think that a doctor's office would be equipped for clients with handicaps. She managed for a while and was happy because at least she could make herself understood. I also found her German-speaking friends at a nearby community centre. They had weekly gatherings, coffee and cake and she enjoyed every bit of it. Bob, the volunteer driver would come to pick her up and then return her home after the party. I would drive her shopping and to the local library so she could select books and magazines of her liking. All those things had to be squeezed into Saturdays, the only time off for me as Mefisto would take care of the store while I also did the house cleaning, and the laundry and whatever else had to be done. It was a busy, fast-paced life.

Mr. Merdura came by every so often to check on things and pick up his rent check. In his opinion, the store was empty. The shelves were not full enough.

"You guys made a boutique out of this place," he said. "Sure enough, it is nice, it is clean and bright but your shelves should be fuller. People like to see lots of things, even if they don't buy. The more clutter, the better."

He was right to an extent. We should have bought a lot more merchandise but we had financial limitations and weren't quite sure what else to bring in. Normally, we would go get an item when a customer asked for it, to make sure we had it the next time someone wanted it. Why bring in stuff that would only collect dust on the shelves, I pondered. Besides, it did not take long before the store received the visit of numerous sales representatives for the most varied articles: stockings, greeting cards, magazines, books, knick-knacks, lighters, more candy and chocolate, baskets, souvenirs, etc. It was quite an enterprise to keep track of everything, re-ordering products and hope that the next day would prove better than the previous one. The best days for business for a typical variety store were Sundays and holidays, when the other bigger stores in the area remained closed. We would sell out even the canned goods. Rarely would a customer object to the price, but it happened with those used to barter in the old country.

"How come so expensive, the other guys up the street (the big grocery store) sell it for a lot less."

"Oh yeah, those guys buy a lot more than we do and, therefore, get a better discount."

"So why don't you guys buy a lot, too?"

"Why? Will you guarantee me to come and buy the stock if I do?" I asked. "Besides, why don't you go down the street and buy the cheaper one there?"

"They are closed today," the man said.

"Aha! There you go. We are open, for your convenience. That's where the name comes from, Convenience Store."

The man picked up a couple of cans and left without a word. Another time, a customer walked in the store and placed an open box of milk on the counter.

"This-a milk is a sour. I need replacement." He had a heavy Italian accent.

"When did you buy this milk?" I asked.

"Jest a few days ago."

"Where did you buy it from?"

"I don't know. It could have been from here or the other store. It is-a milk, whats-a difference?"

"Well, it is indeed milk, but not the brand we sell. Our supplier will not take back sour milk that is not theirs. You better return it to where you bought it from."

"I suggest you take-a back, otherwise I will not buy here anymore," the man said.

There were those exceptional few who believed that by cheating their fellow men it made them look smarter.

Even though I had never seen that customer before, and it was not the brand of milk we carried, to avoid any possible confrontations, I took back the sour milk and gave him a new box. It is said that the customer is always right, but I wondered if that applied also to those pulling a fast one. At that point, I was losing money twice because unlike large grocery stores, the small variety / convenience stores are not granted volume discounts. We had to sell the milk below cost to be able to sell it at all. The dairy distributors were not at all sympathetic with our dilemma and practically laughed it off by saying, "Oh, well, it is what it is. You'll make up for the difference elsewhere, with your cigarettes and trinkets, for example."

Another problem we had to deal with were the ones coming in with puppy eyes, trying to buy on credit. Even though aware of such plague, we all fell into their tricks at one time or another.

One case was that of a young man in his early thirties. He was tall, had curly black hair and was blind in one eye, which he had lost in a gun accident and for that reason, had been living on a disability income. A regular customer buying the typical items such as Coca-Cola and cigarettes, he lived on the third floor of a three-storey building, right across from the store. Initially, he always paid on the spot. Then one day he suddenly realized that he had left his wallet at home and promised to pay the next day, first thing in the morning. He was punctual the first three or four times. Then, something happened for he did not show up for a few days and Peter had to run after him. I began worrying when he dropped into the store begging for "just one little pack of cigarettes," along with the promise of paying everything on Saturday, when he was supposed to get his disability check. He begged so convincingly, that I fell for it. Saturday came and went and he did not show up, but I saw him walking on the opposite side of the street with a cigarette in one hand and a twelve-pack of beer under his other arm. It was only after several visits to his apartment and the threat of calling the cops, that I finally got paid. From that day onwards, the young man had lost all his credit privileges at the store.

Another welfare case was Jim, who was also addicted to nicotine and booze, even though he had never entered the store under the influence. He was also constantly broke, waiting for his welfare check to pay the bills; he owed a little everywhere in that area of town. At least he had the decency of offering a form of guarantee in exchange for the goods, such as his gold-plated watch or his stained dentures, and besides, he always came back to pay and take back his possessions. He tried to work offering his services as handyman—as he did not seem to be able to find a permanent position anywhere. Jim also had heart-breaking stories to tell about his life on earth and confessed, with some shame and hesitation, that when things got really tough, he would collect earth worms at night to sell and along the way, eat half a handful of them himself for the protein.

Then there was Ken, the redhead. In his late twenties, he had no fixed address. He moved along with the wind, which often blew him into the store. He was actually a handsome young man had it not been for his dirty, tangled red hair. He had beautiful blue eyes and at least shaved his beard every so often. His dress code was the standard soiled, crumpled blue jeans and worn out runners. Not because he could not afford better clothing he would say, but so people would feel pity for him and not bother him too much. Most of the time he would walk into the store swaying like a palm tree while his spoken word was incomprehensible slurred gibberish. I was intrigued by him and his choice of life and tried prying open his shell, but he did not remember much of anything due to his alcohol and drug abuse.

He told me that welfare did not pay him enough, even though he would register in different parts of town, borrowing addresses from acquaintances. He had to take care of himself the only way he knew and that was by jumping in front of cars in the evening, when the visibility was bad and the driver could not spot him fast enough, and then sue the poor driver for negligence.

"How on earth do you get away with a thing like that?" I asked. "Don't they find out that you were staging the whole thing?"

"Who said I was faking? I broke arms and legs before." Ken gave me a mischievous smile.

"And you could have died, too."

"Oh, well. That's the risk you take when you want to make good money."

"And did you ever make good money?"

"Oh yeah, a fair bit."

"And what did you do with it?"

"Can't tell", he replied with another of his cynical smiles.

Ken returned to the store another two or three times and then disappeared altogether. Throughout the following months, many other colorful specimens walked through the store's door, some pleasant, some rude, others just regular citizens picking up an item they forgot to buy at the supermarket.

It was a hot, humid Saturday in August. Mefisto had just come to replace me so that I could leave to take care of the house chores, run the weekly errands and do some cooking for the weekend. I was in the middle of chopping onions for the Feijoada (Brazilian black bean dish), when a phone call came in from a customer at the store, telling me that Mefisto was not feeling too good and needed me to come down right away. I dropped everything. I was alarmed because it was not Mefisto's style to have someone call for help on his behalf. I quickly explained to mother the reason for my rush in leaving, then grabbed my purse, jumped in the car and rushed down to the store. Mefisto was pale and definitely looked very ill.

"What do you want to do?" I asked. "Do you want to go to the emergency?"

"No, no. I just want to lie down. I need to lie down. I'm going downstairs to lie down." He headed to the basement.

"Let me know if you want to go to the hospital, ok?" I insisted.

Mefisto had always been stubborn and did things his way. Up until then, he could not accept the idea of being ill. He attributed the weird feeling that day to the combination of heat, the coffees he had been drinking, the cigarettes he had been smoking and the overall stress in his life.

I was nervous and could not concentrate on the few customers that had walked in. Instinctively, I prepared a sign for the door, saying the store was closed for emergency. Suddenly, Mefisto appeared at the top of the stairs.

"I think we better go to the hospital after all. I don't feel right."

I quickly emptied the cash register and left the drawer open. It was in clear view of aspiring thieves and meant that the loot was gone, so don't bother to break in.

I drove as fast as traffic permitted while Mefisto was lying back in the passenger seat and having breathing problems. Luckily, the Scarborough General was not far. We rushed to the reception and as soon as he mentioned having breathing problems and a strange chest pain, two nurses came running over and whisked him away into a cubicle. I remained at the front desk to take care of the usual paperwork and the registration process. In the meantime, they had pumped some oxygen into Mefisto's lungs and hooked him up to an ECG machine. It turned out that he had suffered a heart attack. I couldn't believe what I was hearing and just stared like frozen in time. Nothing had prepared us for that incident. After a while, they transferred him into the ICU where he had suffered a second minor heart attack. Like an after shock after the big one? I wondered. While he was being taken care of by a small army of nurses, I slipped out to make a phone call home and informed mother, who in turn informed the kids as soon as they returned home. Nakina actually had tried to call the store and as there had been no reply, she became alarmed and called Oma to find out what had happened. When she learned about Mefisto, Nakina screamed out in anguish. She had always been very close to her father and the news about his illness distressed her deeply. A little later in the day, the kids joined me at the hospital. They stood there, transfixed, watching Mefisto breathing through an oxygen mask and dozing in and out from his slumber. There was nothing any of us could have done to help. Mefisto was in the hands of competent professionals. Slowly, we walked back to the car and returned home. It was then clear that exhaustion, heat, coffee and cigarettes had played a big role in the incident.

I checked on Mefisto every day. As soon as the kids returned from school, they would take over the store so that I could run over to the hospital. Those were hard times for the family and I often cried myself to sleep or drowned my sadness in a few too many glasses of wine.

When Mefisto finally returned home, he was to avoid any strenuous activity. No more lifting milk baskets or pop cases. It was now my task to do my best and find the strength to carry on, even though it was becoming more and more difficult. Mefisto thought that the answer would be to close the store. I approached Mr. Merdura, explaining the new situation, but he was anything but sympathetic to our problem. We had to finish the lease or find a new tenant, agreeable to Mr. Merdura's demands, at our own expense. To make things even more difficult, he had decided to increase the lease to make it less appealing for a new tenant to take over. My nerves were tense as violin chords but I had to bite my tongue and use diplomacy when dealing with stubborn mules such as Mr. Merdura. Many possible buyers showed up but only one couple seemed to be serious about taking over. Not only were they shrewd merchants, used to heckle, they even forced me to run the store for them for an extra two weeks, if I wanted to get the agreed amount for the merchandise and the equipment left behind. It was a clever blackmail I did not know how to fight. At the very end, they short-paid us by almost $2,000 and practically pushed me out the door while Mr. Merdura looked on, impassively.

I felt like screaming. So much work, effort and sweat, for nothing. When I finally left the store, without looking back once, I jumped into my car and stepped on the accelerator. The sooner I left that street, the better. Tears bathed my cheeks and blurred my vision. I stopped momentarily at a MacDonald's parking lot further down the road and sobbed bitterly. Why was destiny being so harsh all the time? There was anger in my heart against Mr. Merdura, against Mefisto's heart attack, against myself and the whole entire world. Once I calmed down a little, I slowly drove back home.

To this day, I carry a bitter memory of our inconvenient convenience store days, and, therefore, have great respect for the individuals serving me at any of our neighborhood variety stores. It is a 24/7 demanding, heartbreaking struggle for survival. No wonder these stores often change ownership.

Life, however, had to go on. We quickly needed a source of income. For a few days, I leafed through papers, replied to a few ads and even showed up for interviews. Each time, the salary offered was extremely low for the amount of work involved. Tired of knocking on the wrong doors, I went to the local employment center. After filling in forms and a chat with an extremely pleasant employment agent, I was given the address and phone number of a company that was looking for a secretary.

24

Artistic Glass Sculptures Inc.

It was drizzling when I left the employment centre on Thursday morning. It had been easier than expected and I even enjoyed the tiny rain droplets on my face. I rushed back home and phoned the number they had given me. After a brief conversation, I was invited for an interview that same afternoon.

While driving to the appointment, I tried to match the warm, baritone voice with the mental picture of its owner. Perhaps he was tall, handsome, and knowledgeable. Experience, however, had taught me that telephone voices could at times be very deceiving.

Upon my arrival, I was greeted by a very handsome young man who reminded me of Pierce Brosnan, the actor. He was tall, lean, had dark brown hair with a casual curl dropping down his forehead, and grayish green eyes. He introduced himself as Leo. The voice corresponded to the mental picture I had made, but he was not the new employer. Before Leo could say another word, a short, slim man stepped forward, unceremoniously pushing Leo aside, and introducing himself as "the boss," Nemo. He invited me to take a seat right in front of his desk. As he spoke, I recognized the familiar accent of Sicilian origin. He later confirmed it and was pleasantly surprised that I also spoke Italian.

Nemo talked uninterruptedly for a good half hour, explaining the type of work he was doing and the type of cooperation he was expecting from his new assistant / secretary. My first impression of the man was positive and the creative type of work he was doing fascinated me even more. An amateur artist myself, I could envision the possibility of not only learning a new trade, but also contributing with my own ideas whenever an occasion called for it.

Nemo showed me around in the large plant where plate glass was custom-cut, polished, beveled, drilled and sandblasted. He was particularly proud of the showroom, cluttered with dozens of sandblasted and sand-carved glass and mirror panels. Nemo's style recalled figures of Michelangelo and Leonardian fashion. As Nemo went on describing each panel, I noticed a sparkle in his eyes and the urge in seeking approval and admiration for each masterpiece.

Nemo introduced me to his partners, Zack, also of Sicilian origin, and Norris, a gentle giant with a big smile. A Paul Newman look-alike was in charge of the order desk and the production schedule. An elderly lady, Beth, worked as their bookkeeper and was about to enjoy retirement. Once finished the introductions, Nemo quickly terminated the interview saying that he would contact me with his decision the following Monday, as he still had other applicants to interview. I had the distinct feeling that he had already made up his mind but wanted to play a little longer with my expectation. Nonetheless, I was satisfied and hoped to get at least a week off to relax a little.

Next Saturday morning, I was preparing myself for the usual shopping ritual when I received a call from Nemo announcing that I could start working on Monday. While I was happy with the good news on one hand; on the other, I was disappointed with the early call. Goodbye to a little time off and the idea of catching up with sleep and some homework, but I had to set priorities, as usual, and securing a weekly income at that point was a necessity. While slowly recovering, Mefisto took on a small delivery service for a local pharmacy. It was not so much the little money he was earning as the psychological need to feel useful and needed once more.

Working for Nemo at the beginning proved to be a little boring because as usual, I would not postpone or stretch out work to be done. Whatever was requested was completed right away. As on previous occasions elsewhere, I busied myself by leafing through the files to become familiar with the company's correspondence, filing system and order processing. As time passed and Nemo and I got to know each other better, most of my time was filled with Nemo's dissertations on family, art and life in general. He also demanded that I observed his dexterity in the process of drawing or preparing a panel to be sandblasted.

I watched, amused, at the genuine enthusiasm with which Nemo would trace a drawing and cut the stencil with large, theatrical gestures. Each line drawn or cut was followed by an equal amount of pauses and explanations. I listened and watched attentively. I understood that Nemo was the type who not only loved, but needed to be surrounded by admiration, praise and a little adulation—gifts I had mastered throughout my previous working experiences.

In time, I learned more about my daily activities and about Nemo's colorful personality. He was 59 years "young," he claimed.

"I don't care about age. My art makes me feel young. I am an artist and the best in the trade in all of Canada and even the United States, I dare to say."

Nemo believed this so intensely and matter-of-factly, that no one dared to even slightly mention the names of other great and famous glass sculptors, such as Lalique, whose remarkable works of art constantly adorned the pages of well-known interior design magazines. Nemo's eccentricity drove him to compare those artists to himself, not the other way around.

What Nemo lacked in height and muscles, was compensated by his unfaltering verbal energy. Most days, I had to sit in front of his desk and listen attentively to the different subjects he felt like tackling, trying my very best not to yawn. He complained about the boring life he had to lead at home and for a moment, I felt sorry for his wife. Actually, there were days when not even I could stomach his endless chatter. I often wondered why most short people were always the noisiest in a crowd, the most opinionated, drove bigger cars, chose a central table in a restaurant, and relished in telling tall tales no matter how ridiculous they sounded to most listeners.

One afternoon, Frank Sinatra's voice came through Gavin's radio and Nemo commented how well he knew the crowd the actor/singer hung around with.

"By the way, I have known some big shot godfathers myself in the past," he said. "You see this?" he showed the stump of his right ring finger, "you get a little out of line, and you end up in trouble." He didn't get into further details.

Whether to believe the tale or not was yet another story. To avoid having to listen to more tales, I would often find an excuse to go next door to help Bob with the order desk or do some filing for Zack. I had to let my ears rest, at least for a little while.

Nemo's partners, Zack and Norris, dropped over on and off. It was not known whether those visits were to keep an eye on Nemo's work progress or a simple courtesy visit. Fact is, that Nemo would immediately interrupt any conversation, jump to attention, and pull a chair for whichever wanted to sit and chat. They rarely accepted his invitation, though Zack occasionally would sit for a short while to smoke a cigarette while Nemo, to underline his apparent buddy-buddy status with Zack, rattled away in Sicilian. They both smoked like chimneys, filling the air with dense clouds of cigarette smoke. With the exception of Bob, the Paul Newman look-alike and Norris, every person in that company smoked, including me. The fact that Nemo always jumped up at the sight of one of his partners and pretended to do something other than chatting with his secretary, gave me the feeling that he was not as great of an authority within the company as he claimed to be.

Aside from his repetitive stories, he would on occasion come up with some humor as well. He was, unquestionably, a good comedian, at least he thought so. My presence alone was not sufficient. He needed a greater audience and often also called Gavin, his fellow-artist-assistant, who would always blush when told a spicy joke. Nemo seemed to relish Gavin's embarrassment.

Gavin was a tall, slim young man with reddish blond hair and brown puppy eyes. He was extremely shy, well mannered and a very hard worker. Nemo was very proud of his performance, which he naturally attributed to his superior guidance. Gavin was also very grateful to Nemo for having been given the opportunity to learn the fine art of glass carving from an Italian Maestro. Less grateful he was when invited by the Maestro to participate in meetings that were nothing but futile chatter.

Nemo's creativeness usually kicked in after the nine to five schedules. That was because he preferred to chat, if not with me or Gavin, then with the partners next door. The bad thing was that he expected Gavin and me to make up for the time he lost in chatting, after the regular hours, and without overtime pay. He set up his working schedules according to his mood of the day. Some days he would immerse himself in a given project with only a few breaks for a quick story or a joke. Then around ten minutes to five, he would beg me to remain "just for one last cigarette" and the usual chatter session, which normally dragged to about 6 p.m.

Nemo hated to buy food off the coffee truck. "I can't stand that garbage. They mix toothpicks and nails into the squished eggs and maybe, if they are pissed off for some reason, they even spit into it," he once said very seriously. He also hated to bring sandwiches from home because it was not becoming to his image of corporate executive director, as it said on his business card. He loved to go eat in restaurants where mainly Italian food was served. Pizza Nova was one such place. Some pasta and a glass of wine made him a happy, executive camper. The only problem was that he hated to go alone and as everybody else was trying to avoid him, his new target was me who, initially, took it as a privilege to be invited by the boss, but soon realized that it was not such a great idea. He always refused my offer to pay for my portion of the food bill.

"Don't even mention it, my dear," he said It is my pleasure, also because who else would be so kind to keep me company?"

Such lunch intermezzos would produce more dissertations about work, his dreams, the old country and food. Nemo proclaimed to be the best cook in the world.

"No one can make a dish of tripe the way I do it," he said. "I guarantee you would lick all ten fingers of yours."

My stomach made a somersault at the simple idea of having to just look at tripe, let alone eat it. I knew that it was considered a real treat in certain countries' finest restaurants and had also been my grandfather's favorite dish, but I could not bring myself to touch it. Nemo continued to describe recipe after recipe, between spoonfuls of minestrone or pasta. His eagerness to show off his incomparable ability did not allow me to cut in with my own comment. He was the type who asked and answered his own questions.

Nemo's frequent interruptions often irritated me and I had to resort to all my inner strength to maintain my self-control.

"I do not understand how you have never anything to say," Nemo remarked.

"Well, let's put it this way..." I tried to explain, but was interrupted once again.

"Oh, I know. I understand perfectly. You would be surprised if I told you that I know you better than you know yourself. That is because you are like an open book to me and you don't even realize it. Let me just tell you this, my dear...." and Nemo went on and on and on, rattling away, describing my personality, qualities, defects and all the while making comparisons with past employees or members of his own family. Many times I had to hold back my annoyance at his exaggerations, indiscretions and offensive remarks. Some of his statements were really light-headed but he hardly noticed his gaffes.

"I am honest and-a sincere," he said. "I swear in front of-a God. What I think-a, I say. Straight from-a de heart." he justified himself.

He did so indeed, when one afternoon he decided to offer both Gavin and me a lesson in world history. Simply ignoring the fact that Gavin was an Englishman, Nemo proceeded to describe his aversion of the English language and the people.

"It is nothing but a bastard language, and look at the country; it was nothing but a land of pirates and barbaric plunderers," Nemo said, and continued his insensitive historic dissertation.

Gavin sat there, frozen in time, helpless, not believing his own ears. After a moment his blood started to flow again, his face turned red, and he was ready to react and defend his own grassroots.

"How can you just say things like that, Nemo? I was born in England and..." Gavin tried telling him.

"You don't know world history my friend because you are ignorant of the facts," Nemo interrupted, ignoring Gavin's protests and determined to finish his lesson and get old resentments off his chest.

"How come you chose to move over here if you are so terribly prejudiced and unhappy with the English culture?" I asked.

"Because of the children and-a big-a bizziness connections," Nemo said. "But there is nothing better or comparable to my native Sicily." Tears flooded his eyes while he reminisced about the good olden days.

There had been absolutely nothing under the sun Nemo hadn't seen, heard, touched or experienced, except maybe, illness. He always bragged that he had never been ill one day in his entire life. After a full day's work, Gavin's back would be sore from the constant bending over the artwork that had to be traced first and then cut.

"Ah, that is no pain my friend," he said. "It is nothing more than a figment of your imagination."

According to Nemo's philosophy, there was no such thing as pain or illness. Those were conditions germinating in people's brains and the best way to neutralize them was to use the power of mind over matter. Even when I told him about Mefisto's heart attack, which led him to stop smoking, Nemo just smiled.

"Nonsense, my dear," he said waving his hand. "I have an old acquaintance who not only had had a heart attack, but also a triple bypass. To mock destiny, that fellow recovered beautifully due entirely to his willpower and even returned to smoking, drinking and eating to his heart's content. Against the doctor's prevision, he lived happily for many more years. It's all in here, my dear." He pointed his index finger to his head.

Even though masking it superbly, Nemo was vulnerable to pain and could barely hide the droplets of sweat on his forehead and the teardrops flooding his eyes after having been pressed against the floor by a 400 lb. pane of glass. While standing between a large cutting table with a dolly sitting against it, and another dolly in front of him holding that piece of glass, Nemo, with a bold movement of his hand, attempted to remove the vinyl stencil, by pulling it off the surface of the glass. However, he failed to check whether the wheel brakes of the dolly were secured because one pull must have been too strong as the large pane of glass suddenly started to tilt and fall over him, squeezing him against the dolly behind him, which was luckily stopped by the heavy, bolted cutting table.

Typing at the front office, all I heard was a muffled "help, help, help" sound. At first, I thought the boys in the back were just joking around again. At a second cry of help, however, I decided to investigate and there I saw Nemo, his 5'2" fragile frame under the heavy piece of glass, gasping for air and help. Before I could even open my mouth, three men from the shop rushed over and immediately freed Nemo from the glass. He was visibly shocked and in agony for the impact but no one could convince him to have himself checked out at the hospital.

"These bastards have not registered me for health coverage or workers compensation," he said, referring to his partners. "They would get into deep trouble if I went to spill the beans to the authorities." He took a swig from the cognac bottle he kept in his drawer for emergencies. All the while he massaged his knees and shoulders. I helped him clean his pants from the dust and debris. His bloodshot eyes were trying to hold back tears and to hide them from the people around. He rushed to the bathroom to splash cold water on his face and over his head.

Later, when the worst pain had subsided, he desperately tried to find the one to blame for the accident. Somebody should have put on the breaks on the dolly. There was no one in particular assigned to that task. The glass could have broken, fatally injured the man and he could have bled to death. The thought terrified him. It was an accident that was definitely not a figment of his imagination. For several days after the accident, Nemo was sore, blue and black, and walked with a slight limp and for even more days, kept recalling the incident telling about it to most of his friends and acquaintances.

Nemo was always terrified about making mistakes. The simplest drawing at times became an extremely complex one and he would call me and Gavin to witness and confirm the correctness of his calculations. In case of error, he could always blame one of us.

One such incident happened with three large, carved mirror panels for the ceiling of a new, classy restaurant. Each of the three panels had a slightly different size to accommodate the design and the framework. The carved area was spread across all three pieces. Nemo had them lined up side-by-side on a huge cutting table. The painted side was face up because the carving had to be done on the back of the mirror. Not being a tall man, Nemo had to climb up onto the table and move around on his knees to fit the stencils. He enjoyed having me standing around to hand him pencils, markers, erasers, etc., like an assistant nurse to the surgeon. I had to drop everything each time the phone rang because it could have been an important call, maybe even an order. After a while, I just remained at my desk, sure that the Maestro was more than capable of taking care of his work. After all, he had almost forty years of experience in that line of activity.

Somewhere along the line, however, Nemo had for some unknown reason, switched the sequence of the panels. The end result was truly beautiful as the three carved panels sat side by side on the dollies. I was particularly happy, as the design composition had been mostly my creation, even though Nemo signed the artwork because he contributed with minor touch ups and was, after all, the artist boss.

All hell broke loose when the installer called saying that one of the panels was the wrong size and wouldn't fit into the assigned framework and broke.

"Jesus Christ, Jesus Christ. Damn, damn, damn," Nemo shouted into the phone. "How could that happen? I checked and double-checked. I'm positive they were right. I even followed the labels. Oh, God. Jesus Christ, Jesus Christ." He continued running up and down in the shop while holding his head in disbelief.

"George, Robin, Gavin, come over here right now. You guys saw me drawing up the stencils. You saw I did it right. You are my witnesses." He was almost screaming in despair.

They all surely saw him working on the panels but were not aware of the details and were unable to vouch for his assertions. But everybody saw him switching panels as they had to help him to do so and George reminded him of that.

"Impossible my friend; I only switched them because they were wrong in the first place," Nemo said.

Nemo's panic was evident. He called and asked me to be his witness, but I was not present at the switching scene and could not affirm whether he was right or wrong. I was puzzled with his desperate need to be exempted as the guilty party in the apparent mishap. Mistakes happen, even with the best of Maestros, but his pride was far greater than his humility. Nemo was simply furious, desperately trying to find a scapegoat, pacing up and down, chain smoking and swearing. How on earth could he, the famous artist, have made such a terrible mistake? It was simply unacceptable, inexcusable and most of all, impossible.

He spent the rest of the afternoon phoning friends to tell them about his ill fate, caused by the incompetent shop crew. He came to the point of insinuating that perhaps Gavin had sabotaged his masterpiece for envy. Maybe such mistrust on the part of Nemo added to the list of reasons for which Gavin decided to call it quits. In the meantime, they replaced the broken mirror a week later and the whole incident was buried in the "To Forget" file.

When Gavin left the company, Nemo had to look for another assistant capable of sandblasting and carving glass. An ad was placed in the paper and soon enough a string of qualified artists filed through Nemo's door. He was picky, critical, and not afraid of hurting anyone's feelings with his superfluous and unnecessary comments. He ended up choosing Chris, a tall, slim man in his late twenties. His portfolio was filled with a vast array of cartoon characters and he assured Nemo that he was an experienced sandblaster. He was indeed good at it but had a lot to learn about the art of sand-carving glass. Nemo gave him several smaller pieces of ¾ inch thick plate glass to practice and was actually nice and patient with Chris during his initiation period. What Nemo did not like, however, was Chris's sloppy attire and the long, unkempt hair, which Nemo had asked him to cut or to wear in the form of a ponytail.

"Not only can long, loose hair get in the way when using some machinery and cause an accident, but he gets all sweaty when wearing the sandblaster's helmet and then stinks it all up," Nemo said. "How can I use it afterwards, don't you see? So gross." he explained.

Even though proclaiming to be a real gentleman, Nemo often lacked diplomacy, not only with his own employees, but even with some of his customers. One Italian lady, who had been referred by an acquaintance, had come to see him for some sandblasted glass door panels. Nemo showed her the pieces he had in the showroom and hoped that she would go for some of his three-dimensional carvings, but she just wanted a very simple floral motif. Ignoring her wishes, Nemo kept imposing his own artistic views for her doors, to the point that the lady, somewhat annoyed with his insistence was about to leave altogether. I understood the situation and intentionally dropped a folder containing various sketches of floral motifs. The lady's eyes immediately fell onto a delicate cherry blossom composition and wanted to know what it would cost her. Nemo sat down to do some calculations and came up with his usual exorbitant prices just so he could offer the client a likewise super discount and make her feel that she was getting a fantastic deal. It was a drawing that would take about two hours, with two more was to cut the stencil and another hour to sand carve it. Even if he had dragged it out, it would have taken him only two days to complete the job, but to justify the price structure, he told her it would take two weeks instead.

Nemo was all smiles when the lady returned two weeks later to check on the panels and pay for them.

"Here they are, my dear. You now have a real work of art." He pointed to the panels.

The lady was very satisfied and pulled out her check book to pay for the pieces. Gawky, as only Nemo could be at times, he looked on as she wrote up the check.

"Look at this beautiful lady," he said, trying to be funny. "Not only is she beautiful but she can also write."

The lady just glanced at him briefly and did not seem to have appreciated his totally uncalled for stupid observation. She simply handed over the check and requested that the panels be delivered to her house and installed by the company installers as soon as possible. She left without a smile.

One day, Nemo received a phone call from a TV station that wanted to do a piece on him and his art for the Italian channel. I had never seen him so excited. Fame and recognition were finally at his doorstep. He immediately engaged my assistance to help him write the speech he planned to give.

"But Nemo, this is going to be more like an interview," I said. "All you have to do is answer questions. There won't be enough time for a long dissertation."

"I don't care. I have to prepare myself, so just take notes."

I had almost three pages of handwritten material, sufficient to start his biography. I had to type those pages several times, adding and deleting and changing the contents. He probably did not sleep at night from the excitement.

The day before the appointment he had everybody help with the cleaning of the premises and made sure the driveway was clear for the TV crew. The day of the shooting he came in early morning, all dressed up in suit and tie. Pacing back and forth, holding a cigarette in one hand and the typed pages in the other, he tried to memorize what he had dictated. When the TV crew finally arrived, Nemo placed a quick call to a friend for the simple purpose of appearing like a busy executive. He then met with the Italian newscaster who would conduct the interview. They chatted briefly while the camera crew set up the lights and positioned the camera. A young lady applied some make-up powder on the faces of both, Nemo and the newscaster. Considering himself a real macho man, Nemo fought the make-up idea because that was "stuff for females." But he was told that it was necessary to cover up the shine of the skin and render the faces more attractive. The trick worked because Nemo was vain. He then praised the Italian newscaster for his work at the Italian channel and compared him to a beloved Italian showman and presenter named Pippo Baudo. It was like comparing apples to oranges, yet in Nemo's mind, it worked out to be a huge compliment to the newscaster who simply looked on with an expression of "what the hell is this guy talking about?"

Finally, the lights went on and....action. The interview did not last more than ten minutes, if that, and Nemo did not have a chance to say all the things he had planned to say. Under the camera lights, he appeared shy, insecure and almost humble to those who did not know him well. For a few days, all Nemo did, was to rehash his TV appearance even though the final transmission lasted not more than three to four minutes. He definitely had dreams of grandeur, almost as big as the fame of Michelangelo and Leonardo, his favorite artists, and his ego was just as gigantic, yet he was unable to create something original, of his very own. He simply copied from the classics and I often wondered if he ever did go to art school as he claimed he had. He refused to produce sample pieces for Leo to show designers.

"If the salesman is good, he doesn't need sample pieces to carry around. He could forget it somewhere and then someone may steal my ideas," he once said, angrily. Leo did not succeed either in persuading Nemo to produce at least one miserable sample piece, which discouraged not only the clients but also, and mainly, Leo, who often butted heads with Nemo. He argued about Nemo's stupid sales techniques and the complicated, ridiculous price list, which turned out to be frequently incorrect and was re-done according to Nemo's mood swings.

There came a time when Nemo was requested over to the partner's offices for a series of important meetings. I noticed that he would always return upset but I did not bother to touch the subject. It had never been my habit to poke my nose in people's personal matters. If they wanted to confide in me, I would listen; otherwise, discretion was the best tool to live peacefully alongside other people. Then one day, Nemo himself approached me.

"I should not be telling you this, but I trust you," he said. "I know you will not go around telling on me. Anyway, those bastards want me to produce $20,000 per week. How the hell am I supposed to do that?"

The company's budget desperately needed to increase its sales and Nemo's contribution at that point was close to nil. As the fire was burning under his feet, Nemo decided to go out and try to play the salesman himself. Miraculously, he succeeded to get an order for a beautiful and intricate motif to be carved on a ¾ inch thick large glass panel. Nemo prepared the drawing, had it approved, enlarged and applied it to the stencil. For one day, he did some cutting and even I helped. I had by then acquired the handle on stencil cutting. Nemo had taught me the best way to hold the cutting knife and guide my right hand with the left hand to obtain perfect curves and circles. I loved that part of the job, even if it left me with a very sore back at the end of the day. Reassured that everything was running smoothly and that there was plenty of time to deliver the artwork, Nemo flew to New York for a week.

Not being disturbed by his chatter, I decided to surprise Nemo by cutting the rest of the stencil. I even pitched in with some overtime. I figured that the sooner the piece was delivered, the sooner he got paid and his partners would get off his back and be happy with the revenue. When Nemo returned one week later and saw the finished panel, instead of showing gratitude he was taken over by anger.

"What on earth are you trying to do to me? How can you just betray me like that? You put me in a bad light in front of my partners. Now they are going to think that I am not capable of doing my job, thanks to your unnecessary eagerness to finish the piece."

"It's not finished yet," I said. "You still have to carve it don't you?"

"Well, that is true. Anyway, please don't do such a thing ever again."

You better believe it, I thought to myself. I would think twice before trying to be nice and do that little slimy, gutless big mouth another favor. That episode made me lose a fair bit of respect for Nemo. He was nothing but an insecure, megalomaniac who shrank and shriveled when facing higher authorities such as his own partners.

Having established a nice rapport with Zack and Norris, I finally found out that Nemo was not really their partner but merely an employee, without decision-making powers even though he had the arts department under his name and was allowed to sign his employee's payroll checks. Zack had given him the opportunity to join the company hoping that through his ability as a great artist, he would also generate additional income for the company. Nemo, however, had revealed himself a failure and was becoming a financial burden to his partners. He was therefore given an ultimatum. Either his sales were to go up or he was out of the picture entirely.

Nemo felt the pressure mounting and his frustration was taken out on his co-workers. He started to pick on Chris because he would always spend considerable time in the toilet.

"I wish I knew what that boy does all that time, closed in the toilet. He could be masturbating or smoking marijuana," he argued, seriously.

He would pace up and down, checking his wristwatch every ten to fifteen seconds and stop only after Chris came out of the toilet. One afternoon, he even dared ask me to go knock on the door with the excuse of checking if he was all right.

"Shouldn't you be doing the knocking, considering that he's a guy?" I replied, wondering why loudmouth couldn't do such a simple task himself.

Then one day, Chris called in sick. Nemo's eyes acquired a mischievous glow.

"Let's go Isabel. Let's go check out the washroom and see what that hairy bum is hiding in there."

We approached the washroom and with the aid of the tip of his middle finger, Nemo cautiously pushed the door open. Contrary to Nemo's expectations, there was no evidence of drug paraphernalia, but there was an old issue of Playboy, a Comic book and a small cardboard box containing pencils, erasers, markers and colored pencils. Nemo examined everything very carefully, cursing all the while.

"That long haired bastard," he shouted." Look at this, just look at this. He even dared steal my good pencils and there's my eraser, too. I was looking for it. Go get Norris and Zack. They must see this right away."

I went over to call them. Norris wasn't in but Zack came running. Cursing in Sicilian, Nemo immediately showed him all the precious things Chris had stolen from him. Zack just smiled, holding back laughter at Nemo's silly behavior.

"And now that you touched everything and also leafed through the magazine, you could be infected, too," Zack said trying to fuel Nemo's apprehension of contamination by some strange illness.

"Jesus Christ, Jesus Christ; Isabel, go get the alcohol or some disinfectant, quickly," he yelled while rushing to his own washroom. He splashed alcohol all over his arms and hands. "That pig. Now we know what he was doing. One more time, and he's gone, finished, finito."

Zack rushed out from the office because he could no longer refrain from a hearty laughter and so did I. Some people read in a toilet, Chris was drawing cartoon characters and naked ladies based on Playboy pictures, and the sketches were very good, too.

Among Nemo's many hidden talents, there was woodworking. He had proclaimed to be an expert in furniture design and manufacturing, a knowledge he had acquired back in the old country. So when a client came to order a carved glass table top, he convinced her to let him build the supporting structure, made of two half circles on each end. For days, he worked feverishly, sketching and calculating.

"Come here, Isabel. What do you think of this drawing? Do you like it?"

"Sure, looks Ok to me."

"Just ok? Do you think that the base is strong enough to hold this table top?"

"Well, I don't know. I have no experience in furniture making."

"What does that have to do with it? All you need is to use your logic."

"I don't think logic alone will do the trick, Nemo."

Once Nemo was fixated on something, however, there was no way to deflect his attention to something else. He kept pestering me for a logic opinion, which I was unable to give because I was not an expert in furniture-making and absolutely not willing to be blamed for a possible mishap. He then recruited the help of a professional cabinetmaker who helped him build the dreamed-of masterpiece.

There came a time when business shrank to a dangerous low and his meetings with Zack became more frequent and intense. He and Norris were no longer willing to finance Nemo's extravagant work methods. His prices were out of proportion and many customers decided to cancel their orders or skip the concept of artwork altogether.

"Those cheap bastards, what do they know about artwork? Offending my intelligence, that is what they are trying to do. Should I decide to leave this place one day my dear, in loyalty to my person, you should resign, too," he told me. At that point I really wished he was gone.

Somehow, Nemo found a customer and convinced him to do some important artwork on his eight-panel front door. The man was a wealthy dentist and had just built a deluxe villa and asked Nemo to show him sketches. Nemo immediately sat down and started sketching his favorite muscular figures surrounded by chubby little angels, clouds and flying birds. He then took the drawings to Paragon to have them enlarged for easier viewing and then called the customer to the showroom to approve it. The first reaction of Mr. Pirelli was that of shock as he saw Nemo's plan but out of respect, did not disclose his real feelings and told Nemo that he had to discuss the matter with his wife. Mr. Pirelli's expected phone call did not come through and Nemo took a week off because he had things to do in New York.

During Nemo's absence, Mr. Pirelli called and told me that naked bodies and angels were out of the question. His wife wanted a floral motif or even a park scene as the door opened towards a beautiful front garden. I promised I would let Nemo know as soon as he returned from his trip.

That evening, leafing through my picture books, I began to doodle and ended up with a stylized version of Monet's garden scene, suitable, in my opinion, for sandblasting and carving. I hoped Nemo would appreciate my efforts in trying to save the job with a new design but Nemo did not show any particular interest in my sketches and just wondered who that Monet was.

"He's a famous French painter," I explained.

"Ooh? I'm not too familiar with the French people," he said. That was the extent of his interest in my sketch, and in Monet.

He lived in his own space in time or time in space and had no intentions in changing. It would have been a truly beautiful masterpiece, spread across the eight panels, but Nemo hyper-calculated the cost, as usual, and the project fell through.

Soon after, another project went sour for the same reason. Nemo pushed the customer to consider the picture of Venus emerging from a shell. He dragged on the first sketch because for some unknown reason he could not get one eye right. I tried helping him by sketching the eye on a separate piece of paper, taking away the bulge he had created. Nemo tried to re-trace it on his own sketch but kept falling back into his initial incorrect lines. It looked like someone had stuck a big black olive half way through the eye socket of the subject and for a while he was unable to fix it.

"I have to put it aside for a day or two," he said. "Sometimes things just don't fall into place as I wish they would," he said.

In the meantime, more pressure built up because both Zack and Norris were sick and tired of his broken promises and inefficiencies. He had to go.

"I don't need these bastards who totally ignore art and keep offending my intelligence, and you Isabel, you have to come with me. I'll build ourselves a new studio, with new machines, not this Mickey Mouse equipment they have here, and we are going to make lots of money. And you owe me this loyalty for all that I've done for you."

I did not say a word. I just listened and smiled, pitying the poor man who was clearly losing it. I was afraid that Nemo was dead serious about his intentions to start a new company, dragging me along with that idea. I did not react to his words because I did not want to fuel his hopes about me joining him in his new venture. Yet that same evening, I sat down to make a list of all the cons and pros of Nemo's proposition. How much longer would I be able to cope with his endless chatter, with his constant intrusion in my personal life? His wilful ignorance of employee rights and benefits was irritating and so was his excessive possessiveness in the areas of professional and personal friendship.

If unable to generate income from his work while having a solid back-up through his so-called partners, how would he possibly succeed on his own? His sales tactics were poor. His portfolio was obsolete; it contained nothing new and attractive and he refused to come up with new drawings in his very own style—if he ever had one—to create at least a few sample pieces as promotional tools to assist in the sales process. Even though he urged his employees to assist him with suggestions and opinions, he denied anyone the possibility to express his or her views for the simple fact that he was unable to listen. He answered his own questions. He had no need for other artists or co-workers with fresh, new ideas because he, the Maestro, was the one and only who knew it all.

His endless superficial chatter was taking a toll on everybody's nerves. He could spend a whole day chatting with one or the other, wasting not only his own but also the listener's time. The signing of the pay checks was another agonizing weekly issue. He would open the folder, look at the two or three miserable checks and then close the folder again because that very instant, something else came into his mind. He would drag on a conversation for another ten minutes before finally signing them with the usual large theatrical gestures and remarking each time, "I'm used to sign a lot of checks and in amounts hundred times bigger than these." In essence, he was always right and everyone else was always wrong.

One morning, Nemo called saying he would not come in because he had business to attend to. I didn't bother to ask for details. It was not my place to question the boss. That same morning I was approached by an extremely happy Norris.

"Isabel, I don't know if you heard, but Nemo will be leaving us soon. Has he offered you a job yet or would you like to stay with us here?"

The question caught me by surprise because Nemo had not mentioned anything to me at that point.

"Aside from telling me that I owe him my loyalty and should quit my job in case he did the same, he never mentioned leaving this company," I told Norris. "Why are you asking? Did he resign?"

"Not exactly, but he will soon be gone. That's why I'm asking if you would like to remain as our secretary?"

"I think I'd like to stay with you guys."

"Ok then. It's a deal," Norris said, giving me a healthy handshake.

When Nemo came back the day after, he told me that he had submitted his resignation and that I was supposed to do the same. I told him that I could not afford to simply give up a job because he wanted me to do so.

"I will give you a job as soon as I get organized because I don't need these "nobodies." Just don't listen to them; don't fall into their trap."

Nemo left the next day repeating endlessly what I should or not do; the evil that would surround me if I stayed with his ex-partners and the wonderful career I would have if I decided to join him in his new enterprise.

That evening at home, I pondered and pondered some more, but no matter how I looked at the possibility of working for Nemo again, a big red flag kept flapping in front of my eyes. There were definitely more cons than pros and I no longer had patience to deal with his idiosyncrasies either. I definitely needed a break from Nemo and his space in time.

25

Glass & Mirror Inc.

I was wrong in thinking that by Glass & Mirror dismissing Nemo, I would no longer hear from him. He did not give up very easily and when he could not reach me by phone in the office, he would pester me at home.

"I now have registered my new company and you and your family are invited to attend the grand opening. I have a brand new property around the Keele and 401 area."

"Congratulations," I said, curtly.

"I was hoping to receive a phone call from you, anytime, even late at night, Saturday, Sunday, wouldn't matter. How come you never called me?"

"Well, you see...."

"I know why," Nemo interrupted. "Because you didn't have the guts to call me and because you were ashamed. You felt guilty for what you did, isn't it?"

I did not expect that verbal assault and somewhat perplexed, did not know what to say or how to react. Even if I did want to say something, Nemo would not have given me the chance of breaking into the one-way dissertation.

"I loved you like my own sister." (*Poor sister*, I thought.) "Those are sacred feelings in which you do not believe because you're not used to it."

Tired of listening to Nemo's confusing, endless ranting and raving, I simply hung up the phone. He probably would not have noticed it anyway, at least for a little while, distracted as he was in carrying on his recriminatory tirade. Thanks to call display on my set, I did not answer when he called back a little later, nor did anyone else in the household. He tried to reach me several times after that, unsuccessfully. Then one Saturday afternoon, Mefisto told me that a lady on the phone wanted to talk to me. It could have been the doctor's secretary or a friend of mine. As soon as I grabbed the phone and greeted with my usual happy "Hello, Isabel speaking," I recognized Nemo's voice. He had tricked me by using his daughter as decoy.

"Isabel my dear, I beg you not to hang up. You have to hear me out. I've been always very honest and sincere with you. I'm only sorry that for money, you returned to work for those bastards, those frauds at Glass & Mirror. First, they stole that cuckold Leo from me and now they stole you. I would have given you more money and 10 percent shares in my new company. I would have even given you a car to drive back and forth to work. I just bought the very best and most modern glass-cutting equipment from Michigan. It should arrive shortly. I wish you would come and see this. I can show you all the documentation, so you don't call me a liar. I can work with my tie on, so clean everything is around here. Unlike Glass & Mirror's dirty pigsty with their old equipment dating back to the twenties and thirties. They don't even know how to use their computerized cutting machine."

I could almost not believe what I was hearing and had to let out a hearty giggle just thinking about getting more money from him in addition to 10 percent shares in his new company. He was not a rich man according to his own past disclosures. All he owned was a two-bedroom apartment somewhere on Keele and 401 and an old beaten up Lincoln for a car. How would he manage with the new modern equipment if he feared to touch an electric typewriter or adding machine? My ears were burning and my patience fading. The more he tried to talk me into joining his company, the more I rebelled against his presumption and insistence.

"I only hope they will not use my Glass Sculpting trademark. That would then really become an explosive issue, because I have documents to prove everything, and if I wanted, I could destroy Zack like an insect, because I am younger and more capable. That bunch of miserable beggars, offending my intelligence."

I took advantage of a brief break into Nemo's monologue.

"The reason for which I did not call you was simply because I had nothing to tell you and was not planning to sit for an hour with an ear glued to the phone to listen to a one way conversation. Besides, you have no right to insult, criticize or reprimand me because you are nobody to me. The reason for choosing Glass & Mirror over you is nobody's business, except my own." I said it all almost in one breath, disallowing Nemo from cutting into my speech.

"Far from trying to convince you to join my company, I am an honest person. I am. I swear to it. I am not a number of the many you have known in your life."

I wondered what he meant by that. Did he refer to my previous bosses, and did he consider himself to be the one and only perfect boss? I had to let out another chuckle. How much more conceited could a person be? Nemo was definitely very confused and delirious. His every sentence was a contradiction to a previous one.

"If you are an honest, good woman, from this day forward it will be you who will call me. If you don't, that means that you are not being sincere with me and have been nothing but an opportunist. Should you change your mind, however, I will have a chauffeur at your disposal, more money and a real future for yourself. I also want to apologize for taking so much of your time and give my best regards to your family."

Those were Nemo's famous last words because after I hung up, I never heard from him again or about his super modern, famous Glass Sculpting Studio.

In the meantime, Glass & Mirror had received several orders requiring sandblasted artwork and with Nemo and Chris gone, there was no one else capable of doing it. I suggested calling back Gavin who, knowing that Nemo was no longer around, would most probably consider returning.

"Why don't you give him a call, Isabel?" Norris said. "See if you can convince him to come back. Tell him we'll treat him right, also financially."

"I'll see what I can do," I replied.

A few days later, I succeeded in catching Gavin at home. We made an appointment to have lunch in a small eatery on Ellesmere Avenue. I explained to him what Norris and Zack were looking for. I only did not know about the wages as that was a personal matter between Gavin and his new employers. He promised to think about it and would let me know about his decision within the next few days. His decision turned out to be a positive one. Everybody was happy to welcome him back to the shop.

Life at Glass & Mirror was quite different from what I had been used to during Nemo's reign. The salary was not bad, the hours were good and it was not far from home. I had no reason to feel bored as my days proved to be very busy and there was rarely any time for a quick social chat. I was in charge of the reception, as they had just lost their receptionist, the typing of correspondence for Norris and Zack, quotations for Leo and Gavin and invoices for Bob. I also had to issue purchase orders, take orders over the phone, send and receive fax messages and file most of the documents.

Some days were more hectic than others and it was difficult to concentrate on calculations while the phones were ringing off the hook. Luckily, Bob, the Paul Newman look-alike, often took pity on me and grabbed many of the calls which were meant mostly for him anyway. There were customers checking on the status of their orders, or changes had to be made to a pre-existing order, etc. Bob was the production manager and knew exactly what was where and when it was expected to be ready. He was the one to turn to when a miracle was needed. As it often happened with a fair number of contractors, a lousy bunch that enjoyed leaving everything to the last minute, due to negligence, ignorance or disorganization, orders were phoned in and were inevitably stamped as Rush Orders. Bob often wished he could strangle them but the company needed the bloody orders and he always did his best to comply and simply slammed doors and drawers to vent his anger and frustration instead of protesting verbally.

When upset, Zack would chain smoke, yell behind closed doors and then leave the office to take care of some business elsewhere or to have lunch with a buddy at the Tapps Restaurant. Gentle giant Norris rarely raised his voice. Only his face, when turning red, revealed his anger and disappointment. He was always busy, always had things to do. His mind was constantly churning out new ideas and plans. He was enthused when I created the Glassblast Design Catalog, something with pictures finally, that could be shown to designers and allow them to choose from a series of sandblasted motifs.

Both Norris and Zack approved of my promotional designers contest. I had Gavin carve a tri-dimensional sleeping lion on a ¾ inch thick, 12x10 inch piece of clear glass and he did a fantastic job. The contest generated a few orders and the lion was ultimately won by one of the designer participants. Norris thought that the bi-monthly company newsletter was yet another good promotional tool to keep in touch with most of our main customers, and helped me gather material for it.

Leo, the Pierce Brosnan look-alike—without the British accent though— was another interesting character. Always busy, always running. His desk was submerged with folders, correspondence, drawings, take-offs, writing pads, sticky notes with messages, magazines, coffee mugs, in and out boxes and ringing telephones.

To chat with Leo was always a treat. He knew everything about just anybody and anything. There were very few things he hadn't seen, heard of or experienced. He was the typical "been-there-done-that" guy. He was an extremely smooth talker and for that reason, also a great salesman. He never did get along with Nemo because of Nemo's hostile character and inability to come up with a straight answer to help him close a deal. Leo then decided to work entirely for Norris and Zack instead. Unlike Nemo, who constantly had to re-calculate his commissions to see if he could shave off a cent or two, Glass & Mirror paid Leo a fair commission on his sales, upon complete payment of invoices.

Another salesman was Gordon, an older gentleman who loved to brag about his past sales achievements and describe in a garbled confidential, whispered manner, his secret sales techniques. He had been with the company for almost twelve years and had become an icon to be respected.

After having changed a number of bookkeepers, they hired a tall, good-looking girl of Italian descent, named Geena. Not only did she know her profession inside out, but was also a very dedicated and hard-working individual, reasons why the bosses forgave her chronic tardiness in the morning. In time, Geena and I became good friends.

I also had a good relationship with the shop personnel. On many occasions, I spent lunchtime with the boys and learned about their lives, problems, hopes and frustrations at work and in their personal lives. Whenever Bob and the bosses were not around and a problem would come up, such as an emergency order, they would never refuse to help me out. When the weather was inclement, one or the other would always give me a ride, sometimes as far as my front door, since I still had no car of my own at the time.

I loved my job and my surroundings and never spared time and effort to make sure that everything was under control and to the satisfaction of everyone. There came a time, however, when the amount of work increased considerably and the company had to hire a receptionist to take care of the phone calls and help out with some of the typing and filing. It was up to me to select the girls, but it was Norris' final decision to hire one or the other. For some inexplicable reason, we were not lucky in selecting the right candidate.

It was my task to train the elected one to the company's standards. Most applicants showed up with secretarial course certificates, diplomas and fabulous, carefully typed résumés, yet somehow, lacked the skills of a true secretary. They were hired on a three months' trial basis. It proved to be a time consuming process, between training them and trying to do my own job at the same time.

One of the girls was dismissed in her second month because not only was she unable to follow orders but phoned in sick for a day every week and broke down in tears whenever she had an argument with her boyfriend over the phone. She was so distraught after each of those calls that she was unable to attend to her receptionist duties. A personal drama for which there was no place at Glass & Mirror.

A second girl thought that keeping her own working area clean and tidy was not part of her job description. She would keep customers on hold while finishing her own personal phone calls during regular business hours. A third and last one was extremely fast in doing everything, including typos, misspellings and misfiling of documents. She was also a staples maniac. Instead of removing the five previous staples from a set of documents, she would enthusiastically staple it for the sixth time and even seventh, for good luck perhaps. Punctuality was also a rare commodity to be found among some of the aspiring secretarial work force. I always wondered how things had changed and were oh… so dissimilar in the different parts of the world.

I would have never dared arrive late for work, or have my breakfast at my working desk on company time. Likewise, I would have never dared to rudely interrupt the boss in his office without knocking first, if there was a door, or waiting in front of his desk, until he finished whatever he was writing or doing.

Collecting money was a task most people shunned. Leo was one of the few who did not mind and neither did I. There were so many pleasant ways in discovering whether a check had been mailed already. I had never encountered any particular difficulties in begging for what was rightfully ours, pay for work or material delivered, except for one contractor, who with the excuse of holdbacks, also held Glass & Mirror's payments back. On my own initiative, I put that contractor's orders on hold one day, but Norris was not happy when he found out what I had done.

"You can't do that Isabel; I can't afford to lose an account like that," he said very seriously and ran out to the shop to reverse my orders.

I had a hard time in figuring out the logic behind Norris' reasoning. If the customer already owed $10,000 and was dragging out the payment for obvious financial difficulties, adding another $5,000 to the bill would only help Glass & Mirror to get into a deeper hole altogether. I had the feeling that Norris' reaction was that of panic and that it would develop into a more serious financial situation. In addition to some receivable problems, there had been some estimating screw-ups and incorrect take-offs for which Zack was furious and Norris close to pulling his hair out. The work had to be redone, with more financial loss.

On a personal note, I also had problems to deal with at home. My mother needed to go back and forth to doctors because of her back problem. She was having trouble walking, let alone climbing one flight of stairs to her German doctor's office. He probably had a good deal on the office lease and did not expect to treat handicapped people. He was kind enough to refer her to another physician, closer to home, and to an orthopedic surgeon as well, but even their equipment was not entirely "handi-friendly."

Due to the polio in her left leg, mother wore custom-made orthopedic shoes that had to be lifted every so often to adjust the difference between her right and left leg. Then in her later years, she developed scoliosis of her spine. No matter how hard she tried dieting, she would not lose the few extra pounds plaguing her body. Because of mobility problems, she could not run or jog or do exercises like able people and so the entire weight of her body fell onto her right leg. A full x-ray showed that her left leg was a lot longer than her right one and most doctors were amused by it as they believed that the polioed leg was the one that should have been shorter. She had started to walk with the aid of a cane and needed extra help when negotiating stairs. Even just a few were difficult for her. She would always step on with her stronger right leg and then drag her left leg up behind it. She had no strength whatsoever in her left leg, which in her opinion, was a useless appendix, good only to help her stand up and hold her balance. She always complained about why builders did not make friendlier steps to climb. Unfortunately, the standard height of most stairs in Toronto was eight inches, just like those little stool steps in all doctor's offices. They invariably asked the patient to step up on it in order to sit on the narrow examining table, which most probably for economic reasons, did not have features that would allow it to be lowered for handicapped patients. Each time, it required the assistance of the doctor and a nurse, or the doctor and me to help mother climb up the stool, slowly turn her around and then ease her butt onto the table. It was also not easy to help her lie flat on her achy back and then pull her up again. The same ritual repeated itself over and over. The orthopedic surgeon's office was no different. For several months, she swallowed anti-inflammatory pills and got cortisone injections in her back. Because not even the injections would help to alleviate the pain, her specialist decided to do surgery. I rushed back and forth between work, home and hospital because mother did not speak English and needed my translator skills.

Mother never quite regained the mobility she had five years before she landed in Canada, but she was finally free of pain and couldn't be more grateful to Dr. Chapman who, in her eyes, was an angel sent by God to help her. She was sixty-eight years old and undergoing the normal aging process. She also had to submit to a yearly colonoscopy, due to the malignant polyps they had removed years before in Germany. For that procedure, I had found a Hungarian-speaking doctor with whom she could communicate freely about her concerns. She was very happy with the procedures conducted at the hospital because unlike her ambulatory experience in Germany, the Toronto ones were totally painless. The only unpleasant part of the procedure was the preparation—having to drink a fair amount of Citromag to cleanse the bowels. After mother's back surgery, I arranged for her to have nursing help through a local community agency that would care for all her personal needs in the house such as bathing, bed linen changes and the cleaning of her room and the bathroom.

Mother was, therefore, well taken care of and I did not have to miss work except when I needed to drive her to see doctors or go for tests. The home care personnel could not drive patients to doctor's appointments because of the liabilities involved. Besides, to handle mother was somewhat complicated. To get into a car, she would stand on the passenger side with her back to the car seat. She then slowly eased herself into the seat by holding on to the back of the seat with her right hand and to the dashboard with her left hand. I would then lift her left polioed leg into the car first, followed by the right good leg, and at the same time, turning her in the chair into the forward position. With the power of her good, right leg, she would then push herself into a comfortable position. She also needed an additional pillow on the seat of the car to bring it to the height more suitable to her needs.

In the meantime, Mefisto and I had scraped together enough money to put a down payment for a house in the eastern section of Scarborough. With the help of the kids and their friends, we completed the move in one day. There were plenty of rooms for everybody and so much lawn to take care of.

It took a while until all the rooms were settled and the contents of the many boxes put away in their proper place. Slowly, throughout the following years, we would introduce our personal touches in the different parts of the house by adding marble, granite, slate, hardwood, new windows and so forth.

Tired of working for others, rather successfully, Mefisto decided to work on his own by becoming a distributor of glass, ceramic and stone products. He reserved one bedroom to act as office. Both kids had good jobs at the time. Nakina worked for Ford and Peter for GM. They both were hard workers and proud of their achievements.

For some time, both Mefisto and I had contemplated the possibility of going back to the old country for a visit. The timing coincided with the famous Bologna Floor and Wall Coverings Exhibit, an opportunity for Mefisto to see what the market had to offer. Norris seemed happy when I notified him of my intentions. Business was slow and not much money was coming in anyway. They had been downsizing a fair bit and by me taking holidays, they would save a few bucks also.

My restlessness ceased only once I fastened my seatbelt and the plane finally reached the highest cloud in the sky. A shot of scotch on the rocks finished with my lingering anxieties altogether. Some people interpreted that anxiety as conceitedness or indispensability syndrome whereas it was far from it in my view. All I worried about was that those left behind would find everything in proper order, without having to scramble and bitch about it later just like I had to experience similar situations a few times in the past. Luckily, Geena, Bob and Norris were aware of my filing system, general working procedures and I had also left notes everywhere with instructions. I strongly believed in teamwork and sharing information among colleagues was part of it, so that if an emergency ever occurred, the others could easily replace me. I never feared losing the job per se. Just as most companies did not consider their employees totally indispensable, so it was the other way around, too, I figured. Maybe I was naive, but it was my habit, wherever I worked, to create a small "manual of operations" for my particular position at the time.

I even underlined details such as punching holes in a document, because most people do not care much about such details, whether one sheet of paper is more centered than the other in a binder. Date stamping on incoming documents was another neglected item by most people. Unlike so many secretaries I had known, even some with high score diplomas, who would plant the stamps quickly just about anywhere on a document, even upside down at times, whereas I liked to stamp the documents always in the same direction, preferably where there was plenty of space for quick identification. The elimination of unnecessary staples was considered by most a waste of time, but I just couldn't live with bumpy, messy, casually stapled documents that would require additional filing space because of the thickness caused by excessive metal staples, not to mention injuring one's hand while handling the documents.

The Air Canada flight to Milano was a pleasant one. The first portion of our trip was dedicated to the Bologna event. Mefisto had booked a Hertz car ahead of time and we drove right away to Bologna. As usual, the show was a great event, attracting buyers from all over the world. The variety of products on display was unbelievable and posed a real decision- making problem for countless buyers. The exhibition grounds were enormous and required serious legwork and by the end of the day, both Mefisto and I were exhausted.

Once finished with business, we drove back to Milano and booked into a hotel close to the downtown core. The next day we paid a surprise visit to Mefisto's brother Franco, wife Gina, and nephew Giuseppe. Hugs mixed with tears celebrated the happy reunion. There was so much to tell on both sides, and we talked throughout dinner and some more after, till very late.

The next day, Mefisto and I decided to stroll in the downtown core. We visited Piazza Duomo, where the magnificent cathedral, Duomo di Milano, stood, with the golden Madonnina (little Virgin Mary) statuette towering over the city. It was the landmark I was introduced to when I first landed in Milano and it was in that same cathedral that Mefisto and I got married in February, 1967. Nothing had changed throughout the years, except for the cleaning of the outside walls that had been insulted by the smog caused from the exhaust of chimneys and vehicles. Once again I admired the majestic colonnades, the leaded glass windows, the smell of Frankincense, the echo of voices, and the sound of footsteps of an incessant stream of tourists snapping pictures. Then there was the Galleria with all its fancy stores, sidewalk cafés and expensive designer boutiques and fashion shoe stores. There was the La Scala Opera House and many other familiar places we used to visit while living in that city.

I noticed, however, that some things had changed in the city after all. There were many more foreigners populating streets where once one could only see typical Italian faces. A tapestry of Orientals, African and East European nationalities were clearly feeling much at home in Milano. So were a happy group of gypsy kids, running excitedly towards an elderly lady, circling her in a ring-around-the-rosy fashion, while the most talented of the bunch exercised his un-official right to pickpocket the poor unaware victim. A scuffle erupted, yelling and screaming followed and legs running in every direction ended the performance.

The gastronomic palette had also undergone changes. Chinese and Japanese foods had become a popular item and so did African and Brazilian cuisine. I noticed that the overall neatness of the city had been altered, too, for the worse. Milano no longer looked like the spic 'n span, swept and groomed city of the sixties, seventies and even eighties. It had become an even greater metropolis since, a true international melting pot.

On our way back to Franco's, we came across a local street market. I always enjoyed shopping at those open markets. The produce was always fresh and so pleasing to the eye and the palate. That afternoon, we found beautiful, fresh *Porcini* mushrooms (*Boletus Edulis*), with their large brown hat and light yellow, plump stems. Even though in season—it was the end of October—they were rather pricey, but Mefisto and I could not resist. Porcini mushrooms could not be found anywhere in Toronto other than in a dried form and even then, only in a few selected grocery stores. We purchased three or four pounds and I took it upon myself to prepare them. Cleaned, sliced and then simmered in olive oil, garlic, salt and pepper, a sprinkle of parsley and the final divine blessing, a little white wine for that extra punch. Franco enjoyed it so much that Mefisto and I decided to repeat the folly the day after, along with some fresh chestnuts to be roasted later. It was the perfect recipe for a good time together.

We then drove to Bergamo, Mefisto's birthplace, to visit his four sisters, another brother and the many cousins, relatives and acquaintances that lived spread out through the area. Their joy in seeing us was enormous and each one of them went out of their way to turn our short two-week stay into a memorable event.

As always, leaving home for a change was a good thing but returning home was even better. There was always a sense of renewal, a reason for celebration, stories to tell, pictures to show and gifts to give. The famous jetlag would balance itself out over the weekend.

Monday arrived fast and I returned to work bright and early.

"Hey, welcome back, Isabel. How was your trip?" Norris asked with his usual friendly smile. I took a seat and told him briefly about the trip. Norris listened with apparent great interest. Then when I finished my narrative, he blurted out the bad news.

"You know, Isabel," he said clearing his throat from some imaginary phlegm. "Unfortunately, we have to let you go. There is no more money to pay anybody." My smile froze and for a moment, I even stopped breathing.

"What happened, Norris, so suddenly?" I asked, slowly recovering from the initial shock.

"Long story my dear. I'm not happy about it either, however, I'm sure that you will not have any difficulty in finding another job. Just let me know if you need a reference letter and it will be my pleasure to give you one."

As usual, Zack was unable to play the bad guy and face the employees with the bad news, so he left the task to his partner. Leo and Gavin were also told to look elsewhere. The situation was serious. Geena had been the only one aware of what was going on, but as a true professional, kept matters confidential, until I approached her with questions.

"How can something like this happen in such a short period of time?" I asked. "It did not seem like there was any serious trouble when I left."

"But there was, and it has been brewing for quite some time," Geena said. "It only takes a few screw-ups to get into the hole and if in addition the banks refuse to loan you more money, people don't pay because they went under and so forth, there's nothing much you can do. There was more money going out than coming in and nobody was willing to take a pay cut either."

Unfortunately, there had also not been any liquidation money. Quietly and swiftly, the company dissolved into thin air. With a heavy heart I left the place of work I had been loyal to for almost five years and without much ado, began my search through the *Toronto Sun* and *Toronto Star* newspapers. There was, however, nothing interesting for me at the time and I decided to just lie back for a little while, meditate on my destiny and enjoy the upcoming holiday season. I wondered why so many companies, aside from the financial aspects, always chose the holiday seasons to lay off personnel. It was a devastating emotional and psychological experience, not mentioning the financial deficit caused by the lack of income. But then again, what could the employer have done, if there were no more funds?

January came all too soon. Ford Motors was hiring people with manual dexterity for an electronic assembly line. It seemed like an interesting experience, to observe the methodology used to measure a person's promptness, agility and speed in assembling bits and pieces of electronic parts. Only a robot could have done a better job and a lot cheaper, too. The pay was excellent, in addition to an unbelievable benefits package. No wonder the cars cost so much, I pondered. The hours however, could vary and turn into graveyard shifts for the newcomers.

Then one Saturday afternoon, towards the end of January, I received a call from Norris.

"Isabel my dear, I'm now working for the glass division of a large store fixtures company and I need a secretary. What about joining me?"

The running salary for a secretary / receptionist, at the time, was $24,000 per year. About the same I had been earning with Glass & Mirror. Nakina who worked for Ford was making $35,000 per year plus benefits and a lot more when she did overtime, but it wasn't my intention to work graveyard shifts or do overtime because I had mother to look after and had to be available when she had an emergency call.

"Listen, just write down this address and think it over," said Norris. "At least, come and check it out, ok?"

I wrote down the address, phone number, and then shared the news with mother who felt that I should consider Norris' offer.

"Big companies can also go bankrupt or downsize and then lay you off or fire you altogether and then the big buck becomes a no buck." Mother was referring to Ford. "Besides, remember, in a large company you are nothing but a number, a punch-in card whereas in a smaller environment you are still considered a human being. Keep that in mind."

I called Norris on Monday morning and made an appointment for the day after.

Theme Store Fixtures (TSF) had just moved from a smaller place into much larger premises and they were still in the process of setting up shop and decorating the offices. Norris was happy in seeing me and immediately showed me around the place. I was pleasantly surprised with the fact that he had also cared to find a job for another five former shop employees, among them Zack's own brother. The gentle giant cared about his people after all.

Finally, Norris introduced me to Arthur, the owner of the company, a 6'6" tall, handsome devil about my own age. I was impressed with the powerful sound of his operatic voice, a beautiful baritone. We chatted briefly about our origins. When Arthur later said, "I hope you will consider joining my company," I knew that I would. His handshake was firm like that of a person of courage and integrity and I liked that. Needless to say, I withdrew my job application from Ford to join TSF.

26

Theme Store Fixtures

A new chapter was to begin in my life when I joined MG-Glass, a division of Theme Store Fixtures (TSF), on February 4, 1994. Temporarily, Norris and I had to work out of an office that had previously been a storage room. Norris' task, aside from supplying TSF with glass tops, shelving and mirrors, was to find more customers for the new company. As on previous occasions, my task would be that of assisting him, organizing files, taking care of orders, invoicing, some correspondence and naturally, the telephone.

As the glass department did not really keep me busy all day, I was requested to pitch in as receptionist at TSF's front desk during lunch hour and coffee breaks. Later on, I also helped with the filing of vendors' invoices, working alongside Maggie, the bookkeeper, who had joined the company two weeks earlier. The girl was an extremely shy, quiet and hard-working individual, who assisted Harvey, an extremely busy Jewish accountant with a clearly South African accent. Always cracking jokes, he appeared to be a very happy man most of the time.

Then there was Bill, an older Scottish gentleman with a goatee who was in charge of the production schedules. There was Kelly, Arthur's personal secretary and Kami, a tiny, fragile-looking Chinese receptionist who treated all new arrivals with a fair amount of suspicion. She had been working for Arthur for a number of years and had become very protective of her boss and his company. Also part of the company was Rudi Mahler, a proud Prussian who gladly defied the winter elements mainly because he did not drive and did not own a car. He was a salesman and an event organizer. These were the main characters I had to interact with on a daily basis.

Arthur would often come to visit Norris in our little office, mostly during morning hours, hoping to receive good news about the glass business. Norris seemed to have a lot of plans and job prospects, but the success story was still in the making. Arthur promised that soon we would be transferred to the other side, TSF's main office. It was a large open concept with only one partition separating the various desks. Artie had his own spacious office as did Harvey. There was also a large boardroom, a computer programming area, a small kitchen and washrooms for both guys and dolls. The manufacturing plant in the back was divided into the various, wood, metal, glass, painting and assembly departments. Even though each department had its own supervisor, Arthur was the one directing and overseeing every phase of the operation.

February and March were quite cold and because our office had no heating outlets, Norris had to arrange for a couple of heaters to keep at least our feet warm. I could wear nice, cozy sweaters but I was unable to type with gloves on. I had to constantly breathe on my fingertips to keep the circulation flowing.

Arthur's secretary, Kelly, liked to come over to chat with one or the other and tell us horror stories about her boss' despotic behavior. She openly declared her hatred for him and I wondered why such an unhappy person did not quit, instead of spreading ill feelings within the company. However, she did not have to make such effort as she was dismissed soon after and replaced by a nice and competent young lady named Gloria.

Weeks went by and then months, and suddenly, summer knocked on the door. The windows in the storage room could not be opened and not even with the only door wide open onto the corridor, was there the slightest breeze flowing through. There were days when the little office was more efficient than a Scandinavian sauna.

"Let's hope they won't charge us for the privilege of working in a Sauna environment," Norris observed with good humor. When the heat became unbearable, I often slipped over to the TSF office, volunteering for whatever clerical work was available just so I could enjoy the pleasant air-conditioned surroundings.

One morning, Norris brought in a large picnic cooler filled with ice. He also brought a large salad bowl, which he then filled with ice cubes. He placed the bowl in a corner of his desk, put the desk fan behind the bowl and directed the highest setting in my direction.

"How does that feel now? Better?" he asked with a satisfied grin.

What a genius. Who else would have ever come up with such a brilliant idea? I did not have the heart to laugh or to tell him that it didn't make much difference at all. The fan still only stirred up the existing warm air. Perhaps if the chunk of ice had been bigger, a lot bigger! Meanwhile, all I had to do was to convince my mind to believe that the air was cooler—mind over matter, as Nemo used to say.

Arthur walked in as usual one morning to introduce the new Plant Manager, Floyd Fourlet, a handsome, soft-spoken man in his late forties or early fifties. His balding crown enhanced his chubby pink cheeks and his flirtatious blue eyes. It was time that Arthur had some help in rowing the boat that was becoming way too heavy for one man alone.

Floyd did pop in several times more, to chat with Norris and learn further about the glass shop operation as well as the paperwork involved in the various transactions. Norris generously explained every step of his operation. It never occurred to him that Floyd could somehow interfere with his position and perhaps eliminate it altogether.

Around November, Arthur finally transferred Bill to the estimating department and freed up enough space at the very end of the big office for Norris and me. For another while, I kept my old IBM Wheelwriter3, at least until I became more familiar with the Microsoft world.

Rudi was among those hesitant, almost hostile to the idea of adopting a computer as his working tool. He had no interest in, nor did he believe in the effectiveness of electronic devices. He preferred the direct, human touch when dealing with a customer. He did not need a car because there were cabs and airplanes as traveling means. He had a keen eye for art and interior design, which he applied not only to design shows and exhibits, but also to the simple choice of the company's Christmas cards, which were invariably chosen from the MOMA (Museum of Modern Art) collection. He also enjoyed organizing the company's Christmas parties to the tiniest details. The folding of a napkin was for Rudi cause for great study and contemplation. With a characteristic modesty, he would merely smile when praised by everyone for another success story. He would walk around with his head up straight, his brown hair fastened in a ponytail, wearing one of his favorite striped shirts with a white collar. Rudi was a very private person and rarely opened up to anyone. Sometimes I chatted with him briefly in German and it was during one of those chats that he revealed to me his three main passions: Jazz, the Catskills and his beautiful two daughters.

Another person I liked very much was Neeta, Arthur's wife. Beautiful, refined, tall and slim, she had natural blond hair and blue eyes. She used to come in on a part-time basis to help with some filing and the computerized payroll. I loved to chat with her because we had many things in common, including an interesting European cultural background. Arthur was yet another interesting character to chat with. I learned that he too, had stumbled a few times in the past and had to re-start everything from scratch. He was a born optimist who did not easily accept defeat and above all, he was a hard worker who did not refuse to get dirty to his elbows when needed.

"If you want to be respected as a leader, you have to act like one," he once said.

Christmas and the New Year came and went just as fast and with it came changes, new plans and hopes for everyone. Maggie had mixed feelings about Harvey's resignation and the arrival of a new accountant boss. Harvey was a good person even though he could be very demanding most of the time and had the tendency of dragging things out, leaving them for the last minute so that Maggie was often kept till late in the evening. She was much too shy and respectful to dare complain about it. She hoped that the new accountant, Gus Bono, would introduce a less hectic working system.

To get better acquainted with the people surrounding him, Gus called each employee into his office for a chat. He asked questions about their work and about family. He was a very friendly person, always smiling, always courteous. He was slim, of medium height, balding crown and inquisitive blue eyes. Maggie spent a couple of weeks introducing him to the various accounting issues and company procedures.

MG-Glass started the New Year with a busy schedule. To allow Norris more time to source clients for the company, he was allowed to hire a glass shop supervisor. Ron Reeves was a fast-talking individual with all the credentials to become such supervisor. He wore a military crew haircut and a very thin moustache. He was familiar with every aspect of glass cutting and polishing. My sympathy for Ron diminished considerably when after having been introduced to his beautiful young wife, Rita, Ron verbally insulted her for no apparent reason. He seemed to have had a desperate need to affirm his authority and supremacy over her. His attitude did not seem to bother anyone in particular. The important thing was that he executed his job well and did not recoil when faced with trouble and difficulties, which he did face, almost daily.

One of the installers had been on site waiting for a pair of glass doors to be delivered. When after much delay the panels had finally arrived, Sal the installer realized that the lock holes had been drilled incorrectly. They were located in the middle of the door as opposed to the end of the door, behind the cylinder, as requested originally by the owner. Norris, who had received different information from another source, had instructed the tempering company to drill the holes "dead in center." It was a clear case of miscommunication. Then there was a case where a distraught customer called to complain that the center panel of a three-panelled door had fallen out and needed immediate servicing. Ron had to juggle such problems efficiently and fast.

Incorrect measurements did also require prompt action which meant re-measuring, re-cutting and re-tempering the glass, resulting in obvious monetary loss, and there had been quite a few of those cases. Promised deliveries failed to be delivered or were delayed by an entire week and I had to intervene by trying to pacify the irate customers. Almost half of the orders placed had a hot red rush tag attached and for the sake of getting the order, the client was promised to get the material for the day it had been requested. MG-Glass could be a hectic place most of the time, where almost everything was a balancing act, especially when a pair of tempered glass doors were installed half an hour before the grand opening of a store while the owner was close to having a heart attack.

Too often, Ron Reeves was paged to deal with problems related to installations and defective materials. He also had the habit of running through the main office from one shop door entrance to the other. There was no need for him to walk through the office other than to show the boss that he was busily running from one point to another. Floyd therefore decided to call a meeting with Norris where he expressed his concern about MG-Glass' installation jobs interfering with the completion of orders to TSF's own out of town customers, which required absolute priority. Kami and I were given instructions to screen all Ron's incoming calls and relay messages to him only every hour or so, because the constant interruptions seriously interfered with his performance. Rush orders had to be screened as well, because not only were they disrupting the regular flow of order processing, but it was found that the many mistakes and screw-ups were mainly caused by the constant hurry mode in which the glass shop seemed to be operating.

As Norris was mostly on the go, in search of new customers, I decided to compile a weekly activities log, with copy to Floyd, to keep him updated on the developments within the glass shop. Everybody seemed to be very busy all the time and the days, weeks and months just flashed by relentlessly.

For some time, I had suffered with lower back pain and needed prescription medication, and had to visit my doctor to have the prescription renewed. Because the doctor's office was not open on Saturdays, I had to excuse myself from work for a few hours. I would make the time up by skipping lunch or working a little longer in the evenings. It was a matter of principle and honesty.

Another Christmas came, another wonderful party organized by Rudi and Neeta, who always put so much effort and personal touches in everything she undertook. Arthur made sure that everybody under his roof got a little extra in their pay check envelope. It was the festive mood to trigger generosity and gaiety among all.

Many changes came yet again with 1996. On a personal note, due to disagreements within the family nucleus, mother decided that it would be best to live on her own. She had her own ways to deal with issues and live life according to parameters she grew up with, and expected everyone else around her to follow as well. It was important to her that our behavior was proper at all times, that we observed traditions and rules, that we dressed in decent clothes and not in those awful blue jeans; that our hair was properly coiffed and not in a ponytail or drenched in gel, etc. She was certainly not shy when criticizing other family members, often triggering unpleasant reactions from the targeted person or the ones who disagreed with her. She had this uncontrollable urge to constantly compare us with other people. How nicer their garden was, or cleaner their yard or better their cars or how hard-working the neighbor's wife or husband was, and so forth. It was very irritating at times. The situation precipitated one day when she chose to bad-mouth Mefisto to Peter and Nakina.

"Say whatever you want but don't offend or touch my father," Peter told her.

"Besides, if you don't like it here, you can go live somewhere else," Nakina said. "Nobody is forcing you to stay here."

Having kept things bottled up for too long, due to their respect toward an elderly person, both kids had lost their self-control that day and felt the need to vent their anger and frustration with their meddling grandmother. It was then always my task to intervene by standing in the middle of the battlefield trying to diffuse the tensions and placate tempers, often unsuccessfully.

While on one hand mother's decision of moving out brought a sense of relief to the family, on the other hand it would only add another burden to my already hectic schedule. I had to run around to find proper housing for her. Considering that she was a handicapped senior citizen with a minimum foreign pension income, she was lucky in being approved for subsidized housing in a nice, clean apartment building some ten minutes from my house. I also arranged to have a telephone and cable installed, found a family doctor nearby the building with Lab facilities and other countless minutiae which the other family members did not care to worry about. I also arranged for her to have help with the housecleaning, laundry and bathing. The shopping, banking, medical appointments and a string of other chores, however, were still my duties.

I was happiest when at work. It kept my attention focused on other things than the family bickering and my mother's illnesses, pains and moody episodes. There were moments of good humor and laughter, mainly centered on Kami who, maybe never realized she would be the main character in a one-woman show most of the time. Her trademark expression was, "I just can't take it anymore." She was also in charge of the couriers and made sure that whatever parcel was entrusted to her, got to its destination in a timely fashion. She was not shy in keeping the drivers on their toes.

"What the hell are you Fedex people trying to do to me? You are becoming just as bad as the UPS guys. What are you trying to do? Become a new company called the Fedups? Oh, I just can't take it anymore."

One day, while stamping my envelopes at the front desk, I noticed the strange way Kami did her photocopying. She would place the paper on the glass plate, lower the lid, press the start button and quickly run behind a wall or behind the counter. After the third time, I could not resist satisfying my curiosity and asked her why she was running every time she pressed the start button.

"Have you ever heard of radiation?" she said, very seriously. I had to refrain from giggling and returned to my desk.

For reasons unknown to me, Gus Bono quit, leaving the throne open to Fred Mortimer, a young, fairly handsome man in his mid-thirties. He was soft-spoken, clean cut and well- dressed all the time. He was selective in the choice of people that surrounded him. He was also very cynical, grumpy and moody. I had a hard time guessing when there was a good enough moment to ask him a question without being ignored or jokingly insulted. I often brushed it off as an immature reaction from a still growing, spoiled brat. Arthur seemed to be satisfied with him and that was what counted anyway. With Maggie's assistance and patience, he soon got a handle on the company's procedures and accounting system. Initially, I did not have to deal with him much and that was a good thing.

Happy with my busy days, I would often arrive as early as 7:30 in the morning, unlike the other girls who preferred to observe the classical nine to five regimen. Norris preferred to show up early also, tour the glass shop quickly, check his messages, give me a few instructions and then disappear for the rest of the day. On and off, Arthur would ask about his whereabouts and I would tell him that Norris was out on appointments. At least that is what Norris made believe. I mentioned to him that the boss had been asking for him.

"Oh yeah, did he say what he wanted?" was all Norris had to say.

I wondered why they were playing tag with each other. In a way, it appeared as if Norris was avoiding meeting with Arthur, but I could not figure out why. Then one afternoon, Arthur again asked about Norris.

"I believe he is out on appointments," I said.

"Well, you better tell him that I need to see him first thing tomorrow morning," Arthur said, visibly annoyed. "It is very important."

I had a strange feeling that something was brewing and could hardly wait to give the heads up to Norris when calling in for messages.

"Did he say anything in particular, why he wanted to see me?" Norris asked.

"No, he did not, but he seemed nervous and irritated," I told him.

The next day in the morning both Arthur and Norris made an early appearance in the office. While I took over the receptionist's duties until Kami's arrival at 9:00 a.m., Arthur had a conversation with Norris behind closed doors. Some twenty minutes later, Norris walked by the reception desk with his head hanging down, red faced, and a barely audible voice saying, "Bye," without even looking at me.

"Why bye, what happened?" I asked, worried.

"I was fired," were Norris' last words and he walked through the main front door without looking back. Sometime later, Arthur felt compelled to justify Norris' dismissal to me.

"He was a very good man. He meant well and I liked him as a human being. Unfortunately, he was not bringing in enough business to justify his salary. I had to let him go."

There was nothing else to ask or say.

For reasons unknown to me, Arthur's secretary, Gloria, also left the company and was shortly after replaced by Sally Bryce, a married woman in her mid-thirties. She was of medium height, had curly, reddish short hair, and no trace of make-up. She wore eyeglasses with thick lenses that made her eyes appear smaller than what they really were. Her daily attire was blue jeans, an unpretentious top and a gray jacket. It appeared that she was the fastest typist in town because whenever she sat down to type whatever report or document for Arthur, her keyboard would rattle away impressing most people in the office.

Kami was one of the few who was not too impressed with Sally and preferred not to express an opinion at that point. She had to worry about her own many problems.

"Ohi, you can't be safe in your own home anymore," she complained. "The robbers climb all over your house and slip in through the ceiling."

"How would you know that?" I asked.

"Oh, I know, I know. Whenever I find black curly hair under my bed, it's because the robbers have been in the house," Kami explained very seriously, without realizing the hilarity of it all.

In the meantime, the old MG-Glass telephone lines were disconnected, and the company incorporated into TSF. Floyd was now overseeing the glass shop and I joined Maggie in the accounting department to take care of the accounts payable section. It was definitely a much larger operation than what I had experienced in the past, but I did not hesitate to embrace my new task with great enthusiasm. I had to interact with Rami, the purchaser, Axel the woodworking supervisor and several others to get vendor invoices approved and initialed before processing and paying them. They often neglected or forgot to bring me copies of the purchase orders or corresponding packing slips and so I had to go fetch them myself. In doing so, I had to walk by the front desk where Kami always had a quick comment to make. She often mumbled to herself when upset, confused or bothered with something. That particular afternoon she was upset because she could not hold the phone to her right ear and type at the same time. I suggested that she get herself a headset, so she could talk hands free.

"Oh, I don't know if the boss would approve of such a device," she said.

"I can't see why not," I said. "It's not a great expense."

"Oh, I don't know. To run around like ET..."

"Well, if it bothers your right ear, why don't you hold the phone to your left ear instead?" I suggested.

"I can't, I'm saving my left ear for more important things," Kami replied.

I wondered what those special issues could be that only her left ear had the privilege to hear. I liked to share some of Kami's antics with Neeta who would then also enjoy a good laugh.

The two people I preferred to stay away from were Floyd and Fred Mortimer. Floyd had the power to make a person feel like a total idiot and a nuisance. Most of the time, while approaching the doorstep to his office, waiting for his green light, Floyd would briefly glance in my direction, roll his eyes to the ceiling, drop the pen he was holding onto the desk and bark a dry "what?" Floyd was mostly running around the plant inspecting the work carried out in the different departments while huffing, puffing and cursing everyone "for fuck sakes." Initially, I resented the four-letter word Floyd used every few seconds, but in time, I got used to it and tried it out myself when on the edge. It seemed to act as a powerful relief valve.

Fred Mortimer instead, required all his underlings to ask questions when in doubt. Certain payments required approval and, therefore, I had to dare disturb his peaceful existence which most of the time, was not a good idea. It was also not advisable to submit checks for signature when he was grumpy. It was always a damn if you do and damn if you don't situation.

It was definitely not easy to please everyone in a large office environment. Sally was another difficult character to deal with. She had the constant urge to affirm her competence and professionalism and took an almost sadistic pleasure in demeaning other female co-workers. She was one of those "been-there-done-that" types, only a lot better than all the others were. There would never be a topic, on which she would totally agree or disagree. Black had to be white and vice-versa, just to be different.

"I am sure you know, because it is common knowledge...," was her favorite opening to any conversation, practically calling the listener an idiot if she or he was not aware of the topic Sally intended to tackle at the time. She was also intolerant towards older folks and frequently underlined the age factor by initiating the conversation with a "Maybe you're not familiar with the issue as it isn't from your time." She also liked to point out the fact that, "You will have noticed that I am the only professional in this office."

Neeta would often invite the girls for a quick lunch at the Mandarin or another nearby eatery. It was always a happy get together where people could talk about most anything; personal issues, happy or unhappy events, problems, frustrations and even crack a few jokes. Neeta, for the sensitive great lady that she was, also invited Sally who, invariably, declined the invitations.

"I don't enjoy all that funny food you guys eat," she said. "I love plain, simple foods such as plain boiled potatoes, plain boiled carrots, plain broiled steaks and plain Chicken Cacciatori"—which if prepared properly, is not that plain at all. She said she had never tasted butter because her mother raised her on margarine alone. She had never touched Chinese food or any other ethnic foods for that matter. Sally was also very selective about the surroundings she lived in.

"My neighborhood is exclusive and mainly white," she said. "The handfuls of ethnics that live around my area are much selected and mainly a product of better families. You know, engineers, lawyers and doctors."

She also had her own ideas about the meaning of family.

"I really don't believe in all the family sort of things," she once said; yet she was over-protective of her daughter and carefully coached her to stand up to the teachers when defending a principle, as only she knew how.

Sally once confessed that she had a hard time getting along with her mother, yet she always drew a perfect picture of her by praising her numerous abilities and hidden talents. The focal point of her life, however, was her husband, the engineer who did not have to get dirty because all he had to do was to go from site to site and inspect the work done by others. Sally was a romantic who dreamed steamy dreams based on Harlequin type love stories, which she practically devored at a rate of almost two paperbacks per week. Yet her enchanted prince somehow did not manage to rake in sufficient funds to allow his princess to enjoy life instead of traveling one hour in each direction and spend eight hours hammering away on an Acer keyboard. Maybe he could at least give her the chance to change that gray jacket once in a while.

Unlike previous offices I had worked in, TSF did not allow the use of radios on the premises. Arthur was of the opinion that it was a source of distraction and disturbance, especially when more than one person tried to express their musical preferences. "The only music you will hear in here is Isabel's whistling," he once said to one of the girls. The various telephone conversations echoing through the office were noisy and disturbing enough, as was the paging system, whenever Kami's crackling voice invited Rami to take a call on one of the lines.

"Oh, I just can't take it anymore," Kami said.

"What happened this time?" I asked while passing by her desk.

"Oh, all these phone calls to the same person every day." She was referring to Rami who, for obvious reasons, received many phone calls from suppliers or people who wanted to pitch a sale for a new product. Kami's interpretation was a more colourful one. "You know, if they call more than five times a day, they must be gay."

As in every company, there are highs and lows, and sometimes it becomes necessary to re-organize and re-shuffle policies and personnel. TSF had to downsize a little, at least temporarily and therefore laid off some of the laborers and reduced to part-time some of the office personnel as well, including me. Working part-time wasn't such a bad deal after all. I could very well use some down time and did not bother to look for an alternate occupation. I did, however, hope that business would pick up again and things would get back to normal.

By the time I returned full-time again, business had improved but Maggie was still overworked, Fred remained moody and grumpy; Floyd was still running around for "fuck's sake," and Kami could still "not take it anymore."

Rumors of a union trying to infiltrate the working group were growing in a hush-hush mode. The funny thing was that only a few people were not aware of the big secret. I began to worry. I knew that once a union took a foothold in a medium-sized company, it could represent the downfall of the entire company. Union dues on top of the other benefits and contributions carried by the employer would burden even more the company's coffers and curtail the laborer's income—but there were people who evidently had different viewpoints and it was not my business to change them.

One day grumpy Fred was less grumpy. He was actually feeling good to the point of inviting Maggie and me for lunch at a Japanese eatery named Mikasa. I had always loved the refined simplicity, yet so tasty Japanese cuisine. Outside the office surrounds, Fred was surprisingly pleasant, and to an extent, even entertaining. The usual snobbish aura that lingered around him dissolved as per magic. He was actually a very nice guy after all; too bad only at lunchtime.

In the meantime, I continued experiencing back pain. It seemed that the facet joint injections were not as effective anymore. I received prescription anti-inflammatory medication, painkillers and sleeping pills for when I could not rest properly. One alternative to the problem was surgery, but I was afraid of the possibility of paralysis, should something go wrong accidentally.

Luckily, my type of work did not require lifting, pushing, pulling or standing for long periods of time and when sitting was becoming painful, I always had a reason to walk over to Rami to pick up a document or bring one to him for initialling.

"Back pain again Isabel baby?" Kami asked, noticing my stiffness.

"Yeah and pretty soon I will be the one saying *I just can't take it anymore*," I said.

"By the way, what's wrong with Fred Mortimer?" Kami asked. "Is he sick or something?"

"I wouldn't know. What makes you think he is sick?"

"Oh, I don't know, but he seems to hang out a lot in the bathroom," she said. How she would know that was anybody's guess. It was one of those typical Kamiish puzzles. She sat at the front desk in the reception area, divided from the office by a solid wall. Unless she had a secret third eye somewhere, she could not see who was going where and when. She then answered her own question, as usual.

"Oh, well. Everybody is sick these days I guess," she said with a hearty chuckle. "Just look at me. I'm sick in my head and everywhere else, too."

I liked Kami a lot, including her idiosyncrasies. In many ways, she made a lot of sense, blaming it all on the ancient Chinese wisdom that she inherited from her forefathers. Her little doll face was graced by a happy smile most of the time. It took her a while to trust a person, but once she did, she remained a friend forever. She was also very generous with everyone; rich or poor, it did not matter. She was happy when she could make others happy, too, and she was always ready to lend a hand to whoever needed help. She could, however, also be very stubborn and feisty and feared no one, not even Goliath, had he appeared at her doorstep.

A few days later, Kami complained about a dent in her car.

"Ah, gosh, who would just do a thing like that?" I observed.

"Oh, it was not just anybody," Kami said with a tone of certainty. "It was Harley for sure."

"Did you see him do it?" I asked.

"No. But I know it was Harley because whenever you have a disagreement with him, he dents your car," Kami punched her left palm with the fist of her right hand.

Harley, who did not always see eye-to-eye with most anybody, was in charge of the packaging and logistics department. He reminded me of the Spanish actor Cantinflas, without the moustache. He was a very capable, hard-working individual who suffered a perennial fatal attraction when it came to the better-looking female gender. He had an uncontrollable urge to touch his privates with a constant quick stroke. Such action was probably so deeply ingrained in his brain that he hardly even noticed it, if at all. He loved to flirt, especially with Maggie, who decidedly brushed off his advances. Maggie was a serious girl, who raised a son by herself after having left an abusive relationship and had no time for nonsense such as Harley. She had a circle of good friends, including me. On occasion, we would slip out for lunch and have a little chat about our lives in general. Kami could not stand Harley either, but she had bigger problems to worry about.

"So what is your problem this time, Kami?" I asked.

"The fax paper is jamming again," she said, visibly upset. "It is not receiving."

"Well, then stop the machine, clear the jam and re-set the whole thing."

"Well, I'll try because it could be something confidential, stuff that nobody is to see, you understand?"

"More so, stop the machine, clear the jam and reset it," I said.

Kami removed the cartridge and examined it from every possible angle.

"You see, these new cartridges just don't work too well. They just don't make them as well as they used to." Kami replaced the cartridge and reset the machine and soon after, the much-expected message came through with information on traveling destinations, which she immediately shredded, angrily.

"There you go, just wasting my paper with these stupid offers. Does it look like I have time to take a trip?" She continued rambling about a different subject. "Take these carpets for example. I don't know why they can't come up with a system to keep them clean other than vacuuming. They should come up with something like a pillowcase, just slip it off and throw it away each year."

I interrupted her dissertation by returning to my desk where I continued sorting through a pile of packing slips and Invoices. Sally, with her rapid steps and head tilted to one side, dropped off a fax on my desk. It was an invoice that required Bruno's initials before it could be processed. On my way to his desk, passing by Kami's, I asked her to stamp it with her usual date stamp. Kami examines the document very carefully.

"Now, are we sure this is not a Sally Bryce document?" she argued.

"Sure, sure, just stamp it; Bruno is waiting for it," I said.

Kami ranted about the need to know exactly which packing slip goes where.

"This is a faxed invoice that only requires Bruno's initials for payment approval," I said. "All it is lacking is the date stamp, which you have."

"Oh, yes. Now I see. This is an invoice." While screening the document one more time, she rubbed the stamp against the inkpad and then also hit it several times to soak it well before splashing it onto the invoice. She just wanted to make sure that it was an invoice and did not belong to Sally. It was obvious that she preferred to avoid anything that had to do with the girl.

Then there was Dena, the wife of one glassworker, who was constantly phoning her husband. I took some of those calls, which were really unimportant for normal people, such as wanting to know where the husband had put the soccer ball, the shoelaces, and so forth. Later, however, I came to know that the poor soul, after her fourth child had become mentally unbalanced to the point that for a while she had to be interned for treatment. Her husband had to work part-time to enable him to take care of the kids. She never did totally recover. Informed about Dena's health problem, Kami decided to go easy on her.

"I think I won't pick on Dena anymore. They have three or four kids, and kids nowadays are difficult to raise. I have the impression that she wants to talk to someone; just that I have no time. And to be a housewife these days is almost like being in solitary confinement." She sounded very serious.

It seemed that every aspect of life within the TSF walls was somehow connected with ever-present Kami. One of her tasks, which she had taken upon herself voluntarily, was to prepare a fresh pot of coffee for when Mr. A (that is how she addressed Arthur), came in first thing in the morning. It had to be piping hot and had to have a certain amount of freshly ground coffee; otherwise, it wasn't any good. The fresh pot ritual continued throughout the day.

One afternoon, while on hold on the phone, I witnessed her coffee cup dance. She had barely left the kitchen, balancing a cup of coffee in her hand when the phone rang. She turned around, heading towards the closest phone. She put down the cup of coffee but by the time she had reached for the phone, it stopped ringing. She grabbed the cup and proceeded towards the reception. The phone rang again, and again she turned around, walked to the closest phone, put down the cup, reached for the phone and again it stopped ringing. By the third time, she accelerated her steps and finally grabbed the phone in time but her "Hello" did not get an answer.

"Oh, these crazy people; if they want to talk to me they shouldn't be hanging up," she muttered while walking back to reception.

Later on, when I walked by her desk to use the copier, she remarked, "You know Isabel, brokers work in mysterious ways. You have to be very careful because sometimes they charge you twice." She then answered a call and put the caller on hold while leafing through the same two piles of courier invoices in search of double billings. Only when the phone buzzed did she realize that there was someone still on hold and immediately fixed the problem by apologizing.

Problems were not confined to work alone. Mother also had problems which required my attention and intervention. They were a never-ending sequence of events and no one volunteered to help. I was the only liaison between mother and her family doctor. I was the one driving her for blood tests to the hospital, hoping that the nurse would find her vein without torturing her too much and causing her arm to become blue and black. I was the one to arrange for a colonoscopy, which always took some six hours from start to finish, to get prescriptions from the Pharmacy, etc. Mother had a collection of pills to take every day and often, I wondered if those were truly all necessary, such as the water pill for example. She took one type to drain the water from the body, but at night, she was to take another one to refrain her from going to the toilet because she had a hard time getting out of bed and dragging herself via walker to the bathroom. I argued with the doctor about the contradictory orders my mother's body was getting through those pills, but he did not change anything. On one occasion, even the pharmacist argued with the doctor, but no one reached a conclusion. Aside from the medical problems, there were other needs to be filled, such as ordering dresses from a mail order catalog and then returning everything if it did not fit properly or was not what mother had visualized in her mind. She could not find shoes for herself as she needed orthopedic ones and the few offered at the various shoe specialists were an aesthetic abomination in the only color available, black. So we finally found a shoemaker somewhere on Eglinton Avenue, who applied extra soles to heighten her own shoe to the required height. She also decided that she needed a new wheelchair and a lazy-boy chair. The heating and the A/C needed to be inspected, as it could not be set from inside the apartment. It was a rather strange system, and a real problem. The temperature, as per the superintendent of the building, was regulated from the main panel downstairs. The folks on the lower levels felt cold and those on the fifth floor, like mother, were broiling. Then there were those unexpected calls around 5 o'clock in the morning because the fire alarm went off in the building. Not being able to move on her own, mother was always afraid of the fire alarms, even when just a drill. She would then call me, terrified. I would jump out of bed, dress quickly and rush over to her side. Luckily, the building was only 10 minutes away. Many elderly residents would stand around in the courtyard, dressed in their housecoats and pyjamas. Elevators were blocked and firefighters were walking around checking the situation. Accompanied by a firefighter, I would run up the stairs to the fifth floor with my heart pounding wildly. With the exception of only one episode, where an elderly lady left something on her stove, all other alarms were unfounded. Mother would sit in tears close to the main window; she would shake from head to toe and was very close to a nervous breakdown. Somehow that sound triggered in her memories the sirens she had heard during the war. I would calm her down with a shot of Scotch and would stay until the situation was totally under control, and her fear and anxiety had dissipated. Then I would rush back home and complete my dressing and coifing. A quick coffee or tea would take care of my shaken nerves before heading to work to concentrate on my several tasks of the day.

Apparently, I was not the only one who had to look after an elderly parent. One day Kami took off the morning to drive her father to the hospital because he had not been feeling too well.

"They put the poor man through a math test to see if he was responding. I thought that was very disrespectful on the part of the nurse and I told her that she should take that test out on me, not on my folks.

Kami perhaps did not realize she was not the one who needed to be checked out. "After all, you are born with only that many brain cells and once you get old and the

Cells are used up, you can't think straight anymore," she said.

Kami and her ancient wisdom might just have had a point there.

Even though business was not the best, Arthur and Neeta kept up the Christmas tradition with the beautiful tree in the lobby, the poinsettias on the office desks and the reception counter. The snowflakes slowly blanketed tree branches and rooftops and intensified the spirit of the season. Sally was very busy sending out Christmas cards while Rudi planned the setting for the Christmas party. With the exception of Arthur, Floyd and Maggie, the employees were given a week off, which was always a welcome intermezzo from the regular routine throughout the year.

With the holidays over, you would expect everyone to return eagerly to their position and start a new year with more energy and enthusiasm. Kami was one of those, arriving as usual, loaded with several plastic bags containing coffee, sugar and milk.

"Oh, hi, hi, Isabel baby; Happy New Year," she said, almost out of breath. "How's it going?"

"Good, good," I replied, while redialing a fax number.

Kami dropped the bags on her side of the counter and began rambling about the driver who had cut her off at a major intersection. All the while, she started to unpack her goods, one item at a time. She placed the first pack of coffee on the counter, turned around, moved two steps forward, turned around again and took two steps forward. She grabbed the same pack of coffee, holding it for a few seconds, still rambling, and placed it right back where she had grabbed it. She repeated the operation for another three times before realizing that her action did not produce results. Yet she seemed to be happy because a smile soon materialized on her dolly face.

It took a few days to update everyone's curiosity on how each of us had spent the holidays, and it took the same amount of time to get into the regular working pace and frame of mind. Once in gear, time began to flash by at the speed of light, except for me, because my back had given me more problems than I could handle.

One morning when trying to get out of bed, I experienced an excruciating sharp pain. No matter how I tried to turn or move, it made me shriek. I was almost afraid to breath. I told Mefisto about my condition and asked him to boil some water for the water bottle. It wasn't a matter of simple muscle ache and so not the case to apply one of the different pain relief gels or cream rubs that would only stink up the body and the surroundings. Yet the warm water bottle, even if only psychologically, would give me a temporary feeling of relief. I also asked for a glass of water to wash down three of the #3 Tylenol pills. The pain in itself did not relent, but I dozed off for a while. In the meantime, Mefisto called TSF to inform them that I would not be able to make it in that morning. Later on, upon awakening, I had the urge to use the washroom. It was either out of bed or pee in it. Every slight movement caused me so much pain, that I screamed out while tears swelled in my eyes. Yet somehow, I managed to drag my body to the washroom and back to bed where I remained immobile for the rest of the day. Later that afternoon, after much trying, I reached Dr. Chapman's secretary and arranged an urgent appointment for three days later. The other alternative would have been to go to the hospital's emergency, where as usual, they would initiate a new file and diagnosis, although they already had all my information from previous visits, and then proceed with more prodding and painful probing. I chose to stay in bed instead.

On the third day, I was able to move and went to see my surgeon. I had finally brushed aside hesitation and fear and decided on the surgery.

"Ok then, I'll have my secretary book you and send you all the necessary paperwork and instructions," said Dr. Chapman with a reassuring smile. "You don't worry. By the time I'm finished with you, you'll be as good as new."

The healing time, the fusion of both facet joints with bone graft taken from the right hip, was estimated around three months, for some sooner, for others, later. And so on February 16, 1998, I finally had the much-needed surgery. Only the first night did I struggle with pain all night because I could not tolerate the morphine, which triggered the urge of having to constantly throw up. I begged the nurse to give me #3 Tylenol pills instead, but there were no physicians available at one o'clock in the morning to authorize the switch. Every nerve in my body seemed to be on the edge. Even the laughter and chatter of the nurses at the nurse's station bothered me as did the rhythmic tip-tap of their footwear along the corridor. Maybe all that noise was intentional, to keep them awake during the night shift.

The next morning, Dr. Chapman popped by to see me and check on the incision. He seemed to be quite satisfied with the result and agreed to switch the morphine toTylenol-3. He tried to make me sit up but I was too sore.

"That's Ok," he said. "Don't worry. We'll try again tomorrow. The sooner you get up, the sooner you heal."

The next day I got up and took a few steps in the corridor. It was still painful and so I returned to bed but continued the exercise throughout the day and the next four days.

I was pleasantly surprised with the group visit one morning, of my co-workers: Neeta, Fred, Maggie and Kami. They had all come for a short visit bringing flowers and get-well cards. On the fifth day, I was released, ready to go home. Modern surgery was truly amazing as was the healing ability of the human body. I spent a full month recovering. I busied myself with reading, writing, watching TV and slowly walking, bigger stretches around my neighborhood. After only one month and a half, I was able to return to work. When tired of sitting, I would just walk over to Rami and back, enough to decompress my back.

For a while I was unable to help mother with the various doctor's appointments as I was not to lift, push or pull heavy objects, and the wheelchair with mother sitting in it was one of the things to avoid. Already before surgery I had trouble in wheeling her to the doctor's office because, amazingly enough, their medical building's entranceways were not handicap friendly. I always hoped that someone would walk by and hold the door open for me. It was otherwise a struggle to keep the heavy door open with one foot while twisting my entire body to push the wheelchair through it.

Tired of the building's administrative ignorance and insensitivity to the handicapped needs, I wrote to the MP in charge of the area at the time and got him involved. Months later, after mother could no longer leave the house for the regular visits, the first automatic door had been installed on the lower level and soon after, a second one on the upper street level of the medical building.

In the following years more attention was given to the handicapped's cause and more establishments were equipped with proper doors and access ramps, but the narrow examining table with the step stool was still a rigid, permanent fixture in most doctors' offices. The patient, therefore, had to be examined while sitting in a chair or in the wheelchair itself. How good of an examination that could be was pure speculation, but there was never much else to be inspected other than the blood pressure and the tour with the stethoscope, which did not require a specific stretched position anyway.

In the meantime, work at the office proceeded at the usual pace; some days fast and chaotic, others slow and almost boring due to the repetitive nature of the job. The only interesting character was Kami.

"Fred Mortimer wants you to courier this envelope by Fedex overnight," I said.

"Ok, where to?" Kami asked.

"Address is on the envelope," I replied.

"When must it be there?"

"Well, if you call today, the recipient might get it by 9 a.m. tomorrow morning," I said.

"No way, you're lucky if they get it by 10 a.m. But it is going to cost you about 25 bucks."

"That's Ok, Kami. It's the assessment moneys. We may have to pay a penalty should it not get there in time. You know how these government people operate. They can be very intolerant when it comes to deadlines and expect the taxpayer to follow the rules, or else."

"That's right," said Floyd, who happened to pass by and overheard the conversation. "Better twenty-five bucks courier charges than $1,000 penalty."

"Well, I'm just asking because Bernie can do that, too, or take the P&P guy for example," said Kami. "He also does same day deliveries."

"Oh, whatever, just make sure they get it before noon tomorrow," Floyd said and walked away.

"Ok, ok. I just have to understand the situation and the urgency first. They'll get it. Don't you worry." Kami trailed behind me and Floyd as we quickly walked away.

We both had business to attend to and wished that Kami would not drag out her concerns that much.

One afternoon, Maggie asked me to drive to the bank to make deposits. It was a half- hour drive back and forth and I did not mind running errands, as they broke up the uniformity of the daily routine. It was a beautiful warm, sunny July day with a cloudless blue sky and I found it a pity to spend it among the four walls of an office with artificial lights instead of the sunshine.

"It's gorgeous out there," I remarked while walking by Kami's desk.

"Yeah, you're right," Kami said. "I wish I could be out there and get a tan."

"Why don't you?"

"Have no time."

"What do you do on weekends? You have no kids, dogs or cats."

"Yeah, but I get a lot of junk mail."

"Dump it."

"I can't."

"Tell me why not?"

"All those credit cards they send me."

"Cut them up."

"Sure, but it takes time."

"Well then do it later, when it is cloudy," I said between amused and annoyed.

"Can't, because later I have to eat and that takes time also," said Kami.

It certainly was not an easy situation. Somebody should demand that credit card companies stop sending out all those cards so that receptionists can have time to tan, I thought while refraining from laughing aloud.

As fast as summer had arrived, so it disappeared and was replaced by the beautiful fall season. The air was clear and crisp but Kami always had a reason to complain about something.

"I do not believe in double-paned windows," she said one day. "There isn't much difference at all. Cold is cold and warm is warm, whether you have one or two panes. I wish we had only a one-paned window. At least I would have some air to breath."

"Darn, Kami," I said. "You are lucky we have double windows, especially during winter. Sometimes we freeze with double panes let alone single ones."

"Well, I really prefer it cooler. I hate having to perspire from my head because it makes my hair grow so much faster. Just like plants that need water, because my hair grows like grass."

She had her very own philosophy on most anything and was always eager to share it with whomever was willing to listen.

One of the major events that year was the departure of Fred Mortimer. Apparently, he received a great offer from a major accounting firm and could not afford to turn his back on it. It was, however, doubtful if his co-workers would ever miss him, as nobody did really feel sorry to see him go. Once more, Maggie, who was definitely not happy with yet another new situation, had to train a newcomer, Morrie Rosen, a very pleasant middle-aged gentleman. As on previous occasions, Maggie hoped it would finally be the last one.

Another significant event that year was the theft of a computer from the CAD department. It apparently happened in broad daylight, but not during my reception duty between eight and nine in the morning as I would have noticed someone carrying out a computer—a very unusual occurrence, and, therefore, highly noticeable. All repairs were carried out on the premises by an in-house technician. The news spread like wildfire and soon everybody was commenting and speculating. Because the stolen computer's memory contained sensitive CAD drawings, most people assumed that it could only have been of interest to a competitor manufacturer. Detectives and psychology analysts interviewed and tested all employees, apparently without significant results. To add insult to injury, the insurance company refused to cover the theft. They were only interested in collecting the premiums. When it was time to help the victim, they were able to twist and argue ad infinitum, just to avoid having to dish out a penny. The incident meanwhile remained shrouded in mystery.

I always wondered about the amount of paper that circulated in an office. Both Neeta and I were in charge of filing documents. One small order at times generated ten to fifteen pages and just as many staples to hold it all together. Harley, in particular, was an obsessed stapler. The more staples he could apply to a set of documents, the happier he was. I hated staples and whenever I had a little more time, I would gradually remove them all and replace them with only one; even though Floyd considered it to be a waste of precious time.

"Oh, Isabel, good you are filing," Kami said. "Can you help me find an invoice?" She pointed to some notes on her pad while the phone just started ringing. She ignored the phone and continued to explain her reasons.

"The phone, Kami," I reminded her after a while.

"I know," she said and continued talking. After the fifth ring, she finally picked up the receiver: "Hello, hello, hello?" Since she could hear no sound on the other end, she grabbed the receiver and banged it a couple of times on the edge of the desk. She tried again. "Hello, hello, hello? Strange, there is nobody there." She seemed puzzled with the mysterious caller who most probably, was not patient enough to wait so long.

"Oh, well. If it is important, they'll call again, I guess," I said with a chuckle.

"You know, it could be Joe, the guy who calls in sick on Thursdays to tell me that he will for sure be in for work on Monday," Kami said.

"And who is Joe?" I asked.

"Oh, he is some guy who works in the back. He is also very rude and confusing. And you have to watch it because being dark skinned, when he gets really angry, he tends to lose color." Kami was very serious.

Never before had I heard of such peculiar phenomena. Maybe Kami had the ability to see what other people could not.

Arthur's every wish or simplest request was Kami's command, privilege and pleasure. She would drop everything and run to attend to her boss's needs. The same applied to when Neeta, the "lady boss" needed something. In the opinion of some people, Kami's extreme promptness, bordered on servileness. In reality, however, it was nothing but pure affection and respect on her side.

"I need you to watch the phones for me," she said hurriedly one day.

"Ok, what's the rush"?

"I have to run to have some film developed for Mr. A," she said. "He needs these pictures today."

"Ok, ok," I said. "Just forward the calls to me, as usual."

"Yeah, but you have only one intercom," said Kami, inspecting my phone close up.

"You just don't worry, Kami. It wouldn't be the first time that I take care of the calls from this end."

Kami, however, was stuck on her train of thoughts, and there was nothing much anybody could do to change her mind.

"Yeah, your phone is not equipped," she mumbled while running back to her desk, forgetting that she had so many times in the past forwarded the calls to my set. She must have undergone a momentary memory freeze, I figured.

Working with Morrie, the new accountant, was quite pleasant. Unlike young, moody Fred Mortimer, Morrie was relaxed; always smiling; he totally lacked the arrogance and self-importance so typical of some of the younger professionals. He also enjoyed a good chat, revealing a far better cultural background. In reality, the company did not need an accountant at that point, because Maggie had studied and improved her accounting knowledge throughout the years and had become proficient in every aspect of the department.

When it came to the yearly evaluation, however, it was always up to Floyd, not the accountant and not Arthur, to decide who got an increase and who did not, and my failed increase was always due there being no more room for it in the budget. Not even for an inspiring twenty-five cent increase.

In the meantime, to the shock of everyone, Rudi Mahler had passed away over one weekend. The Thursday before, as I sat across from his desk, I noticed an unusual pallor in his face. It looked as if he was wearing a white wax mask over his face and I felt goose bumps running over my back. I mentioned the fact to Neeta, who also walked by his desk and confirmed having seen the same, scary death mask. Nobody knew what was wrong with Rudi except Maggie. He had been confiding in her for some time, but as the loyal, discreet person she was, Maggie never disclosed anything, not even to me. As eerie as it sounded, I had a dream that Saturday, in which Rudi appeared to bid farewell. He did not seem to be ill at all in my dream. In fact, he appeared happy and his pink cheeks, with dimples on both sides, had turned into a radiant smile. Rudi was missed by many people, especially around Christmas.

A young, talented computer geek, who also had extremely good taste in design, and later became a very essential part of the TSF team, took over Rudi's place. Not only was Johnny Dyp smart, but he was also very funny. He would announce his little electronic mishaps by emitting a brief, loud scream.

That was the only sound signaling that hard working, dedicated Johnny was still alive and well. Even selective Kami liked Johnny, maybe because he was as funny as she was.

One afternoon, Kami walked down the office sniffing the air very carefully.

"Funny smell in here, I find," she commented while stopping at my desk. "It smells like poop," she clarified.

"Could be mouse shit, too," I said. "They do run around sometime."

"Well, that too, but it is mainly people's shoes. They must walk their dogs and maybe some of us step into it and bring the smell inside."

I quickly lifted both my feet in Kami's direction who took a quick peek.

"There, check my shoes; t'wasn't me, eh?" I said.

"Well, the other day even Mr. A's parking spot stank. I made it a point to go out there and smell it myself after he had left. And did it ever stink."

"And did you find out after all what that stink was all about?" I asked while struggling to hold back laughter.

"Well, it's all these guys in the back. They do it on purpose. They have no respect. Oh, I just can't take it anymore."

Kami continued talking to herself while heading back to her desk. I could certainly not always follow Kami's train of thoughts. Perhaps this was because sometimes she only partially expressed a certain thought orally and kept the other portion within the deep recesses of her mind.

In May 1999, my son, Peter, got married to his longtime sweetheart, Gerry, a beautiful, intelligent girl who had studied to become a teacher. She was the hands-on, hard-working specimen who had also worked at GM, where the two had met. Unfortunately, the Eglinton Avenue plant had closed down for good and the whole structure was demolished. Peter stood there, heartbroken, because he loved his job; with tears swelling in his eyes as he and I passed by the area one day and nothing else was left but rubble. The company had then put him on a recall list and for about two years, he worked at the Oshawa location. Then new layoffs took place and once more, his name appeared on a recall list. Tired of the unreliable yoyo system, Peter decided to join his father in his small home-based distributorship, and in the process learned a new trade and gained a useful hands-on experience.

The wedding was a memorable family event. Even my brother, Frank, whose Parkinson's disease had slowly worsened, managed to fly over from Vancouver to celebrate the event. He enjoyed every bit of the happy reunion and even dared to dance, very slowly, with me. Mother enjoyed the role of proud grandmother and definitely had a great time until the wee hours of the morning.

That year brought along much unrest among the TSF workers who were planning to sign up with a union. The idea of a possible union intervention with a consequent strike disrupted the free, relaxed atmosphere that had reigned in the company up until then. New security and disciplinary measures had to be put in place and enforced by an otherwise lax management. Safety glasses and boots were necessary and so were hearing protection devices. There would be no more quick smokes outside, lunch and coffee breaks or munchies and pop cans at workstations. There would be no more barging into the offices for a phone call, a chat, or any other reason without obtaining permission. Working hours had to be respected as well. The workers knew that should they decide on a strike, they would no longer receive wages or be entitled to unemployment insurance benefits. It was sad and very disturbing. I was deeply affected by those new events and hoped that it would not come to a real strike, but the workers ultimately signed up with the union anyway.

One Monday morning, I was surprised to see Sally that early, having a cigarette outdoors.

"Eh, how come so early, Sally?"

"Just thought you should be the first one to know that I am quitting," she said, curtly and clearly. She was tired of traveling and tired of working for Arthur. She had other plans for her immediate future. As I had no personal interest in Sally, I didn't bother to ask questions either. I was, however, puzzled with the fact that she had elected me to be the first one to know about her leaving TSF. She was kind enough to take it upon herself to select and personally train her successor who had to be, if not as perfect as Sally herself, at least very close. The choice fell on Mary Lynn, a very reserved, mature woman who was just as fast a typist as Sally. Arthur seemed very satisfied with the choice as well, and that was after all, what counted in the matter.

The year 2000 had been a difficult one for TSF. Rather than contacting the management to arrange a return to the bargaining table, the union and a majority of plant personnel decided to go on strike without giving notice. On a Monday morning, therefore, and for the very first time in my life, I had a close encounter with a democratic concept I had not experienced first hand before. A picket line greeted me at the entrance of the company's driveway. They were all carrying signs with the name and number of their union, which would have been more appropriate for a shipyard environment than for the manufacturing of fine store furnishings.

I was deeply disturbed and close to tears. Knowing Arthur's background and the hard work he had put into the creation of the company, I felt sorry and angry at the situation. A million thoughts crisscrossed my mind. Where, on earth was it written that an individual had to create a place of work for another to be employed and that such employment was to be tailored to the specific needs and wishes of a given employee or employees? Yet it does happen, when some greedy unions step in to help the poor workers fight the horrendous monster boss who built a company for the sole purpose of engaging the workers into slavery, and by keeping them in a Gulag of incredible sufferings, where benefits are only basic and the boss's wealth is not equally shared among them. Strikers would certainly not lack sympathizers if they were tied up in shackles to their work stations, being whipped whenever the production was slacking, being held at gunpoint at their work bench or being paid Third World country wages without any form of benefits. No one had prevented them from leaving, in search of a better job or better pay. Obviously, the most virulent group, exhorted by the most talented of instigators, knew that unskilled laborers did not have a very good chance in today's competitive markets and hoped that by electing a union and declaring a strike, they would be able to hold on to their old cushioned, overpaid, unskilled positions.

The strike continued for days and then weeks, causing disruptions in the supply of orders and inflicting even more loss in an already precarious financial situation. The vicious attack of the union stooped so low as to contact a number of TSF's clients in Canada and the United States, threatening to picket their stores if they dared purchase TSF products. As a result, orders were suspended or canceled altogether.

As the strike progressed and no solution seemed to be in sight, the democratic fighters decided to make things more interesting. In one instance, a striker jumped in front of the car of an opponent to be intentionally hit, hurt, and trigger a public opinion reaction. Luckily, the other party had fast reflexes and good brakes. There were death threats to non-sympathizers, slashed tires, broken car windows and scratched paint. Entranceways were defaced and littered. Vulgarities were uttered and middle fingers rose at the passage of any office employee. Some of their gangster-like practices included following cars and delivery trucks, and throwing nails on the ground with the purpose of puncturing tires. Couriers tried to avoid crossing the picket lines because, belonging to unions themselves, they did support the actions of the TSF workers. Many cars honked to signal solidarity. Even the cops assigned to monitor the strike process belonged to a union, and were extremely cautious in how they could "serve and protect" the parties. Arthur had to hire a security service to watch over the leased building, the parked vehicles and the safety of the individuals who decided to return to work. He had also arranged for a shuttle service for all employees to avoid damages to their vehicles. Kami was one of the few who would occasionally, still drive in to work.

One morning, she walked in huffing and puffing, carrying a tree branch in her hand. "Oh, I just can't take it anymore," she said. "Look what I just found behind my car."

She showed me and Floyd a small stick. "Those union guys planted this thing right behind my car so that when I back up, the stick scratches the paint." she explained very seriously.

"Oh, come on now," Floyd said. "How would you know it was the guys out there and why would they use a little thing like that just to scratch your car?"

"Ah, because the stick was pretty erect," she replied.

Floyd couldn't hold back a hearty laugh and had to leave the scene right after that. I wondered if Kami was at all aware of how hilarious at times some of her observations turned out to be. It was certainly a welcome break of good humor during those difficult times.

Work at the plant was reduced to just a handful of people and their supervisors. Delivery trucks were held up as much as twenty minutes at a time. Because they could not produce and deliver on schedule, TSF had to face some hefty penalties, which in turn minimized the expected income and consequent cash flow. This also compromised their ability to pay bills and purchase materials for new orders. No orders meant no income which translated into lay-offs, temporary or permanent, extreme downsizing and ultimately the total collapse of the entire company. Obviously, the clever striking forces did not see it that way; so typical of an uneducated proletariat. In their eyes, and limited comprehension, TSF's coffers were an endless fountain of overflowing richness. The boss' Mercedes, even if second-hand, was for them the ultimate proof of the man's wealth. He was a millionaire. I wondered if it had ever occurred to them that they were free to create something of their own, just so that they also could purchase a Mercedes. All it would take were guts, sacrifices and a lifetime of hard work—but perhaps striking was easier.

Every now and then, I would walk over to the reception window and peek out to the driveway. It had been a very cold winter and the picketers had filled drums with pallet wood set on fire to keep warm. Once in a while one of them would run across the street to pick up coffee and donuts. Others believed in a more efficient heating system by lacing their coffee or tea with some Captain Morgan. Hopping around to keep the circulation in their feet, they did not seem too depressed. They talked a lot and laughed, probably telling jokes to each other.

"Oh my, oh my, what a mess this is," I remarked gloomily.

"Don't you worry my friend, they got what they wanted," Kami said while joining me at the window. "Look at them. They are happy, laughing their heads off, unlike us, who have to work and worry. Just look at my problem. Here I am trying to page this guy Maurice, to give him a message. But it is getting dark out there and Maurice ain't that fair either."

It was indeed getting late and time to go home. I grabbed my bag and was about to leave.

"Say, Kami, how do you say Sayonara in Chinese?" I asked.

"Well, I don't know." Kami giggled. "We don't really have such a word in Chinese because you see, we are not as emotional as the whites, but if you really must say something, just say "takecare, takecare."

Kami said the words in a quick succession so that they ended up sounding like an exotic, foreign word. I left the premises laughing and with a new greeting à la Kami.

One morning I had missed the shuttle and decided to drive in. I was stopped at the picket line for about fifteen minutes. I overheard one of the men asking the individual blocking my car, "Oh c'mon, let her pass already. She is a secretary." The other guy replied with a firm "No, she works for the asshole." It was then that I lost my patience and jumped out of the car.

"Listen, you. I work in the office. That is my job. I do not interfere with your democratic right to strike. You should not interfere with my democratic right to work. I have absolutely nothing in common with your motivations. Just remember this, if we do not keep this boat afloat, you will be sitting out here for many more months to come, by yourself, in the cold, freezing your ass off, with no job at all because you guys are doing your very best to sink the boat." I shook from head to toe.

Very slowly, the guy stepped aside and waved me through. Even though upset by the incident, I was surprised with my audacity in standing up to the hostile party. It took a while for me to regain control of my emotions and direct my focus towards my scheduled tasks.

Later in the day, I checked on the strikers' movements. The second entrance was unattended. They were probably huddling in the coffee shop, and I hoped that they would remain there until I was ready to leave. Walking by the reception desk, I grabbed a candy from Kami's courtesy basket.

"I should never stop here, because whenever I do, I grab one of your candies," I told Kami.

"Oh, don't you worry. I take two and a half spoonfuls of sugar each time I grab a coffee or have some tea," she replied.

"Yes, but I am supposed to watch my sugar intake because of the diabetes problem..."

"Ohi, never mind diabetes," Kami interrupted. "Don't believe everything they tell you. Look at me, I might even have something they haven't found a name for yet. Do you see me worried?"

Kami had a point. Maybe I shouldn't believe everything the doctor tells me. Maybe all they were doing was poisoning me with a bunch of chemicals. And on top of all that, expected me to give up some of the yummiest items in my life such as Lindt Chocolate, cakes from Fabian's, Cabernet Sauvignon, Gorgonzola cheese, Szegedi Salami and other such delicatessen. How fulfilling could life otherwise be, without a few earthly pleasures? At least to partially counterbalance the otherwise numerous hardships one had to battle each day, I pondered.

I had no difficulty in leaving the premises that evening, but I decided to avoid driving in and continued using the company shuttle instead. The strike was dragging on and patience often ran thin, resulting in verbal abuse and intimidation. One had to be extremely careful not to fuel the striker's anger because not even the cops could do much to protect anyone unless physical injury occurred, possibly in front of witnesses. It would then become evidence of violation, which could lead to a court-imposed injunction against the union, and so forth, endlessly.

On occasion, Arthur would join me at the reception window. He would sadly gaze over the driveway, which had slowly acquired the appearance of a war zone, or look at the empty work stations and the silent machinery in the back of the shop. I could just imagine the turmoil the man was facing; yet there was nothing I could have done to help aside from assuring him of my solidarity.

"Somehow, and God willing, we will overcome this ordeal," Arthur said, hopeful.

In the meantime, the company had suffered enough financial damage, totally crippling their ability to offer any form of job security to anyone. There were no more contracts and work dwindled down to a very few jobs which made yet another downsizing of personnel necessary. I was one of the office forces replaced by Neeta who was by then familiar with every aspect of my job.

In time, many strikers had changed their minds and returned to work. The union had been ultimately defeated because due to their own greedy, inconsiderate actions, TSF never fully recovered from the financial damage. A lifelong effort in building a company, a dream nurtured throughout the years, crumbled merciless in just a few months.

Weeks later, I resigned from TSF to join Peter and Mefisto at AllRock Inc., a family company that needed my moral support and secretarial expertise.

27

AllRock Inc.

"So how does it feel like being self-employed?" Maggie once asked me over the phone.

"It has its pros and cons," I said. "The worse is that I can't call in sick to get a break once in a while," I added with a chuckle.

Self-employment, however, had many advantages; I did not have to get up early; I saved on gasoline and traveling time; I did not have to dress up; I could set my own hours; I could also run errands for the house, and combine office work with house chores. But as easy as it was to set our own hours, it was also easy to override them when the prospect of a good sale came in after regular working hours.

What Mefisto had started as a one-room basement operation, spread out to three rooms on the upstairs level: two offices and a samples room. He had also rented a large warehouse some three minutes down the road from the house, where we kept a fair amount of stocked goods. The office doors never closed for the weekends or holidays and the sound of an incoming fax was always irresistible and had to be checked out immediately. If it was an order and the item was in stock, Mefisto made sure that the order was filled and packed, even on a Sunday or a holiday, and shipped the next business day. AllRock's promptness to satisfy its customers was notorious and greatly appreciated.

Even though Mefisto was a serious no-nonsense, demanding boss, the atmosphere at AllRock was a relaxed one. Lunch breaks could be a pleasurable event on the back porch of the house, while watching squirrels and bluejays competing for a handful of peanuts. Just as easily, however, lunch breaks could be skipped due to a particularly busy day.

Business was booming and later on, when Ford had once again laid off Nakina, she too, joined the family business on a part-time basis, initially to help out with the sampling and doing stock checks for the customers. Those were the good days, when not much pressure existed except on packing and shipping days. Not plagued by financial difficulties, the family often reunited for a pleasant meal in one of our favorite restaurants and Mefisto always beamed with pride when he could take care of the bill. He also enjoyed escorting visitors from Italy, mainly relatives and friends, to visit all the noteworthy tourist sites in Ontario. The CN Tower and Niagara Falls were always elected as the most impressive and unforgettable experiences of them all.

One very special event that year was the birth of my first grandchild named Mikaela. Peter beamed with pride and joy as he introduced his beautiful baby daughter to us grandparents. It was not that long ago that he had been a baby himself and now he had one of his very own. How amazing the human life cycle was, I pondered.

Aside from the regular daily office work, I also had to contend with mother's various needs such as doctor's appointments, medical tests, arranging for hair perms and toenail clippings, order and pick up medications from the pharmacy, take care of the weekly shopping, set her letters to friends in proper German and so forth. I always tried to use after-work hours to run such errands to avoid possible conflicts with Mefisto who, as a typical son-in-law, never did see eye-to-eye with his mother-in-law. He was of the opinion that my mother was exploiting and abusing my goodwill, patience and time, stealing away my attention from his domain.

Another happy event that year was Nakina's wedding on September 16, 2000. Mother was overcome with joy and even more so when her grandchild and my niece, beautiful fifteen-year-old Lara, came from Vancouver for the very first time, to participate in the wedding.

On the wedding day there was much animation in the house. Music filled the air, flutes of champagne and appetizers crowded the kitchen table while the girls, giggling, were getting ready in their hunter green maid-of-honor outfits. I was in charge of Nakina's hairdo, which turned out into a professional-looking classic chignon. Needless to say, Nakina was the happiest and most beautiful bride that day.

I then rushed over to pick up mother, because once again, anything concerning her was my load and I was alone to deal with it. A few pictures were taken in front of the garden immortalizing the reunion of four happy generations. Slowly, the line of cars began to move, honking their horns all the way to the Country Golf Club where the ceremony and later the dinner party were to take place. Handsome, tall, blue-eyed Chris was proudly awaiting his bride, who marched solemnly on her father's arm towards the Gazebo's altar.

Mother's wheelchair was positioned on top of the stairs from where she had an unobstructed view of the function. There was no pathway down to the Gazebo and to push the heavy wheelchair across the bumpy lawn was impossible, at least for my back. Nevertheless, mother enjoyed the party, as did all the other participants to the event.

Monday morning, it was back to work, back to the company's modest ambitions; modest in the sense that, as long as everyone had a roof over their heads, food on their tables and a decent salary, life was good. Up until then we ignored greed or the obsession of becoming millionaires, but times change and opportunities materialize. AllRock dealt with contractors, some designers, architects, and a number of manufacturers and distributors of a wide range of materials such as marble, granite, slate, porcelain, ceramics and glass tiles and mosaics. Among Mefisto's business acquaintances, there was a certain Rocco Towers, C.E.O. of Deco & Screen Ltd., which specialized in the silk-screening of selected patterns onto plain ceramic tiles of various sizes and colors. Rocco, known for his mechanical abilities, enjoyed creating and building machinery for his own company's use. He also claimed to have invented a special system to manufacture tiles from recycled glass of all sorts, mainly leftover discarded glass of all shapes and shades. One day, Mefisto brought home a 6x6 inch sample piece.

"What do you think of this?" he asked me.

"Yuk. I hate the color; looks like la mierda," I said, grimacing.

"They can make it in all sorts of colors. It is a very good product, meant for commercial use in very heavy traffic areas. Rocco is thinking of lobbying the government to finance the recycling project and help buy the proper machinery."

"So they don't have the machinery yet?"

"No, but Rocco has the patent to it."

"And who is going to do the lobbying?" I asked.

"Rocco said he has connections."

As usual, Mefisto was taken over by enthusiasm.

"I can't see why the Government would refuse helping us. After all, we would clean up the landfills of discarded bottles and other glass items."

Mefisto saw a great potential in Rocco's plan and for that reason, convinced both, Peter and me to join Rocco Towers and his partner, Patrick Griggio by forming a new company. I tagged along one day to get to know those geniuses at last. Mefisto introduced me to Rocco, a short, thin individual with inquisitive blue eyes peeking out from over the rim of his eyeglasses. He must have worked hard by then as his handshake lacked energy. Patrick Griggio was a tall, handsome fellow, also in his early sixties who by profession was a graphic designer and did most of the company's artwork. The two reminded me of the odd-couple characters.

I was shown their collection of printed patterns but there was nothing exceptional in my view that would stand out from among the various tiles. I had serious trouble in visualizing the best way to present those large, heavy 6 x 8 inch ceramic pieces to an architect or designer in an attractive binder format. Initially, I did not dare point out my reservations because I would invariably be called the usual pessimist, who always planned to cross bridges long before arriving at the site. The fact that we would have to move offices and warehouse to Concord, to accommodate the new partners, also contributed to my hesitation. It would be a forty-minute drive each way in good weather. Something deep inside me triggered restlessness, worries, and Nakina shared my anxiety and fervently hoped that the deal would not come through, but once the boys made up their minds, there was no holding back.

Busy days followed, between meetings with lawyers and accountants in preparation for the great move. Rocco was in charge of finding a suitable location, large enough to house the two companies under one roof and renamed Cerglass Distributors, Inc. In the meantime, we would still work out of our former premises, which gave me another few weeks to adapt to the idea of change.

The day had just begun. Mefisto, Peter and I had just gone over that day's work schedule when the phone rang.

"It's for you. It's your mom," Peter said.

I ran to the living room to take the call so the other two could continue talking undisturbed.

"You better put on the TV and check the news," mother said somewhat excited.

"Why?" I asked. "What's all about?"

"I don't know. I don't understand all that is being said, but it seems serious."

I turned on the CBC News channel. The screen showed the replay of an airplane flying straight into a tall building causing a spectacular explosion. For a moment, I thought it was another Hollywood mega-stunt and so did Peter when summoned to the living room to have a look. The newscaster, however, announced that it was for real and soon enough, a second plane crashed into the second building. It was definitely a shocking experience to witness such a catastrophic event, live on TV. It was September 11, 2001 and the two buildings were the Trade Center's twin towers in New York.

For the rest of the day, I was unable to concentrate on work and remained glued to the TV screen. It defied my comprehension, how anybody could be so evil to plan such a murderous scheme which caused thousands of innocent people to lose their lives. Fanaticism fueled by rage and vice-versa. A tragedy that would become the main topic of conversation for most people for many months, if not years, to come, and a haunting memory for anyone directly and indirectly involved in that heartbreaking, tragic experience.

As disturbed as I felt in the days ahead, I had to focus on the business and start packing documents, folders, binders, sample boards and so forth for the big move. I had not seen the inside of the new premises yet, but Mefisto assured me that I would like it. As usual, my approval was irrelevant and I only hoped that a miracle would reverse the entire situation. But apparently, life had to teach me, us, a few more lessons.

28

CERGLASS Distributors

The moving day had finally arrived. Peter and Mefisto worked hard, packing and moving pallets and driving them to the new location. Then it was my turn to see the new premises. The front of the building was clad in red bricks. Once I walked through the front entrance, I could see the office—a very small space. I couldn't see how we could all fit in there with the respective desks, filing cabinets and shelves. But there was a lot "more space" in the back, I was told. I felt a cold ripple travel down my back as I opened the door to the "more space" and warehouse in the back. It was an approximate 5,000 sq. ft. area covered in an inch or more of sawdust left behind by the previous tenants who were in the millwork business.

One of the two existing toilets marked *Ladies*, was soiled all over: counter, floors, walls and sink, which also had a leaking faucet and the warm water shut off. The guys' washroom was even more soiled, with graffiti all over the walls, urine puddles on the floor and the door off the hinges. It resembled a third world country's public washroom. It was decidedly and surprisingly unusual for otherwise proud, clean Italian landlords.

Rocco who had dealt with the property owner should have made sure that the premises were clean, or at least swept clean, holes in the walls filled and painted, windows washed and the hundreds of dead flies removed from the windowsills at the time of take-over by the new tenants. There had also been a mistake made by the property owner's realtor in switching unit numbers. Instead of number one, as shown on the door, their documents indicated number two. Based on the initial information, Cerglass had already printed all new stationery and business cards and notified customers and suppliers accordingly. The realtor, accompanied by the landlord's son, could not understand the reason for all the fuss about the unit number.

"Oh, what's the difference?" they said. "A number is just a number. One or two doesn't make any difference."

The nuisance, however, was that Cerglass' correspondence was being delivered next door and when the neighbors were not around, we were unable to have access to our mail, which most of the time included a much-awaited check. After considerable argumentation, they finally agreed to refund one third of our printing expenses but refused to take responsibility for the clean-up, the dangling wires, the broken warehouse toilet door, the dripping women's washroom faucet and the defective heating system. Apparently, Rocco had not requested any of those things to be taken care of.

For a few days I was angry with Rocco, the spineless little coward who left Mefisto to do all the talking during the complaint session. Regretfully, there was no going back. I had to put my heart at ease and take the good with the bad. I admired Peter for his tireless energy. Sure enough, he was half my age, trained muscles and prompt reflexes, and he was still forgiving and trusting. I could not let him down so I rolled up my sleeves and pitched in by helping him to erect a wall to close the large opening towards the warehouse, which was the famous "more space" to be used as additional office space. For my own satisfaction, I did document, photographically, the before and after of those premises. We then filled the countless holes in the walls and painted them all in a pale green color, soothing to the eyes at least. I then washed the dusty windows and eliminated the dead flies crowding the windowsills. Peter painted the cement floor in a metallic gray and cut out runners from an old recycled gray carpet that had been lying around. Meanwhile, Mefisto ran around to purchase used office furniture: desks, chairs, filing cabinets, photocopiers and so forth. After a few weeks, the premises looked like real offices and everyone was buzzing around with plenty of things to do. Interestingly enough, our partners never pitched in with any of the clean-ups and run-arounds.

Initially, I traveled with Mefisto back and forth to work because I disliked driving on the highway. Soon enough, however, I acquired the necessary confidence to travel on my own. Once I became familiar with alternate routes as well, the daily trip became almost boring. So I invented an entertainment system. Some days I would pretend to be a jazz crooner, other days an opera singer and let my voice do the traveling. When tired of singing, I would invent a fictional passenger and build entire stories around it. I promised myself that one day, I would take time off to write down those stories. Only heaven knew when that time would materialize. I had not married into a well-to-do family and always earned every penny and every inch of peaceful happiness and it didn't look like the situation would change anytime soon.

Working days were busy. Mefisto and Peter were mainly on the road, visiting designers, architects and retailers while Rocco and Patrick spent the days in the warehouse. Patrick did the measuring and mixing of glazes and Rocco took care of the printing and firing process. Rocco's assistants were Tobias, in his early seventies, known as the sausage man because of his home-made salamis and sausages, and Gregorievic, a Russian ballet dancer who, due to the lack of other skills, including the knowledge of the English language, had a hard time in finding work on the job market.

As time progressed, it became necessary to hire a bookkeeper. After a number of interviews, Mefisto and Peter selected Lynn, an ever-smiling Chinese lady in her mid-thirties. I spent time teaching her all that she had to know, but even at a distance of several weeks, Lynn still needed guidance. I repeated the instructions and Lynn kept interrupting with her usual quick: "Ok, Ok, Ok, I know, I know," just to forget everything a few days later. I noticed that whenever Lynn was nervous or in a hurry, her speech became scrambled, unintelligible. I also had to teach her telephone manners. One day, I had just returned from running an errand when I witnessed Lynn grabbing the ringing phone.

"Nobody heee," she happily announced.

"Never say 'nobody here,'" I said. "Say the person you are calling is momentarily not available. Then ask for his or her name and telephone number."

"Ok, ok, ok," she replied, still very happily.

Lynn also had a little struggle with her "Rs." Occasionally, out of courtesy, she would ask me if I cared to share her bowl of "flied lice" (fried rice). With Lynn's friendly smile it actually sounded cute and I often overlooked her shortcomings because of her willingness to pitch in anytime and anywhere help was needed. As the bookkeeping did not absorb her entire day, because I still took care of the payroll, the payables and receivables, Lynn was put in charge of the samples department. She soon became an expert in the use of the glue gun and very fast in assembling sample swatches and binders.

Telephones often rang off the hook and it was becoming difficult to cope with the amount of calls for stock checks, pricing, technical information or simply messages for one or the other partner. A receptionist was hired. Vivian Gold had impressed most everybody because of her preparedness at the time she showed up for the interview. She had been the only candidate that had taken the time to find out about the company and its products. She was the typical image of an eager beaver. Once again, it was up to me to sit down with the girl and train her accordingly.

Even though Vivian had the healthy habit of keeping notes — she had a small booklet filled with instructions written in Hebrew, her mother tongue — she also possessed the bad habit of calling my name every five minutes to ask questions or simply confirm a certain action or information. The nature of the business was indeed multi-faceted and it would take time to master the countless details involved. Every so often, I had to conceal my frustration because the idea of having to look for a new person and train her all over again simply terrified me.

With Mefisto and Peter gone most of the days, it became necessary to hire a Shipper/Receiver to take care of the incoming merchandise and the subsequent packaging and shipping of orders to customers. After a fierce selection, a tall, well-built young man with puppy eyes and kiddie mannerisms was hired. His secret nickname was Morenometer. The first portion of his name, Moreno, referred to his intense suntanned complexion and the second half of his name referred to his metering the hours left for clocking out. He showed he was a very peculiar character. Just as he appeared to be big and strong, he was also fragile at the same time. When not taking a nap in his car during lunch break, he would come into the office, sit in a chair and complain about how ill he felt, how sleepy and tired he was or how broken his back felt after packing a few boxes of tile. He did not seem to have had health issues at the time he applied for the shipper's position. Any other work to fill his ample idle moments did not fit his "job description," so Morenometer decided to try elsewhere and left Cerglass. One less moocher on my payroll, I thought. Characters like him usually chose to work or pretended to work for a company for three to four months, then cleverly triggered a situation that would call for a layoff or even firing, just to be able to receive unemployment benefits and take a relaxed holiday for a few weeks or months before repeating the scheme all over again elsewhere. Revolting as it sounded, the unemployment system, aware or not, allowed this type of immoral activity.

In the meantime, Rocco required another helper for his printing operation and hired yet another Russian ballet dancer named Yuri, who apparently back in Russia had a degree in petrol engineering. Whatever that was equivalent to, only Rocco knew. He could have been a gas station attendant for all that mattered. As long as he did his job right, Peter observed, he had no problems with the guy and as the dancers were not always very busy, Peter decided to borrow Yuri for some packaging on a part-time basis. It appeared, however, that the engineer did not consider the low packaging position appropriate enough for his rank and reacted with a poorly concealed hostility. When Peter noticed that he was not doing a proper job, he dismissed Yuri and did the packaging himself.

"If you want the job done right, you better do it yourself, always," I said.

Sales calls were the most important feature of the company, which had a considerable overhead. We needed to hire additional help and after a series of interviews, the men decided to hire Wayne Swansea, a young chap in his early thirties. He had an impressive résumé and a good presence. He had been referred to Peter by an acquaintance. During the initial training period, he also tagged along with Peter to learn hands-on about the presentation details. Some three weeks into his training period, I noticed some strange behavioral changes taking place. Wayne would sit in a meeting, listening intently and scribbling something on a note pad. I came across that note pad one afternoon and all Wayne had written were three or four illegible words in handwriting similar to that of a five-year-old. Interestingly enough, Rocco also had a similar handwriting, which I considered very unusual given his degree of education. Was Wayne bluffing? I decided to keep a closer watch on the guy. Sitting at a computer one afternoon, I noticed Wayne's transfixed look. He wasn't even typing. His head was slightly bobbing up and down and then his eyes were closing intermittently. I asked him if he was feeling all right. He jumped to attention but only for a short period of time. He soon fell back into a trance-like state. I notified Peter, who also began observing the man. It could be something temporary. Maybe he was not feeling good, had taken some medicine that caused drowsiness or was sleepy because of late night orgies or moonlighting elsewhere. The possibilities were almost infinite.

One day, Wayne closed himself in the warehouse washroom. Had it not been for Yuri having to use it, nobody would have noticed that it was occupied by Wayne. Yuri first, and then Rocco knocked on the door several times. Each time, Wayne's voice came through with an "I'm Ok, just a minute." Then finally, the door opened and Wayne walked out, a little precarious on his feet, and headed to the office. I had that awkward feeling that maybe the guy was on some sort of drugs. In that case, the company could not afford maintaining an unproductive element and Peter approached him in that respect. Wayne obviously denied having any kind of health problems. The last straw came when he fell asleep while standing up at the coffee machine. His body was swaying back and forth and his knees were bending slightly. His eyes were shut and he was unable to snap out of it. Peter immediately called his girlfriend who worked somewhere in the area nearby, and asked her to remove him from the premises because he was in no condition to drive.

There were many things we could have done such as calling the police, an ambulance or firing him on the spot and let destiny take its course. Instead, we were nice enough to let him slip out quietly. A few days later, Wayne called to apologize and as Peter declined his request to return to work the next Monday, he had the audacity to ask if he was getting his vacation pay. Peter said no, and hung up. Wayne never called or showed up again. Later, it was found that his résumé was a big fake. Some of the companies listed were not real and a couple of others had never heard of him. It was probably in Cerglass' karma to be unable to find serious help, with very few exceptions, naturally.

Around 11:30 a.m., Patrick would walk around the office with hanging shoulders emitting agonizing sighs.

"What's with those sad eyes, Pat?" I once asked.

"I got to eat something, fast," replied Patrick. That 6'2" man explained that he and Rocco could not function without food and were accustomed to their punctual daily half hour lunch break. They satisfied their taste buds in a small Italian eatery around the corner from the office; the restaurant served home-style, freshly cooked meals. On occasion, Peter and I would join them for lunch. The food was truly appetizing, abundant and considerably cheap.

While working on a creative piece of art one day, I asked Rocco to fire a 4x4 inch piece of black glass tile which had on top broken pieces of red, yellow and white colored glass chips that formed the figure of a butterfly. Rocco obliged and the piece turned out beautifully. I used it as the centerpiece in a composition inspired by the Madame Butterfly opera. I donated the artwork to the Canadian Opera Company who exhibited the piece in their art gallery and subsequently sold it for $350. Enthused about my successful experiment, I continued composing such panels in my rare spare time. The theme of most panels was abstract in a pleasant combination of colors that could suit most dining room walls or corridors and halls in hotels, restaurants and other places. As no one had time enough to promote my work, the panels remained hanging on office walls or stashed in corners collecting dust.

Because Rocco did not come up with any new developments of his own and the recycled glass project had also been pushed aside for a number of mysterious reasons, I took it upon myself to do experiments with the glass tiles to create pretty accent pieces. For one reason or another, Rocco was suddenly unable to figure out the correct kiln temperature for a proper firing job. Whether it was merely bad luck or he failed on purpose, was anybody's good guess. Months later, Patrick told me in great confidence, that Rocco had never taken my creations seriously and thought they were a joke and not worth being pursued.

When summertime came around, Rocco insisted in taking four weeks holiday. It coincided with the Bologna Fair in Italy. With the excuse that he would also attend the exhibit to check out new products for the company, he had Cerglass pay for his air ticket and his deluxe restaurant bills because that is what one did when visiting Italy—check out every possible food outlet and indulge in a gastronomic heaven on earth. Patrick was a more conscientious fellow and dared take only one week off. Everybody else remained at the rudder because that is what bosses normally do, when they care about their own company.

Rocco returned with samples of a beautiful ceramic tile line with colors as vibrant as only the Mediterranean Sea and landscapes could offer. The enthusiasm on all parts was great and we ordered a generous amount of items selected for import. It was a considerable investment and everybody was confident that the product would fly after being introduced to designers, architects and retailers. Most everybody showed great interest but considered the product overpriced, even though Cerglass had applied a minimum mark-up just to launch it on the market. It failed, however, to produce real orders, just as Cerglass had failed to take into consideration that most homeowners in Ontario were the conservative type, playing with the usual neutral safe colors such as earthy grays and other pale palettes. Rarely would we encounter a client who had the guts to choose character colors because most owners eventually planned to re-sell their homes, and strong hues could dissuade the prospective buyer from closing the long-awaited deal.

Rocco had also checked into purchasing machinery worth about half a million dollars. The idea, however, was botched right at its birth because of the existing financial limitations. Only former AllRock had a solid financial reputation and could have obtained a loan from their bank. Rocco did not own anything aside from a beat-up-car and smelly old clothes. Patrick was not comfortable in using his house as collateral and was out of the game also and so, for my peace of mind, the machinery purchase was canceled altogether. Besides, Rocco's poor production performance and inability in creating new products did not warrant such a great investment.

Another bad import choice was a face-meshed glass mosaic from Brazil. Initially the product seemed promising. The price was competitive, but even with an extensive publicity campaign, the product, probably more suitable for warm climate country murals, did not fly as expected in Canada. Moreover, the supplier, Farofeiro Mosaics Ltd., refused extending credit, even after months of prompt payments. The typical Brazilian bureaucratic hurdles and the expensive shipping costs discouraged not only Cerglass, but other distributors as well, from pursuing the import of the mosaics. Collecting dust, the material would sit on the shelves for many years to come, because not even at $4 per square foot, for a product that normally retailed for $23, could we find a willing customer. The manufacturer refused the notion that such material could not be sold in Canada, but the reality, however disappointing it must have been for everyone, was that aside from Cerglass, there was no other distributor in Canada and only one in the entire U.S.A. Maybe this fact spoke for itself. Peter was so angry at that product that I had to keep him from tossing the hundreds of useless sheets into the garbage. From that moment onwards, he made it a point that all our efforts would concentrate exclusively on our Canadian supplier whose products were far superior quality wise. Despite being a little pricier than off-shore manufacturers, this supplier was more reliable with overall performance.

Office life in the morning started with Peter and me enjoying an espresso in our makeshift mini bar/coffee shop, a little corner right outside the office, in the warehouse. There was also a kettle, a microwave oven and a small fridge. We used to exchange information, which included personal and work-related matters. Invariably, Patrick liked to barge in, too, with comments, a joke or an anecdote. Patrick was a friendly, easy-going fellow who liked to take life one step at a time. He enjoyed dissenting and arguing about a given subject, just like Mefisto did occasionally and appeared to come across forcefully when presenting his own ideas and tastes, but was smart enough not to hold a grudge if the listener did not follow his suggestions, and wrapped it all into a big smile.

Once Patrick finished with his usual mixing of glazes, he would dedicate time to his graphic design projects—a skill he commanded very well. Sometimes he would approach me for a chat. He was passionate about certain subjects he would not talk about with just anybody, such as the paranormal, exobiology, meditation, UFOs and art in general. We exchanged information on these subjects as well as on book titles and the occasional recipe because Patrick, who, like most Italian males loved to eat, considered himself to be, if not the greatest, one of the best cooks on the planet. For a moment, I imagined Patrick, Nemo and Mefisto in the same room, arguing about who was the best gastronomic connoisseur. It would have been a cacophony of sounds, one shouting over the other's voice.

The first year of partnership passed fairly quickly and without major complications. Among the few thorns in Mefisto and Peter's side was the fact that Rocco insisted on switching accountants. He wanted to use his own for the business operation whereas Mefisto preferred to retain Nina, a competent, caring professional who had looked after his books for well over ten years. Strangely enough, it had also been Nina who had warned Mefisto against the partnership with Rocco. It seems, however, that some people need to experience a mistake in person to understand its true nature. To avoid further frictions, they finally agreed to switch over to Angela, also very competent but unlike Nina, a very expensive professional.

The first year's financial analysis was disappointing. A closer look at the figures revealed that Rocco's department was an under-achiever and needed an urgent adjustment. Peter called for a meeting to address the situation. They studied a way to increase the pricing by at least a few cents per tile printed. Up until then, fearing to lose his best client to the competition, Rocco had under-priced himself. I suggested Peter keep a closer eye on Rocco's activities in general. Their part of the operation was supposed to generate enough income to cover their own high salaries as well as the wages of their laborers. The only person who was not on a regular payroll was old Tobias, who needed the job to keep himself busy and at a healthy distance from his nagging wife. Tobias was a good man who, in his spare time, did what most Italian men of a certain generation do: make their own wine and sausages. One day he even brought in a small homemade salami and proudly offered it to Mefisto who enjoyed every bit of it. I tasted it out of courtesy but did not care for meat products any longer.

The second year of partnership did not improve much either and I was annoyed at the fact that the main reason for that partnership had been totally swept aside. The famous recycled glass project had never been tackled and no progress been made because Rocco was obsessed in pleasing his cheap clients first. I pointed this out to both Mefisto and Peter who called for yet another meeting demanding action on the matter from the partners. I also asked that a sample be made in a more attractive color but Rocco said he no longer had access to the machinery. Suddenly, the entire recycled glass project became a muddled mystery.

I began to feel restless and developed an ill feeling towards Rocco. He was not being sincere and was definitely hiding facts, even though he had what appeared to be official documents on the machine for which he had Cerglass pay for the annual patent renewal fee. Many times, I surprised Rocco and Patrick whispering in the back of the warehouse. On seeing me walking by they would immediately interrupt the conversation and pretend to be busy.

When sometime in May, Rocco declared that he was taking four weeks off, both Mefisto and Peter got upset. Nobody could afford to take so much time off, especially when the company was not doing too well, but Rocco was adamant and had already booked his air ticket to Italy. This time Patrick joined into the protest because it meant that he had to cover Rocco's ass by skipping his own holidays. Tough luck, I thought. He had picked him for partner and up until a few weeks back, they were whispering buddy-buddies. I no longer felt like sitting at the same table with them and declined any further invitations for lunch.

Restless and worried, I decided to do my own little investigation. AllRock had entered the partnership with a total of $140,000 including cash and inventory. Deco & Screen contributed $90,000 in so-called technical "Know-how" and machinery. At that point, Rocco and Patrick's salary had long passed the ninety thousand dollar mark, barely covered by their silk-screening operation. That meant that Mefisto and Peter's side of the operation was covering everything else: the wages of their employees, supplies and all the overhead. It was a financial burden that could not last for too long. My heart rate increased and I had to fight the rage that was slowly building up inside me. I researched the figures even deeper, put it down on paper and showed it to Mefisto and Peter. Needless to say, it was a shocking revelation that required extreme, immediate action.

Peter called for yet another meeting. Both Rocco and Patrick seemed concerned, wondering what earful they had to put up with this time. Mefisto and Peter explained the situation but Rocco could not believe those figures and decided to do his own, three pages long calculations. Peter suggested that everybody should hit the road and do sales calls as well as follow up on the interested individuals who had sent enquiries through the Info-Link publication. In the meantime, they had to let go the laborers in the back. Tobias was the only one left for another little while.

For many days, the phones were busy and Patrick even took a trip to the east coast trying to establish new retail accounts. Business-wise the trip was not as successful as expected, but he had collected a noteworthy list of the best restaurants in the area.

The fragile situation of the company did not deter Rocco from his second planned holiday trip to Italy. He had to go at all costs even though Mefisto had warned him about the possibility of his position no longer being available on his return. At that point, Rocco was in vacation mode and could care less about what was going on at Cerglass. It was definitely not the right attitude for a serious business partner. Therefore, Peter and Mefisto decided that the best thing to do was to dissolve the partnership. Rocco and Patrick failed to stand behind their end of the bargain and were no longer in the position of demanding anything. They were only draining the last resources of the other two partners.

In addition to my work-related problems, I also had to worry about mother, who was definitely not happy in the nursing home she was living in. She wanted to leave at all costs, forgetting that she could no longer manage anything on her own and needed help 24/7. To get her out of bed they had to use a small lifting device similar to a crane because she was too heavy for the nursing staff. Like other normal people, she hated the fact that the nurses could not expedite changing the urine-soaked pads and definitely hated the innate rudeness of some of the caregivers. I tried to explain to her that she had to be patient a little while longer, until the new nursing home was ready and where she would then once again enjoy all the used to amenities. It was, of course, easier said than done, for an outsider.

I had planned to surprise her on Sunday with a visit along with Nakina and our pooch, Figaro. I would also bring her tomatoes, fresh from the garden, but mother was tired of fighting and living. After I finished my Saturday chores, and had returned from my usual errands, I received a phone call from mother's best friend, Gertrude.

"Your Mom is in the hospital. They just took her, hurry up. She does not want to live anymore."

My heart started pounding wildly. I quickly explained the situation to Mefisto and we were about to leave for the hospital when Nakina's car drove into the driveway.

"Where are you guys going?" she asked.

"To the hospital, grandma is very ill," I said.

"I felt I had to come by for some reason," Nakina said, surprised and puzzled. "I just didn't know why or what for."

We then drove to the hospital. Mother was laying on a gurney in the emergency department, unconscious. I held her hands and spoke to her in a whisper.

"I'm here mom, I'm here with you. Can you hear me?" I repeated the words over and over again, but mother would not react.

In the meantime, Nakina had also notified Peter who drove back to town with the family and joined us at the hospital. I was in shock, even though I knew that soon enough, mother would give up the fight. Three, they say, is always a charm and that had been her third respiratory failure. I could not avoid guilt feelings. Why did I leave her in that nursing home she hated so much, even if it had been only a provisory arrangement? Why did I not go visit her that morning before doing my chores and running errands? Why-why-why; could've-should've-would've. The ER physician who was looking after her explained that there was really not much they could do for her at that stage. To revive her meant to intubate her, but she would never quite regain consciousness I was told. I remembered her previous episode of respiratory failure, which she barely survived and had begged me already then to be released from the poking and prodding, the weeks hooked on IVs to have the liquids drained from her body, more medication and more daily pain and struggles. "Should I ever come to the point of leaving this earth, please, do me a favor, don't let them resuscitate me," were the words she had entrusted me with.

It took me a lot of courage, even though my heart was breaking while viewing her peaceful face, to answer the doctor's question with a whispered "release her." I hoped I was doing the right thing and that mother was finally happy, truly freed from the earthly bondage of daily physical and emotional pain and suffering. Deep in my heart, I formed a mental image of mother running freely over the green prairies of heaven, with a smile on her face at last. She passed away at 10:45 p.m., on August 23, 2003.

A most unusual episode took place on the other side of the country that same day. My brother, who had also been living in a nursing home due to the deterioration of his Parkinson affliction, somehow found his way out from the premises and ended up on a main road. When a short time later Frank was found and returned to the home by police, with minor scrapes and bruises, he explained to the supervisor that he had to look for a phone to speak urgently to his mother. In my view, mother was definitely trying to send a message to Frank, who in his fragile, sensitive state of mind captured it and desperately tried to reach out to her by trying to talk to her over the phone. He had never been told about his mother's illness or hospital recoveries to avoid burdening him further psychologically and emotionally.

As desired, mother was cremated and her ashes buried next to my father's in a plot reserved for them in a most beautiful, peaceful cemetery in Vancouver, B.C. Magnolia's help in taking care of the details was remarkable and I was not only extremely grateful to her but grew even closer to my sister-in-law as time went by. We were both sensitive souls, who believed in peace, art, beauty and infinity.

When Rocco returned three weeks later, all happy-go-lucky from his Italian vacation, he came running to Mefisto.

"So, here I am. What do you want me to do?"

"Nothing; there is no more work here for you, unless you go out selling and bring in some money, because I have no money to pay you," Mefisto snapped.

"Well, what am I gonna do?" Rocco pleaded. "I need to work!"

"You should have thought of it before taking four weeks vacation when you were fully aware of the fact that the boat was sinking," Mefisto said. "I'm sorry, I can't help you." He returned his attention to his paperwork.

Visibly enraged, Rocco stormed out of the premises never to be seen again. He did, however, have the guts to ask his lawyer to demand a $60,000 shareholders chunk that in his opinion was due to him. The entire company laughed at that request. In the meantime, Mefisto had switched back to his former accountant, Nina, who was kind enough to refrain from saying: "I told you so." The company's finances were in shambles and a copy of the statement was also sent to Rocco's lawyer who was sensible enough to realize that the cow had been milked to its last drop, and settled for a $5,000 goodwill severance pay. In a way, Rocco was lucky that Mefisto and Peter weren't the revengeful types and did not sue him for misrepresentation and misleading business information that practically brought the company close to bankruptcy. Rocco had nothing worth suing for; he was a nightmare we hoped to forget and never to encounter again.

Patrick was in the same boat. Aside from the sales aspect, which was not his forte, there was no other work for him, mainly because the company was unable to finance his salary. Patrick was no dummy, and understood the situation and accepted the $5,000 goodwill check without arguing. Not long before, he felt the need to confess that he and Rocco never had it so good while on their own. Before the partnership, there were weeks when they could not even take home a salary. Rocco had no credit and no collateral and neither did Patrick, who did not always see eye-to-eye with his partner. Finally, Tobias was also let go. There were no more printing jobs for him.

"I don't know why you guys did that to Mr. Rocco. He was always such a great gentleman," he once told Mefisto.

"Yeah, right," Mefisto snapped, visibly irritated. "A liar and a cheat he was, your gentleman. Had it not been for my son and me, you would have left already six months ago. Your gentleman is the reason why we are at the brink of bankruptcy."

We then notified the landlord of our intentions to move and immediately contacted a real estate agent to sublet the premises and find a smaller place back in Toronto. We were lucky to find a beautiful office with warehouse in a business plaza closer to home. From the old machinery brought in by Rocco, only the picturesque clanking, rattling printing machine and kilns were sold for a ridiculously low price. Hauled over to the new place were the wobbly, rusted platform ladder, the half-rotten four-wheeler cart, a drill and a saw, because nobody was willing to purchase them.

"Hey, Nakina, don't fall from the $90,000 ladder," or, "Don't cut your fingers with the $90,000 saw," were sarcastic remarks and a constant bitter reminder of a mistake we hoped never to repeat again.

29

PAG Distributors Inc.

Beaten psychologically, emotionally and drained financially, Peter, Mefisto and I had to once more follow the survival instinct and dig deep into our reserves of hope, courage and perseverance. We incurred more expenses and had to borrow heavily to keep up with the overhead and suppliers' expenses. Wherever money we could save, we did. As before in Concord, where I had vacuumed carpets, dusted furniture and cleaned soiled washrooms, so also in the new location I had to use my "Molly Maid" expertise. I did not mind pitching in even though I hoped that one day soon the company would do well enough and be able to hire a proper cleaning service.

Lynn, the Chinese bookkeeper, remained with us for another while and continued doing some of the bookkeeping and the sampling. Vivian Gold, after a few months into the new location, became restless. The company was unable to raise her salary at that point and she was literally fed up with the order desk functions. She also disliked filling the UPS paper work and honestly expressed her feelings to Peter. She told him that she was aiming higher in her career and hoped to get into the sales field. As the sales aspect of the company was covered by Peter and Mefisto and the only opening at the time was the order desk and reception position, Vivian quit and decided to try her luck elsewhere.

It just happened that during that same time period, Nakina was recovering from a nervous breakdown due to work-related stress elsewhere. To get back on her feet was essential and so PAG hired her to replace Vivian. Nakina picked up everything very quickly and easily, as all young, hardworking bright people do. Aside from her moody moments and temperamental outbursts, she became a great asset to the company and relieved me from part of the daily burden. She took initiatives which none of her predecessors had ever taken.

She organized the samples room in a manner so that even a color-blind person could easily find a sample piece. She was neat, fast and strict with whoever dared mess up her work area and she was very good in dealing with the clients and the public in general. In the meantime, Mefisto kept brewing new ideas. He had always been a very active person who could never sit on his behind for more than a few minutes.

"You know," he often told me, "I created AllRock that has become Cerglass and now PAG Distributors and practically belongs to Peter. But what am I going to leave behind for our little girl?" referring to Nakina. "I have this dream," he said, lifting an arm towards the sky. "I want to create a store, a very special, unique store. It will be the best store in town and will end up saving us all from hardship, and I will leave it to Nakina."

Mefisto's enthusiasm was so genuine, that no one dared dissuade him from his plan. Peter offered to prepare the initial sketches and as those took form and color, it became much easier for everyone to visualize and appreciate Mefisto's dream.

During that same period of time, Peter's old buddy, Joe Pezzo, decided to take a break from his financial consulting job and joined PAG as sales representative. Like Sweeney before him, Joe underwent a period of training, which included site trips with Peter to architects and designers, pitching the versatility and beauty of the company's various custom products.

Mefisto meanwhile pursued his dream. He found the location and he found the financing but he needed help with everything else, and so PAG pitched in by helping with the many details that went with a store opening such as providing display materials, setting up the computerized invoicing system and so forth. The 2004 grand opening was a successful event and Mefisto was more than proud of the achievements as were the rest of the family, friends and acquaintances.

That same year, I was happy to have my niece, Lara, spend a few days with the family in Toronto. Her father's health was deteriorating ever so fast and it was emotionally devastating for her, at age 19, to witness his fading away, day after day. To be in the company of a happy crowd could only help her, even if just for a short period of time, to take her mind off the pain and suffering her family faced daily.

Peter was preparing the BBQ to grill some fresh salmon, when the sad news reached us. Frank had passed away. Lara was devastated by the news and so was I. For a few days, Lara and I shared our pain, tears and memories. We flew back to Vancouver together. Magnolia once again showed off her organizational ability. She had planned a most extraordinary memorial for Frank. It lasted well over an hour between prayers, readings and Frank's favorite classical arias. Lara, Magnolia and I sat on the bench across from the open casket, huddling, holding hands and comforting each other whenever a particular memory, triggered by a reading or a piece of music, became overpowering. Even though Frank had provided for his own burial ground, Magnolia could not part from the urn containing his ashes and kept it in the house. Her heart alone would determine when to bury the urn, and only the urn, because the memories connected to it would forever dwell in her heart.

Back in Toronto, it was business as usual. With a considerable amount of attention and efforts directed to the new store, PAG had neglected its own business operations and had to catch up with its sales plan. More and more customers, retailers in particular, were changing over to the less expensive Asian offshore products. A few of our U.S. customers also followed suit, especially Rizzo Tile with whom we had an ongoing large project for several years. To keep the customer happy and preventing him from defecting to the other side, PAG's mark-up, in addition to the dwindling American dollar, was marginal at best. When Rizzo Tile dared ask for an additional discount, Peter had to finally put his foot down and sent him to deal directly with the manufacturer.

"There you go, another good example," I said. "You give them a finger and they eat up your hand; you give them a hand and they eat up your arm. It is a vicious circle, a never-ending story you can end only by putting your foot firmly on the ground."

After a few months of hands-on experience, which included the heavy, less glamorous packaging process in the dusty warehouse surrounds, Joe Pezzo decided to return to his former, clean consulting desk job. PAG was unable to match the high salary he was going to earn on the other side.

Aside from the various problems that kept adrenaline flowing on a daily basis, Mefisto was having more heart problems and had to have an angiogram. He was also told to take it easy from then on. Because Joe Pezzo's wife, who also joined the company for a short period of time, did not feel comfortable in taking care of the store in the evenings, especially in winter, or on weekends, and as the budget available could barely afford one only employee, she had to leave the company. Nakina's husband, Chris, took over and successfully carried on for an entire year. He certainly came across many interesting situations in the store and liked to tell the family about the most significant ones.

In one instance a client had walked into the store and after endless choosing and matching of colors, had decided on one of the porcelain floor tiles. Some six weeks later, after the product had already been installed in her home, she returned to the store and demanded a refund equivalent to the difference she would have paid less in another store, which by the way was the original supplier for Mefisto's store as well. They sold equally to the public as well as to other retailers and distributors, creating havoc in the marketplace. There was no reasoning with the woman who delighted in tormenting Chris by phoning every half hour and quickly hanging up. The few times she decided to speak, she uttered threats and words comparable to toilet discharge. Peter suggested Chris give that particular person a refund just to get rid of her harassment. In her unbalanced state of mind, she could only cause damage and harm if not satisfied, maybe even throw rocks against the storefront windows. The police in such cases would just brush it off because no one was harmed or killed yet. It truly wasn't worth the hassle. Luckily, such incidents were rare.

It reminded me of the day when someone walked in very quietly in our showroom and took the liberty to check out Nakina's office while I finished answering a phone call in my office and was preparing to shut down the computer to leave for the day. Surprisingly, I heard a noise and went to check it out. I almost collided with the stranger at the end of the corridor.

"Whooow, where did you come from?" I asked the stranger.

"I was just wondering if you guys wear overalls in this business," he said stuttering and blushing at the same time. I explained that we did not need overalls. He then asked questions about the tiles while slowly moving towards the exit door. He was a tall fellow, in his thirties, reddish blond hair in a ponytail, grayish blue eyes and overall well-dressed. He definitely did not give the impression of a thief even though I felt rather uncomfortable with his presence. He then quickly slipped out and moved on foot down the driveway. I locked the front door and instinctively walked back to Nakina's desk. The money that I remember having seen earlier that day on her desk was gone. I called Nakina who confirmed that she had left the money on top of her desk. My heart began pounding wildly. I quickly checked the drawer in the desk opposite to Nakina's workstation. There we kept some cash from customer deposits, mostly small amounts, and it was also gone. I ran to the door, looked out and saw the tall man walking into another door, or so it seemed from my point of view anyway. I locked the door behind me and walked down the driveway and into the office where I thought the stranger had entered, but there was no trace of him anywhere. The people in that office confirmed having seen the tall man with his ponytail who was about to enter their premises but for some reason changed his mind and quickly ran back out. I was shaken and felt violated. Never before had we been unlawfully invaded and robbed by a thief. I immediately called Peter, Mefisto and again Nakina, who urged me to call the police. I waited and waited and waited. The cops were too busy and couldn't make it that evening. Luckily, Mefisto and Nakina rushed over to keep me company till my nerves settled. I then called the police again and asked if I could at least have a copy of their report just to be told that it was available for pick up at a downtown location and, to add insult to injury, would cost $40. So much for the famous "To Serve and Protect" motto, I thought, very upset and disappointed.

"Hey, listen, no matter what consider yourself lucky," Nakina said. "What if the guy had physically attacked you? What if he had a knife or a gun?"

She was right. It would have been a lot worse than losing a couple of hundred dollars.

Scarborough was no longer that peaceful, clean borough I so much loved; not too far from downtown, and still blessed by a huge greenbelt. Slowly but steadily, all surrounding farmland, orchards and animal refuges disappeared under a relentless building plan of new establishments, retail outlets and two storey dormitories. The cement and brick jungle was here to stay.

Lynn, who had also left the company months earlier, came in for a brief visit one afternoon. She had been diagnosed with lung cancer and decided to get treatment in China where, she said, they were far more advanced in the various techniques. I never heard from her again. The need for a part-time bookkeeper was imminent. This time we concentrated on professionals who did not require much baby-sitting and were familiar with the user-friendly Quick Books system. We received over 100 applications, each résumé more impressive than the other. Everyone had excellent references and curriculums so much so, that Peter and I had a hard time selecting. They all asked between $25 and $35 per hour fees, which if they were really good at the job, was reasonable after all. We only hoped that Kim Lear would prove to be as efficient and knowledgeable as she claimed to be. Five weeks later and shortly after Christmas, she left a voicemail saying that she had received a good offer from another company and was unable to resist accepting it and would therefore not return. It had only been a short period of time and yet that so-called professional had caused enough havoc in the books by incorrectly applying payables and receivables even though she had been instructed accordingly.

On September 14, 2005, my third grandchild, beautiful Cassandra was born to Nakina, the happiest mom on earth. We all missed her efficient hard-working presence during her one-year maternity leave. How lucky she was, I thought, to enjoy her baby for an entire year, unlike the three months I was granted in Italy and Brazil back in the seventies.

Peter and I were busy even though business in general had slowed down considerably due to the increasing influx of competitive offshore products. We definitely needed a greater sales force and hired Talia Landy, a lady in her early forties, who was to visit architects and designers, keep their library updated and mainly follow up on job specifications. For a while, she also helped out at the store level one day per week as a design consultant.

More and more designers and architects decided to specify PAG products in their projects because of their quality, beauty and because they decidedly stood out from the regular crowd. Both Peter and I hoped that it would be the beginning of better days for the small family enterprise. Maybe it was PAG's fate, however, to be constantly in the wrong place at the wrong time, because good luck seemed to avoid the company with great persistence.

In the meantime, Mefisto's health deteriorated even more. He had a pacemaker implanted and a while later was diagnosed with colon cancer and had to undergo surgery, which thankfully, was successful and did not require chemotherapy or irradiation. After that, he just could no longer focus on the store and neither could Peter nor I. Our resources were already stretched thin enough. Mefisto's dream, had regretfully become a nightmare and there was nothing else left to do but to get rid of the store. To re-pay at least a portion of the small business loan we owed to the bank, Mefisto and I had to re-mortgage our house. Luckily, Nakina returned to her post in September 2006 to efficiently take over the order desk, reception, in-house sales, sampling, courier transactions and whatever else it took to run a smooth operation.

Nakina had a special talent in dealing with customers, especially with some of the most demanding, obnoxious and self-centered all-knowing designers who would pop in unannounced hoping the entire staff would jump to their feet in adoration. Even though I would keep my cool with that type of character, I preferred to hand the arduous task over to Nakina. It was nonetheless very interesting to observe their behavior.

Some would walk in and immediately exhibit a business card and with a commanding tone announce, "I am an interior designer." It would follow with "I'm working on a large project and need samples." Nakina would oblige, running back and forth to pick the samples and label them accordingly. Sometimes it was, as announced, an interesting, large project. Other times it was just a small 20 by 30 square foot backsplash. There was a definite difference of behavior among the various designers and contractors. Some female designers were definitely very difficult to deal with, irritated if not receiving a timely follow-up call and just as pissed if called upon more than once or twice. Luckily, only a handful had such hormonal issues and other emotional insecurities. The true talent was humble and respectful and cared to listen to all the details on the various products as well as the corresponding installation procedures. Others were too conceited in their apparent knowledge. Such was the case of a young designer who argued that there was no difference between glass tiles. "Glass is glass," he said. "What difference does it make?" He laughed at the explanation that there were different types of glass products, recycled or pure glass, different firing procedures, different textures, etc.

Nakina was the only one to comfortably deal with walking, living ignorance. Her patience thinned only when clients called in five minutes before closing time to have samples couriered to them, possibly the same day or, when they showed up to pick up an order after she had already set the alarm. As annoying and irritating this could be, it was the cost of doing business.

The real problems, however, did not occur in the day-to-day struggle but on the battlefield of sales, where only the fittest "big boys," knew how to manipulate, win and flourish. Many times PAG would lose a specified job because a sub-contractor would wilfully procrastinate the ordering of the designated product just so he could tell the general contractor that the item was not in stock and then use a replacement tile, mostly a sub-standard product at a slightly lower cost but still profitable in his own pocket.

There have been cases where the specifying designer also, for one reason or another, pressure or attractive payola, would not stand behind his or her special creative process, and close one eye to substitutions. Unfortunately, this situation required constant vigilance and follow-up calls to designers and contractors, to make sure that, at the end of the day, PAG could still count on some bread and butter on its table.

They used to say that in war and love everything was allowed. Well, they will have to add business to it as well. There had been a case where a subcontractor lied shamelessly about a PAG product just so they could use their own sourced material and thus increase their profit margin. Peter found out about the replacement days after the installation had taken place. Anger, disappointment and the sense of helplessness were feelings that would affect the entire family every time we were betrayed by those who had dared look straight in our eyes while planning mischief behind our backs. Due to the ever-growing competition within the construction industry, it had also become a fertile ground for lies, deceit, greed and corruption, accepted and sanctioned by the notion of free enterprise.

Considering the current competitive glass and ceramic tile markets, PAG made an extra effort to offer the lowest possible quotes just to get the jobs specified and generate income. But some of the so called "big boys" in the industry, had the tendency of turning a $20 per square foot product into a ridiculous $60 per square foot item, scaring off the end user who naturally was then willing to switch to a lesser product, price-wise and quality-wise as well.

"Is there no law to regulate this sort of shady maneuvering?" I once asked one of our loyal contractors.

"You don't want to end up in a cement mixer now do you?" he replied, almost in a whisper. "Some people you better don't touch. They know all the tricks and short cuts of the trade." He could certainly not have been more explicit.

There were days when everyone became discouraged, especially Peter, who was often very close to throwing in the towel. Some blame was also to be laid on Talia Landy, the architectural rep who should have followed up the quoted projects on a weekly or at least bi-weekly basis, instead of just leaving voice mails, hoping that someone would eventually return her calls. She had not been aggressive enough as not even the sales figures had changed from the previous year. Without sales, there was no income, not for PAG and even less for Talia who left the company shortly after a review of her failed accomplishments.

All the small family enterprise could do was keep on toiling, tighten its belts, downsizing the premises, cut salaries to a minimum essential, recycle paper, boxes and whatever else there was recyclable. The only thing we could not avoid was paying the overhead bills, which included the incredible variety of high bank and credit card fees and interests as well as the various government remittances. I would often spend sleepless nights wondering if there would be enough money to pay the bills of a particular week and wept bitterly whenever customers would fail to pay their bills, were on the run by ignoring our pleas or went bankrupt altogether. It was becoming more and more difficult to give credit even to those with apparent great references. Life was certainly not a piece of cake on the challenging business stage. With the economy in shambles, more difficult days seem to build up at the horizon, but even with all the struggles and the heartbreaks, we must not and would not give up, because after hitting rock bottom, it would be time to rise again, God willing, to the top.

EPILOGUE

Someone once told me that most events in our life are predetermined; for one reason or another, they are meant to be. I often wonder if it was my destiny to meet all the people populating the twenty-nine chapters of my story.

I certainly keep fond memories of most of the protagonists, and thank them for the opportunity to work for them, with them or alongside them. From each one I learned a valuable lesson.

Throughout the years I have tried to remain connected with as many people as possible and I can still see their faces in the picture book of my mind. From time to time, I call my first boss, Lilli, who is in her late eighties, still living in Petrópolis and always so happy to chat with me. Father Anthony would have been ninety-seven had he not passed away three weeks before his birthday in May 2009. Father Joseph, who had introduced me to Father Anthony, is also gone. Bill, the Gentle Giant, also died five years ago in California. Luckily, Father Nielsen, who is now eighty-nine, is still very much alive; with all the irons in the fire, as he liked to say. He promised to come visit me in Toronto next year. Morton, who suffered Parkinson's disease for several years, passed on and I don't know what happened to Paula. For a while I kept in touch with Father Francis and Father Thom. Both priests later married, divorced and vanished.

From the Italian group I exchange e-mails with my good friend Elly, who lives in Tuscany and my dear friend Danny, who recently moved to Florida.

In Toronto I often meet with Neeta for a chat over an espresso at a Starbucks coffee house. We exchange news with Maggie via e-mail and Kami comes to visit me at the office occasionally. Floyd Fourlet had a heart attack a few years ago and passed on and so did Nemo; and it wasn't a figment of his imagination neither.

For several years now I have kept not only a diary on my various employment experiences, but also pictures, letters, birthday, Christmas and farewell cards. Some of the reference letters I collected almost embarrass me as they sounded too good to be true. For that reason, I never used them.

Now that I have a business of my own, I can better appreciate my former employers' various situations and sympathize with their screaming and cursing. It certainly was so much easier to just punch the clock on the way out from work and forget about it all until the next morning. I now know what it means to be plagued by all sorts of worries, especially those concerning the company's cash flow. How difficult it is when clients don't pay and avoid your phone calls and messages—worse when they decide to jump the fence and disappear altogether. It certainly leaves a bitter taste in your mouth; yet we cannot give up. Life must go on and I still have so much more to do and many more exciting stories to tell, time permitting.

LaVergne, TN USA
27 January 2010
171234LV00001B/6/P